D0983346

MARY CHURCH TERRELL

A COLORED WOMAN IN A WHITE WORLD

AFRICAN-AMERICAN WOMEN WRITERS, 1910–1940

HENRY LOUIS GATES, JR. *GENERAL EDITOR*

Jennifer Burton *Associate Editor*

OTHER TITLES IN THIS SERIES

Charlotte Hawkins Brown	*"Mammy": An Appeal to the Heart of the South* *The Correct Thing To Do— To Say—To Wear*
Jessie Redmon Fauset	*The Chinaberry Tree*
Jessie Redmon Fauset	*Comedy: American Style*
Zara Wright	*Black and White Tangled Threads*
Maggie Shaw Fullilove	*Who Was Responsible? Stories*
Mary Etta Spencer	*The Resentment*
Fanny Jackson Coppin	*Reminiscences of School Life and Hints on Teaching*
Frances Joseph-Gaudet	*"He Leadeth Me"*
Gertrude Pitts	*Tragedies of Life*
Anne Scott	*George Sampson Brite Case 999—A Christmas Story*

MARY CHURCH TERRELL

A COLORED WOMAN IN A WHITE WORLD

Introduction by
NELLIE Y. MCKAY

G. K. HALL & CO.
An Imprint of Simon & Schuster Macmillan
New York

Prentice Hall International
London   Mexico City   New Delhi   Singapore   Sydney   Toronto

G. K. Hall & Co.
An Imprint of Simon & Schuster Macmillan
1633 Broadway
New York, NY 10019

Library of Congress Catalog Card Number: 96-6242

Printed in the United States of America

Printing Number
1 2 3 4 5 6 7 8 9 10

Library of Congress Cataloging-in-Publication Data

Terrell, Mary Church, 1863–1954.
    A colored woman in a white world / Mary Church Terrell ; introduction by Nellie Y. McKay.
       p.   cm.—(African American women writers, 1910–1940)
    Includes bibliographical references and index.
    Previously published: New York : Arno Press, 1980.
    ISBN 0-7838-1421-6 (alk. paper)
    1. Terrell, Mary Church, 1863–1954. 2. Afro-Americans—Segregation.
3. Afro-Americans—Civil rights. 4. Afro-Americans—Biography. 5. Civil rights workers—United States—Biography. 6. Afro-American women social reformers—Biography. I. Title. II. Series.
E185.97.T47A3   1996
323'.092—dc20   96-6242
[B]   CIP

This paper meets the requirements of ANSI/NISO Z39.48.1992 (Permanence of Paper).

C O N T E N T S

General Editors' Preface   *vii*

Publisher's Note   *xiii*

Introduction by Nellie Y. McKay   *xv*

A COLORED WOMAN IN A WHITE WORLD   1

GENERAL EDITORS' PREFACE

The past decade of our literary history might be thought of as the era of African-American women writers. Culminating in the awarding of the Pulitzer Prize to Toni Morrison and Rita Dove and the Nobel Prize for Literature to Toni Morrison in 1993 and characterized by the presence of several writers—Toni Morrison, Alice Walker, Maya Angelou, and the Delany Sisters, among others—on the *New York Times* Best Seller List, the shape of the most recent period in our literary history has been determined in large part by the writings of black women.

This, of course, has not always been the case. African-American women authors have been publishing their thoughts and feelings at least since 1773, when Phillis Wheatley published her book of poems in London, thereby bringing poetry directly to bear upon the philosophical discourse over the African's "place in nature" and his or her place in the great chain of being. The scores of words published by black women in America in the nineteenth century—most of which were published in extremely limited editions and never reprinted—have been republished in new critical editions in the forty-volume *Schomburg Library of Nineteenth-Century Black Women Writers*. The critical response to that series has led to requests from scholars and students alike for a similar series, one geared to the work by black women published between 1910 and the beginning of World War Two.

African-American Women Writers, 1910–1940 is designed to bring back into print many writers who otherwise would be unknown to contemporary readers, and to increase the availability of lesser-known texts by established writers who originally published during this critical period in African-American letters. This series implicitly acts as a chronological sequel to the Schomburg series, which focused on the origins of the black female literary tradition in America.

In less than a decade, the study of African-American women's writings has grown from its promising beginnings into a firmly established field in departments of English, American Studies, and African-American Studies. A comparison of the form and function of the original series and this sequel illustrates this dramatic shift. The *Schomburg Library* was published at the cusp of focused academic investigation into the interplay between race and gender. It covered the extensive period from the publication of Phillis Wheatley's *Poems on Various Subjects, Religious and Moral* in 1773 through the "Black Women's Era" of 1890–1910, and was designed to be an inclusive series of the major early texts by black women writers. The Schomburg Library provided a historical backdrop for black women's writings of the 1970s and 1980s, including the works of writers such as Toni Morrison, Alice Walker, Maya Angelou, and Rita Dove.

African-American Women Writers, 1910–1940 continues our effort to provide a new generation of readers access to texts—historical, sociological, and literary—that have been largely "unread" for most of this century. The series bypasses works that are important both to the period and the tradition, but that are readily available, such as Zora Neale Hurston's *Their Eyes Were Watching God*, Jessie Fauset's *Plum Bun* and *There Is Confusion*, and Nella Larsen's *Quicksand* and *Passing*. Our goal is to provide access to a wide variety of rare texts. The series includes Fauset's two other novels, *The Chinaberry Tree: A Novel of American Life* and *Comedy: American Style*, and Hurston's short play *Color Struck*, since these are not yet widely available. It also features works by virtually unknown writers, such as *A Tiny Spark*, Christina Moody's slim volume of poetry self-published in 1910, and *Reminiscences of School Life, and Hints on Teaching*, written by Fanny Jackson Coppin in the last year of her life (1913), a multi-genre work combining an autobiographical sketch and reflections on trips to England and South Africa, complete with pedagogical advice.

Cultural studies' investment in diverse resources allows the historic scope of the *African-American Women Writers* series to be much more focused than the *Schomburg Library* series, which covered works written over a 137-year period. With few exceptions, the authors included in the *African-American Women Writers* series wrote their major works between 1910 and 1940. The texts reprinted include all the works by each particular author that are not otherwise readily obtainable. As a result, two volumes contain works originally published after 1940. The Charlotte Hawkins Brown volume includes her book of etiquette published in 1941, *The Correct Thing To Do—To Say—To Wear*. One of the poetry volumes contains Maggie Pogue Johnson's *Fallen Blossoms*, published in 1951, a compilation of all her previously published and unpublished poems.

Excavational work by scholars during the past decade has been crucial to the development of *African-American Women Writers, 1910–1940*. Germinal bibliographical sources such as Ann Allen Shockley's *Afro-American Women Writers 1746–1933* and Maryemma Graham's *Database of African-American Women Writers* made possible the initial identification of texts. Other works were brought to our attention by scholars who wrote letters sharing their research. Additional texts by selected authors were then added, so that many volumes contain the complete oeuvres of particular writers. Pieces by authors without enough published work to fill an entire volume were grouped with other pieces by genre.

The two types of collections, those organized by author and those organized by genre, bring out different characteristics of black women's writings of the period. The collected works of the literary writers illustrate that many of them were experimenting with a variety of forms. Mercedes Gilbert's volume, for example, contains her 1931 collection *Selected Gems of Poetry, Comedy, and Drama, Etc.*, as well as her 1938 novel *Aunt Sarah's Wooden God*. Georgia Douglas Johnson's volume contains her plays and short stories in addition to her poetry. Sarah Lee Brown Fleming's volume combines her 1918 novel *Hope's Highway* with her 1920 collection of poetry, *Clouds and Sunshine*.

Th generic volumes both bring out the formal and thematic similarities among many of the writings and highlight the striking individuality of particular writers. Most of the plays in the volume of one-acts are social dramas whose tragic endings can be clearly attributed to miscegenation and racism. Within the context of these other plays, Marita Bonner's surrealistic theatrical vision becomes all the more striking.

The volumes of *African-American Women Writers, 1910–1940* contain reproductions of more than one hundred previously published texts, including twenty-nine plays, seventeen poetry collections, twelve novels, six autobiographies, five collections of short biographical sketches, three biographies, three histories of organizations, three black histories, two anthologies, two sociological studies, a diary, and a book of etiquette. Each volume features an introduction written by a contemporary scholar that provides crucial biographical data on each author and the historical and critical context of her work. In some cases, little information on the authors was available outside of the fragments of biographical data contained in the original introduction or in the text itself. In these instances, editors have documented the libraries and research centers where they tried to find information, in the hope that subsequent scholars will continue the necessary search to find the "lost" clues to the women's stories in the rich stores of papers, letters, photographs, and other primary materials scattered throughout the country that have yet to be fully catalogued.

Many of the thrilling moments that occurred during the development of this series were the result of previously fragmented pieces of these women's histories suddenly coming together, such as Adele Alexander's uncovering of an old family photograph, picturing her own aunt with Addie Hunton, the author Alexander was researching. Claudia Tate's examination of Georgia Douglas Johnson's papers in the Moorland-Spingarn Research Center of Howard University resulted in the discovery of a wealth of previously unpublished work.

The slippery quality of race itself emerged during the construction of the series. One of the short novels originally intended for inclusion in the series had to be cut when the family of the author protested that the writer was not of African descent. Another case involved Louise Kennedy's sociological study *The Negro Peasant Turns Inward*. The fact that none of the available biographical material on Kennedy specifically mentioned race, combined with some coded criticism in a review in the *Crisis*, convinced editor Sheila Smith McKoy that Kennedy was probably white.

These women, taken together, began to chart the true vitality, and complexity, of the literary tradition that African-American women have generated, using a wide variety of forms. They testify to the fact that the monumental works of Hurston, Larsen, and Fauset, for example, emerged out of a larger cultural context; they were not exceptions or aberrations. Indeed, their contributions to American literature and culture, as this series makes clear, were fundamental not only to the shaping of the African-American tradition but to the American tradition as well.

Henry Louis Gates, Jr.
Jennifer Burton

PUBLISHER'S NOTE

In the *African-American Women Writers, 1910–1940* series, G. K. Hall not only is making available previously neglected works that in many cases have been long out of print, we are also, whenever possible, publishing these works in facsimiles reprinted from their original editions including, when available, reproductions of original title pages, copyright pages, and photographs.

When it was not possible for us to reproduce a complete facsimile edition of a particular work (for example, if the original exists only as a handwritten draft or is too fragile to be reproduced), we have attempted to preserve the essence of the original by resetting the work exactly as it originally appeared. Therefore, any typographical errors, strikeouts, or other anomalies reflect our efforts to give the reader a true sense of the original work.

We trust that these facsimile and reprint editions, together with the new introductory essays, will be both useful and historically enlightening to scholars and students alike.

INTRODUCTION

By Nellie Y. McKay

> "'I am always getting ready to write something, . . .
> but I am never prepared to begin. I am more like
> George Eliot's Casaubon than anybody either in
> fiction or out of it with whom I can be compared.'
> If I had lived in a literary atmosphere, or if my
> time had not been so completely occupied with
> public work of many varieties, I might have gratified
> my desires to 'tell the world' a few things I wanted
> it to know."
>
> —*A Colored Woman in a White World*[1]

Mary Church Terrell was almost an octogenarian when she transcribed these words from one of her diaries into her autobiography: a comment on her desire to write long fiction. But although she lived for another fourteen years, in the grand scheme in which one suspects she saw her life, that wish to write novels was not to be. For her such a denial was a loss, since the wish was not a frivolous gesture. Terrell was so impressed by Harriet Beecher Stowe's *Uncle Tom's Cabin*, and moved by certain popular perceptions of its impact on the race and slavery issue in the country, that she longed for a comparable achievement of her own. On the other hand, in spite of her regrets, she was not unaware that the other writing she did was significant. For Terrell was the daughter of former slaves, members of a group for whom, for more than two hundred years, the achievement of literacy was mostly by theft, while unprescribed speech was unequivocally forbidden on pain of cruel and often inhuman consequences. We know, too, that in the writings of Terrell and many of her peers the challenge of the word was to bring its force to bear more fully, positively, and powerfully on the lives of black Americans than their ancestors had been able to do.

Africans and their descendants in America, even when forbidden, had used the word. Among earlier generations, a number audaciously claimed ownership of speech and the written language of the master and used them in defiance against the status quo. Many suffered as a result of those acts; a few, more fortunate, gained voice and successfully gave their own meaning to a besieged black life; and for the majority, the urge to resist through the word grew stronger and more insistent with time. But while pragmatic concerns dictated strategies of cautious resistance in how blacks, even those who escaped, used the word during slavery, the women and men of the postbellum generation revised such approaches and gave full vent to their feelings. In the personal narrative in particular, although subsequent black writings in that genre follow in the tradition of black resistance established in the slave narratives, later writers told the "world" a great deal that they wanted it to know in unambiguously direct language.[2] Readers of Mary Church Terrell's autobiography will agree, however, that as loquacious as she was, Terrell's text suggests she had more things to say than time or her medium allowed.

Although it was unfortunate for Terrell personally that she never found the time or opportunity to indulge her desire to write fiction, her nonfiction prose was a powerful avenue of communication for her, and its value to the struggle for black rights was not lost on her. In the autobiography the earliest evidence that we have that she saw writing in her future comes in her recall of the first time she saw her name in print, in a children's magazine, *St. Nicholas*, when she was nine or ten years old. Although this occurred as the result of her correct response to a puzzle that appeared in the magazine, she claimed boundless delight at such a recognition. As a student at Oberlin College in the early 1880s, she used her authority as an editor of the school's magazine to address readers at different times. This was the beginning of her journalistic career, which came to maturity in the late nineteenth and early twentieth centuries and continued into the late 1920s. In those years her opinion pieces appeared regularly in a number of black newspapers and periodicals, including the *New Era*, a women's uplift magazine published in Boston; the *Colored American* of Washington, DC; the *Afro-American* of Baltimore; the *New York Age*; the *Norfolk* (Virginia) *Journal and Guide*; the *Chicago Defender*; the *Howard Magazine*; and the *Voice of the Negro*, the first black magazine to appear in the South. At the same time, her articles also appeared in the white news media in such publications as the *Washington Evening Star*, the *Boston Globe*, the *Washington Post*, and the *North American Review*. Each of her columns and essays addressed issues of racism and racial oppression against black Americans.

Readers today can understand and respect the tension Terrell felt between her achievement and the goals she never attained. Nevertheless, her accomplishments were large, including the many speeches and addresses she gave that were never published. More than most people of her race and gender, hers was a powerful voice that was widely heard in her time. A quintessential race woman, who fully met W. E. B. Du Bois's standards for the Talented Tenth as well as those of the black club women's "lifting as we climb" ideal, Mary Church Terrell spent her life and major energies in speaking out and writing words she hoped would improve the lives of black people less fortunate than herself and as a race relations mediator between her group and the white world. By all standards, she was a remarkable woman, who chose, in spite of the advantages of her economic class separating her from the majority of black Americans of that era, to spend her life in the struggle for justice for all black people.

Mary Eliza Church Terrell (Mollie to her family and friends) was born on September 23, 1863. In the narrative two opposite events frame her birth. First, sometime during the months before she was born Mary's mother, reportedly in a fit of depression, unsuccessfully attempted to commit suicide: "[B]y a miracle she was saved" (Terrell, 1). Second, the circumstance of her birth date served as a fortunate omen for the baby girl, granting her a seeming favor that accompanied her throughout her life. As it is, with no further mention of the suicide attempt, her story unfolds with almost fairytale qualities in her descriptions of her early years. Later on, when she was a young woman, the material advantages of those years, especially her education, seem to have afforded her the self-confidence consciously to shape much of the course of her adult life. These advantages gave her more access, more freedom, and more opportunities to be heard than most black women (and men) of the first generation born after slavery.[3]

Mary Eliza Church and her younger brother, Thomas, were the children of Louisa and Robert Reed Church, both mulattoes, both former slaves, who then lived in Memphis, Tennessee. Little is known of Louisa Ayers Church's early life, nor did she speak much about slavery to her children. She was taken from her mother and raised in New Orleans as a companion to her white mistress, her master's daughter (Jones, 8). In response to her children's questions about her life in servitude, she told of a master who not only taught her to read and to write but who also gave her lessons in French. She also told them of the splendor of her wedding trousseau, chosen and purchased in New York by her master's daughter, who arranged a "nice" marriage for her. Louisa's mother, Aunt Liza, the only grandparent the Church children knew, appears to have conveyed two kinds of stories to her grandchildren: "thrilling" adventure tales, and stories that described the brutality perpetuated against slaves.[4] Mollie admired her grandmother's gift of storytelling, and was deeply moved by the sufferings of the former slaves.

Like his wife, Robert Reed Church spoke little about slavery to his children and Mary Church left home before she understood the relationship between her parents and that institution. Her father, the son of his master and his master's sixteen-year-old slave woman, was born in Holly Springs, Mississippi. As a boy and a young man, he worked on his father's steamboats on the Mississippi, rising from dishwasher to steward. Although not cruel to his son, the elder Church did little to indicate he considered the son other than a slave, including neglecting to teach him to read and write. After the Civil War Robert and Louisa Church moved from Holly Springs to Memphis, where Robert, who was self-taught in reading and writing, used his aptitude for business to open a saloon that soon turned into a hotel. At the same time, Louisa, whom her daughter described as an artist of wide reputation in her trade, established the first hairdressing parlor for black women in town, a venture that was an instant success. While Robert Church is thought to have been the first black millionaire in America, Mary Church makes note in the autobiography that her mother's contribution to his meteoric rise to fortune was not insignificant. The money she made from her business immediately after the war bought their first house and the first carriage they owned, setting the standard of living for which they both subsequently strived. By the time Mary and her brother were old enough to appreciate their social status in the community, at around the same time that millions of other black children across the country were gaining their first consciousness of the link between race and poverty, the Churches were members of the Memphis black elite, living in an interracial suburb of the city.

But the economic security of the Churches was not a guarantee of family stability. When Mary was six and her brother four, her parents separated and later divorced. Louisa Church gained custody of the children. Reasons for the breakup are nowhere discussed in the autobiography, nor is the disruption it caused in the family ever mentioned. We are left to speculate on the connection between Louisa's attempted suicide and the end of her marriage six years later. It is also interesting that all later references to her qualify her as a "ray of sunshine all the time," a remark on the infectiousness of her "hearty, musical laughter," and assure us that not only was she never depressed but no one else could be so afflicted in her presence. Nevertheless, whatever the subsequent relations between the two adults, according to Mary Church, Robert Church actively involved himself in his children's growing-up years and gave generous financial support to them throughout his life. While the autobiography also reveals nothing about Mary's brother's reactions to the divorce, the daughter presents herself as having warm and loving relationships with both parents. Toward the end of her life, a still sunny and always cheerful Louisa Church, who suffered financial reverses and apparently did not remarry, lived with her daughter in Washington, DC, for fifteen years before she died.

Soon after her parents separated, the poor quality of the public schools in Memphis prompted them to send six-year-old Mary north to attend school in Yellow Springs, Ohio. At the same time, Louisa sold her Memphis establishment and moved to New York City with her son. There she reestablished herself and once again made a success of the black beauty culture business for many years. Mary meanwhile remained in Ohio for close to fifteen years. First, from 1869 to 1871 she attended the "model school," a private kindergarten connected to Antioch College. In addition to her regular classes, her mother, who believed that children should learn several languages, engaged a private tutor from the college to instruct her in German. Mary then attended public school in Yellow Springs for two years, followed by five years at the Oberlin Academy (high school) from which she graduated in 1880. She was a student at Oberlin College from 1880 to her graduation in 1884.

Although separated from her family except during some summer vacations, in *A Colored Woman in a White World* Terrell describes her years in Yellow Springs in idyllic terms.[5] Living with a warm and generous black family, she presents an image of herself as adjusting readily, easily, and well to the new life, and writes with exuberance of the natural beauty of the environment, which well suited her aesthetic tastes. These were also the years in which she came to understand the meaning of race and her connections to the black slave past. While these latter discoveries were unpleasant and even caused her mild trauma when they occurred, they seem not to have damaged young Mary's self-esteem. Instead, they motivated her determination to resist racial oppression and to work actively to change the negative social perceptions that white people had of black people. For one thing, she learned to stand up for herself without fear when schoolmates or even adults exhibited racist behavior toward her or spoke disparagingly of black people in general. Once, when a teacher, in casting a school play, assigned her the role of a black character that she felt compromised her race, she refused to take it. At the same time, she was a lively child, fond of play including climbing trees and engaging in harmless pranks. She also loved to study and did well in school.

While at Oberlin College Mary Church distinguished herself socially and academically in a number of ways: she was unanimously elected freshman class poet and to read at Class Day activities; she joined a literary society and was chosen twice, as a sophomore and again as a junior, to defend her group in a public debate against the rival women's literary society. She was especially proud of this peer-group expression of confidence in her abilities, as the honor of representing the group was usually reserved for seniors. She also served as an editor for the *Oberlin Review*. However, her most outstanding academic achievement was in graduating from the classical course of study, then known at Oberlin as the "gentlemen's course" because it was considered too rigorous for women, who instead generally took the literary curriculum. The "gentlemen's course" was a year longer, required the study of Greek, and awarded students a diploma rather than a certificate. Against the advice of her friends, who argued that too much education would ill equip her for securing a suitable marriage partner, Mary chose and successfully completed the classical course. Most likely her desire to prove that blacks were not intellectually inferior to whites motivated her persistence. In her ability to master Greek, which she had first studied in high school, she may have proved that point to at least one person. When the English writer Matthew Arnold visited Oberlin during her time there, she did so well in her recitation of the Greek lesson of the day that he openly admitted to believing previously that the African tongue was too thick to pronounce Greek correctly (Terrell, 41).

Although Robert Church fully supported his daughter's decisions regarding her education, he strongly disapproved of her desire to enter the working world after she graduated from Oberlin. His perspective on working women was interesting for a man whose rise in financial and social status was greatly enhanced by the contributions of his wife's successful work efforts. In addition, knowing the favorable situation Louisa had been able to create for herself following their divorce should have helped him to understand how important it was for women to be as independent as possible in all areas of their lives. Instead, his views of women's place in the world, based on his status as a wealthy man at the time, were firmly rooted in the nineteenth-century cult of domesticity. He expected his well-educated and talented daughter to return to Memphis, and to be a social hostess in his newly built, well-appointed house until she married. For one thing, he argued against her acceptance of paid professional employment on the grounds that such positions should be left for young women for whom employment for wages was a financial necessity. In his mind "real ladies did not work," and having the financial means to support that belief, he wanted his daughter to be such a lady.

Not wishing to offend her father, whom she loved, but also out of a sense of gratitude for his support of her during her college years, Mary Church remained with him for a year. Soon after that he remarried, and although her next act created a rift between father and daughter for a time, she accepted a teaching position at Wilberforce University. She writes of being so thoroughly convinced of how wrong it was for her to squander her training and her obligation to do useful work in the interests of her race, that she risked estrangement from her father to pursue her professional objectives.

A scant 56 pages at the opening of the 427 in *A Colored Woman in a White World* cover Mary Church Terrell's story of her birth, family, education, and the beginnings of her career life. Later, brief chapters entitled "Learning to Cook and Entertaining Guests" (although she tried, we are told that she never acquired the art of the former) and "My Children and I," both in twenty pages, provide the only other portions of the text with a brief sustained narrative of her nonpolitical life. Rather, she devotes the remainder of the work to accounts of the activities that mark her career as the race woman she was.

Mary Church left Memphis in 1885 to assume a teaching position in the preparatory department at Wilberforce University. For $40 per month she taught five courses ranging from French to mineralogy, served as secretary to the faculty, played the organ for Sunday and weeknight services, and gave one night of her time each week for choir rehearsals, except just before commencements, when the choir rehearsed several times each week. For reasons not explained in the text, at the end of two years an invitation to teach at M Street High School, the "colored high school" in Washington, DC, was more appealing to the young woman than remaining at Wilberforce. She immediately accepted the offer and moved to the nation's capital at the end of the school year. It is reasonable to suspect that on the one hand, the nature of her appointment at Wilberforce, where she was forced to teach subjects of which she knew little and sometimes nothing, and to perform several ancillary duties, made that job so onerous that she was happy to leave it, and on the other, that Washington, which already had the reputation of a magnet for black intellectual and social life, was a more attractive place to be. At the M Street school her duties were to teach Latin and German, subjects in which she was fully trained. One of the first people she met in Washington was the head of the Latin department, Robert Heberton Terrell, whom she married two years later. Robert Terrell was a longtime resident of Washington, a commencement orator, and one of seven and the only man of color in a class of 300 to graduate from Harvard University with honors in 1884, the same year that Mary Church graduated from the classical course at Oberlin. Too much education had not spoiled her chances for the kind of man she wanted to marry. They were together until his death in 1925.

Over the course of the fifty years covered in the remainder of the autobiography, from the time she goes to Washington until the end of the 1930s, Mary Church Terrell outlines many of the triumphs she had and the obstacles she overcame in her struggles for equal justice for black people in America. Most prominent among the themes that run through the whole are those of the compelling drive for racial uplift on the part of educated black women, her sense of a great need for better interracial understanding between whites and blacks, and meditations on the phenomenon of passing. Hers is a fascinating story of an educated middle-class black woman's struggle for liberal reform against racism and sexism.

Although the offer of a teaching position provided Terrell her opportunity to reject the cult of domesticity, getting married soon ended that part of her career. In those days only unmarried women were permitted to teach. But with one door closed to her, she quickly found another path to which she could passionately commit her time and energies: involvement with women's issues. She was drawn initially to women's organizations through the suffrage movement meetings she attended in Washington where she associated with women like Susan B. Anthony, Carrie Chapman Catt, and Harriet Stanton Blatch. In that organization she also had her first opportunity to speak on politics in public. However, speaking to white women in their organization, urging them to recognize black women, was too limited a role for Terrell. Nevertheless, in the insights gained from these associations she perceived a model of organization that could be useful to black women. Although black women organizing among themselves was not unknown among this group, since this strategy had been used effectively for almost a century, such organizations were mostly contained within the black church. Concluding that nonreligious organizing by black women was of crucial importance to the advancement of the community, Terrell threw in her lot with the Colored Women's League, founded in Washington in 1892. One of the first activities of that group was the establishment of a program of education for women for which Terrell taught (without pay) German and English literature.

But the Colored Women's League was not the only group of black women attempting to organize along these lines at the time. In reaction to the racism of the late nineteenth century, black women on the East Coast, in Boston, New York, and Philadelphia, and in cities farther west such as Kansas City, Chicago, and Denver, recognized the need for a network of support among themselves. By then these women were also beginning to look for even wider support than the local groups provided. The momentum for larger networks began with a successful call from Mrs. Josephine St. Pierre Ruffin (another leader in the club movement), in 1895, that brought a number of women from several states to Boston to discuss matters of common concern. At a follow-up meeting in 1896, in Washington, the National Association of Colored Women (NACW) came into being.

The generation of young black women who came of age in the 1890s—which also included such stalwarts as the educator and outspoken feminist Anna Julia Cooper, who graduated from Oberlin at the same time as Mary Church; Mary E. Cary Burrill, playwright and teacher; Nannie Helen Burroughs, educator and feminist leader; and Pauline Elizabeth Hopkins, journalist and fiction writer—did not aspire to the ideal of the pedestal associated with the cult of true womanhood. Although the black women's club movement supported efforts on behalf of moral purity, suffrage, temperance, and self-improvement, these women redefined themselves as "New Women": independent, purposeful, and capable of effecting social change. Educated and self-reliant, they estimated that their training and abilities entitled them to a role in the public debates and in activities concerning the advancement of women and the "colored" race. To that end, they organized to consolidate their strength and challenged social prescriptions that circumscribed the lives of all women and men of color.

One of the leaders in this generation, Mary Church Terrell is most remembered for her founding role in and her work with the national black women's club movement in the 1890s and the early twentieth century; for her civil rights activities, which included acts of civil disobedience; and her support of the suffrage movement. At the 1896 meeting that resulted in the founding of the NACW, she was elected its first president. She served in this capacity from 1896 until 1901, winning reelection twice, and presiding over the association's first three biennial conventions: in Nashville in 1897, in Chicago in 1899, and in Buffalo, New York, in 1901. In those years, in addition to other issues of interest to her and/or NACW, Terrell worked aggressively to promote programs that especially aided black women: kindergartens, day nurseries, and Mother's Clubs. The NACW also established homes for girls and young women on their own, for aged black people, and for other various groups of those in need. The organization also provided a conduit through which new groups of black middle-class women leaders could come.

The NACW, the first national black organization to tackle the problems of black people as a group, flourished strongest between the 1890s and the 1920s. By 1916 its membership was 50,000 strong and the organization handled its multifaceted programs without the assistance of white philanthropy. Its achievements by then were phenomenal, especially in education, in helping young women from the South to find employment in northern cities, and in organizing health care for black women and children. The issue of poor and homeless young women in the cities was especially vexing to the membership of the NACW, since many of these young women became the victims of unscrupulous labor contractors or fell into prostitution. Among the most prominent women in the association were Mary McLeod Bethune, Lugenia Burns Hope (the wife of John Hope), Victoria Earle Matthews, and Charlotte Hawkins Brown. Each of these women, and dozens more, left a legacy that affected younger black women for many decades. Held together by the ideals of self-help, racial pride, and adherence to racial unity, they weathered the conflicts (regional, personal, and ideological) that at times threatened to erode their solidarity. A large number of educated women in business, social work, and the professions, with interests in women's issues and family matters, were part of the membership that worked hard to assist those less fortunate than themselves. Part of their motivation derived from knowing that white America judged their race (and its women in particular) by what they considered its "lowest elements." It was therefore their responsibility and privilege to help their social inferiors, to train the lower classes to adopt attitudes, manners, and behavior applicable to middle-class mores. In this way, they believed, white perceptions of the race would improve. Not surprisingly, the best results were visible in the local clubs where self-help efforts to uplift the community were more easily quantifiable. However, by the mid-1930s a combination of factors, including generational changes and the Depression, took a toll on the effectiveness of the association. With the creation of the National Council of Negro Women (NCNW) in 1935, the NACW went into decline. But it had done much to shape the leadership and many of the institutions of major importance in the black community. Paula Giddings, evaluating the success of this organization, concludes: "[T]hey had defended the race when no one else had. They had defended themselves when their men had not" (Giddings, 135). Theirs was a great achievement, and Mary Church Terrell was one of those responsible for the successes.

In addition to discussing her work with NACW, Terrell writes in detail in her autobiography of her career on the lecture platform. Her debut in the 1890s came through presentations to members of the NACW and the National American Woman's Suffrage Movement. Not long after, she was booked by the Slayton Lyceum Bureau and made a name for herself at a time when even few white women were on the lecture circuit or engaged in public work. Again, this was not a new field for black women, but the circumstances for Terrell were vastly improved over those of earlier nineteenth-century black women lecturers. In 1836, in Boston, Maria Stewart, black abolitionist and women's rights advocate, did what no American woman of any color before her had done: she raised a "political argument before a 'promiscuous' audience," which, as Marilyn Richardson suspects, made her the first black woman to lecture in defense of women's rights (promiscuous here means a mixed audience of women and men).[6] Stewart was followed by many such women in the nineteenth century. Among them the abolitionist and women's rights and temperance advocates were almost always lettered women with connections that served them in their travels. More precarious was the situation of the itinerant preachers, who had little in terms of erudition or financial resources, and who sometimes had to travel distances of hundreds of miles from one place to another on foot. All, however, without organized support, created their own religious or secular platforms while few white women were engaged in public speaking.

Terrell was on the lecture platform, she tells us, for a period of thirty years. Most of her lectures revolved around the intellectual and cultural achievements of black women, the successes they had made in education and other areas, and the obstacles they continued to face. She also made appeals to her white audiences for justice for black people. Terrell traveled both within the United States (in the North and the Jim Crow South) and in Europe with a message she hoped would raise the awareness of her listeners to situations that diminished the humanity of those who were not white or male. She spoke without notes, memorizing and rehearsing speeches that she had previously written and revised. In her autobiography she cites several speeches that were favorably reviewed in the white and black news media. The lecture bureau paid her between $15 to $20 plus expenses for each lecture she gave, hardly enough, even then, to make it a lucrative vocation.

During her years as a public lecturer Terrell was invited to speak on many prestigious occasions at a large number of important institutions and to various kinds of audiences. Such events included the twenty-fifth anniversary of Spelman Seminary (later

Spelman College); meetings of the American Missionary Society; and to students at such institutes of higher learning as Wellesley College, Radcliffe College, the Liberal Club of Harvard, and Cornell University. Even more honorific for her were invitations to appear abroad: to represent black American women at the International Congress of Women in Berlin, in 1904, where she was the only American speaker to address the multilingual audience in English, German, and French; to lecture to the Quinquennial International Peace Congress in Zurich in 1919, which she attended as a member of the U.S. branch of the Women's International League for Peace and Freedom; and in 1937 to represent the women of her race at the International Assembly of World Fellowship of Faith in London. Her travels abroad, especially under the auspices of the organizations with which she was associated, brought her into contact with a large number of internationally known figures and dignitaries from various European countries with interests in human rights. As a spokeswoman of color, she was treated by these people very differently from what black women were accustomed to in America. On the continent as well as in England she was respected and admired for her intelligence and her dedication to the work she was doing, and at no time there did she feel denigrated for reasons of her race. Among her friends abroad she included the British writer H. G. Wells (who wrote the Preface for her book) and his wife, at whose home she was a house guest, and Lady Astor (an American raised in Virginia and the first woman member of Parliament to take her seat at the House of Commons), who invited her to tea on the terrace of the House of Commons and secured her a ticket to the "Stranger's Gallery" where she could hear the proceedings in the House. But perhaps the two people she was most pleased to meet abroad, both of whom she saw in England, were the renowned African-English composer Samuel Coleridge-Taylor, and Ethiopian emperor Haile Selassie, who was living there in exile in the 1930s.

Not all of Terrell's time was spent on the lecture platform or on activities specifically related to the NACW. In the 1890s her interest in education on the local level landed her an appointment as the only black woman on the District of Columbia's Board of

Education. Other members of the board consisted of four white and two black men, and two white women. Initial fears that the white members of the board, especially the white women, would refuse to work with her, proved false. She served for almost six years and resigned when a matter coming before that body posed the issue of a potential conflict of interest for her. Interestingly, at that time she was the only member of the group who had actually taught in Washington's public school system. In addition to acting with her fellow board members in the best interests of the District, its personnel, and students, Terrell did her best to support "colored" teachers who often faced charges of which they were innocent. In 1897 she introduced a resolution to the board that February 14 (the birthday of Frederick Douglass) be designated "Douglass Day" in public schools, and that "songs of freedom be sung, essays be read, declamations given by the pupils and orations delivered by distinguished men and women touching the career of Frederick Douglass" (Terrell, 134). The resolution was carried. It was the first time, Terrell wrote, that any city had set aside a day on which "colored" children could learn about the careers and deeds of distinguished black people.

In this and other self-appointed duties Mary Church Terrell outlines the trajectory of the life of a black woman who deliberately chose to be a public person, not for personal political gain, but to serve in the large cause of the right of all Americans to be treated as human beings. In such a position, however, it was inescapable at times for her not to make decisions on or take sides in political controversies. Trusting in her own good judgment, she took pride in being a politically independent thinker. For instance, in the 1890s the Terrells were great admirers of Booker T. Washington and his Tuskegee project. In fact, Robert Terrell's 1901 appointment to a judgeship (the first held by a black American) in Washington by President Theodore Roosevelt came most likely as a result of Washington's influence. At the same time, as the debate over the merits of industrial training or higher education for the black masses heated up between Washington and W. E. B. Du Bois at the beginning of the twentieth century, in spite of her admiration for the former, Mary Church Terrell proved her independence of mind by disagreeing with Washington's emphasis on industrial training to the exclusion of higher education. Her disagreement with Washington was clearly manifest when she joined the NAACP as a charter member at its inception. In fact, she hastily abandoned a lecture tour she was on in New Orleans in order to attend the first meeting of the new organization, and in 1919 she became vice-president of the Washington branch. The goals of the NAACP, to bring people of different races and "colored people of all shades" together, complemented her personal interests in working for positive interracial relations. This was an organization for which she saw great need, and she bestowed some of her highest compliments on those whose hard work and dedication made it the longtime success that it was.

Mary Church Terrell's life and work as depicted in *A Colored Woman in a White World* are another reminder that over time black women in America, coming from diverse backgrounds and perceiving the world from many perspectives, often sublimate their differences to shared concerns about the lives of all black people and the plight of women, particularly black women. Terrell's class privilege makes her especially interesting in this context. Her background was unusual, especially in the era in which she was growing up. For example, few young women of any race at that time had the breadth of education she acquired, and perhaps only a few, had they been given the chance, would have considered it an asset to their lives. Not only did she attend and graduate from Oberlin College, when there were still only a small number of blacks who were attending white colleges and universities, she had the extraordinary opportunity to study German and French for a year in Europe (a gift from her father). In that year her exposure to the cultures of these countries greatly enhanced her understanding of differences between groups and gave her a different education on human nature. Europe also gave her more choices for determining the future course of her life. Among these, she might have married and remained there, where, like many other black Americans of the time, she believed she would have been freer of the racial prejudice that at times demoralizes even the most self-secure among the race in America. Instead, she returned to the United States and turned her efforts toward the struggle of her people.

At the same time, although Terrell rejected domesticity and chose neither to cross the color line for convenience (which she might have done at different times) nor to marry a European (white) man and make her home in Europe (she had three marriage proposals while there), she was not a political radical. While she believed strongly that the enslavement of Africans and the racism inflicted on the descendants of slaves were unjust and unworthy of America's democratic goals, she never questioned the white assumption that black Americans should conform to the standards and behavior of middle-class white Americans as a prerequisite to social acceptance by whites. To this end she dedicated her life's work, as she outlines it in *A Colored Woman*, to help to bring the lowliest of her race within the desired elevated sphere. Part of her work included the missionary zeal with which she strove in her contacts with whites to be an ambassador from her group: to impress on them through her actions that there were black people who were similar in all other ways but their race to the best of white people, and that given the chance all other black people would do likewise. In fact, *A Colored Woman in a White World* is a missionary text bent on convincing whites that if given the advantages of education and better economic opportunities (such as she had had), black people as a group would be as civilized in their behavior as their white counterparts, and to showing black people that whites will accept them when they acquire the accoutrements of Euro-American culture.

Nor was she alone in her opinions on the meaning of racial uplift and the importance of raising the lowest class of black people toward standards that she believed would make them acceptable to the dominant group. Almost all of the elite women responsible for the success of the black women's club movement held the same philosophy of blackness and black culture in relationship to the superiority of white culture. These were not settlement house workers, even if many of the goals of the two groups often overlapped.[7] Nor can these women be wholly blamed for the condescension and paternalism they brought to the good work they did for those less fortunate than themselves. Terrell's generation not only was a group that barely missed having been born slaves, some were sufficiently fortunate to have gained opportunities for education and social privileges well beyond those of even most white Americans at that time. Still, their proximity to the "peculiar institution" was too close for them to be comfortable in situations that called for identification with the roots of African culture. In part, this autobiography is the story of the public life of a race-conscious black woman who, although she took the high moral ground on issues of racial oppression, never seemed to comprehend the extent to which her politics granted the superiority of whiteness.

In addition to this problem in her text, one wishes Terrell had seen fit to construct a more inclusive narrative, one that might have better illuminated the manner in which women of her station and time coped with the frustrations and disappointments of their day-to-day lives; revealing more of how they integrated their public and private lives. For instance, in the first five years of her marriage Terrell lost three children, who died shortly after birth. In these years she was engaged in the suffrage movement and with the beginnings of the black women's club movement. It must have been extremely difficult to synchronize the dualities embedded in the many spheres of her experiences. How did she do it? Later she had one child who lived, and she adopted a second. We know nothing of how she perceived balancing the duties of wife and mother of two alongside of her very visible public roles. Similarly, we know nothing about her relationship with her husband, of how both managed successfully to conduct demanding and stressful careers while raising their family.[8] Some insight into these issues would have added a valuable dimension to the narrative.

Mary Church Terrell published her autobiography in 1940. She was seventy-seven years old. She lived for another fourteen years and died on July 24, 1954, at the age of ninety-four. According to her biographer, Beverly Washington Jones, Terrell expressed a desire to write about her life as early as 1910, but could not give time to it then because of other pressing public obligations. Not until 1927 did she begin work on her autobiography, and she spent the next ten years writing and rewriting the manuscript, which she completed in 1938. In the autobiography, she reveals herself as a woman who took meticulous care in how she presented herself to the world in writings and lectures. She must have been even more so in shaping the presentation of her life's story. But her efforts met with astonishing disappointments to her, as one publisher after another rejected the book for their lists. Finally, determined to get her narrative out, she turned to a vanity press, Ransdell Company of Washington, DC. Pricing the book at $2.50, she marketed the narrative as she lectured to civic organizations in various cities, and by eliciting the assistance of family and friends in a campaign to make it known. It sold well, as many as 1,000 copies in 1942, and most reviews were laudatory. But even so she could get no commercial publisher to agree to handle it (Jones, 62–4).

Two months before Mary Church Terrell died, on May 17, 1954, Chief Justice Earl Warren announced the decision of the Supreme Court in Brown *v.* Board of Education in favor of Brown. For Terrell, who had made the improvement of interracial relations one of the key items on her agenda to uplift the oppressive qualities of black life in America, this must have been one of the most gratifying moments of her life. Interestingly, Terrell had dropped out of public life between 1940 and 1946, and when she emerged, it was with a more radical stance than she had ever taken before. Instead of confining her criticism of racism and other oppressive factors directed at black life to the lecture podium and newspaper articles, in the wake of an emerging new stance among more aggressive blacks she participated and lent her respectability to direct action against the American court system through actions like picketing, boycotting, and sit-ins. At age eighty-three, in a challenge that lasted for three years, she attacked the AAUW-DC on its membership policies that discriminated against black women. In 1949 she won her case. Terrell continued to participate in these public acts of confronting the system almost until her death. Most notably, she campaigned for the Equal Rights Amendment (ERA) in the 1940s, and in the 1950s she led the successful charge against segregated eating places in Washington. Photographs of Terrell, past age ninety, on picket lines, dressed in hat and gloves, a "Don't buy at —" sign in one hand, the other holding the cane on which her weight rested, testify to the stamina and determination of one black woman's crusade for justice.

Mary Church Terrell's original title for her autobiography was "A Mighty Rocky Road" (Jones, 62). No one will deny that the life of any black woman in America has been other than a journey on which many obstacles make it a perilous path. Terrell was more fortunate than most, and could have avoided a large number of hardships had she chosen the life her father envisioned for her. Instead, she joined the struggle to uplift the race and gave her entire adult life to its demands. As a "colored" woman in a white world, however, with the resources she had at her disposal she had a front-row seat from which to observe and engage the action on both sides of the arena. If, as it does at times, her narrative reveals elements of snobbery and even a low estimation of the "unwashed masses," her intentions were embedded in nothing less than a strong will to remove the stigma of inferiority from the race with which she cast her lot. She was the product, however unique she might have been, of the white and black worlds of her time and she used her advantages well. *A Colored Woman in a White World* is a text that deserves serious consideration in the black autobiographical tradition. It has much to teach us about the complexity of black life in this country and it helps us to better comprehend the many roles that black reformers, women and men, played in shaping the politics that led to the black explosions of the 1950s and 1960s in the black revolution of this century.

NOTES

[1]Mary Church Terrell, *A Colored Woman in a White World* (Washington, DC: Ransdell, 1940), 237. Hereafter cited in text as Terrell.

[2]See the early chapters in William L. Andrews, ed., *To Tell a Free Story: The First Century of Afro-American Autobiography, 1760–1865* (Urbana: University of Illinois Press, 1988) for a discussion of the strategies, and the effectiveness of those strategies, that fugitive slaves used in telling their stories. For Terrell and others like Anna Julia Cooper and W. E. B. Du Bois, there is no subterfuge in how they address their white audiences.

[3]"[The] fairytale qualities of her early life" refers to the unusual circumstances of Mary Church's childhood in comparison with most black children of her time. She experienced no financial hardships. Her parents

ch Terrell's original title for her autobiography was
cky Road" (Jones, 62). No one will deny that the life
woman in America has been other than a journey on
obstacles make it a perilous path. Terrell was more
n most, and could have avoided a large number of
l she chosen the life her father envisioned for her.
oined the struggle to uplift the race and gave her
fe to its demands. As a "colored" woman in a white
er, with the resources she had at her disposal she
w seat from which to observe and engage the action
, of the arena. If, as it does at times, her narrative
nts of snobbery and even a low estimation of the
asses," her intentions were embedded in nothing less
will to remove the stigma of inferiority from the race
he cast her lot. She was the product, however unique
ve been, of the white and black worlds of her time
her advantages well. A Colored Woman in a White
ext that deserves serious consideration in the black
ical tradition. It has much to teach us about the com-
ck life in this country and it helps us to better com-
many roles that black reformers, women and men,
ping the politics that led to the black explosions of
1960s in the black revolution of this century.

NOTES

Terrell, *A Colored Woman in a White World* (Washington,
1940), 237. Hereafter cited in text as Terrell.

chapters in William L. Andrews, ed., *To Tell a Free Story:
tury of Afro-American Autobiography, 1760–1865* (Urbana:
Illinois Press, 1988) for a discussion of the strategies, and
ess of those strategies, that fugitive slaves used in telling
For Terrell and others like Anna Julia Cooper and W. E. B.
e is no subterfuge in how they address their white audi-

ale qualities of her early life" refers to the unusual circum-
ry Church's childhood in comparison with most black chil-
ime. She experienced no financial hardships. Her parents

At the same time, although Terrell rejected domesticity and chose neither to cross the color line for convenience (which she might have done at different times) nor to marry a European (white) man and make her home in Europe (she had three marriage proposals while there), she was not a political radical. While she believed strongly that the enslavement of Africans and the racism inflicted on the descendants of slaves were unjust and unworthy of America's democratic goals, she never questioned the white assumption that black Americans should conform to the standards and behavior of middle-class white Americans as a prerequisite to social acceptance by whites. To this end she dedicated her life's work, as she outlines it in *A Colored Woman*, to help to bring the lowliest of her race within the desired elevated sphere. Part of her work included the missionary zeal with which she strove in her contacts with whites to be an ambassador from her group: to impress on them through her actions that there were black people who were similar in all other ways but their race to the best of white people, and that given the chance all other black people would do likewise. In fact, *A Colored Woman in a White World* is a missionary text bent on convincing whites that if given the advantages of education and better economic opportunities (such as she had had), black people as a group would be as civilized in their behavior as their white counterparts, and to showing black people that whites will accept them when they acquire the accoutrements of Euro-American culture.

Nor was she alone in her opinions on the meaning of racial uplift and the importance of raising the lowest class of black people toward standards that she believed would make them acceptable to the dominant group. Almost all of the elite women responsible for the success of the black women's club movement held the same philosophy of blackness and black culture in relationship to the superiority of white culture. These were not settlement house workers, even if many of the goals of the two groups often overlapped.[7] Nor can these women be wholly blamed for the condescension and paternalism they brought to the good work they did for those less fortunate than themselves. Terrell's generation not only was a group that barely missed having been born slaves, some were sufficiently fortunate to have gained opportunities for education and social privileges well beyond those of even most white Americans at that time. Still, their proximity to the "peculiar institution" was too close for them to be comfortable in situations that called for identification with the roots of African culture. In part, this autobiography is the story of the public life of a race-conscious black woman who, although she took the high moral ground on issues of racial oppression, never seemed to comprehend the extent to which her politics granted the superiority of whiteness.

In addition to this problem in her text, one wishes Terrell had seen fit to construct a more inclusive narrative, one that might have better illuminated the manner in which women of her station and time coped with the frustrations and disappointments of their day-to-day lives; revealing more of how they integrated their public and private lives. For instance, in the first five years of her marriage Terrell lost three children, who died shortly after birth. In these years she was engaged in the suffrage movement and with the beginnings of the black women's club movement. It must have been extremely difficult to synchronize the dualities embedded in the many spheres of her experiences. How did she do it? Later she had one child who lived, and she adopted a second. We know nothing of how she perceived balancing the duties of wife and mother of two alongside of her very visible public roles. Similarly, we know nothing about her relationship with her husband, of how both managed successfully to conduct demanding and stressful careers while raising their family.[8] Some insight into these issues would have added a valuable dimension to the narrative.

Mary Church Terrell published her autobiography in 1940. She was seventy-seven years old. She lived for another fourteen years and died on July 24, 1954, at the age of ninety-four. According to her biographer, Beverly Washington Jones, Terrell expressed a desire to write about her life as early as 1910, but could not give time to it then because of other pressing public obligations. Not until 1927 did she begin work on her autobiography, and she spent the next ten years writing and rewriting the manuscript, which she completed in 1938. In the autobiography, she reveals herself as a woman who took meticulous care in how she presented herself to the world in writings and lectures. She must have

been even more so in shaping the
But her efforts met with astonish
one publisher after another reje
Finally, determined to get her narr
press, Ransdell Company of Wash
$2.50, she marketed the narrative
zations in various cities, and by e
and friends in a campaign to make
as 1,000 copies in 1942, and mo
even so she could get no commerc
it (Jones, 62–4).

Two months before Mary Ch
1954, Chief Justice Earl Warren
Supreme Court in Brown v. Board
For Terrell, who had made the i
tions one of the key items on her
qualities of black life in America,
most gratifying moments of her
dropped out of public life betweer
emerged, it was with a more rac
taken before. Instead of confinir
other oppressive factors directed a
um and newspaper articles, in the
among more aggressive blacks
respectability to direct action agai
through actions like picketing, k
eighty-three, in a challenge tha
attacked the AAUW-DC on its me
nated against black women. In 194
tinued to participate in these publi
almost until her death. Most no
Equal Rights Amendment (ERA)
she led the successful charge agai
Washington. Photographs of Terr
lines, dressed in hat and gloves, a
hand, the other holding the cane o
fy to the stamina and determinatio
for justice.

Mary C
"A Mighty
of any bla
which ma
fortunate
hardships
Instead, s
entire adu
world, ho
had a fron
on both si
reveals ele
"unwashe
than a stro
with which
she might
and she us
World is a
autobiogra
plexity of
prehend tl
played in
the 1950s

[1] Mary Chur
DC: Ransde

[2] See the ea
The First C
University o
the effectiv
their stories
Du Bois, tl
ences.

[3] "[The] fai
stances of N
dren of her

indulged her on many levels, including shielding her from the worst manifestations of racial oppression. This good fortune stayed with her. Her education in the North took place under circumstances she describes as extremely positive and comfortable. Later she married the man who must have been one of the most eligible black bachelors of the time, and who supported her choices for work and political activities. Except for her race, Mary Church's life, from her autobiography, has much more in common with the white middle class of her day than with the black American experience.

[4]Although Mary Church met her paternal grandfather when she was very young, and everyone knew he was her father's father, the former slaveowner appears to have had no familial relations with his slave son's family.

[5]It is difficult to tell from the autobiography just how much time Mary Church spent with her family while she lived in Ohio as a child, but it does not appear to have been very much. Some summers she remained in Ohio for the entire vacation; in others, she made brief trips east, to visit with one or the other, and in a few instances, both parents. What surprises the reader is how calmly she took the separations, and how accepting she seems to have been of her situation from a very early age. There is no hint of resentment on her part for this treatment of her. On the other hand, her brother seems always to have been with his mother during his childhood.

[6]Marilyn Richardson, ed., *Maria W. Stewart, America's First Black Woman Political Writer* (Bloomington: Indiana University Press, 1987), xiii.

[7]The settlement house movement originated for the benefit of white immigrants to U.S. cities at around the same time that the migration of blacks from the South to the North began in the late nineteenth and early twentieth centuries. Discrimination against blacks in white houses led concerned black women to organize similar housing situations for blacks. The goals of settlement house workers were much like those of the women in the club movement that was getting underway at the same time. But settlement house workers lived in the houses in which they worked and had continuous intimate contact with those they served. Whatever their feelings about the migrants or the aged and the infirm, their integration into the individual communities they served gave them an image of greater identification with the needy. Some of the settlement house workers were also club women and worked with both organizations.

[8]Robert Terrell graduated from Harvard magna cum laude in 1884. He began his career as a teacher in Washington, DC, and for a period was the principal of the M Street High School. He received an LL.B. from Howard University in 1889, and an LL.M. in 1893. After these degrees he

worked for the U.S. Treasury Department, practiced law in Washington, was elected to the Board of Trade, and then was appointed a judge of the Municipal Court of the District. Terrell continued to serve in this capacity until his death in 1925.

BIBLIOGRAPHY

Andrews, William L., ed. *To Tell a Free Story: The First Century of Afro-American Autobiography, 1769–1865.* Urbana: University of Illinois Press, 1988.

Hine, Darlene Clark, ed. *Black Women in United States History.* Brooklyn, NY: Carlson, 1990.

Richardson, Marilyn, ed. *Maria W. Stewart, America's First Black Woman Political Writer.* Bloomington: Indiana University Press, 1987.

Terrell, Mary Church. *A Colored Woman in a White World.* Washington, DC: Ransdell, 1940.

A COLORED WOMAN IN A
WHITE WORLD

Mrs. Mary Church Terrell

A

Colored Woman

in a

White World

By
Mary Church Terrell

RANSDELL INC.—PUBLISHERS—WASHINGTON, D. C.

Contents

Chapter		Page
	Preface	i
	Introduction	vii
1	My Parents	1
2	Early Childhood	13
3	I Am Sent North to School	18
4	My Parents Send Me to Oberlin, Ohio	29
5	I Enter Oberlin College	39
6	Activities During College Course	49
7	I Go to Memphis, Teach In Wilberforce and Washington and Go Abroad	56
8	I Study in Germany	72
9	In Europe with Mother and Brother	81
10	I Leave Berlin and Go to Florence	91
11	I Return to the United States	100
12	With Frederick Douglass and Paul Dunbar at the World's Fair	109
13	Buying a Home Under Difficulties	113
14	Learning to Cook and Entertaining Guests	120
15	The Commissioners of the National Capital Appoint Me a Member of the School Board	127
16	The National American Woman Suffrage Association Invites Me to Speak	143
17	Club Work	148
18	On the Lecture Platform	157
19	Notable Lecture Engagements	164
20	Prince Henry of Prussia, Dr. Booker T. Washington and Tuskegee	189
21	In Berlin, Germany	197
22	Distinguished People I Met Abroad	209
23	My Efforts to Succeed as a Writer	221
24	My Children and I	238

25 My Experience as a Clerk in the Government Department........ 250

26 Efforts in Senate to Prevent Judge Terrell's Confirmation....... 260

27 The Secretary of War Suspends Order Dismissing Colored Soldiers
    at My Request.. 268

28 Harriet Beecher Stowe Centenary and My Sally into Spiritualism.. 279

29 Trying to Get a Colored Girl into an Academy in the North..... 287

30 Traveling Under Difficulties............................... 295

31 Political Activities—Charged with Disorderly Conduct......... 308

32 Work in War Camp Community Service.................... 318

33 Delegate to the International Peace Congress................. 329

34 Meeting Old Friends and New—Plus a Dose of Race Prejudice
    Administered by My Countrymen....................... 337

35 A Week-end Visit with Mr. and Mrs. H. G. Wells—I Meet Other
    Distinguished People in England........................ 348

36 Employed by Ruth Hanna McCormick to Help in Her Campaign
    for the United States Senate. Abroad with my Daughter...... 355

37 A Few Cases of Friction................................. 359

38 Crossing the Color Line................................. 372

39 The Colored Man's Paradise............................. 383

40 Social Activities.. 397

41 Address the International Assembly of the World Fellowship of
    Faiths in London and Meet Haile Selassie................. 402

42 Carrying On.. 407

PREFACE

I HAVE BEEN ASKED to break my obstinate refusal to write prefaces for books; it is a job that always gives me that Uncle Pumblechook feeling, and generally I think a Preface does a book more harm than good. Among other things it is a usurpation of the reviewer's job which he may very naturally resent. But this is not an excursion into criticism. This is an exceptional occasion. I have known and liked the author for very many years, and I take her desire rather as a friendly wish to confer upon me the honour of godfather of her literary offspring, than to extract from me any proclamation that here is a great work of art, a polished, pre-eminent and memorable piece of writing, towering above other books and commanding the awe and admiration of the cultivated world.

I will not write anything of that sort. It would not be true. Nevertheless, I would not blue-pencil it, I would not rearrange it; if anything, I would rather one or two things were put in that I know almost certainly have been left out. The percipient reader of the opening sections may guess what they are. Apart from this discreet faltering from explicitness, this book, in its class and quality, could hardly be better. I am very proud of my godchild and very pleased to contribute my silver mug to its baptism. Its essential value lies in its revelation of the character and mental reactions of its writer and of the changing social atmosphere in which she has lived.

I doubt whether her book is one to read continuously from cover to cover. I think the seasoned reader will begin with the first three or four chapters and then go on dipping into it and reading to and fro. He will find himself recalled to earlier passages. He will want to verify certain impressions. Gradually the personality and the scene will become real to him, in just the same way that people and places we hear about and get a glimpse of and then come to know better become distinct and real. When, as my reward for this Introduction, I get the book nicely printed and inscribed, I shall put it on my shelves not among the masterpieces of art, but as the living Mary Church Terrell, the most subtle, almost inadvertent, rendering of the stresses and views and impulses that characterise the race conflict as it appears in America.

I might almost say the human conflict. I suspect that Mrs. Church Terrell, to this day, still believes that there are somewhere happy, lordly people so serenely secure that they can afford to be fair, generous and unresentful to all the world. One or two figures in her story, as she sees them, have that unchallenged quality. But—and here I follow Adler—the desire to extort some admission of our own superiority over other people seems to be almost ineradicable in the human animal. Safety, success, the advantages of race or position, simply make that demand for acknowledgment more aggressive. We must have our admitted "inferiors" to touch their hats to us, make way for us, say "Sir," and listen respectfully. And the "inferior" who, for all our delusions of racial purity, is made of the same flesh and blood as we are will get it back somehow if he can, by revolt, by sabotage, by derision behind the master's back, by turning his humiliation on to *his* inferiors, and so on.

The struggle of the assertive self is unending, and the greatest triumph of civilisation and moral education, is so to sublimate the self-respect of the individual that he will put his pride into behaving like a gentleman and an equalitarian, in spirit and in truth. Mrs. Church Terrell has lived her life through a storm of burning injustices; but if she had been born a sensitive and impressionable white girl in a village on some English estate, destined normally to be an under-housemaid and marry an under-gardener, she would have had almost the same story to tell, if not in flamboyant colors then in aquatint. She would have struggled to independence and self-respect against handicaps less obvious but more insidious. She would have discovered parallel frustrations. She would have found her brothers and cousins barred, very effectively if not quite so emphatically, from education and opportunity. She would have realised that the mutual antagonism of classes, the conflict of the old school tie with the rank outsider, the monopolisation of business and jobs, the contemptuous treatment of the lower-class girl, the victimisation of the little man, were all going on—not in terms of blood and fire, but in monochrome—which may at times become a dingy grey, more dispiriting perhaps than the hot sunshine on a hot plantation.

"That is all very well," Mrs. Church Terrell may say, "but the fact remains that the colours of the inferiority and superiority struggle in Europe are not so intense as in the American scene, that the contrasts, as I saw them on my various visits to Europe, seemed to be fading." The prospect of a world, equalitarian in spirit, based on the Rights of Man and a mutual give and take seemed nearer to the Europe of those happy visits. We cannot say that now, and that leads to one of the most important of the many threads of interest that run through this volume of realities. There are many little items in it to sustain the idea that the civilisation of America is declining. The colour antagonism of America is increasing; it is not diminishing. It is sharper and more widespread.

Mrs. Church Terrell is much concerned with that, as well she may be. One can explain it only as a consequence of a steady deterioration in the general moral and intellectual quality of the United States, parallel with, if not so rapid as the contemporary moral and mental collapse of Europe. Every phase in such a general decline of social order is necessarily accompanied by a release of aggression, intolerance and original sin. So far back as 1906, I did a book of journalism, *The Future in America*, long since out of print, in which I discussed the American outlook with a frankness for which America has never been sufficiently grateful. And a year later, a much profounder critic than myself, Henry James, produced *The American Scene*, a book I rarely see quoted by American writers, in which he brought substance and experience to bear upon the same question.

Since *The Future in America* is out of print, I will quote something here which I quoted in that book. They are the words of a certain president of Cornell University, President White. He was a member of the class of 1853, and he made a great oration to the Yale alumni in 1883. He said:

"To a few tottering old men of our dear class of '53 it will be granted to look with straining eyes over the boundary into the twentieth century; but even these can do little to make themselves heard then. Most of us will not see it. But before us and around us, nay, in our own families, are the men who will see it.

The men who go forth from these dear shades tomorrow are girding themselves for it. . . .

". . . What, then, is to be done? Mercantilism, necessitated at first by our circumstances and position, has been in the main a great blessing. It has been so under a simple law of history. How shall it be prevented from becoming, in obedience to a similar inexorable law, a curse?

"Here, in its answer to this question, it seems to me, is the most important message from this century to the next.

"For the great thing to be done is neither more nor less than to develop other great elements of civilisation, now held in check, which shall take their rightful place in the United States, which shall modify the mercantile spirit. . . which shall make the history of our country something greater and broader than anything we have reached, or ever can reach, under the sway of mercantilism alone.

". . . We must do all that we can to rear greater fabrics of religious, philosophic thought, literary thought, scientific, artistic, political thought, to summon young men more and more into these fields, not as a matter of taste, or social opportunity, but as a patriotic duty; to hold before them not the incentive of mere gain or of mere pleasure or of mere reputation, but the ideal of a new and higher civilisation. The greatest work which the coming century has to do in this country is to build up an aristocracy of thought and feeling which shall hold its own against the aristocracy of mercantilism. I would have more and more the appeal made to every young man who feels within him the ability to do good or great things in any of these higher fields, to devote his powers to them as a sacred duty, no matter how strongly the mercantile or business spirit may draw him. . . .

"In the individual minds and hearts and souls of the messengers who are preparing for the next century is the source of regeneration. They must form an ideal of religion higher than that of a life devoted to grasping and grinding and griping, with a whine for mercy at the end of it. They must form an ideal of science higher than that of increasing the production of iron or cotton. They must form an ideal of literature and art higher than that of pandering to the latest prejudice or whimsey. And they must form an ideal of man himself worthy of that century into which are to be poured the accumulations of this. So shall material elements be brought to their proper place, made stronger for good, made harmless for evil. So shall we have that development of new and greater elements, that balance of principles which shall make this republic greater than anything of which we can now dream."

I will add no comment of my own to that. Turn over the pages of this plucky, distressful woman's naive story of the broadening streak of violence, insult and injustice in your country, through which she has been compelled to live her life. If President White came back to Cornell, and happened upon this book and began to ask questions, what answer would America give to him?

H. G. WELLS

London, England
April, 1940

INTRODUCTION

THIS IS THE STORY of a colored woman living in a white world. It cannot possibly be like a story written by a white woman. A white woman has only one handicap to overcome—that of sex. I have two—both sex and race. I belong to the only group in this country which has two such huge obstacles to surmount. Colored men have only one—that of race.

White women of Great Britain showed what a serious handicap they considered their sex by the desperate methods they used to obtain the suffrage. The white women of the United States proved they entertained the same view by working continuously and hard for more than seventy years to secure the rights which citizenship usually confers upon men. I wonder what they would have done if they had been obliged to overcome two handicaps instead of one.

In relating the story of my life I shall simply tell the truth and nothing but the truth—but not the whole truth, for that would be impossible. And even if I tried to tell the whole truth few people would believe me. I am well aware that truth will be interpreted by some to mean bitterness. But I am not bitter.

I have been obliged to refer to incidents which have wounded my feelings, crushed my pride and saddened my heart. I have touched upon this phase of my life as lightly as I could without misrepresenting the facts. I do not want to be accused of "whining." I have not tried to arouse the sympathy of my readers by tearing passion to tatters, so as to show how wretched I have been. The many limitations imposed upon me and the humiliations to which I have been subjected speak for themselves.

I have recorded what I have been able to accomplish in spite of the obstacles which I have had to surmount. I have done this, not because I want to tell the world how smart I am, but because both a sense of justice and a regard for truth prompt me to show what a colored woman can achieve in spite of the difficulties by which race prejudice blocks her path if she fits herself to do a certain thing, works with all her might and main to do it and is given a chance.

Some of my white friends tell me that colored people must work out their own salvation. I hope the efforts which I have made will convince them that I have tried not only to work out my own salvation, but to help others in my group to work out theirs.

I do not want to wage a holy war or any other kind of war upon a group which is strong and powerful enough to circumscribe my activities and prevent me from entering fields in which I should like to work. I wish to insist upon this with all the emphasis which I can command. No colored woman clothed in her right mind who has had as many genuine friends in the dominant race as I have had and who has been given by them as many opportunities to render the service which I have tried to give could be bitter toward the whole group.

CHAPTER 1

MY PARENTS

To TELL THE TRUTH, I came very near not being on this mundane sphere at all. In a fit of despondency my dear mother tried to end her life a few months before I was born. By a miracle she was saved, and I finally arrived on scheduled time none the worse for the prenatal experience which might have proved decidedly disagreeable, if not fatal, to my future.

I distinguished myself as a baby by having no hair on my head for a long time. I was perfectly bald till I was more than a year old. I have a picture of myself taken in those days when my little head looked for all the world like a billiard ball. I have often wondered why my mother, who usually had such excellent taste about everything, wanted to hand down to posterity such a bald-headed baby as I was. While I would hate to think that my mother was ashamed of her baby, I am sure she did not take the same pride in exhibiting me to her friends that she would have felt if my head had been covered by a reasonable amount of hair.

But babies who are born under far more favorable conditions than those which confronted me when I was ushered into the world do not have all the blessings of life showered upon them. Bald-headed though I was, the fates were kind to me in one particular at least. I was born at a time when I did not have to go through life as a slave. My parents were not so fortunate, for they were both slaves. I am thankful that I was saved from a similar fate.

I learned about my father's antecedents in a very matter of fact, natural sort of way. It was his custom to take me in his buggy to see Captain C. B. Church Sunday mornings when

I was four or five years old. Captain Church always welcomed me cordially to his beautiful home, would pat me on the head affectionately, and usually filled my little arms with fruit and flowers when I left. "You've got a nice little girl here, Bob," he used to say to my father. "You must raise her right."

As for myself, I simply adored him. "Captain Church is certainly good to us, Papa," I said one day, just after Father had left his house. "And don't you know, Papa, you look just like Captain Church. I reckon you look like him because he likes you," I added, trying to explain in my childish way the striking resemblance between the two men. Then my father explained the relationship existing between Captain Church and himself, and told me how kind Captain Church had always been to him. "He raised me from a baby," said he. "He taught me to defend myself, and urged me never to be a coward. 'If anybody strikes you, hit him back,' said Captain Church, 'and I'll stand by you. Whatever you do, don't let anybody impose upon you.'" And my father was very obedient in this particular without a doubt.

Hanging on the wall of our home in Memphis, Tennessee, where I was born, near the close of the Civil War, there used to be a picture of Captain Church dressed as a Knight Templar, and near by one of my father wearing the same uniform. They looked exactly like the picture of the same man taken at different periods of his life. I have heard my father say that Captain Church's sympathy was on the side of the Union, even though he was a slaveholder, and that he suffered financially because he took this stand.

My father was so fair that no one would have supposed that he had a drop of African blood in his veins. As a matter of fact, he had very little. A few years ago I received a letter from a white man of whom I had never heard before, saying:

"Your grandmother Emmeline was my mother's nurse and life companion. My own mother died some two years ago at the age of 78 and but a short time previous to her death gave a sketch of some of her early life. I did not take down any of the scenes described, but one of them I remember very vividly, because there was such a beautiful touch of the polished fiction in real life connected with it. It was something of the early life of your great-grandmother as well as of your own grandmother, Emmeline.

"Your great-grandmother was not an African or of African descent, but a Malay princess brought over from the Island of San Domingo in captivity by a slave ship, bound for the United States from the shores of Africa. After the ship had secured its cargo of slaves, it touched at one of the ports of an island in San Domingo, at a time when the island was in a state of revolution. The revolution had in this particular instance overthrown the royal family, and had them in captivity.

"When the captain of the slaver went ashore, he found this state of affairs, and the Rebels had given the royal family, then in prison, the choice of either being sold into slavery or beheaded. Among those then in prison was a beautiful Malay girl, about 14 years old, a member of the royal family. Her complexion was a deep red and her hair was very straight and black. She had around her neck a beautiful coral chain attached to a gold cross, which her captors allowed her to retain. The captain of the slaver made a trade for her. She was not placed among the African slaves, but given a place in the cabin.

"Upon arrival at Norfolk, Va., one of the favorite ports of both entry and sale for the slavers in those days, she was sold to a rich tobacco merchant at what was then considered a fancy price. My grandfather had three plantations in Virginia at that time, and it was his custom to go down to Norfolk upon the arrival of these slavers and purchase more or less of these wild Africans. By distributing them among the other slaves on the plantations, they would in course of time become civilized. It was only after a very spirited bidding did he let the young princess go to her purchaser.

"She was taken into the family of this merchant as seamstress to his daughters, a position in those days of promise and distinction to any slave. In the course of a few years, after her daughter Emmeline was born and but a little girl, this tobacco merchant failed in business, and his slaves all had to be sold, including your grandmother and her mother.

"My grandfather went to Norfolk, and after assuring your great-grandparent that her little girl would be raised among his own daughters, he bought the very little girl, Emmeline, and gave her to my mother, who was then his baby girl. My mother's name was Rosalie and she and the little girl, Emmeline, were brought up more as two sisters than as mistress and maid.

"A planter from near Natchez, Miss., bought Emmeline's mother and she was given the position of seamstress to the household in his family. In fact, she was never treated as a slave and never had to do menial work. Besides speaking her own native language she had learned French while on the Island of San Domingo. All through her life she retained her talisman, the coral chain and cross, which her captors in San Domingo had allowed her to retain.

"My mother was married at the age of sixteen, after moving from Virginia to Holly Springs, Miss., and thence to Arkansas. Twenty years of her life were spent in New Orleans, where your grandmother, Emmeline, learned the French language and always passed as a creole. I have often heard my mother say she was the most beautiful type of creole she ever saw. The affection which existed between Mother and Emmeline was more on the order of sisters than mistress and maid. When Emmeline died Mother said she could never see as much sunshine in after years. Emmeline was a communicant of the Episcopal Church at the time of her death.

"You know we Southerners take much pleasure in watching the advancement and prosperity of even the younger generation of those whose parents were connected with our household and children's growth. I hope this little memo of history will be interesting to you. If it does, may I ask you to send me a photo of your own family, if possible, if not, of you and your husband. Now I wish you and yours many blessings of the future.

"I am most respectfully yours,"

When he wrote me this letter the man who says his mother owned my grandmother lived in Mammoth Springs, Ark., and so far as I know, his family resides there now.

Many a time I have lived over that parting scene when Emmeline, my grandmother, who was then only a small child, was sold from her mother never to see her again. Often have I suffered the anguish which I know that poor slave mother felt, when her little girl was torn from her arms forever.

When slavery is discussed and somebody rhapsodizes upon the goodness and kindness of masters and mistresses toward their slaves in extenuation of the cruel system, it is hard for me to conceal my disgust. There is no doubt that some slaveholders were kind to their slaves. Captain Church was one of them, and this daughter of a slave father is glad thus publicly to express her gratitude to him. But the anguish of one slave mother from whom her baby was snatched away outweighs all the kindness and goodness which were occasionally shown a fortunate, favored slave.

My father was employed in various capacities on Captain Church's boats. From being a dishwasher he was finally elevated to the dignity of steward, which was as high a place as a slave could then occupy. In this capacity he naturally became accustomed to buying in large quantities. And the habit thus acquired followed him through life. In supplying his own home he never bought a little of anything. My earliest recollection is of seeing barrels of flour, firkins of butter, and large tins or wooden buckets of lard. He would buy turkeys and chickens by the crate. Bunches of bananas used to hang where we could easily get them in our house, and there was always a goodly supply of oranges and nuts.

My father was an excellent cook and enjoyed nothing more than coming into the kitchen to prepare dishes he liked. When I came home from school during summer vacations, one of the first things he used to do was to broil me a pompano, a fish which has a delightful flavor and is caught in the waters near New Orleans.

Although my father never went to school a day in his life, since there were no schools for slaves, he was unusually intelligent and thoughtful and reasoned exceedingly well. He learned to read by constantly perusing the newspapers and always kept abreast of the times. He taught himself to write his name legibly—even beautifully—but he never wrote a letter in his life to my knowledge. I do not know whether he would not or could not do this, but he always had an employee or a member of his family write his letters for him.

In conversing with my father, few would have suspected they were talking to an uneducated man except for an occasional mistake in grammar or the mispronunciation of a word, to which even educated people in the South are often addicted. I was never ashamed to have my father converse with anybody, no matter how highly educated or renowned that individual might be. I was always sure he would have something worth while to say and that he would express his thought very well.

When I was a mere slip of a girl I sometimes pitied other girls of my acquaintance because their parents made so many mistakes when they talked. But as I grew older I was not at all disturbed by the lapses in English made by those who were not responsible for their lack of education.

My father was rather reserved in his manner, was rarely familiar with anybody, and had a certain innate culture which men deprived of educational opportunities, as he was, rarely possess. He had business ability of high order and gave proof of that fact over and over again. It is a great temptation to say much about my father, for he was a remarkable man in many respects. I am not trying to paint him as a saint, for he was far from being one. He had the vices and defects common to men born at that time under similar circumstances, reared as a slave, and environed as he was for so many years, from necessity rather than choice, after he was freed.

My father had the most violent temper of any human being with whom I have come in contact. In a fit of anger he seemed completely to lose control of himself, and he might have done anything desperate in a rage. He was one of the most courageous men I have ever known. If it ever has been true of a human being that he knew no fear, it can be said of Robert Reed Church during the major portion of his life. As he grew older and feebler, he lost some of the fire and dash of youth, as was natural, but even then he had plenty. I could cite a number of cases in which my father faced danger fearlessly, but I shall refer only to two.

Shortly after the Civil War what is commonly called "the Irish Riot" occurred in Memphis. During that disturbance my father was shot in the back of his head at his place of business and left there for dead. He had been warned by friends that he was one of the colored men to be shot. They and my mother begged him not to leave his home that day. But he went to work as usual in spite of the peril he knew he faced. He would undoubtedly have been shot to death if the rioters had not believed they had finished him when he fell to the ground. Till the day of his death there was at the back of his head a hole left by the bullet which wounded him, into which one could easily insert the tip of the little finger. He suffered terribly from excruciating headaches which attacked him at intervals and lasted several days. Sometimes the pain was so great he threatened to take his life. Doctors told him these headaches were caused by the wound he received during the Irish Riot when he was a young man.

I want to relate just one other incident showing the fearlessness of my father. He had bought an unusually beautiful sleigh on one of his trips to the North, not because he needed it in the South, but because he admired it. His friends considered it a huge joke that he had brought such a sleigh to Memphis, but he insisted that he would have occasion to use it some day. And he did.

There came a heavy fall of snow in Memphis one winter, and everybody who owned a sleigh brought it out. My father drove up and down Main Street in his beautiful sleigh several times. It was drawn by a horse that was decidedly a high stepper. People were enjoying the unusual fall of snow immensely and were throwing snowballs at each other in the street with great glee. As Father drove up and down Main Street a shower of snowballs struck him. At first he took it good-naturedly and laughed with the crowd, although they hurt him and frightened his horse. He soon discovered that the innocent-looking snowballs were stones and rocks covered with snow and thrown at him to injure him. After he had been pelted with these missiles several times, a large rock was hurled at him and struck him in the face. Then he pulled out a revolver and shot into the crowd of men who had injured him. It was a desperate thing for a colored man to do anywhere, particularly in the South, and it is a great wonder he was not torn limb from limb, even though he was shooting in self-defense.

In temperament and disposition my mother was as different from my father as one human being could well be from another. She irradiated good will and cheer upon all with whom she came into contact. She was a ray of sunshine all the time, and nobody, no matter how depressed he might be, could withstand the infection of her hearty, musical laugh. She had troubles of her own, to be sure, financial, domestic, and otherwise. But she could have said literally and truthfully with St. Paul, "None of these things move me."

Before her death she lived with me fifteen years in Washington, after she left New York City, which had been her home for a long time. I cannot recall that I ever saw her depressed but once, although she had lost all her worldly possessions and was in poor health. If I was gloomy or worried about anything and went to Mother's room to talk matters over with her, when I left her presence I always felt like a child who had hurt its finger and had its mother "kiss it well." She had a way of really convincing me (and I am not so easily "convinced") that the matter was not so bad as I thought it was, that the prospects didn't begin to be as gloomy as I had painted them, and that everything would turn out all right in the end.

As I look back upon my habit of confiding my troubles to my mother, I reproach myself severely for placing upon her mind and heart any burdens which she, herself, was not obliged to bear. It seems to me it was a weak and inconsiderate thing for a daughter to do. The only reason I can forgive myself for imposing my woes upon my mother was that she never seemed to let anything worry her at all.

She possessed artistic talent of a high order, and I believe she would have acquired considerable reputation as an artist if she had had a chance to study in her youth. When I had completed my sophomore year in college, I spent the summer vacation in Oberlin, Ohio, where I had been attending school. My mother came to see me and began to take lessons in painting. She was thoroughly absorbed in her work and did nothing from morning till night but paint. So enthusiastic and industrious was she in the pursuit of art, I was really concerned about her and feared she might be losing her mind. She painted pictures of birds, butterflies, and flowers, ad infinitum on little trays and articles of various kinds, till her room fairly overflowed with them. I have today a beautiful screen on which she painted wisteria, which has been highly commended by artists.

My mother also possessed remarkable business ability, and established a hair store in Memphis which was a brilliant success. I am sure she was the first colored woman in Memphis and among the first in the entire South to establish and maintain a store of such excellence as hers undoubtedly was. The élite of Memphis came to "Lou Church's" store to buy their hair goods. And 'way back in the 70's women had to buy a quantity of false hair to keep up with the prevailing style. There were waterfalls and curls galore hanging coquettishly under their chignons at the side of their heads. So fearfully and wonderfully made was the coiffure of the 1870's that my lady who could afford it always secured the services of a regular hairdresser and rarely attempted to do her hair herself for any important social function.

Lou Church was considered an artist, and her reputation as hairdresser spread far and wide. She used to relate with pride that when the Duke Alexis came to Memphis, some of the ladies who were to attend the big ball given in his honor came to her store as early as seven o'clock in the morning to have her dress their hair, because when they put in their order she had so many engagements ahead of them that she had to start early and work hard all day till nearly midnight, so as to fill them all.

Mother's hair store was in the most exclusive business section of Memphis, right off Court Square. If she were alive today I doubt very much whether she or any other colored woman could rent a store in such a prominent business section.

To her husband Mother was a helpmeet indeed, for it was she who bought the first home and the first carriage we had. She was the most generous human being I have ever known. There are several people living who can testify to that fact. I am sure she would cheerfully have given away the last cent she possessed, if she had thought it was necessary. And the individual who wanted to get it would not have had to argue or persuade much to convince her it was necessary. But, alas, she had less conception of the value of money or the necessity of saving it than anybody I have ever known. She lavished money on my brother and myself in buying us clothes and giving us everything

[9]

the heart of children could desire. Not only did she spend money freely on her own children, when she happened to have it, but she delighted in making presents to her friends.

My mother and father separated when I was quite young. This pained and embarrassed me very much. In those days divorces were not so common as they are now, and no matter what caused the separation of a couple, the woman was usually blamed. The court gave my brother, who was four years my junior, and myself into the custody of my mother. My little brother had been living with my father, and Father wanted to keep him, but the court refused to grant his request.

I remember very distinctly the day the "hack" drove up to Mother's house on Court Street, a block below her hair store, and deposited my little brother, bag and baggage on the sidewalk in front of our home. My joy knew no bounds.

Mother finally sold her store in Memphis and moved to New York City, where she established another on Sixth Avenue which she managed with brilliant success.

Although Mother had been a slave, she never referred to that fact. When I questioned her about it, she would usually say that her master had not only taught her to read and write, but had also given her lessons in French. She enjoyed relating that her wedding trousseau had been bought in New York by "Miss Laura," her master's daughter, who had gone there on a visit, and that she had been given a nice wedding at which a delicious repast had been served.

I cannot leave my forebears without saying a word about my dear grandmother on my mother's side. In complexion she was very dark brown, almost black, with a straight, shapely nose and a small mouth. In her manner she was quiet, refined, and reserved; she always spoke in a low tone of voice, and tried hard to teach her granddaughter to do the same thing. My grandmother was called "Aunt Liza" by everybody, black and white, old and young, and was generally beloved. When people in the neighborhood were ill, they always sent for "Aunt Liza." And she never failed them.

She could tell the most thrilling stories imaginable, and I listened to her by the hour. I wish I had inherited her gift. The story I liked best was the one which she told about a "hoop snake" which had spied some children walking through a wood, had decided to give them a good scare for being so far from home alone, and had put its tail in its mouih and rolled after them "jes' as hard as he could." One of the roving children happened to look back, saw the "hoop snake" pursuing them, and warned the others of their danger.

My eyes were as big as saucers and my hair stood on end at Grandmother's realistic imitation of the agonized tones of the eldest child as he called out, "Run, chillun, run, the hoop snake's after you! Run for your lives!"

Occasionally Grandmother told me tales of brutality perpetrated upon slaves who belonged to cruel masters. But they affected her and me so deeply she was rarely able to finish what she began. I tried to keep the tears back and the sobs suppressed, so that Grandmother would carry the story to the bitter end, but I seldom succeeded. Then she would stop abruptly and refuse to go on, promising to finish it another time. It nearly killed me to think that my dear grandmother, whom I loved so devotedly, had once been a slave. I do not know why the thought that my parents had once been slaves did not affect me in the same way. "Never mind, honey," she used to say to comfort me, "Gramma ain't a slave no more."

She had an unpleasant experience herself which it pained me to hear her relate. She was reared in the house and was the housekeeper for "ole miss," so she rarely came into contact with the overseer. But one day she went into the field on an errand and the overseer challenged her about something. She resented what he said and he threatened to whip her.

"I dared him to tech me," she said. "Then he started toward me raising his whip. I took out and run jes' as fast as ever I could and he right after me. When I got to the kitchen door I picked up a chair and said, ef you come a step nearer, I'll knock your brains out with this here chair. An' he never come a step nearer, neither."

James Wilson, my father's brother, was as fair as a lily, with eyes as blue as the sky, and was as perfect a specimen of the Caucasian as could be found anywhere in the world. Uncle Jim was forced to fight in the Confederate Army very much against his will. Although he was usually cool and calm, nothing riled him so quickly as a reference to what he considered that painful and disgraceful episode in his life.

Not many people have fewer relatives than myself. Until my father married a second time, for many years our entire family consisted of my mother, father, brother and myself.

CHAPTER 2

EARLY CHILDHOOD

DURING MY CHILDHOOD my parents lived in what was then called the suburbs of Memphis, where I was born near the close of the Civil War. The first playmates whom I can remember were German children who lived near by. My mother says that sometimes she could not understand what I wanted, because I would call things by their German rather than by their English names, having heard my playmates talk about them in their mother tongue.

Although I was christened Mary Eliza Church, neither my family nor my friends called me Mary. I was known as Mollie Church to everybody who was acquainted with me. The name of one of Captain Church's daughters was Mollie. Perhaps that may have influenced Father to give me that nickname. But Miss Mollie Church was deaf and dumb. As a child, I talked a great deal and was never quiet of my own free will and accord, if I could find anything to do, which I generally did, or could discover anybody to talk to. When he heard me chattering like a magpie, Father used often to say that nothing could have been more inappropriate than that his little daughter's namesake should be dumb. But he would usually wind up by saying that honors were easy, after all, for I talked enough for both of us.

One of my earliest recollections is of a terrible scene which I should like to forget, but cannot even unto this day. I must have been very young, not four years old, I think. During my mother's absence from home a cat caught her canary bird. A woman who worked for us decided to punish the animal, called some of her friends together for that purpose, and with their assistance beat it to death. I remember well how I fought and scratched and cried, trying to save the cat's life. When I found I could not do so, I fled from the awful scene before it succumbed.

As I look back upon that shocking exhibition of cruelty to animals, I can easily understand why those ignorant women were guilty of it. They had all been slaves and had undoubtedly seen men, women, and children unmercifully beaten by overseers for offenses of various kinds, and they were simply practicing upon an animal which had done wrong from their point of view the cruelty which had been perpetrated upon human beings over and over again.

While I was very small and still lived in the suburbs, my father employed a man by the name of Dan, who often looked upon the wine when it was red and got into trouble as a consequence. As Dan was an excellent workman when he was sober, Father used to pay his fines when he was arrested for intoxication.

One day the police came to our house to arrest Dan for some slight infraction of the law, and, after searching all over the premises, they were about to leave without finding him. But, just as I saw them close the front gate behind them, I called out, "Mister, I know where Dan is. He's hiding under that big tub yonder." When I saw the officers taking Dan away and realized what I had done, I was inconsolable, for I loved him very much. I cried so continuously and begged so piteously that Dan be allowed to come back to the house that my father was forced to pay his fine again, although he had previously vowed he had taken Dan out of jail for the last time.

I can scarcely recall going to school in Memphis at all. Just one incident stands out prominently in my mind which proves I did. One day my father came to the school, which was in a church near a bayou, to bring me a doll, and found me tied to my teacher's apron strings. She was somewhat embarrassed to have my father see me in such a plight and explained that, while I was really a nice child and meant well, it was utterly impossible for me to keep still.

"Mollie suddenly disappeared a short while ago," she said, "and I was greatly alarmed, because in looking around the room I could find her nowhere. As I walked down the aisle, I spied her crawling on the floor under a seat to get to a girl in front of her." I can recall hearing the teacher remonstrate rather mildly with my father for bringing me a doll to school. But Father left it with me nevertheless. I presume he had seen the doll in a store, remembered he had a little daughter who would enjoy it, bought it, and brought it to the school without thinking there could be the slightest objection to it, since he knew nothing whatever about schools himself or school discipline on general principles.

I can recall another incident of my childhood which my mother used to enjoy relating very much. In my day and time little girls who were very active were called "frisky," and that adjective was often applied to me. I was chosen "Queen" for some Christmas exercise and wore what I thought was a beautiful red tarlatan dress which stood out stiff and straight. I had to sit on a very high throne. For some reason or other (perhaps because I grew tired of sitting alone on such a high perch) I decided to leave that distasteful eminence and suddenly jumped to the floor, to the horror of those in the audience who saw me take such a dangerous leap. Mother could never understand how I could jump such a distance on a hard floor without breaking my leg, at least.

The first time I remember having the Race Problem brought directly home to me was when I was going North with my father, who used to take me with him everywhere he went. I could not have been more than five years old. There was no Jim Crow car law in the state of Tennessee then, so that although there was a separate coach for colored people and they were expected to occupy it, there was no law on the statute books to force them to sit in it. As a rule, therefore, self-respecting colored people would not go into the coach set apart for them.

When my father boarded the train he took me into the best coach, but soon afterward went into the smoker. So far as I can recall, as a child, whenever I saw my father in the company of white men, they talked with him as they did with other men and treated him, in general, as they did each other. I call attention to this fact particularly, because the period to which I refer was so soon after the emancipation of the slave. It seems remarkable that in their relations to each other both the ex-masters and the ex-slaves could adjust themselves as quickly as they did in some instances to the new order of things.

My father had been in the smoker but a short time when the conductor passed through the coach to collect tickets, glared at me, and asked who I was and what I was doing in that car. I replied as well as a frightened little girl, five years old, could be expected to answer under the circumstances. But I did not placate the irate conductor, who decided then and there to put me into the coach "where I belonged." As he pulled me roughly out of the seat, he turned to the man sitting across the aisle and said, "Whose little nigger is this?"

The man told him who my father was and advised him to let me alone. Seeing the conductor was about to remove me from the car, one of my father's white friends went into the smoker to tell him what was happening. My father returned immediately and there ensued a scene which no one who saw it could ever forget.

In that section at that time it was customary for men to carry revolvers in their pockets. Fortunately, no one was injured and I was allowed to remain with my courageous father in the white coach.

Naturally, this incident agitated my young mind considerably. I plied my father with questions. I thought of all the sins of omission and commission against which my mother had warned me before I left home, but I could think of nothing that I had done wrong. I could get no satisfaction from Father, however, for he refused to talk about the affair and forbade me to do so.

In relating the incident to my mother, when I reached home, I asked her why the conductor had wanted to take me out of a nice, clean coach and put me into one my father said was dirty. I assured her I had been careful to do everything she told me to do. For instance, my hands were clean and so was my face. I hadn't mussed my hair; it was brushed back and was perfectly smooth. I hadn't lost either one of the two pieces of blue ribbon which tied the little braids on each side of my head. I hadn't soiled my dress a single bit. I was sitting up "straight and proper." Neither was I looking out of the window, resting on my knees with my feet on the seat (as I dearly loved to do). I wasn't talking loud. In short, I assured my mother I was "behaving like a little lady," as she told me to do. Trying to suppress her tears, my mother patted me on the head and comforted me by saying she was sure I was behaving myself, but she explained the incident by telling me that sometimes conductors on railroad trains were unkind and treated good little girls very badly. Seeing their children touched and seared and wounded by race prejudice is one of the heaviest crosses which colored women have to bear.

[16]

I can recall vividly just one more incident which took place during my early childhood, before I left Memphis to go to school in the North. My grandmother, Eliza, was very religious and attended the Baptist Church regularly. On one occasion when she wore a new spring bonnet which my mother had just given her, she was so impressed with the sermon that she began to shout. When I saw her jumping up and down and clapping her hands together, I became greatly alarmed on account of the damage it might do to the new spring headgear. I tried my best to stop her by holding on to her dress, and I cried aloud: "Oh, Grandma, please don't shout, you're knocking off your new spring bonnet and you'll ruin it." It is unnecessary to describe the effect which this plea for the preservation of that precious piece of millinery had upon the congregation.

CHAPTER 3

I AM SENT NORTH TO SCHOOL

Rᴇᴀʟɪᴢɪɴɢ that the educational facilities for colored children were very poor in Memphis at that time and that she could not rear me as she wished, Mother decided to send me North to school, when I was about six years old. Two of her friends had sent their daughters to Antioch College in Yellow Springs, Ohio, and she decided to send me there also. Mother took me there herself and arranged to have me board with a family by the name of Hunster, consisting of the parents, two grown daughters—"Miss Maggie" and "Miss Sallie"—and two grown sons, the elder of whom was a cripple and used crutches. He kept a candy store in the front room of the large house and I patronized it very well, for my father allowed me five dollars a month for sweetmeats.

No little girl could possibly have been happier than I was so far away from home, for I became a member of that family in every sense of the word. I called Mrs. Hunster "Ma" and Mr. Hunster "Pa." Miss Sallie, petite, vivacious, and amiable, was my favorite and I loved her fondly. The young man she married later was attending college in Yellow Springs, and it was one of the greatest privileges of my life to be allowed to carry notes from one to the other.

In Yellow Springs I was sent to what I believe was the forerunner of the kindergarten in the United States. It was called the "Model School," and as I look back upon it today, I feel sure it deserved the name "Model." This school for children was connected with Antioch College, of which Horace Mann, the great educator, was first president.

Mrs. Hunster lived in a very large house and kept a hotel, called the Union House. It was the best, in fact it was the only hostelry in Yellow Springs when I was a child. Many were the gay sleighing parties which came from Springfield and the surrounding towns. In the summer there was an ice cream parlor and I considered it great sport to be allowed to serve the patrons sometimes. One of the most delightful recollections of my life in Yellow Springs is the ride I used to take with Pa Hunster in the wagon very early in the morning, when we went to get cream from a farm quite a distance away. For the Hunsters' ice cream was made from the pure and unadulterated article, if you please.

I was allowed to eat just as much cream as I wished, and I dare say I ate too much, for I have never cared a great deal for it since. I have regretted this exceedingly many times. It is very embarrassing for a woman accustomed to attend social functions not to like ice cream. She must either refuse it altogether, leave it untouched on her plate to annoy her hostess or force herself to partake of something she does not like. Many a time when I have felt obliged to eat ice cream to be polite, I would have much preferred a sandwich.

The distance between the Hunsters' hotel and Antioch College was quite long for a little girl my age, and on one occasion I narrowly escaped freezing to death. I had bravely trudged through the snow until I reached the college grounds, which were enclosed by a high fence. By the time I had pulled myself to the top rail I was so exhausted and so numb with cold I could go no farther. And there I sat for what seemed to me an interminable time, unable to move on that bitter winter morning, slowly freezing to death. Fortunately for me, a man happened to pass by and rescued me from my perilous perch.

While I was attending this model school, my mother, who believed that children should learn at least two foreign languages, decided to have me study German and engaged a young woman student to give me lessons. I have no idea whether I made any progress in German or not, but I enjoyed going to my teacher's room in the dormitory. It thrilled me to see the young women walking through the halls, to and from their rooms, and I decided then and there that some day I would have a room in a dormitory myself. Since my teacher taught me just before noon, she always seemed hungry, and ate an apple which she shared with me, so that whether I learned any German or not I looked forward to my lesson with pleasure.

After I had attended the Model School for several years the Hunsters advised my mother to send me to the public schools. I enjoyed the work here as I always did when I went to school. I cannot recall that I ever had to be forced to study. I was ambitious to stand at the head of my class and I was willing to pay the price. I do not deserve one bit of credit for this, however, for getting my lessons was a sort of indoor sport for me and was a genuine joy. I was always curious to know what "my books" were going to say next. But by no possible stretch of the imagination could anybody call me a "goody, goody girl," for I played and romped every minute I could. Climbing trees had to be done a bit surreptitiously, but I climbed them just the same. I used to pick cherries for the people who would let me, and enjoyed disputing the fruit with the birds. Sometimes it was very hard to get permission from the lady with whom I boarded to climb trees, but occasionally she relented to allow me to pick cherries for a neighbor.

The night before our class was to be examined in geography I learned word for word certain passages about which I thought it likely the class would be questioned. I guessed right and my paper was marked 100. I must have exhausted my store of geographical lore in this examination, for I have known practically nothing about geography from that day to this. Ever since I was a little girl I have traveled a great deal in the United States, but it is very difficult for me to bound the states through which I have passed many times and which the average normal human being under similar circumstances could locate with ease and would know by heart. I believe I possess as little sense of direction as anybody, not mentally deficient, could possibly have. If there is any bump of geography or topography in my cranium, its growth has been arrested. I once read that Mark Twain was similarly afflicted and it comforted me considerably.

In the public schools of Yellow Springs I learned a fact that I had never known before. While we were reciting our history lesson one day, it suddenly occurred to me that I, myself, was descended from the very slaves whom the Emancipation Proclamation set free. I was stunned. I felt humiliated and disgraced. When I had read or heard about the Union army and the Rebel forces, I had never thought about my connection with slavery at all. But now I knew I belonged to a group of people who had been brutalized, degraded, and sold like animals. This was a rude and terrible shock indeed.

"Here you are," said a voice ironically, "measuring arms with these white children whose ancestors have always been free. What audacity!" I was covered with confusion and shame at the thought, and my humiliation was painful indeed. When I recovered my composure I resolved that so far as this descendant of slaves was concerned, she would show those white girls and boys whose forefathers had always been free that she was their equal in every respect. At that time I was the only colored girl in the class, and I felt I must hold high the banner of my race.

When I grew older, however, the stigma of being descended from slaves had lost its power to sting. For then I discovered that with a single, solitary exception, and that a very small one, no race has lived upon the face of this earth which has not at some time in its history been the subject of a stronger. If history teaches one lesson more than another, it is that races wax and wane. The conqueror may lord it over his subject for a time, but he is himself conquered in the end. Holding human beings in slavery seems to have been part of the divine plan to bring out the best there is in them. In being descended from slaves, therefore, I learned that my group and I are no exception to a general rule. This fact not only comforted and consoled me, but it greatly increased my self-respect. I felt I had the right to look the world in the eye like any other free woman and to hold my head as high as anybody else.

I had only one disagreeable experience in the public schools of Yellow Springs. Once when I had really done nothing wrong, a nervous little teacher accused me of whispering and boxed my ears. So well did she do her work that I was deaf from the effect of her blows for several days, and I doubt that my hearing has ever been as good as it previously was. This so incensed the Hunsters that they went to the superintendent to get redress. After questioning the children who sat near me and investigating the matter thoroughly, he was convinced that I had been punished unjustly and directed the teacher to apologize to me. I have often regretted this occurrence for the sake of the teacher. I do not wonder that she made a mistake. It was quite natural that my teacher should take it for granted that I was whispering on this particular occasion, since I had sinned in that respect so many times. It was extremely difficult for me to keep still in school from the day I entered till I received my degree from college. In a great throng which was surging through one of the buildings at the Centennial Exposition in Philadelphia a few years after this little episode I happened to spy my teacher who had punished me unjustly, and I was as glad to see her as though nothing of a disagreeable nature had happened.

It was at Yellow Springs that I was obliged to make my first decision with reference to the Race Problem. I was the only colored girl in my grade and one of the few colored girls in the public school. In the town at that time there were only two colored families with whom the Hunsters associated, for there were then but few representatives of the race in that small village.

A play was to be produced at the close of the public schools and the pupils were being selected for their parts. It was an amusing little play in which several nationalities were to appear. I was invited to take the part of a Negro servant who made a monkey of himself and murdered the king's English, but I refused to do so without discussing the matter with anybody at home or asking anybody's advice. I decided not to take the part. I knew this role had been assigned me solely because I was a colored girl, and I was embarrassed and hurt.

Before this, while I was attending the Model School, I had had an experience which indelibly impressed my racial identity upon me and about which even to this day I do not like to think. Every noon I went into the cloakroom to get my wraps preparatory to going home. One day when I entered, a group of young women were chatting there and several of them were posing before the mirror, joking about their charms.

"Behold my wonderful tresses," one was saying. "But look at my sparkling eyes," challenged another. "My rosebud mouth," called out a third, "is the admiration of the world." After putting on my coat I heard somebody speak to me, as I passed the mirror, and not knowing what else to say, I imitated the young ladies, as a small girl sometimes will, by asking "Haven't I got a pretty face too?" "You've got a pretty black face," said one of the young ladies, pointing her finger at me derisively.

The shout of laughter that went up from that group of young women rings in my ears to this day. For the first time in my life I realized that I was an object of ridicule on account of the color of my skin. I was so shocked, embarrassed, and hurt I was glued to the spot and could not budge an inch. I seemed to lose the power to think as well as to move, so I could not say a word. It dawned on me with terrific force that these young white girls were making fun of me, were laughing at me, because I was colored. As I stood motionless, a pathetic little figure in that large room, the laughter died down considerably. I had not yet put on my hat and it slipped to the floor. When I had recovered sufficiently to stoop and pick it up, the change of position seemed to restore my power to think and to revive my courage. I ran to the door, stopped, turned around, and hurled back defiantly, "I don't want my face to be white like yours and look like milk. I want it nice and dark just like it is." As I ran down the hall, I heard them clapping their hands.

That experience taught me a lesson which I have never forgotten. From that day to this, not only have I never laughed at any human being because of any physical defect, but I have never had the slightest inclination to do so. It is amazing how many people who are otherwise kind, considerate, and well bred have the bad habit of making fun of people, if one or more of their features are not exactly in proper proportion, or pleasing to the eye, or if they carry themselves in some peculiar way.

Whenever a Chinaman passed by and children, black as well as white, sang out derisively, "Ching, Ching Chinaman, do you eat rats?" I invariably reminded the colored children that just as they made fun of Chinese, many people made fun of us. Or I would run up to white children and declare with too much emphasis and feeling, perhaps, that I liked the Chinaman's pretty yellow complexion better than I did their pale, white one. Of course there were always consequences of various kinds after such a speech, which were often decidedly unpleasant. But I made up my mind to stand them, whatever they were. I remembered the scene in the cloakroom and I could hear the voice of ridicule crying out, "Your face is pretty black."

But some people are natural-born game-makers. I have heard very homely women poke fun at the personal appearance of another who was quite pretty, if the latter had the slightest physical defect which they could detect. It is amazing that it never seems to occur to game-makers that there is anything the matter with themselves. They apply their high standards of pulchritude to everybody but themselves and do not sigh with Robbie Burns: "Oh wad some power the giftie gie us to see oursels as others see us."

In Yellow Springs I saw the beginning of the great temperance reform. It puzzled us children to see the good ladies sit on camp stools in front of a little grog shop all day till quite late at night. And some declared that the ladies who were trying to close this objectionable resort remained in front of it all night long. I, myself, had been reared to believe in taking liquor in moderation, and this idea of not drinking anything at all was something new under the sun to us children who looked at these pioneers in temperance work.

Until I was sent away to school, my father gave me a "toddy" for my health every morning. It was all right except when he put garlic in it, which frequently happened, and then it was more or less an ordeal. In my generation many parents believed it was a great mistake not to give children liquor at home. They argued that if they were not taught to drink in moderation there, they would go to extremes when they first tasted it among strangers.

Few people who saw women taking turns standing or sitting before those saloons, when I was a child, dreamed that in forty years an amendment to the Constitution would be passed prohibiting the manufacture and sale of ardent spirits all over the United States. By many the temperance reform was then considered a joke, and those who believed in it were regarded as cranks. There could be no better illustration of the saying that "it is the unexpected which happens" than the passage of the Volstead Act. Although many criticisms were hurled against the methods used to accomplish the temperance reform, even those who opposed it wished it were possible to put the cause of so much poverty, sorrow, and crime beyond the reach of the multitude.

During the period when an effort was being made to enforce the Volstead Act, whenever I saw a young man of exceptional ability or who gave promise of having an unusually brilliant career, I used to say to myself, "Whatever may be the obstacles which you will be obliged to overcome and whatever may be the temptations which you will have to resist, the saloon with its allure will not be one of them. Even if you have inherited the love of strong drink, your career will be less likely to be ruined by it, because the opportunity of indulging your taste for it does not beckon you from all sides as it did your fathers before you."

Speaking of drink reminds me of an experience I had when I was quite small. My father kept fine horses for many years. Some of them were such high steppers that races on the boulevard with other steeds of like mettle were of common occurrence. On one occasion my father was taking me out for a drive and met a Mr. McClain, a white man, who owned a horse of which he was very proud. He immediately challenged my father for a race and the two men agreed that the loser was to give the winner a dinner at the Half Way House, as soon as it had been run. My father won the race and the two men with the little girl repaired to the inn to carry out the agreement.

Whenever an order was given to the waiter it was made for three, and in the enthusiastic discussion of the race and the horses, both the host and the guest evidently forgot that one of the three was a small girl. And that little lady, who was nothing if not imitative, did everything she saw her father do with the liquid as well as with the solid refreshments set before her. As a consequence of this, my first dissipation, I was ill several days. I had literally slipped from my chair before my father realized what had happened.

As I think of that dinner given my father by his white friend at a public house near Memphis, Tennessee, I cannot help contrasting conditions which existed when I was a child with those which obtain at the present time. It is but one of the many incidents which might be cited to prove how much closer and more friendly were the relations existing between the two races right after the Civil War than they are today, and also how much greater were the privileges enjoyed by colored men than they are now. I cannot conceive of any circumstance or situation which would induce the proprietor of a public house in or near a Southern city to serve any colored man, no matter how much he might be importuned to do so, or what the emergency might be.

At Yellow Springs the first signs of what talent for public speaking I possess began to manifest themselves. I learned many a poem by heart and loved to recite them to anyone I could induce to listen to me. There was one poem which appealed very strongly to me. I enjoyed nothing more than reciting:

"Give me three grains of corn, Mother,
Give me three grains of corn,
It will keep the little life I have,
Till the coming of the morn."

I used to follow Ma Hunster all around the kitchen while she was preparing the meals, and pursue her into the dining room or out into the yard, or wherever she went, reciting this pathetic poem. And what wonderful patience with me Ma Hunster had! She not only encouraged me to recite to her, but she praised the manner in which I declaimed and said she enjoyed it!

During the summer vacations I remained in Yellow Springs. Learning poems by heart was one of the tasks set to keep me out of mischief. It was then I learned Tennyson's "Queen of the May," which I never tired of reciting. At that early age I acquired a taste for Tennyson's poems which I have retained throughout my life. It was also in that little town that I learned to read good books. Many of them I drew from the library of the Sunday school of the Christian Church, which I attended regularly.

It is the fashion among some people today to ridicule the books which used to be given out by the Sunday-school libraries, because it is claimed they were not true to life and usually made the good die young. But I believe that at the time so few books were written for children, the Sunday school did well to offer its pupils the best in literature that was then available.

The Rollo books were prime favorites with most of us children. When Louisa Alcott's books began to appear, they were received with an acclaim among the young people of this country which has rarely if ever been equaled and never surpassed. I could hardly wait for *St. Nicholas* to appear from month to month. I owe a real debt of gratitude to the editors of that magazine for the pleasure which its contents gave me as a child. There were puzzles in the back of the magazine to solve, and the morning when I feverishly tore off the cover to see whether the solution I had sent in was correct, discovered that it was, and saw my name in print for the first time was a real red-letter day in my life.

My interest in politics began in Yellow Springs, to which the most distinguished campaign speakers used to come. I can remember attending some of the meetings and listening with rapt attention to the spell-binders reel off their eloquence by the yard. Young as I was, I worshiped General Grant and recited with great enthusiasm the following partisan rhyme over and over again:

> "Grant rides a white horse,
> Greeley rides a mule.
> Grant is a gentleman,
> Greeley is a fool."

Since I have read the life of Horace Greeley and know how upright, wise, and good a man he was, I regret exceedingly that my childish partisanship for Grant, which that great general undoubtedly deserved, caused me to rattle off a rhyme so uncomplimentary to his political rival, who possessed so many virtues and towered so high among the notable men of the time.

Fate surely smiled upon me when she influenced my mother to send me to Yellow Springs and place me in a school for children connected with Antioch College. Mrs. Caroline H. Dall has written an interesting brochure about this institution entitled *The College, the Market and the Court*, in which she declares, "A more exquisite model school than the one connected with the college I never saw."

When I contrast what my educational foundation would have been if I had remained in Memphis and had been sent to the school for colored children, poorly equipped as those schools were then, with what it was in this model school, I lift up my heart in gratitude to my dear mother for her foresight and for the sacrifice she made in my behalf.

This chapter would be incomplete if I did not refer to the wonderful Christmas boxes which my generous mother used to send. They were full of everything which would delight the heart of a little girl. There were candies, nuts, and oranges, of course, plus a dress or two, a hat in the latest style, a gold ring, maybe two of them, a beautiful doll, nicely dressed, and other things which Mother thought I would need and like. The first Christmas box which I received not only was full of gifts for myself, but contained presents for each and every member of the Hunster family, including a cashmere dress for each of the Hunster girls.

But one of the gifts brought me no pleasure at all. It was

a hat, beautiful, stylish, and becoming, too. But it was altogether too advanced in style for that small town. Nobody there had anything like it. It had a piece of velvet hanging down the back, and none of the girls with whom I associated had any kind of streamer falling off their hats in the rear. So I cheerfully wore my last winter's hat to Sunday school and to church, and nobody could persuade me to wear my Christmas headgear, so stylish and new. When I was a little girl I had the greatest horror of appearing in anything different from the clothing which my chums wore, no matter how beautiful it might be.

Yellow Springs lies about seventy miles northeast of Cincinnati and fifty miles southwest of Columbus, Ohio, midway between the thriving cities of Springfield and Xenia, about eight miles from each. There was a wonderful glen with a deep ravine, high bluffs, projecting cliffs, and huge disrupted masses of rock which afforded an enchanting variety of scenery. As a child I played in that veritable fairyland, climbing the heights, gathering flowers of great variety and profusion, and gazing in rapture upon a waterfall which plunged down in a cascade ten or twelve feet high. The picturesque beauty of the place made a deep impression upon me. I enjoyed drinking from a far-famed spring which at that time attracted invalids from all over the United States. In addition to a little soda and magnesia, the water is so strongly impregnated with iron that it gives a yellow tinge to everything over which it flows and is for that reason called Yellow Spring. So deep lies the source of this spring that neither drought nor flood changes its volume, nor does heat or cold alter its temperature in the least.

I was so much impressed with the stories I heard about John Brown and admired his courage so much that I named the spring in his honor, and many of my older friends always referred to it as the "John Brown Spring."

I owe much to the instruction given me during the two years I was in the model school and the two years I attended the public schools of that little village. My training there was excellent, and I was started on the right track. From every point of view, my life in that small town was ideal. My love of nature is all the more genuine and intense because, in my childhood, my eyes were opened to its majesty and beauty as revealed in such profusion in that marvelous glen.

CHAPTER 4

MY PARENTS SEND ME TO OBERLIN, OHIO

AFTER I HAD SPENT four pleasurable and profitable years at Yellow Springs, my parents were advised by Mr. Winter Woods, a talented elocutionist, to send me to Oberlin, Ohio. He suggested that they should have me complete the course in the public schools first and then enter college. I wish that Winter Woods, Senior, were living today, so that I might express my gratitude to him for giving my parents this advice.

The superintendent of public schools wanted me to enter the "A Grammar," as it was called then. It corresponds to the eighth grade of the present time. But since the class had finished decimal fractions and I knew nothing about them, he feared I was not far enough advanced to enter that grade. He presented my case to a dear little teacher from New England who wore curls hanging down her back, and she cheerfully consented to stay after school to teach me decimals, if I wanted to do so, in order that I might enter the eighth grade. I gladly accepted her kind offer of assistance, and in a short time I had caught up with my class.

While I liked all the teachers in the Oberlin High School, there was one little woman only a few years older than her pupils, pretty and sweet, whom I adored.

In the Latin class was the daughter of a man who had formerly been a professor in Oberlin College and had later been sent as minister to Haiti. She could put up a pitiful mouth like a child about to cry and make big tears roll down her cheeks whenever she chose to do so. It often happened that this mischievous girl did not know her Latin lesson, so when she had been called upon and failed, she would look at the pretty little teacher with an injured, innocent air, primp up her mouth to cry, and then let the big tears course down her cheeks. Of course I was convulsed, and so was everybody else in the class who saw this exhibition. It was very difficult for the little teacher to keep a straight face when she looked at my friend weeping and saw me shaking with laughter. One day she asked both the naughty girls to stay after class, so that she might talk to us. "You girls say you love me very much," she began, "and you are always bringing me fruit and flowers. Well, if Mary weeps every time she fails and Mollie shakes with laughter, some fine day I'm going to laugh aloud myself, and then I'll be dismissed as a teacher of this school. If you really want me to continue to teach here, don't tempt me to disgrace myself any more." It is unnecessary to state that we behaved ourselves like two angels in that class ever afterward.

Several incidents of the first year in the high school stand out very clearly in my mind. I made 100 in my final examination in algebra. Although I did not care for mathematics particularly and never gave promise of writing a book on the subject, I did like algebra very much and was overjoyed at my mark.

Again, I wrote the first essay I ever attempted. My subject was "Birds," and I began it thus: "There are a great many birds in this world." Then I covered four sheets of paper with the names of all the birds of which there was any record in the encyclopedia which I could consult. "I like birds, and I do not see how anybody can be cruel to them," was the conclusion of my first sally into the field of literature.

In the middle of the first year I got into what then seemed to me very serious trouble indeed. Some good-natured, lazy boys who sat near me prevailed upon me during an examination to pass them the trial paper on which I had worked some examples in algebra before transcribing them on the paper which I handed in to the teacher. These boys had been notoriously and continuously inefficient in the subject. Naturally, when the teacher looked at their papers and saw that they had worked all the examples correctly, she was very much surprised. Then she observed that there was a striking similarity between the methods used by the boys and those which I had sent in. Then, too, the explanation of the steps taken which was given by the boys was exactly like mine. When I was confronted with this incriminating evidence there was nothing to do but confess that I had helped those boys by giving them the trial paper on which I had worked my examples and written out the reason for the method of solving the problems.

The punishment inflicted upon me for assisting the boys in this examination was that my mark was reduced so low that I was just allowed to pass. The boys whom I assisted were marked zero. That was a lesson I never forgot. I have often felt that it was a good thing for me that it happened so early in my course. It was the last time I ever communicated with any human being during an examination.

During the second year in the high school an incident occurred to which I am greatly indebted for my appreciation and love of the best music. Professor Fenelon B. Rice, who was then director of the Oberlin Conservatory of Music, came to the high school to train some girls to sing for our Commencement. Among the nine girls selected, I was one of three chosen to sing contralto. After rehearsing us several times, Professor Rice asked me to wait one day, so that he might talk to me. He then told me he would like to have me sing in either the First Congregational or the Second Congregational Church choir and invited me to join the Musical Union, also. I was sure I could not read music at sight well enough to pass, I said. But Professor Rice encouraged me to believe I could, and I did.

With but few intermissions, I sang in the choir of the First Congregational Church of Oberlin from the time I was in the second year of the high school till I graduated from college, a period of seven years. Most of the time I sang in the Musical Union as well.

To be a member of the choir of either the First or Second Church as well as of the Musical Union was a liberal education in the best choral works of the old masters and of the modern composers, also. I looked forward with keenest pleasure to singing "The Messiah" every Christmas, and I enjoyed taking part in the wonderful oratorio, "Elijah," often rendered during Commencement week. It was a great privilege to be a member of both these musical organizations, and the experience was of incalculable value to me in every way. What greater blessing or more priceless boon could be bestowed upon a human being than the ability to appreciate good music?

While I was in the high school I had to decide what course I would take when I entered college. I chose the Classical Course, which necessitated the study of Greek and which was often called the "gentlemen's course," because it was the one generally pursued by men who wanted the degree of Bachelor of Arts. Few women in Oberlin College took the Classical Course at that time. They took what was called the Literary Course, which could be completed two years sooner than the Classical Course but which did not entitle them to a degree. They simply received a certificate.

Some of my friends and schoolmates urged me not to select the "gentlemen's course," because it would take much longer to complete than the "ladies' course." They pointed out that Greek was hard; that it was unnecessary, if not positively unwomanly, for girls to study that "old, dead language" anyhow; that during the two extra years required to complete it I would miss a lot of fun which I could enjoy outside of college walls. And, worst of all, it might ruin my chances of getting a husband, since men were notoriously shy of women who knew too much. "Where," inquired some of my friends sarcastically, "will you find a colored man who has studied Greek?" They argued I wouldn't be happy if I knew more than my husband, and they warned that trying to find a man in our group who knew Greek would be like hunting for a needle in a haystack.

But I loved school and liked to study too well to be allured from it by any of the arguments my friends advanced. I was very much impressed and worried by the one which warned that I couldn't get a husband. But I decided to take a long chance. I wrote to my father and laid the matter clearly before him, explaining that it would cost more to take the course that I preferred and that few women of any race selected it. My dear father replied immediately that I might remain in college as long as I wished and he would foot the bill.

When I graduated from the high school my subject was "Troubles and Trials." Each member of the class was allotted five minutes and everybody had to speak. Many people in the audience who either were personally acquainted with me or knew what a happy-go-lucky girl I was were greatly amused at the subject. I tried to prove that most troubles and trials are imaginary rather than real, and even if they are real, they can often be removed altogether by hook or crook. But, if that is impossible, the harm they do can be considerably abated by using a little diplomacy. As an illustration I cited the case of a monk who was ordered to walk a long distance in shoes into which peas had been poured. He did so and reached his goal footsore and weary. When he saw another pilgrim upon whom the same penalty had been imposed arrive well and happy, he asked him why he had not suffered from the same ordeal as he himself had. "But, Brother," replied the smiling pilgrim, "I boiled my peas."

In the Oberlin High School I formed a friendship which has lasted throughout my life. To the casual observer no two girls could have appeared much more unlike either in personal appearance or in disposition than my friend Janey and myself. To begin with, we differed in race. She was white and I am colored. She was a pretty blonde with blue eyes and a wealth of golden hair. I was decidedly a brunette. She was quiet, reticent, almost shy, rather hard to get acquainted with, but a delightful companion if you knew her well. On the other hand, I was quick, vivacious, talkative, made friends easily, and was full of fun.

With a girl of my own race I also formed a friendship in that Oberlin High School which has lasted a lifetime and has always been very dear. I started in the eighth grade with these two girls, graduated from the high school with them, then from the Academy, and later from college, having been their classmate for nine years. My friendship with the white girl illustrates a point which I cannot resist the temptation to stress; namely, the advantages of a mixed school. It helped both the white girl and the colored girl to form a close friendship with a girl of a different race. After having been closely associated with a colored girl whose standards of conduct were similar to her own and whose personality appealed to her strongly, that white girl could never entertain the feeling of scorn, contempt, or aversion for all colored people that she might otherwise have had. No matter how strongly representatives of the dominant race might insist that certain vices and defects were common to all colored people alike, she would know from intimate association with at least one colored girl that those blanket charges preferred against the whole race were not true.

It would be difficult for her to believe that her own particular colored friend was the only exception to the rule laid down by critics of colored people as a whole. Intuitively, she would know that there are many such "exceptions," and she could never place such a low estimate upon the mental and moral qualities of the whole race as she would if she did not know from personal experience the desirable qualities of head and heart which at least one representative of the race possessed.

On the other hand, no matter how many sins of omission or commission white people might commit against colored people, a colored girl who has enjoyed the friendship of a white girl knows by this token, if by no other, that there are some white people in the United States too broad of mind and generous of heart to put the color of a human being's skin above every other consideration. No one could make this colored girl believe that all white people are innately hostile to her race and that there can be no common ground of understanding and good will between them. From personal experience, she knows that, as individuals, some white people are lovable, just, and kind.

It is unfortunate that the children of the two races early get the impression that each is the mortal enemy of the other. Few efforts are being made to teach them mutual forbearance and tolerance. It is said that one man cannot hate another if he understands him. The chances of having the two races understand each other better seem to be getting slimmer and slimmer every day. There is a growing tendency even in Northern states to segregate colored people in every way, so that the outlook for mutual understanding does not seem as bright as it might.

During the second year in the high school I was quite ill. By sheer force of will I dragged myself to school, which was just across the street from where I boarded. I practiced the precepts taught by Christian Science long before Mrs. Eddy founded her church, although I did not understand what I was doing. I might easily have given up the ghost. I had grown very thin, and many believed I had tuberculosis. I was boarding with the widow of the first colored man who graduated in homeopathy in Cleveland, Ohio. She gave me the address of one of the leading homeopathists of the city, and I wrote him describing my case and telling him about my work in school, that I was taking the Classical Course and that I wanted very much to live, so that I might get a degree from Oberlin College.

This skillful physician took the time and the pains to travel forty miles to see a young colored girl about whom he knew absolutely nothing except the information gleaned from the two letters I wrote. He had to lose nearly a whole day from his practice to make the visit, because, while the distance between Oberlin and Cleveland was not great, the trains between the two places at that time were comparatively few, and of course there were no automobiles. After the first visit, he came several times to see me over a period of several months. I did not let my parents know I was ill, because I feared they would not allow me to continue in school.

After I had grown better and seemed on the road to recovery I asked my Cleveland physician to send me his bill. When I opened his letter I could scarcely believe my eyes. He had charged only ten dollars! His fare from Cleveland and return had cost almost as much as that, and the time lost from his practice must have amounted to a great deal. Throughout the months he was treating me he wrote me regularly, as a father would write to a child, and sent me medicine for which he did not charge.

During the summer vacation following this illness I went to see my mother, who had left Memphis and gone to New York City. She often allowed my brother and myself to go to Coney Island and to Manhattan and Brighton Beaches, so that we might take a dip in the ocean. Living out in the open nearly all day and taking the salt water baths and eating the good food which my mother provided completely restored me to health. I had left school so emaciated and weak that nobody expected to see me alive again, and returned in the fall as plump as a partridge, with cheeks as red as roses—the very picture of health.

One night during a fit of depression brought on by illness I felt it would be a comfort to write out my thoughts. Without intending or trying to do so, I was greatly surprised to find that I was expressing myself in rhyme. I dared not light my lamp after a certain hour; it was strictly against my landlady's rule. So by the glow from a little stove I wrote a pensive, doleful rhyme. I did not send it to my mother, and I never told her I wrote it.

I always placed a very low estimate upon anything I wrote. I was never satisfied with my essays. I usually felt like tearing them up and was ashamed when I handed them to my teachers.

I certainly had a bad sense of inferiority when I appraised anything I wrote.

Mother came to see me graduate from the high school, and after Commencement I went to Memphis to visit my father and my grandmother, who lived in a little cottage built on the site on which we had lived when I was a child. I was having a delightful time with my friends when the yellow fever suddenly broke out and I was obliged to leave.

One day a German woman who lived near us came rushing into our house in great distress. "Aunt Liza," she called, "please come to see my husband right away. He's just as sick as he can be, and I don't know what is the matter with him." My grandmother was known far and wide as a Good Samaritan, and she cheerfully went with her neighbor to render any assistance in her power. After Grandma had been gone a short while, I decided to follow her to see what had happened. As I entered the room where the sick man lay, I was struck by the color of his face. It was as yellow as saffron. My grandmother came to me immediately, and I could see she was greatly alarmed. "Go home right away," she said. "Don't stay a minute." She told me as soon as she came home that she was sure the man had yellow fever and was dying. She was right, and he died in a few hours.

I had hardly reached home when my father rushed in greatly excited, saying that several yellow fever cases had been reported, that there would undoubtedly be another epidemic as there had been the year before, and that my brother and I must go to New York immediately. Bitterly disappointed that her children could not spend the summer with her, Grandmother packed our trunks right away.

No one who left Memphis that night can ever forget the scene. Some claim that at least five thousand people rushed away from the city, while others declare there were more than that. The whole population seemed to be at the station trying to leave. Naturally, the trains were late starting and the confusion was indescribable. Those who were going were weeping and those who could not go were crying as though their hearts would break. Every now and then a defiant voice would shout aloud: "You all are trying to run away from death. You are leaving us poor folks behind to die. We haven't got enough money to get out of the city. But you had better look out. Death can find you where you are going just as easy as he can find us here with the yellow fever."

Water was being sold at so much per glass or cup, and it was almost impossible to buy it at any price. The next time I visited her, Grandmother related harrowing scenes which she had witnessed during that awful summer. She told me that all through the night trucks laden with corpses passed along the streets. Piercing shrieks of those who were losing loved ones rent the air. Those who lived through the yellow fever epidemics of Memphis in 1878 and 1879, as my grandmother did, recalled them with a shudder.

In spite of the danger my father returned to Memphis, after he had accompanied my brother and me as far as Cincinnati, and became the laughing stock of some very wise business people, because he invested every penny he had saved in real estate which was being offered at a bargain. And bargains there were a plenty during that yellow fever epidemic! The average property owner was in a panic. There had been an epidemic in 1878, people said, and now there was another in 1879. There was no doubt in the world that Memphis was doomed. Nothing could save it. People were willing to sell for a few hundred dollars in cash property worth many thousands. And it was difficult for them to find purchasers, even though they were willing almost to give it away.

Seeing my father invest every penny he had in real estate, some declared that Bob Church had lost his mind. But when people told him that Memphis was doomed, my father would declare that there was no reason in the world why Memphis should not be one of the most healthful cities in the United States.

"Isn't it called the Bluff City?" he would inquire. "That's just what it is," he would say. "It's built on a bluff. The reason why Memphis has epidemics of yellow fever," he explained, "is because the streets are in such a terrible condition. They are now paved with blocks of wood which quickly rot, and there are big holes filled with great pools of stagnant water breeding disease. When Memphis is cleaned up and the streets are properly paved by honest officials, there won't be any yellow fever and it will be one of the most healthful and desirable cities in this country." My father lived to see his prediction fulfilled to the letter.

I have gone into detail in this matter to prove how sagacious, logical and far-sighted my father was. Many men who had graduated from college, perhaps, and who had great reputations for keen business acumen lost practically everything they had in a panic, because they did not use their brains as well as did this unlettered, recently emancipated slave who had never gone to school a day in his life.

When I reached New York after running away from the yellow fever, I was ill several days. I tried to believe that the attack was not even remotely related to the epidemic in Memphis, although I had a high fever and could not help remembering that somebody had said, "It was a great pity that Mollie had gone into the room of that German stricken with yellow fever, while he was dying, because it was more infectious then than at any other time." But again I practiced Christian Science without knowing it, ate lemons by the dozen, and was soon perfectly well.

CHAPTER 5

I ENTER OBERLIN COLLEGE

I N THE FOLLOWING FALL I entered the senior class of the preparatory department of Oberlin College, which has since been abolished. I boarded in the old "Ladies Hall," which was destroyed by fire and has been replaced by Talcott Cottage. The tables in the dining hall seated eight, and it was customary for students to choose those whom they wanted to sit at their respective tables for the term of three months. In the middle of the term some friend would invite me to sit at a table which she was arranging for the one to follow, and I would accept. Somebody else would extend me the same invitation and I would also accept that, forgetting that I had already promised to sit with another group. Each of these girls would send in my name as one of the eight who had accepted her invitation for the following term. Then, when I was seated at one table and failed to appear at another at which I was expected, naturally there would be more or less confusion, and explanations had to be made. The lady whose duty it was to attend to the dining room declared that I gave her a great deal of trouble, because too many people wanted me to sit at their table.

If I were white, it might be conceited for me to relate this. But I mention these facts to show that, as a colored girl, I was accorded the same treatment at Oberlin College at that time as a white girl under similar circumstances. Outward manifestations of prejudice against colored students would not have been tolerated for one minute by those in authority at that time. Occasionally, a colored girl would complain about something which she considered a "slight," but, as a rule, it was either because she was looking for trouble or because she imagined something disagreeable which was not intended. Later on, however, conditions affecting colored students changed considerably.

My associates in college were, naturally, members of my own class. Until I reached the junior year I had only one colored classmate, and she lived at home. I boarded in Ladies Hall three years all together: during my senior preparatory year, when I roomed with a girl of my own race; during my freshman year, when I roomed alone; and during my senior year, when I roomed with my colored classmate. Throughout the whole period in Ladies Hall, never once did I feel that I was being discriminated against on account of my color.

In my senior preparatory year I had one of the best teachers in the entire course—"Prin White," as he was familiarly called, who was principal of the department. Prin White taught us Greek and he was as vivacious, interesting, and inspiring as a teacher could well be. He had very high standards for his pupils. Some thought they were too high, but he succeeded in making most of us live up to them. When a student was called upon to explain the case of a noun or the mood of a verb, Prin White required him not only to give the rule for the construction, but, along with the rule, to give a sentence in Greek illustrating the point.

For a time I was the only girl in this Greek class with 40 boys. It was a joy to read the *Iliad* with Prin White. He entered so enthusiastically into the spirit of that matchless poem that his students caught the inspiration. I still have my recitation card. He marked on a scale of 6. When he handed me my card showing 5.9, he said in his quick, nervous way, fixing me with his keen, blue eyes, "Miss Church, you should be proud of that record." Praise from Prin White was then and still is praise indeed. And I can thrill even now, 58 years after the incident occurred, when I think of it.

I also remember another incident in my college days with pleasure and pride. It was when my Latin teacher complimented me, because I scanned a certain passage in Virgil well. I can recall those Latin lines today, and the genuine feeling with which I read them.

The Greek professor in college was also one of my favorites. He looked like an ascetic, tall and straight and thin. I usually sat on the front seat in his class and drank in every word he said. I took much more Greek than the curriculum required, both because I enjoyed the Grecian authors and because I was fond of my teacher.

One day Matthew Arnold, the English writer, visited our class and Professor Frost asked me both to read the Greek and then to translate. After leaving the class Mr. Arnold referred to the young lady who had read the passage of Greek so well. Thinking it would interest the Englishman, Professor Frost told him I was of African descent. Thereupon Mr. Arnold expressed the greatest surprise imaginable, because, he said, he thought the tongue of the African was so thick he could not be taught to pronounce the Greek correctly.

Later on Professor Frost became president of Berea College. For years before his administration this institution had admitted colored and white students on terms of equality. But shortly after Professor Frost became president the Kentucky Legislature passed a law, with Berea specially in mind, forbidding any school or institution to receive both white and colored students unless the one race or color should be established in a separate department not less than 25 miles from the other: and this on penalty of a fine of $1,000 for the institution, $1,000 for each of its teachers and $50 for each of its pupils. In his autobiography President Frost expressed keen regret that Berea was forced to debar colored students on account of this law.

In my freshman year I attended the Bible class regularly and believe it benefited me greatly. I really looked forward to it with enthusiasm and pleasure, because I was allowed to ask questions about the passages in the Scriptures which troubled me. And no verse came nearer shaking my faith in the justice of God than that one which states, "I the Lord thy God am a jealous God, visiting the iniquity of the fathers upon the children unto the third and fourth generation of them that hate me, and showing mercy unto thousands of them that love me and keep my commandments."

I could not understand why a just and loving father should make children suffer for the sins committed by their forefathers. The injustice of the law of heredity stunned me. It seemed terrible to me that the children of drunkards should inherit a tendency to drink immoderately and the children of thieves might have a hard time to be honest, and so on through the category of vices. The teacher was patient with me and did his best to show me why such a dispensation was just, but I was never able to see it in that light. However, I decided not to try to understand it any longer. I finally brought a semblance of peace to my mind by saying, "I am finite, and if I understood all the plans of the Infinite I should be equal to Him in wisdom, which would be unthinkable and absurd, of course." Even so, my poor brain often whirled and my heart was often sad, as I wrestled with the problem of heredity.

When I tackled geometry in the preparatory department of the college I met my Waterloo sure enough! I struggled hard to do the work, but I did not understand how to go at it properly and I barely pulled through the course. How I loathed plane geometry! It wounded my pride and "hurt my feelings," because it was so hard for me to understand.

I did a little better in solid geometry, but I did not set the world afire even in that. Finally, I grew desperate and decided it was a waste of time and energy for me to try to understand propositions, and I calmly made up my mind to commit to memory the letters on a figure and say "big TAB is to little tab as big AB is to little ab," without having the slightest idea what it was all about. No teacher who wished to show off his class in mathematics would ever have called on Mollie Church to recite in college, any more than a teacher in the public schools would have exhibited my drawing book to display the skill to which her pupils had attained. When visitors came to our class in the public schools and asked to see our books in which we had done free-hand drawing or had copied objects, no teacher ever showed mine. She usually managed to put it at the bottom of the pile.

Try as hard as I might, I could never learn to draw. If I set out to draw a straight line it would turn out to be crooked. And if I wanted to draw a crooked line it was more than likely to be straight. My brother inherited some of my mother's talent for painting and drawing, while I inherited none. My brother, Thomas Ayres Church, wrote a book on *The Roller*, a canary which is taught to sing tunes, and he drew all the illustrations himself. They were exceedingly well done. He was the first person in this country to write a book on this subject. The best publishing houses sold it and it had a ready sale.

In my freshman year I was elected class poet unanimously, and read a poem at the Class Day exercises, which were held a short while before Commencement. I chose as my subject "The Fallen Star," and imitated the hexameter used by Longfellow in

Hiawatha. In the same year I wrote another poem which a class-mate liked so much she quoted one of the stanzas in an essay she read at an exhibition given by her literary society when we were juniors.

Because I had written several effusions of which my teacher approved, I had been rather generally regarded as the class poet. When the time came to elect speakers for the Junior Exhibition, it was the consensus of opinion among the majority of my class-mates that I would be elected class poet. After a classmate had nominated me, another presented the name of a young man who had never written a poem in his life, so far as the class had heard, and had never exhibited any talent in that direction, so far as the class knew. After a great many ballots had been cast, I wanted to withdraw my name, but some of my classmates who sat near me held me down in my seat. Finally the young man was elected. I believe I am justified in thinking that if a white girl had won the same reputation for writing poetry that I had, and had been recognized by the class as I had been in my fresh-man year, she would probably have been elected class poet for the Junior Exhibition instead of a young man who had previ-ously exhibited no talent or skill in that direction at all. Some of my classmates criticized the successful candidate severely, because he did not withdraw in my favor after five or six bal-lots had been cast, as he probably would have done if his rival had been a white girl.

But I did not allow this episode to embitter me at all. On the contrary, it encouraged and comforted me greatly to see how many of my classmates stood by me so long. I knew also that they finally voted for the young man, so as to break the deadlock, after they saw that a few of his friends were determined to elect him. There is no doubt whatever that on this one occasion, at least, the fact that I am colored prevented me from receiving the honor which many members of my class thought my record proved I deserved.

Right after the Junior Exhibition I attended a party which was always given by one of the professors and enjoyed myself immensely. My mother had sent me a beautiful silk dress from New York, which I wore. I am sure that nobody who saw me that day thought I was suffering because I felt I had been a victim of race prejudice in failing to be elected to write a poem for "Junior Ex." I know now better than I did then that "blood is thicker than water" when several racial groups come together to elect a representative for the whole.

But I received almost every other honor that my classmates or the members of my literary society could give me. While I was still in the senior preparatory class, a young woman in the senior college class rushed after me one day and insisted upon having me join Aelioian, the literary society to which she herself belonged. She was one of the most brilliant and popular members of her class, and I felt honored to have such a student solicit my membership in her society. She did not have to persuade me long to gain my consent to join Aelioian. I am glad I began work in this society so early in my course. I was eligible for admission, even though I was only a senior in the preparatory department, because a girl in that class was as far advanced in her studies as one taking the literary course would be in college.

In addition to the literary work required, the drill in parliamentary law was invaluable. All I ever knew about it I learned in Aelioian. After I went out into the "cold world," when I was called upon to preside over meetings of various kinds, I would have been greatly embarrassed if I had not been prepared for this service by the drills given me in Aelioian. The ability to speak effectively on one's feet was also acquired in this society.

I was elected twice to represent Aelioian when it had a public debate with L. L. S., the other women's literary society. The first time I was a sophomore, and the last time I was a junior. I considered the latter selection a special honor because as a rule the society elected a senior to represent it in the public debate held with L. L. S. before Commencement. This was the most important exercise given by the society, so that no greater honor could be conferred upon a member than to be elected disputant to represent it in a debate with its rival on that occasion.

For a while I was one of the editors of the *Oberlin Review,* the college paper, and I was quite excited when I saw the first article I had ever written for publication appear in print.

I enjoyed attending the Thursday lectures, at which either one of the professors or some distinguished man from out of town appeared. The literary societies brought the best orators, the most famous singers, and the finest orchestras to Oberlin, so that when one had finished her college course, if she had availed herself of the opportunities offered her, she would have seen and heard the most distinguished speakers and the greatest musicians in the United States.

A building was presented by a generous woman to the women's two literary societies, and after it was completed a committee was appointed from each society to decide how the rooms should be furnished. Aelioian placed me on a committee of three to represent it. And so, I could cite numerous instances to show that the members of my society did not discriminate against me on account of my race.

Since my college society conferred upon me every honor in its gift, and my classmates failed only once to recognize me as I believe they would have done under similar circumstances if I had been white, I feel I have little reason to complain about discrimination on account of race while I was a student in Oberlin College. It would be difficult for a colored girl to go through a white school with fewer unpleasant experiences occasioned by race prejudice than I had.

I attended all the class receptions and every social function which the college gave and was sure of a cordial reception wherever I went. The sister-in-law of the acting president of the college decided to have a lawn tennis club, when that game was just beginning to be popular, and I was one of twelve girls she invited from the whole institution to become a member of it. If I attended Oberlin College today, I am told, I would not be so free from the annoyances and discriminations caused by race prejudice as I was fifty-six years ago.

Although for many years there was as much "social equality" to the square inch in Oberlin College as could be practiced anywhere in the United States, I have heard the authorities state that there had never been a case of intermarriage between the races in the whole history of the school. The prediction of the prophets and the near prophets in this particular was never fulfilled. All sorts of dire calamities were threatened by those who strongly opposed the admission of colored students. It was predicted that if white and colored students were allowed to associate with each other on terms of "social equality," the most disgraceful things would be happening all the time. There would be intermarriages galore, of course, and the whole tone of the school would be low. The opponents of equal opportunities for

[45]

colored people have proved over and over again that they have not the gift of prophecy.

For a long time I led the singing in a Sunday evening prayer meeting in Ladies Hall. At one of these meetings an incident occurred which made an indelible impression upon my mind. It was customary for those who attended these meetings to bear testimony concerning their experiences as Christians or to offer prayer. On one such occasion I stated that, although I tried to be a Christian, I sometimes did things which I knew a good Christian should not do.

"For instance," I said, "I sometimes whisper in a class, when I don't intend to violate the rule or disturb the order, because I am thoughtless but not deliberately obstreperous. I fear also that I giggle and laugh too much and am not serious enough." And then I expressed the hope that the Christians present would pray for me that I might change my giddy ways and become more quiet and sedate.

As soon as I had finished, a tall, pale, very thin woman, heavily swathed in black, leaned forward from the back seat, fastened her sad eyes upon me, pointed her bony finger at me, and said most impressively, "Young woman, laugh and be merry while you can, and as much as you can. Don't try to suppress laughter and be serious in youth. Some day when you grow older, when the cares and sorrows of life press hard upon you, you'll want to laugh and can't."

About a week after that this woman committed suicide in Cleveland, Ohio, by jumping into Lake Erie. Both her husband and her young daughter had died within a short time of each other and she could not become reconciled to their loss. She had come to study in the college, hoping to divert her mind from grief, but she did not succeed. Many a time since that Sunday evening prayer meeting I have tried to laugh when the sorrows and cares of life have pressed hard upon me, and couldn't.

While I was still in college I had the first bitter experience of inability to secure employment on account of my race, during a summer vacation which I was spending with my mother in New York City. I thought it would be a fine thing then to earn money with a lot of leisure on my hands. I had heard my college friends talk about desirable positions which students were able to secure during summer vacations. One of them had been employed by a wealthy woman who wanted a young, intelligent girl to read aloud to her, write letters for her, and act in the capacity of secretary. I thought I would try to get such a job. Accordingly, I fared forth several times to answer advertisements calling for such service. At least three of the women whom I went to see told me that I possessed just the qualities they desired and were very complimentary indeed. I thought I had secured employment three times, but three times I was doomed to disappointment.

Just as I was leaving her room one of the women who had practically engaged me said: "I observe you are quite swarthy. You speak English too well to be a foreigner, unless you were born in the United States, or came here when you were a baby. What is your nationality?" "I am a colored girl," I replied. If I had told her I was a gorilla in human form, she could not have been more greatly shocked. Never before in all her life had she come in contact with an educated colored girl, she said. She really didn't know there were any in the world.. While she had no prejudice against colored people herself, she said, her servants were white and she was certain they would leave if she employed a colored girl.

On a certain Friday afternoon one of the women whom I went to see engaged me positively and directed me to begin work with her Monday morning. But on Sunday afternoon a messenger brought me a letter saying that her daughter had seen me, as I was leaving the house, and had asked about my nationality. Her coachman would come at seven o'clock that evening for a reply, she wrote. When he came I gave him a note in which I frankly admitted my racial identity. At ten o'clock that night the coachman returned with an answer to my confession of race in which my employer told me she was very sorry to cancel her agreement with me, but under no circumstances could she employ a colored girl.

Months before I graduated from Oberlin I realized that the carefree days of my youth would soon be a thing of the past. I dreaded leaving my friends behind and "going out into the cold world." But the desire to get my diploma and receive my degree was an obsession with me. When I said my prayers at night I used to emphasize the fact, as much as I dared while talking to the Lord, that He could send any affliction whatsoever upon me

He saw fit, if He would only let me live to graduate. I begged Him earnestly not to let me die before Commencement Day.

I do not see how any student could have enjoyed the activities of college life more than I did. Learning my lessons as well as I could was a sort of indoor sport with me. I had my troubles and trials, of course, because occasionally I broke the rules by going skating without permission, for instance, or breaking the study-hour rule, or sitting up after ten o'clock, but that was all included in the course, I thought. I learned one thing outside of the curriculum. Breakfast began at quarter past six in the morning. That did very well in the fall and spring, but in the cold, bitter winter it was terrible to have to arise while it was dark as midnight in a room with a temperature miles below zero, make a fire to keep from freezing to death, and dress in time to be at the breakfast table at fifteen minutes past six.

I did not eat very much at that period. But students were obliged to be in the dining room for morning prayers. So I calculated to a nicety the exact time when the bell would ring for the students to turn from the table to hear the Bible read. I would hop out of bed just five minutes before that happened, and I learned to dress myself so quickly that I was never late for morning prayer during the whole time I boarded in Ladies Hall.

Neither one of my parents came to see me graduate from college. My mother sent me a wonderful black jet dress, for the young women who graduated from the "gentlemen's course" always dressed in sombre black then. She also sent me a pair of opera glasses as a graduation present. While the gift was greatly appreciated, it did not compensate me for her absence on an occasion to which I had looked forward with such anticipation of pleasure for so many years.

CHAPTER 6

ACTIVITIES DURING COLLEGE COURSE

DURING MY FRESHMAN YEAR I had a thrill which comes once in a lifetime. Sticking out from under my door when I came to the Ladies Hall at noon one day was a letter postmarked Washington, D. C., addressed to me in a handwriting I had never seen before. During my college course it was most unusual for me to receive a letter from a stranger, so I tore it open eagerly to see from whom it came. And then I was dumb with surprise. It was an invitation from the wife of a United States Senator to visit her during the Inauguration in Washington. It would require a word artist of the first magnitude to describe my rapture at such a prospect, so that my readers would feel the same exuberance of spirit which I experienced when I received this letter from Mrs. B. K. Bruce, wife of Senator Bruce.

I was certain my father would let me accept the invitation. He and Senator Bruce had been friends for many years. The Senator had a large plantation in Mississippi not far from Memphis, and Father used to purchase mules and supplies for him, since the planter knew very little about doing such things himself. For many years it was Senator Bruce's custom to stop with Father as he passed through Memphis on his way to and from his plantation.

After receiving the permission to accept the invitation I began immediately to study ahead. I knew I could not enjoy myself in Washington if I did not make up my college work before I went. So I read all the Latin and Greek assigned for that term before I started my great adventure, leaving the dreaded mathematics till I returned.

Mrs. Bruce was a tall, beautiful, graceful woman, so fair that no one would suspect she had a drop of African blood in her veins. She lived in what then seemed to me a veritable mansion in what was considered a most desirable residential section of the National Capital. She had a horse and carriage plus a coachman, Meekins by name, who was a constant source of worry to my hostess, but who furnished no end of amusement for me.

On this visit to Washington I had my first taste of Society, spelled with a capital S. My mother had sent me some beautiful clothes from New York bought with the money which Father had sent her for that purpose, so there was nothing to mar the joy of my young heart. With Mrs. Bruce I attended dances and receptions galore, both large and small. Naturally, Senator and Mrs. Bruce took me to the Inaugural Ball, which was the biggest event of all. It has since been thrown into the discard, but for many years some women began to plan, as soon as one inauguration was over, what they would wear to the next one four years off. Styles did not change so rapidly in those halcyon days as they do now.

At the Inaugural Ball I was introduced to so many senators, judges, representatives, and other grandees it made my head swim. Senator Bruce, who was the only colored man in the United States Senate, was highly respected by all the worthwhile people in the official life of the capital and was genuinely liked by many. When the Senator from Mississippi refused to extend to Senator Bruce the courtesy which one senator is expected to show to another from the same State when he makes his first appearance in the Senate, Roscoe Conkling, Senator from New York, arose from his seat and did the honors for the colored man himself.

I recall distinctly how the distinguished representatives of the Government beamed with pleasure upon Senator Bruce as they grasped his hand. On several occasions some of the higher-ups mistook me for the Senator's wife and addressed me as "Mrs. Bruce." The fact that this case of mistaken identity proved that I must have looked a few years older than I was did not disturb my young heart in the least, but amused me very much. The mistake was probably made because Mrs. Bruce was so fair and my complexion more nearly resembled the Senator's than did hers.

But if I had met none of the grandees of officialdom of the National Capital, if I had failed to attend the Inaugural Ball or any of the other social functions, my visit would have been more than worth while, because it afforded me an opportunity of meeting one of the greatest men whom this or any other country has ever produced.

As I was walking down the street with a friend one day, a short distance ahead of us I saw two men talking to each other. Instantly and instinctively I knew that one of the men, who had magnificent, majestic proportions and a distinguished bearing, could be none other than the great Frederick Douglass. Fortunately, my friend was well acquainted with him and introduced me to him then and there, any rules of society to the contrary notwithstanding. And thus began a friendship which I prized more highly than words can portray, because I derived so much inspiration and pleasure from it all my life.

While I studied hard at Oberlin College and availed myself of all the opportunities afforded, I did not deprive myself of any pleasure I could rightfully enjoy. I entered into all the sports suggested by the fertile brains of others and played many of the pranks proposed. I learned early in my course that the fun derived from breaking the rules did not compensate for the trouble into which one was plunged by doing so.

I discovered that one could secure permission to do almost anything within reason, and that seemed much the easiest way to me. During my freshman year I secured permission to sit up till midnight for several months to do some extra work, although girls had to be in bed at ten o'clock and the authorities insisted upon that as a general thing. However, one young woman circumvented that rule in a very ingenious way. When she sat up late, she covered her transom so thoroughly that not a ray of light could shine into the halls. One of her friends who knew she had not reported the violation of that rule, although she claimed to send in honest reports, asked her how she justified herself in failing to do so.

"Well," replied the young woman, "I go to bed every night between nine and ten. I put a cardboard with the figure 9 on it at the head of my bed and place a cardboard with the figure 10 on it at the foot of my bed, so I'm not breaking the ten o'clock rule at all."

During my senior year I secured a permission from Mrs. A. A. F. Johnston, who then had charge of college women and later became dean, which it is claimed she had never given before. Lawrence Barrett and Marie Wainwright were producing Shakespeare's plays in Cleveland, and I wanted very much to go to see them. The girls with whom I discussed the matter advised me not to tell "Madam J," as she was familiarly called, what I wanted to do. "Just get permission to go to Cleveland," they said, "and after you get there you can do as you please. Then you won't be breaking any of those precious rules either."

After thinking about the matter I decided to pursue a different course. For the life of me I could not see how an intelligent woman like Mrs. Johnston could possibly refuse to give me permission to see good artists perform Shakespeare's plays. If she did refuse I wanted to know what reason she would assign. During the winter of my sophomore year I had gone to Cleveland every Saturday to have my throat treated by a specialist, so that I knew I would have no difficulty in securing permission to go to Cleveland.

"Mrs. Johnston," I said, as I entered her office, "I want to go to see *Julius Caesar* and *Hamlet*. My classmate, Miss Gibbs, will go with me. We will attend the Saturday matinee and the performance at night and return the next day." I asked permission to do this as though it were nothing unusual, and looked Mrs. Johnston straight in the eye as I spoke. "If you want to get permission to do anything," the girls used to say, "don't go to Madam Johnston looking like a condemned criminal, but look her straight in the eye, as though you knew exactly what you wanted and expected to get it."

Mrs. Johnston had auburn hair and she wore two pretty little curls, one on each side of her head. Her face became as red as fire, for it was strictly against Oberlin's policy in those days to cultivate the theater. The very audacity of the request silenced her for a second, but when she recovered from the shock, she gave me the permission most graciously and expressed the hope that I would enjoy the plays and have a nice time. This Cleveland episode comes very vividly before me, because it was the first time I had used the long distance telephone. Having such a short time to arrange the trip, I 'phoned a friend in Cleveland to get the tickets for me, and I was quite excited when I heard a voice forty miles away.

The study hour from nine to twelve in the morning, two to four in the afternoon, and seven thirty to ten at night was my salvation. It enabled me to study at the proper time. Without this rule I fear I would have been visiting girls in the dormitory, preventing both them and myself from studying, when we should have been preparing our lessons for the next day. It has since been abolished, and I feel sorry for the girls who are denied the protection which this rule afforded me.

I went to all the baseball games and learned to keep an official score. I contributed my mite to provide a spread for the boys when they won. I skated fairly well and enjoyed it immensely. It was against the rules for girls to dance at any of the college functions, and decidedly against the rules for young men and women to dance together anywhere. There was a girl in Ladies Hall who loved to dance as well as I did, which is saying a great deal. She and I would betake ourselves to the gymnasium every evening after supper and trip the light 'fantastic to our heart's content, priding ourselves especially on the fact that we knew all the latest steps.

Dancing in Oberlin was usually frowned upon by everybody who wanted to be considered intellectual or who sighed to be classified as a highbrow. Nevertheless, several of the teachers who boarded in the Ladies Hall and some very serious-minded young women used to come to see my partner and me dance, and encouraged us considerably by complimenting us. No human being has ever enjoyed dancing more than I did. Throughout my youth I would much rather dance any day or any night than eat. Even now dancing is my favorite recreation.

One Fourth of July a friend and I thought it would be great fun to go horseback riding in the afternoon. Neither one of us felt that we would take a prize at it, but there was nothing else exciting to do, so we decided to try it. My friend said she had been brought up on horses, knew a good saddle horse when she saw one, and would select her mount. I told the livery stable man I would depend upon him to give me a good, well-behaved, kindly animal, so he gave me a cute-looking little white horse whose name was Dixie. Of course I would have preferred a horse with another name, but what's in a name, I said to myself half ashamed.

Now Dixie would undoubtedly have been all right if he had had no competition and had been alone. But, of course, there was another horse, and one who went at a merry clip when he called himself going. Dixie made up his mind in the beginning that he simply would not allow that other horse to get ahead of him. Both of the horses were continually being frightened by firecrackers which the children were shooting off, so that neither was in a particularly amiable frame of mind. My friend's horse had also decided that he would not let a little white horse like Dixie get ahead of him. The more Dixie tried to overtake him, the faster that unmanageable horse ran. I kept begging my friend to rein her horse in, so that he would set a proper example to Dixie. But she kept shouting back that she could not do a thing with him, so long as Dixie tried to overtake him, and advised me to hold Dixie back. So we two girls went galloping down the pike like two madcaps on horses which neither one of us could control. That we finally reached the livery stable with no bones broken is a mystery which I cannot explain.

Occasionally, forty or fifty people would hire "band wagons" and go on a picnic to Lake Erie, usually to Lorain, about ten miles from Oberlin. My father had sent me a guitar in my freshman year and I had taught myself to play chords. So it was my duty to play chords to accompany the singing.

Several times I remained in Oberlin during the summer vacation and went camping on Lake Erie with a party of friends. There were three middle-aged women and a youth near my age, the brother of one of the women. There was one large room with bunks on the side, one above the other, like the arrangement in a Pullman car. We youngsters used to don our bathing suits in the morning and wear them all day, part of the time swimming and splashing in the lake, and part of the time rowing a little boat. It was our duty to row to the nearest town for supplies, and we considered it great sport, although we had to use every ounce of our strength to negotiate the distance both ways and were usually "tired to death" when we returned.

Once we two, John Jackson and I, were invited by a party who happened to anchor near our camp to take a sail out on the lake with them. We jumped at the chance. Such luck we had never dreamed would befall us. It was a glorious afternoon in August when we started, and no two young people in the whole world were happier than ourselves. But after we had gone quite a distance, clouds began to appear, and before the boat could reach shore a terrific storm broke. I had no idea what it meant to be in a sailboat, until I saw the difficulty experienced by the men who were trying to get it to shore.

Terror-stricken, I had to move from one side to the other, while the men shifted the position of the sails and the rudder. Over and over again they failed to direct the boat properly, so that it would go toward the shore headed in the right direction. Sometimes when I was sure they had succeeded and hoped we would soon land, I would hear one of the men say, "No, that won't do, we've got to tack once more." Then they would have to go in the opposite direction again. And so they seesawed back and forth for what seemed to me an eternity. That taught me a lesson about sailboats, and I have never been in one from that day to this.

I have always enjoyed seeing a storm on water, but once while I was camping on Lake Erie I allowed my enthusiasm for this manifestation of nature to carry me too far. I thought it would be great sport to go into the lake while the storm was raging. So in I plunged and was having a delightful time jumping up and down as the big waves rolled in to shore. But, suddenly, when I tried to touch the ground after I had jumped on a high billow, I found there was nothing under my feet but water. I realized that if that kept up long I should be washed out into the lake and drown. There was nobody near me who could swim. I was the only person in the lake at that place. Even if anybody who could swim had been near me, he would have had difficulty in bringing me through the high, rough waves, as they rushed angrily and heavily toward the shore.

I do not know how I saved myself. I can simply remember that whenever I saw a wave coming in I jumped as high as I could and kept thinking I would surely drown if I allowed myself to fall into a panic. Finally, I felt my feet touch land. So great had been the exertion, I barely had strength enough to wade out of the water. Never after that experience was I tempted to risk my life for the sake of a thrill.

CHAPTER 7

I GO TO MEMPHIS, TEACH IN WILBERFORCE AND WASHINGTON AND GO ABROAD

JUST BEFORE I GRADUATED from Oberlin my father wrote me he would meet me in Louisville, Kentucky, with two of my friends after Commencement, that we would have a nice visit there and then go to Memphis, where I was to live with him. When I reached Louisville, my father took the trunk check and gave it to the driver of the "hack," that ancient of days which has gone the way of all flesh, and told him to get my trunk. The driver soon returned with a little black wooden box which looked like a coffin for a cat or a dog, and was about to place it under the driver's seat when I spied it and asked why he didn't get my trunk. "This little box is what your check calls for," he replied. So there I was in a strange city, knowing that I would be invited to all sorts of functions, and there were the pretty dresses Mother had sent me before Commencement locked in a trunk that was nobody knew where! The baggage man had evidently mixed the checks up when I left Oberlin for Louisville, and I was the unfortunate victim of that mistake.

Fine dresses did not occupy so much of a girl's thought then as they do now, so I swallowed my disappointment quite philosophically. Perhaps the reason I thought so little about dresses was that my mother always saw to it that I was well provided with suitable stylish clothes, which she selected with great care. I do not see how a normal girl could have thought less about clothes than I did throughout my college course, although people said I dressed well.

It was very annoying not to have the right kind of apparel

when I appeared at the functions to which I was invited in Louisville, but I explained the reason to my hostess and a few friends and made up my mind to have a good time. It would be much easier for me to extricate myself from such a dilemma today, because, if I had the money, I might buy one or two ready-made dresses which would answer the purpose very well. But ready-made dresses were not so plentiful then as they are now, and I probably would not have thought of resorting to such an expedient if they had been. The day before my visit ended, my trunk came, having been lost ten days, and I had a chance to wear one of my pretty gowns.

Three times my trunk has been lost. Once when I was filling lecture engagements in the South it was gone a month before it was recovered. My anxiety on that occasion was very great. I was living in Washington and a President of the United States was about to be inaugurated. The only clothes I had which were suitable to wear to the various functions which were to be given for the visitors during that festive week were packed in that trunk, which did not arrive until March 2—two days before the Inauguration. "You're very lucky indeed," said the baggage man when I went to get it. "If it had not reached here till to-morrow, when the thousands of pieces of baggage belonging to visitors come rolling in, the Lord knows when we could have gotten it for you."

When I reached Memphis I saw the beautiful Queen Anne home which my father had just completed and furnished. He had sent me some blueprints of the house which he said he was building for me, the winter before I graduated, so that I might see the plan. But a blueprint meant almost nothing to me then and means no more now. It has always been impossible for me to visualize the completed structure merely by seeing a blueprint. My mental apparatus is simply not built that way.

My new house seemed very wonderful and imposing to me, when I beheld it for the first time on a glorious fall day. A delicious dinner had been prepared for our party. Nobody in the world knew better how to order a good dinner and nobody enjoyed ordering a dinner more than Father. He was the very soul, the very quintessence of hospitality. He did not like to accept invitations to dine out himself (it was almost impossible to induce him to do so), but he loved to have his friends break bread with him in his own home. Everything went as merry as a marriage bell. And, indeed, I learned that a marriage bell was just about to ring.

The following January my father married Miss Anna Wright, one of the friends he brought from Memphis to meet me in Louisville. She had been a school teacher in Memphis for many years, performed brilliantly on the piano, was one of the most popular young women in the city, and was generally beloved. Her mother and my mother had been intimate friends from my earliest recollection. One summer, when I was home on a vacation, "Miss Anna," as I called her, was engaged by my mother to give me music lessons. I was well acquainted with her, therefore, and was very fond of her.

When my father told me he was going to get married, named the bride-to-be, and asked me what I thought of it, I assured him that if he had scraped the country with a fine-tooth comb he could not possibly have found anybody who would have pleased me better. Since my own mother and father had been separated for years and there was no likelihood they would ever be reunited, I saw no reason in the world why my father should not marry again. One day Anna herself told me my father wanted to marry her and asked me what I thought of it. I assured her I had no objection whatever.

After being intimately associated for many years with my father's second wife, who died several years ago, I would not change in the slightest way the opinion expressed to him about his fiancée, when he told me for the first time he intended to make her his wife. In temperament and disposition my stepmother and I were entirely different, and yet we never had the slightest misunderstanding with each other, and never had a "falling out" during her lifetime.

I was greatly surprised to see how my pleasant relations with my father's second wife affected some of my acquaintances. They seemed to feel that I should be antagonistic to her and resent her marriage to my father from the very nature of the case. The old saws about stepmothers and mothers-in-law have sunk deep into the consciousness of people on general principles. Many believe they state facts and do not regard the gibes as jokes.

If my own mother had been pained or provoked at my

father's second marriage, perhaps I, too, might have been annoyed or aggrieved. But she had known Anna many years and had always liked her, so she felt my father had made a very wise choice indeed.

On one occasion she certainly proved she meant what she said. For when my father and his wife and two children were visiting in New York, where she lived at the time, Mother entertained them in her home. After she left New York and came to live with me, Father and his family often visited me, and on such occasions the relations between all of us were very cordial indeed. Father's little girl called my mother "Mama Lou."

A few days after he married, Father came into my room and showed me his will, in which he had originally bequeathed all his property to my brother and myself. He then tore it up, saying as he did so, "You know I'll have to change my will now." Even then I did not feel the slightest resentment either toward him or toward his wife. I felt that he had made his money at the cost of much energy and many sacrifices and that he had a perfect right to dispose of it as he pleased. But the trouble is, many people feel that in considering certain situations they are expected to entertain stereotyped opinions prescribed by custom and tradition, whether a particular case warrants any deviation from that point of view or not.

During the year I spent in Memphis after my father's marriage I made up my mind definitely that, since he no longer needed me, it was wrong for me to remain idle there. I could not be happy leading a purposeless existence. Situated as I was, I could not put the college education I had taken such pains to acquire to any good use. I could not engage actively in any kind of work outside of the home, because my father did not approve of my doing so. He would not consent to my teaching in the public schools of Memphis, because, he said, I "would be taking the bread and butter out of the mouth of some girl who needed it." Since he was able and willing to support me, he declared, he did not understand why I wanted to teach or do any kind of work.

Naturally, my father was the product of his environment. In the South for nearly three hundred years "real ladies" did not work, and my father was thoroughly imbued with that idea. He wanted his daughter to be a "lady." But said daughter had been reared among Yankees and she had imbibed the Yankee's respect for work. I had conscientiously availed myself of opportunities for preparing myself for a life of usefulness as only four other colored women had been able to do. In the class of 1884 at Oberlin College an extraordinary thing had happened. Three colored women received the A.B. degree at that Commencement. Previous to that, only two colored women had received that degree from any college in the United States or anywhere else in the world, so far as available records show.

All during my college course I had dreamed of the day when I could promote the welfare of my race. Therefore, after graduating from Oberlin I grew more and more restless and dissatisfied with the life I was leading in Memphis, as the year I remained there rolled by. And so, although the relations between my stepmother and myself were most cordial, I decided that life would be pleasanter for everybody concerned, my own mother included, in spite of her philosophical attitude toward my father's marriage, if I left Memphis and engaged in the work I had prepared myself to do.

The summer following my father's marriage I went to New York to visit my mother. After writing to several schools for colored youth, I secured a position in Wilberforce University. Several desirable positions were offered to me as the result of that correspondence. The heads of institutions for colored youth were beginning to insist that the teachers employed should be college graduates, and there were so few colored women who met this requirement then that it was very easy for those who had to secure desirable positions.

Wilberforce University is situated about three miles from Xenia, Ohio. This was one of the reasons I decided to go there rather than to another school. I knew my father would be less opposed to my teaching in the North than in the South, and I wanted to placate him as much as I could. Years afterward I learned that the president of one of the Southern schools, who had offered me a position, actually waited a week for me at the beginning of the year. But I had not received the letter notifying me of the appointment. The president of this school was a Scotchman and he was eager to place a well-prepared colored woman on his faculty, the rest of whom were white.

At Wilberforce I received the munificent salary of $40 per

month, out of which I was obliged to pay my board, although my room was furnished me free of charge. I taught everything from French and mineralogy in the college department to reading and writing in the preparatory department. In a senior class which I taught, each of the students was older than I. In Oberlin I had had only one year in French, but at Wilberforce I was required to teach a class each of whom had had two years of the language. To make a bad matter worse, two of the students came from Haiti and their mother tongue was French, of course. Literally, I burned the midnight oil, so as to keep ahead of my pupils, each of whom had had a year more French than their teacher. How I cudgeled my brain, strained my eyes, and burdened my memory, trying to learn the stones in mineralogy!

In addition to teaching five classes in subjects totally dissimilar, I was secretary of the faculty and had to write the minutes in longhand, no matter how voluminous they were or how busy with my classes I was. Every now and then students who had been charged with various misdemeanors were brought before the faculty to be questioned. On one occasion several students were accused of throwing a bucket of water on the President of the University. So one after another came before the faculty to tell what he knew, but mostly what he didn't know. Taking this voluminous testimony in longhand was a task which I should never have the courage to attempt again. It covered reams of paper and finally had to be transcribed in the secretary's book.

My position in this particular case was a bit uncomfortable and unfortunate, because, when walking from the recitation building to my boarding place one day, in a burst of confidence a student told me who threw the water on the President. But he had pledged me to eternal secrecy, before I had the remotest idea what he was going to divulge. So, as secretary of the faculty, there I sat through long hours of the night listening to all manner of fairy tales about the bucket of water which I knew were not true. Never, after that, did I allow students to tell me any secrets about their pranks. I stopped them just as soon as they began to unburden their souls.

In addition to teaching five classes and being secretary to the faculty, I played the organ for the church services every Sunday morning and evening and gave a night every week to choir rehearsal. Long before Commencement I had to accompany the chorus several nights a week, while it was either learning new selections or rehearsing old ones for that gala occasion. And Commencements at Wilberforce in those days were really red-letter days for us all! The trustees of the University came, not only to attend the exercises, but to discuss ways and means of financing the institution, and they sometimes engaged in such hot debates that their voices could be heard a long distance from the conference room.

Nobody could truthfully claim that I had many idle moments when I taught at Wilberforce University. I certainly earned my salary. But I enjoyed every minute of my work there. The school is beautifully situated in an entrancing rural spot, and everything in the community centers around the institution, which is a world in itself. At the end of the year I had actually saved $150. I felt richer the day I counted my money and found that I had that large amount than I have ever felt since. If I should discover by hook or crook that I had come into possession of a fortune today, I could not feel happier or richer than I did at Wilberforce with that fabulously large sum which I had saved out of my salary that first year.

During the first year I taught at Wilberforce I heard from my father only once. He was so angry with me for accepting a position to teach, he would not write to me. I had often discussed the subject with him and knew he was unalterably opposed to my teaching anywhere. For that reason I did not tell him I was going to teach in Wilberforce after I left my mother in New York. I had definitely made up my mind I would not spend another year in idleness, and I thought it was better to teach without his permission than to ask it and then accept a position after he had forbidden me to do so. I hoped that when he learned I was working in the North instead of the South, he would be reconciled to it. But my hopes were blasted.

For a few seconds after I read Father's letter replying to mine in which I told him I had gone to Wilberforce University to teach, I was literally stunned with grief. He upbraided me bitterly. He reprimanded me severely for disregarding his wishes and disobeying his commands. His reproaches stung me to the quick. My conscience was clear and I knew I had done right to use my training in behalf of my race. Nevertheless, it pained me deeply to displease my father and for a long time I was very unhappy indeed. But I wrote to him occasionally throughout the school year and did everything I could to appease his wrath. At Christmas I sent presents to him, to his wife, and to a little baby brother who had arrived in October. But nothing came to me from my father—not a line.

As soon as school closed I went to New York to spend the first half of my vacation with Mother, and then I decided to go to Memphis to see Father, so as to patch up our differences if I possibly could. En route I sent him a telegram stating that I would arrive at five o'clock the next morning, and when the train pulled into the station, there on the platform waiting to greet me was my dearly beloved father, who literally received me with open arms. So ended the most serious breach between my father and myself which ever occurred.

Father realized that in doing what I believed was my duty I was simply proving that I was a "chip off the old block." As some girls run away from home to marry the man of their choice and thus brook their father's displeasure, so I left home and ran the risk of permanently alienating my father from myself to engage in the work which his money had prepared me to do. After that Father never objected to my teaching, and at the end of that summer vacation he was perfectly willing for me to return to Wilberforce to resume my work.

At the close of my second year at Wilberforce a very wealthy and delightful woman who was interested in our group came to visit the school, liked me, and invited me most cordially to go abroad with her the next summer. I had long wanted to study abroad and hailed this opportunity with delight. My father cheerfully consented to let me go and promised to give me all the money I needed for the trip. So far did my wealthy friend and I go with the preparation for this voyage that she selected our cabins and talked enthusiastically about the color of some dresses which she thought would be becoming and wanted me to wear. She waxed especially eloquent when she described the colors she wished me to affect when we reached Egypt. Women of my complexion look very well in pink, she said, so I was to have at least one dress in that color.

Then suddenly there came an invitation for me to teach in the colored high school in Washington, D. C. Dr. John R.

Francis, one of the colored members of the Board of Education, had written to the secretaries of several colleges requesting them to send the names of recent colored graduates with their records and addresses, so that he might write them concerning positions in the colored high school.

Mrs. A. A. F. Johnston, the dean of women in Oberlin, wrote so enthusiastically about the three colored women who had graduated in the class of 1884 that Dr. Francis sent for one of the others and for me to come immediately. The third member of the class came to teach several years later.

I regret exceedingly that I have lost two letters of recommendation written by Oberlin professors in my behalf. One was sent by my Greek teacher, Professor Frost, and the other was written by Mrs. Johnston herself. They attributed to me qualities of head and heart which I wish I could believe I possess, and they placed an estimate upon my record of which anyone might be proud.

I wanted very much to go abroad with my wealthy friend, because I knew that the conditions under which I would travel with her as a chaperon would be so extraordinary that it would be practically impossible to duplicate them with anybody else whom I would be likely to meet. But my father promised that if I waited till the following summer, he would go abroad with me himself. That prospect was very alluring indeed. Still, I was tormented by the fear that if I postponed the trip, something might happen to prevent me from taking it at all. "After altering your plan," a little voice kept whispering in my ear, "what if your father changes his mind and decides not to go abroad next year? If he does, you may have to wait a long time before you get another chance. And perhaps you may never be able to realize your dream of years."

I knew Father would not let me go abroad alone, even if I myself had sufficient courage to undertake it. I could scarcely sleep for revolving this momentous question in my mind. Never after that in my whole life was it more difficult to decide what it was best to do than when I was trying to make up my mind whether I should go abroad as I had planned, or postpone the trip a year and accept a position to teach in the high school in Washington. After a nerve-racking period of indecision and torture I finally decided to come to Washington. And there is no doubt whatever that this decision just at that time did change the whole course of my life.

After coming to Washington I was required to take an examination in several subjects, one of which was concerning the best methods of teaching, about which I knew nothing except what I had gained from actual experience in Wilberforce University. I take it for granted that I passed, for I was appointed. Dr. and Mrs. John R. Francis invited me to stay a while in their spacious and comfortable home, till I could get permanently settled, and then I went to live with Mrs. Cox, Mrs. Francis' mother, who was one of the most lovable women in the world.

I had been in Washington only a day or two when I began to hear a great deal about a young man who had graduated from Harvard University the same year I received my diploma from Oberlin. He was an honor man, I was told. When he graduated from Harvard, only those men wore the cap and gown whose rank entitled them to be speakers. In a class of three hundred white men who had had the advantage of him in heredity and environment and also in the wherewithal to finance a college course, this young colored man was one of seven who marched in the Commencement procession wearing his cap and gown.

His father had brought him to Washington from Virginia when he was ten years old, and he had attended the public schools of the District of Columbia. So the citizens were very proud of him indeed. He was quite popular, and people liked to talk about the first colored boy who had graduated from the high school of Washington who had taken a degree at Harvard University.

He was described to me as being tall, very good-looking, a fine dancer, and splendid company on general principles. He was also a great favorite among young women, of course. I had been in Washington nearly a week and had not seen this much-described and frequently discussed young gentleman. Never having beheld a colored man who had graduated from Harvard University, I must confess I was very eager to meet him.

The first Sunday afternoon after reaching Washington I was sitting on Dr. Francis' doorstep and happened to glance down the street. Rapidly approaching the house was a tall, dapper, well-dressed young man whom I knew intuitively and instinctively to be the Harvard graduate, Robert Heberton Terrell, about whom I had heard so much. Immediately I jumped to my feet and rushed upstairs impulsively and exclaimed excitedly to Mrs. Francis, "Mr. Terrell has come." Mrs. Francis, who was calm and unemotional, was very much amused at the commotion into which Mr. Terrell's visit had thrown me, and for a long time enjoyed relating the incident. I tried to explain that the only reason I rushed upstairs was that I was sitting alone and there was no one to introduce me to the stranger. But Dr. and Mrs. Francis poked a great deal of fun at me just the same.

Mr. Terrell had charge of the Latin department in the high school and I was designated to assist him. It is safe to assert that never since the dawn of creation did two teachers of the same subject get along more harmoniously and with less friction than did that head of the Latin department in the colored high school of Washington, D. C., and his assistant. I had some first-year classes and a second-year class. In addition to a first and a second-year class Mr. Terrell also taught the senior class in Virgil. Occasionally he invited me to teach this advanced class and seemed to take pleasure in showing the pupils I was capable of doing so.

When Mr. Terrell himself was teaching a class and a discussion arose concerning the construction of a sentence in Virgil, he would sometimes tell his pupils he did not know whether it was a subjunctive of purpose or a subjunctive of result, but he "would ask Miss Church and see what she thought about it." After a statement like that there were always significant glances around the room and a few suppressed giggles. Then the next day Mr. Terrell would be likely to make a report something like this: "I have talked with Miss Church about this sentence and she thinks it is a subjunctive of purpose. It seems to me it is result rather than purpose, but you had better accept Miss Church's construction, she knows more about Latin than I do." Perhaps some boy a little bolder than the others would remark sotto voce, "We all knew you would think your assistant was right."

Long before the first school year in Washington closed, my father assured me definitely that he intended to fulfill his promise to go abroad with me during the summer vacation. He let me make the arrangements to suit myself. I decided to take one of the Cook tours which included a trip to some of the principal cities in England, Belgium, Switzerland, and France. From

Washington I went to New York to visit my mother and to purchase what I needed before sailing.

There was a very distinguished passenger on the *City of Berlin,* on which Father and I sailed—Mrs. Isabella Beecher Hooker, the half-sister of Harriet Beecher Stowe. From someone on the steamer she heard that I was going abroad to study and she sent for me to come to see her. She became so interested in me that she gave me letters of introduction to some of the most helpful and influential people in Paris and thereby rendered me a service which few others would have or could have given. These letters from Mrs. Hooker were an open sesame wherever and whenever I presented them. By chance I met in Paris an Oberlin man who told me that Mrs. A. A. F. Johnston, dean of Oberlin women, was stopping at the Continental Hotel, and suggested that I call on her. Those who have met an old friend unexpectedly in a foreign land know how happy I was.

It is hard to believe that any woman could have extracted more pleasure and profit from a three months' tour in Europe than I did. I drank in everything of historic interest in great gulps. I could never see enough in one day and never grew tired. Long stairways I climbed eagerly, while some of our company groaned aloud and others absolutely refused to ascend. I can take an affidavit that I never missed a word of explanation which any guide on the trip gave about anything whatsoever, no matter how trivial it was. My father's interest in the historical places we visited and in the rare objects we saw was also unbounded. He insisted upon my sending postals and letters describing these places; which consumed a great deal of my strength and time, but I wish I could lay hands on some of those which I wrote on my first trip abroad, so that I might see today what was my point of view then. The priceless paintings in the Louvre opened up an entirely new world to me. It was the first time I had seen the works of the old masters or the best specimens of the modern school, and I rejoiced in the glorious opportunity of learning something about art.

Few men could have been more wretched than Father the morning he boarded the train in Paris, to take the steamer sailing home, and left me there standing alone on the platform. He had solemnly promised to let me study abroad. I had set my heart on it, and nothing in the world could have induced me to give up this cherished plan. As he stood in the station waiting for the train Father begged me to return with him.

"But my clothes are in the hotel," I replied. "Surely you don't want me to leave all my belongings here in Paris," I said. If I had decided to do that, however, Father would have heartily approved the decision. Although he rarely showed how deeply moved he was about anything, his eyes filled when he kissed me good-bye and left me alone in Paris.

Not a tear was in my eye, however, for at last the time had come when I could do the work which I had planned so long. I was the happiest girl on earth. I am sure I felt as Monte Cristo must have felt when he exclaimed, "The world is mine." Here I was in Paris. I could study French, visit the wonderful galleries to my heart's content, learn something about art, and attend the theaters. In short, here at last was the realization of those radiant dreams which had filled my head and heart for years. Father promised I might study abroad a year, and I knew he would keep his word. There was nothing to worry me. Not a care in the world, bubbling over with enthusiasm and youth!

Just as soon as I could find a suitable pension I left the cozy little hotel in the Rue de Richelieu and went to board with a widow who was highly recommended by one of Mrs. Hooker's friends. She was a typical Frenchwoman who had a young niece, so that it was a decided advantage to me to secure accommodations in such a home. My landlady was a most capable and faithful teacher and worked hard to make my pronunciation and accent correct. By talking with her niece, who could neither understand nor speak a word of English, I learned many expressions used in ordinary conversation and not generally found in books.

Living in Paris was more expensive than I thought it would be. I had to pay much more for my room and board than I cared to spend for those two items alone. Moreover, when I wanted to attend the theater, it was necessary to have a chaperon and pay for her ticket as well as my own, even when she did not expect an extra fee for her services. I chafed under this condition considerably.

Having secured several addresses from an American girl, I wrote to a family in Lausanne and arranged to go there without telling my father that I intended to leave Paris, because I feared he would object to my traveling in Europe alone. I had definitely decided that it would be more advantageous for me in every way to go to Switzerland, and I thought it was better to make the change without asking my father's permission than to do so if he insisted upon my remaining in Paris. I felt greatly handicapped in Paris, because comparatively few American girls, as young as I was, went about the city alone. The little Swiss Republic beckoned me, because I knew American and English girls were accustomed to go about unaccompanied.

Before I left Paris I sent my father my Lausanne address and then waited in fear and trembling for a reply. After reaching Switzerland, every morning when I awoke my first thought would be, "What if you should receive a cable from your father ordering you home, because you left Paris without consulting him!" But no such tragedy occurred. My father assured me most emphatically that he had perfect confidence in me, no matter where I traveled. "I know you can take care of yourself," he wrote, "and that you will do the right thing, wherever you are." After receiving a letter like that from her father, no girl who had a bit of conscience or a spark of honor could possibly have abused his confidence in her by doing anything of which she knew he would not approve.

The family with whom I boarded in Lausanne consisted of the father, mother, and two daughters about my own age. My room was very small, just large enough for a single bed, a little table, and a chair. It had only one little window. But from that single little window what a glorious view I had! I could see the snow-capped Alps towering heavenward and at right angles to them the low-lying Jura Mountains, which somehow linger in my memory as being always brown. Sarah, the younger of the two daughters, was an artist of considerable talent who played the piano exceedingly well and painted much better than the average amateur. She appealed to me all the more strongly, perhaps, because the stern régime under which she lived differed so strikingly from the soft, easy life led by her pampered sister. I have read about favoritism being shown some particular child in the family, but I have never seen such a flagrant case of it as the one I witnessed in Lausanne.

The father of the family, who was connected in some way with the Suisse Simplon railway, enjoyed taking a company of young people on a long hike. Early Sunday morning we would take a train at Lausanne for some near-by town from which we could climb a mountain that he wanted us especially to see. On our way both up and down the mountain, we would stop at some wayside inn and have a light repast which was always topped off by some delicious beverage which Monsieur G. would brew himself. No matter how much we plead with him and tried to bribe him, we could never persuade our host to divulge the secret of the ingredients or the manner in which he made it. There was no use peeping and prying and following him about, trying to surprise him in the act of concocting it. He always successfully eluded us. Of all the cities and towns visited near Lausanne, nothing interested me more than the Castle of Chillon.

In Lausanne I attended a private school for girls. Most of the pupils were younger than I, although I was by no means the oldest. I recited all my lessons in French and was required to write compositions in French like the others. I learned much about the literature and history of Europe that I had not previously known and acquired many new points of view. I lived a long distance from the school and had to climb a steep incline—almost a young mountain—to reach it in the morning.

In the family where I lived the conditions were almost ideal. In addition to the two daughters, a young girl came from German Switzerland, speaking the German of her section, which nobody could understand. We four girls had all the fun that was rightfully due us under our own vine and fig tree.

Following the custom of the country, we drank wine for dinner. But I grew tired of the wine after a while and longed for a drink of nice, cold water, which I heard could be procured from a near-by spring. I told Lizette, the maid, if she would bring me a pitcher full for my dinner, I would make it worth her while. She did so and I drank three glasses of water at the dinner table.

Mme. G. was shocked and begged me not to jeopardize my health in that way. She was sure that cold water would paralyze my digestive apparatus. The girls were almost in tears as they saw me commit suicide before their very eyes so far away from home. It was the first time Mme. G. had ever seen a human being drink cold water during a meal, she said, and she believed I had injured myself seriously. She was so sure that I would be very ill as the result of such disobedience to the rules of health that she made me give her the address of my parents, so that she would have it handy in case she had to cable them during the night. And they were all surprised when they saw I not only lived to tell the tale, but suffered no ill effects from the cold water at all.

After remaining in Lausanne a year I felt that I had spent as much time studying French as I could afford to give it. I had been careful to learn to pronounce certain words as Parisians do, when there was a difference between their pronunciation and that of the Swiss. I wanted to study German and I decided to go to Berlin. I had heard that the purest German was spoken in Dresden. But I had resided in the Capital of the United States and had spent quite a while in London and Paris, so it seemed logical to live in the capital of Germany. I felt that if I learned to speak German as well as it could be taught in Berlin, I would be as proficient in the language as I could hope to be.

With a heavy heart, in spite of the fact that I was doing exactly what I had planned to do, I tore myself away from the delightful surroundings and left my dear friends in Lausanne. I was the closest friend Sarah had ever had, and she was inconsolable. I shed many bitter tears myself when I bade her good-bye. But, after boarding the train, youth's grief at leaving friends was greatly assuaged by the magnificent scenery which was unrolled before my enraptured eyes. Nothing that Nature has ever done could be more wonderful than Switzerland in winter. It is useless to try to paint a word picture of the snow-capped Alps. One may read volumes on the subject without being able to have any conception of the reality.

CHAPTER 8

I STUDY IN GERMANY

O N THE WAY TO BERLIN I stopped in Munich and Dresden. In Munich I employed a guide to show me the city. I had spoken nothing but French for a year, and, although I had spoken German fairly well before I left home, both my tongue and my ear were somewhat out of practice. As soon as I reached Germany, however, I was delighted to see that I could understand what was said to me and could express everything I wanted to say.

My guide, a blond German, suggested that he could carry my Baedeker's guidebook more conveniently than I could. I had bought it before I left Lausanne, so that I could read up on the journey I was about to take and decide what I wanted to see, before I reached the places. It always amused me a bit to see Americans with their heads buried in their guidebooks and their eyes glued to the printed page instead of looking at the works of art or at the structures they had come so far to see.

I forthwith entrusted my Baedeker to the guide's watchful care. As we boarded a street car on our way to a church, a man standing on the rear platform looked at me very seriously and said something to me in German which I did not quite understand, but which sounded like a warning of some kind, as he nodded toward the guide. In thinking about the words spoken rapidly I was sure I heard "Geldbeutel," and I knew it meant "purse." I observed also that the guide looked daggers at this man, who was speaking directly to me as though he were trying to tell me something for my own good. It finally dawned on me that the stranger was warning me against the guide and telling me to watch my purse.

When I settled with my guide that evening I understood perfectly what the man on the trolley car was trying to tell me. After paying him for the time he had given me, I asked him for my book. At first he denied having taken it from me at all. He could not remember doing so, he said. But when I insisted he had, he began to search carefully through the many pockets in his trousers and sweater, as though he were trying to find it. After looking for it in vain, he opined that he must have lost it somewhere during the day. But when I told him in German that if he did not find my Baedeker I would call the police, he fished it from the depths of his sweater, being obliged to insert his hand so far down in his clothing 1 feared he could never bring it up again. But when his hand did finally heave in sight, so did my Baedeker's guidebook. That was one of the very few cases in which an effort was made to steal from me while I was abroad. Sometimes the cabmen or the small tradesmen would try to withhold a few centimes in making change, but they did it so cleverly and had reduced their manipulations and explanations and gesticulations to such a work of art that it was almost a pleasure to be cheated by those skillful gentlemen. No woman of any nationality ever tried to cheat me out of a sou from the time I left the United States till I returned.

When I reached Dresden I was glad I had decided to study in Berlin. The city was full of Americans and English. Wherever I turned on the streets, I heard my mother tongue. I knew that a foreign city full of my white countrymen was no place for a colored girl. I was trying to flee from the evils of race prejudice, so depressing in my own country, and it seemed very stupid indeed for me to place myself in a position to encounter it abroad.

In Dresden I received my first taste of German opera, for there the most noted singers were appearing at that time. I went alone, for it was never unpleasant for me to go anywhere unaccompanied. From the time I first began to travel, I preferred to go by myself, so that I might see just what interested me and stop to look at it as long as I pleased without feeling I was annoying somebody else who was not so eager to gaze on it as I was. On several occasions I have had the pleasure of traveling with people who were interested in the same things that I was, and then "I had the time of my life."

When I reached Berlin I decided to remain temporarily at a pension on Markgrafen Strasse which was kept by a neat, pleasant little Jewess. She had only one vacant room, which was so small I did not see how I could be comfortable in it. There was no place to hang my clothes and no way to heat the room except by a gas stove, and I had always heard that heat from a gas stove was injurious to the health. For that reason I looked at a room in another pension and talked with the proprietor about it, discussed the price, and told him I would notify him at a certain time whether I would take it or not. In the meantime, the guests in the Markgrafen Strasse pension were so agreeable and so eager to have me stay, and the clever landlady made the little room so comfortable and attractive, I decided to remain there. The fact that there were no Americans in the pension to tempt me to speak English was an added inducement for me to stay where I was.

According to promise, therefore, I communicated my decision to the proprietor of the pension who had shown me a room several days before. He claimed that I had definitely engaged the room and that he had saved it for me, and insisted upon having me pay the rent for a month. As the less of two evils, I acceded to his demand. Some American women who had seen me pass through the hall told the proprietor I was quite swarthy and it was barely possible I represented a race which was socially ostracized in the United States by all white people who had any self-respect. I learned afterward on good authority that my countrywomen would have made it decidedly unpleasant for me if I had gone to that pension to live.

When I reached Berlin I had not heard from home for three weeks. Before leaving Lausanne I had instructed Father to send my letters *poste restante* to Berlin. As soon as I reached Berlin, therefore, and decided on the pension at which I would remain temporarily, I started for the city post-office, eager to get the mail which I knew was awaiting me. I received many letters, and when I had finished reading them, I started to return to my boarding house. It was the first week in December, the afternoons were short, and I observed that it was growing dark rapidly. When I looked for the paper containing my new address, it was nowhere to be found. While joyously reading my letters from home, I had undoubtedly lost that slip of paper of such great value to me. So there I was in the great city of Berlin with night coming on, actually lost, acquainted with no one, while practically everything I possessed was in my luggage deposited in an apartment house which I could not locate to save my life. After cudgeling my brain a long time I thought I remembered the name of the street on which my pension was located. I was also able to tell the policeman to whom I related my troubles the name of the car I had boarded to reach the post-office, and I described pretty accurately the corner on which I had taken it. So systematically is everything conducted in Germany that it is quite easy to secure quickly practically any information one needs. The names of people who keep boarding houses are on file, and a stranger may remain in the city only a short while before he is required to register his name and tell everything about himself the authorities want to know, and they want to know EVERYTHING.

And so, after several processes of induction and deduction plus consultations with a certain office, I discovered where I had deposited my belongings. When I finally reached the pension, it was quite dark, and I found that both my landlady and all her boarders were very much alarmed about the inexplicably long absence of the young American girl who had just reached the big city. After such an experience I carefully guarded my addresses in the future and was never lost in a strange city again.

Our family included two brothers, Hebrews, one of whom was a bank official, very learned, very sedate, and mature. The other was much younger and was connected with the stock exchange. He was an entertaining, witty Lothario. Then there was a tall young German with a magnificent physique who was studying something or other which was a dead secret and who was always talking about a girl to whom he was engaged back home. "Meine Braut" was a subject which he never tired of discussing and regaled us with, in season and out. He had been an officer in the army, since he was living in the heyday of German militarism, and he told us over and over again how his fiancée used to come to his house every day, so that she and his mother might look out of the window as he proudly marched by. No human being could possibly be more conceited than he was, and no human being, not even excepting Bismarck himself, could have believed more implicitly in brute force than he did. Not only did he believe in war and all the horrors incident thereto, but he smacked his lips with relish when he told how he intended to whip his children and boss his wife.

There was also an interesting little clerk who was heels-over-head in love with the landlady, who had no idea of marrying a man as poor as he was. Being of a romantic turn of mind, I did everything in my power to soften Fräulein's heart, but she always silenced me by saying that she herself had long outgrown the romantic age, when women marry for love alone. It was the first time I had ever heard a woman declare openly and aboveboard that she did not intend to marry for love, and I marveled at her frankness.

The two Hebrew brothers helped me greatly in learning German and becoming thoroughly acquainted with Berlin as well as its interesting suburbs. They advised me with reference to the books it was best to read, and directed me to various objects of interest which are not generally mentioned in a traveler's guide and which I should not have seen but for them. On several occasions these two brothers and a cousin took me to see the castles in the environs of Berlin. I especially enjoyed visiting the one at which Frederick the Second and Queen Victoria's daughter, his consort, spent their honeymoon.

This Englishwoman was the first person to establish a school in Germany for the higher education of girls. But the German idea of the higher education of girls differed materially from that entertained in the United States. Some of the professors from the University of Berlin delivered lectures at this girls' school which might easily have been digested by children of twelve. But the facilities for the so-called higher education offered women at this institution were greater than those which could be found anywhere else in Germany at that time and they were, therefore, gratefully accepted by many.

I attended this school, and one day when the Empress Frederick, who had founded it, visited it, I curtsied to her in true German fashion like the other girls. Twice and sometimes three times a week I attended the opera while I remained in Berlin. I often attended the theater also, for there is no better way of educating the ear and acquiring the correct pronunciation in studying a foreign language than by listening to good actors. I had a dear little Russian friend who was one of the most remarkable linguists I have ever met. She spoke at least seven languages fluently. We usually attended the opera together and sat in the peanut gallery, which was frequented by students, from whose comments I learned much more about the operas and music on general principles than I could have acquired in any other way.

Thus I became acquainted with the youth of many lands, some of whom were rated as geniuses and expected sooner or later to startle the world with their achievements. Many of them were poor in this world's goods, however rich in talent and great expectations they were. To me it was pathetic to see the desperate struggle to get along and keep soul and body together which many of them made. The schemes which some of them hatched to make life a bit easier than it was were also amusing.

One day my landlady knocked at my door and told me some callers wished to see me. When they were ushered into my room, one of my Belgian friends introduced me to a blind musician from Austria. He had come to propose marriage to me. He had probably heard from some American student that I had African blood in my veins, was very fond of music, and might be glad to marry a promising musician. Since I hailed from the United States, he took it for granted that I had a respectable bank account. He was perfectly willing, therefore, to link his destiny with mine, assuring me that what he lacked in money he more than made up in talent. I learned from a reliable source that this was true. He begged me to marry him and he promised to become a great artist. Several of the friends he brought with him gave glowing accounts of the laurels he had already won as a pianist. He would surely be heard from some day, they declared. There was no doubt about that, and then, they said, I would be proud to be the wife of one of the greatest virtuosos in Europe.

The blind musician explained that he had heard me talk on several occasions, liked my point of view about some of the questions discussed, and thought I had a beautiful voice. He said he had dared to come to propose because one of his friends had pursued a similar course and had succeeded in marrying an American girl with a lot of money.

Although I was greatly amused, and could scarcely conceal my disgust, I felt sorry for the afflicted man and tried not to say anything which would wound his feelings. I declined his offer, however, in no uncertain terms, saying that I had been reared to believe that marrying for anything but love was a sin, and that his cold-blooded proposition shocked me beyond expression.

While I was in Berlin, I was greatly indebted to a young

man of my own race for several musical treats I enjoyed and for information concerning musical people which I could have secured from no other source. And the way I happened upon this friend was very romantic indeed. Shortly after reaching Berlin I walked out with an American girl whom I had known in Oberlin to see the beautiful shops so brilliantly lighted and artistically decorated for Christmas. We had stopped several times to admire the wonderful display. I felt that somebody was following me, and I turned around several times to see if I could discover anyone. Once I thought I saw a man stop suddenly quite a little distance behind me, but I was not sure, so I said nothing to my companion. We continued our stroll, stopping every now and then to discuss the beautiful objects displayed. Just as we drew up to a window I turned around suddenly and saw standing behind us Will Marion Cook, a young man with whom I had been well acquainted for years and who was then studying music in Berlin.

He said he had suddenly spied me, as he turned the corner, and although he felt sure he recognized me, he could not believe the evidence of his eyes, because he had not heard I had left the United States to travel and study in Europe. He was so impressed with the resemblance I bore to the girl he knew at home, however, he decided to follow my companion and me until he could catch a glimpse of my face, and he was just coming up to greet me when I recognized him. This young man had remarkable talent for the violin. At that time Joachim, one of the greatest teachers of the violin of modern times, taught nobody who was not unmistakably talented in that instrument. Neither wealth, power, nor high social position could tempt this great master to teach anybody who was not a presumptive genius. It was rumored in Berlin that more than one member of the aristocracy had implored Joachim in vain to teach his son. But the great Joachim taught this young colored man from the United States, so impressed was he with his superior talent. Instead of confining himself to the violin, however, this young musician has become a renowned composer of popular music characteristic of his race.

I talked with a young colored man who was studying in Europe because he possessed exceptional talent. He seemed listless rather than lazy, and it pained me to hear from some of his friends that he was wasting his time. When I urged this young man to avail himself of the marvelous opportunities and advantages he enjoyed, he replied, "What's the use of my trying to do anything extraordinary and worth while? A man must have some kind of racial background to amount to anything. He must have a firm racial foundation on which to build. What have we accomplished as a race? Almost nothing. We are descended from slaves. How can you expect a people with such a background as that to compete successfully with white people?"

I confessed to him that I myself had once become very much depressed and discouraged when, as a young girl, I realized for the first time I had descended from slaves. But I told the young man that I had recovered my equilibrium immediately, when I learned from the study of history that with a single exception practically every race of the earth had at some time in the past been the subject of a stronger, so that when colored people in this country passed through a period of bondage, they were simply suffering a fate common to other groups. And then I called his attention to the marvelous progress which the colored people in the United States had made in less than forty years.

I could not convert him to my point of view. But no young colored person in the United States today can truthfully offer as an excuse for lack of ambition or aspiration that members of his race have accomplished so little, he is discouraged from attempting anything himself. For there is scarcely a field of human endeavor which colored people have been allowed to enter in which there is not at least one worthy representative.

During the first winter I was in Berlin my mother wrote that she and my brother were coming abroad in the spring to spend the summer with me in Europe, that they would land in Liverpool and she wanted me to meet them.

Just before I left Berlin I was the recipient of a unique gift which I have always highly prized. "Fräulein, what is your coat of arms?" the elder Mannheimer asked me one day. "You know full well I have no coat of arms," I replied. "Well, you deserve one and you shall have one," he said. A few days after that he and his brother brought me an elegant leather portfolio on which a quaint little church had been embossed in an American flag. So I think I have the distinction of being the only person of African descent in the United States who has a coat of arms.

While I was preparing to leave Berlin, I broke a small hand mirror. How wretched I was after that! I did not know till then how superstitious I was. I feared that broken mirror was an omen that some terrible disaster would overtake my loved ones at sea. I reached Liverpool at least ten days before the steamer arrived, and, in spite of strenuous efforts to control myself, I was very apprehensive indeed. I dreaded to read the newspapers, lest I might learn that the steamer had gone down and everybody on board had been lost. The afternoon that I saw the speck far out on the ocean that I knew was the steamer bearing my mother and brother to me was a happy one indeed. I waved my umbrella so vigorously that I broke it into pieces, before I realized what I had done. Never since Mother and Brother arrived safely in Liverpool in spite of the broken mirror have I allowed myself to worry much about any superstition.

CHAPTER 9

IN EUROPE WITH MOTHER AND BROTHER

JUST BEFORE MOTHER STARTED
for Europe she enjoyed a rare visitation of good fortune. A
plumber who happened to be working for her one day persuaded
her to buy a ticket in the Louisiana lottery, which at that time
flourished like the proverbial green bay tree, but has since been
put out of commission altogether. She paid a dollar for it, then
threw it aside and forgot all about it, as she had done many times
before. After a while this plumber, whom Mother had neither
seen nor heard from since he sold her the ticket, came to the
house to tell her that the number on the ticket she had bought had
won the first prize and she was entitled to $15,000. My mother
thought the plumber was joking until he showed her the number
of the ticket, which he had carefully preserved.

But where in the world was that valuable ticket? Who
knew? Mother certainly did not. She had often bought tickets
before from anybody who offered her one, and had promptly
thrown them aside and forgotten all about them. The house was
searched from top to bottom. The contents of all the drawers
were dumped out and carefully scanned. The pockets of every
dress and coat in the house were emptied. Bureau scarfs were
raised in the hope that the little ticket might have been slipped
under one of them and left there for safe keeping. But all in
vain. The valuable little ticket could not be found.

Finally, Anna, a German girl who had been working for
Mother several years, ever since she had landed from the Fatherland, remembered that she had recently cleaned out a drawer
in the buffet, had thrown a lot of trash in the waste-paper basket,
and had not had time either to burn it up or to dump it into the

[81]

trash barrel to be carted away by the city. She ran to this basket and hastily pulled out the papers which had been marked for destruction, and there at the bottom of the pile was the innocent, unobtrusive little ticket which was worth $15,000 in cash!

Mother gave the plumber who notified her of this good fortune $1,000. She gave Anna $300 for finding the ticket and sent me $300 to buy a fur coat. I was in Lausanne at the time and put this money into the bank, resolving not to touch a penny of it till Mother could help me select whatever I bought. The good fortune enabled Mother to travel in Europe with her son and daughter without being worried about financing the trip.

The first thing she did when she reached London was to order a handsome sealskin ulster for herself, selecting her own skins, and another for her daughter at one of the best furriers in the city. Mother's knowledge of materials of all kinds always astounded me. She knew good quality in everything pertaining either to clothing or to the furnishings of a home. In her prime she was one of the best-dressed women I have ever seen. Then three or four suits were ordered right away for my brother, and a dress suit that was made to order for him was the very last word in that article at that time.

Whatever Mother wanted she bought, if she happened to have the money that minute to pay for it. She literally fulfilled the Scriptures and obeyed to the letter the injunction not to lay up treasures for yourself on earth. She valued money only as it administered to her own immediate needs or the needs of those she loved and provided what luxuries she craved. So she freely spent the money she had won, stopping at the best hotels, using cabs whenever she wanted them, and enjoying all the pleasures which travel in a foreign country affords. In vain I tried to persuade my generous, improvident mother not to spend her money so lavishly, especially on me, but she paid no attention at all to this advice. If she saw anything she even suspected I needed or would enjoy, she bought it for me in spite of any protest I might make.

In Paris we had an experience which might have resulted very disastrously indeed. We attended the opera one night and took a cab to go home. We had been driving what seemed to me a long time when I suddenly realized that we were getting into the suburbs of Paris instead of traversing the streets to which I was accustomed and which led to our hotel. When I asked the driver where he was going, he grunted something which gave me to understand he knew what he was doing, and looked out on both sides of the road as though he expected to see somebody. I had heard of strangers being taken by cabmen to deserted spots near Paris to be robbed and sometimes murdered, if they resisted, and I suspected that the cabman was looking for a confederate to help steal my mother's diamonds, which were sparkling in her ears. With all the courage I could summon I told the cabby to turn around immediately, and gave him to understand that if he did not obey my orders, my brother was prepared to force him to do so. Much to my surprise and relief, the cabman turned around at once and drove straight to our hotel, which was quite a distance in the opposite direction from which he was going. Ever since then I have been timid about hiring a cab in a strange city at night.

During the Paris Exposition in 1889 we met a sure enough, flesh-and-blood African prince, who was one of the most courteous, cultured, magnetic, and attractive personalities I have ever seen anywhere in the world. He had been educated in Paris and had acquired the manners of the French, although he was dressed in oriental splendor. My mother always insisted that this prince made such a deep impression upon her daughter that she would undoubtedly have become an African princess if she had only had a chance.

It was very difficult for my mother and brother to secure accommodations to return home in time for the opening of Marietta College, which my brother was attending, because so many Americans had gone to Paris to visit the Exposition and all wanted to leave by the middle of September. While rushing from one steamship office to another I ran into a young colored girl with whom I had been well acquainted in Washington. This was one of many instances which proved to me that the world is very small indeed. I visited very few places, no matter how diminutive in size, in which I failed to meet someone I had either known in the United States or met abroad.

It was finally arranged that my mother and brother should sail from Hamburg on the Hamburg-American Line, and we went there to spend our last few days of vacation together. If I had known how hard it would be for me to say good-bye to them and see them sail away home, leaving me behind on a foreign shore, I might not have had the courage to remain abroad, although I wanted very much to study in Europe another year and my father had given me permission to do so.

As soon as the steamer sailed, I rushed to the hotel, threw my effects into a valise, and took the train for Berlin, where I planned to spend the winter. I went to a hotel instead of to my pension when I reached Berlin, because I did not want any of my friends or acquaintances to see how wretched I was. I had no appetite and could not force myself to eat. I remained in bed, for I felt too weak to dress. At noon on the third day the proprietor came to my room to see what was the matter with me. The maid had told him, he said, that I was ill and had eaten nothing for three days, and he intended to send for a doctor. I assured him that there was nothing the matter with me and that I would be well enough to go out the next day. I had been traveling all summer, I explained, and was a bit shaken because my mother and brother had just sailed home.

"Have you any friends or acquaintances here in Berlin?" he inquired. When I told him I had, he insisted upon my giving him their addresses. I had decided not to return to the pension in which I had formerly lived, because I thought a change of environment would be advantageous to me. For that reason I did not give the proprietor the names of my good friends in the pension in which I had spent such a happy time. I decided to refer him to an Oberlin friend.

She came posthaste the next morning, and insisted that I was simply homesick and that I must come to her pension immediately. I protested vigorously against doing so, because I did not want to live among English-speaking people, since it would tempt me to use my mother tongue too much. 'Way down deep in my heart I feared to board in a house where there were many Americans. I felt I would get into some kind of trouble on account of race prejudice. But my Oberlin friend overcame all objections, promised solemnly that she would allow me to speak English only on the Fourth of July and Christmas, selected a room in her pension for me, made all the arrangements, and moved me there bag and baggage that very afternoon.

I had been in Fräulein von Finck's pension but a few days when I observed that a woman whose complexion was quite swarthy fastened her eyes upon me every time I came into her presence. Finally, she accosted me one evening when we were both in the reception room, and asked me to what nationality

I belonged. "I have heard that you are an American," she said, "but you are rather dark to be an American, aren't you?" I laughingly replied that I was a "dark American." "And I am dark like you, too, you observe," she said. "I am a Spaniard and my husband is German. Every time I see a woman who is not fair, I become very much interested in her indeed."

That was the beginning of one of the most instructive and delightful experiences I had while I was abroad. This Spanish woman was the wife of a general in the German army. Once in a while they left their residence and lived in a pension where there were young people and students of different nationalities, because they enjoyed coming into contact with them. Frau General von Wenckstern liked to talk with them, associate with them, and learn their aims and ambitions in life. Through my Spanish friend I was introduced into several distinguished social circles into which few Americans had entree. And this opportunity came to me because my complexion was dark! It was indeed a rare experience for a colored girl hailing from the United States.

After I had been in Fräulein von Finck's pension a short time, I saw two young American men eyeing me as though they were anything but pleased to behold me in their midst. These two students were studying medicine. One was from Baltimore and the other hailed from Washington, D. C. I observed that Fräulein, who was literally fair, fat, and forty, quite loquacious, and especially catered to Americans, held long conversations with these two medical students, who could neither speak nor understand German very well. But Fräulein could speak English and enjoyed practicing it on Americans who would let her do it.

One day she called me and told me she would like to see me in her room that afternoon at two o'clock. When I entered, Fräulein appeared embarrassed, and it was evident she did not know how to say what was on her mind. "To what nationality do you belong, Fräulein Church?" she began. "I am an American," I replied. "But you are darker than the average American, aren't you?" She flushed a deep red when she asked this question. "Yes, I am darker than some Americans," I admitted. "Can you go to a hotel in the United States?" I knew by that question that somebody had explained to her the disabilities under which colored people labor in the United States. "I certainly can," I assured her. "I have been going to good hotels with my father ever since I was a little girl. But why do you ask me these questions, Fräulein von Finck? What difference does it make to you what my nationality is, so long as I conduct myself properly in your pension and pay my bills? There are several nationalities in your pension. There is an East Indian much darker than I am."

And then Fräulein von Finck threw all her cards on the table and related the whole story from start to finish. "The two medical students from Baltimore and Washington tell me you are a Negro, Fräulein Church," she said, "and that you are not allowed to stop at a first-class boarding house or hotel in the United States. They also say that if I allow you to remain here in my pension, no self-respecting people from the United States will stop with me. I told them that an American girl who was well acquainted with you and had gone to school with you in your own country had engaged the room for you in my house and had persuaded you to come against your will. They explained that by saying there are a few cranks in the United States who are willing to associate with Negroes and for that reason are socially ostracized by self-respecting people. Then I told them that the young men and women who are your friends are highly educated, refined people who associate with the best Americans who live in Berlin.

"But the medical students told me I was greatly mistaken and declared that just as Jews are socially ostracized in Germany, so Negroes are socially ostracized all over the United States. They stated positively that Negroes cannot secure accommodations in decent hotels there. Nor can they buy tickets in the theaters, unless they are willing to sit in a portion of the gallery set apart for them. 'But Fräulein Church is not a Negro,' I insisted. 'She is not black. She is no darker than Frau General von Wenckstern, a Spaniard.'

" 'But she is classed as a Negro in the United States, whether she is black or not,' they said. 'If an individual has only a single drop of African blood in his veins,' those two young men explained, 'white people in the United States consider him a Negro.' "

In short, there was nothing these young men from the United States could possibly tell this German woman which would cause her to reject and repudiate me, which they failed to relate or reveal. I told Fräulein von Finck that I had attended school with white Americans all my life, that I had graduated from a high school, an academy, and a first-class college conducted by white Americans for white and black students alike, that I had been accorded the same privileges and the same treatment in them which white students received. I impressed it upon her that I was by no means the only colored student who had attended institutions of learning in which colored students were accepted along with the white. I explained also that the discrimination against colored people in hotels, theaters, and schools which had been so graphically described by the medical students was practically confined to one section of the United States. At that time this was essentially true. But since then race prejudice has rapidly spread all over the country.

After expressing my opinion freely and relieving my mind, I told Fräulein von Finck I would not embarrass her by remaining under her roof another night. I felt I could not retain my self-respect if I stayed another second in the same boarding house with two young men who were so full of prejudice against my race that they would drive from comfortable quarters a young colored girl who was alone in a foreign land three thousand miles from home.

Fräulein begged me to remain. She assured me that she simply wanted to talk with me, so that I might explain matters to her. When I insisted upon leaving the house immediately, she wept and declared she would never forgive herself for having spoken to me at all, if I left. She assured me she preferred to have me stay with her, but if I insisted upon going anyhow, she urged me not to move for another month at least.

Very much against my will and my best judgment I kept my room a week longer. This incident proved to me that among some Americans race prejudice is such an obsession that they cannot lay it aside even in a foreign land, where there is no danger they will be pestered to any appreciable extent by the objectionable Negro. When these young men saw a colored girl trying to cultivate her mind in a foreign land, the chivalry of southern gentlemen snapped. They did not hesitate to humiliate me and disturb my peace by attempting to persuade my landlady to put me out of the house.

But, after all, I was not sorry that I went to Fräulein von Finck's, for Frau General von Wenckstern made it possible for me to see a phase of life among the aristocracy which I could have observed in no other way. Moreover, she introduced me to a fine young man who was a graduate of Heidelberg University, a counselor at law, and who belonged to an old, distinguished family. One evening she arranged a theater party to which this young man was invited. Between the acts I was quite sure I heard him saying something about me to Frau von Wenckstern. I could not help hearing him exclaim in surprise, "Why don't the Americans like her?" And then in disgust, "What do they claim is the matter with her?" After that some words reached my ears which made me certain he was saying something complimentary.

Herr von D. took me home from the theater party, and, after discussing the difference between the educational system of Germany and that of the United States, he was very much surprised to learn that I had received an A.B. degree from college. Observing that he was quite skeptical about my having studied Greek, I quoted the first line of Homer's *Iliad* to him. He stopped on the street abruptly and was transfixed to the spot. I am sure if I had built a steam engine before his eyes, he could not have been more astonished, not to say shocked, than he was when he heard me quote a line of Greek. "Um Gottes Willen, Fräulein," he exclaimed, "there is not another girl in the whole German Empire who can rattle off Greek like that." But I assured him he was quite mistaken, and that there were many American girls in the German Empire who could rattle off Greek much better than I could and who had graduated from college just as I had.

After leaving Fräulein von Finck's I succeeded in finding a delightful boarding place in the home of a widow of a Court minister who had two daughters about my own age, as had been my good fortune in Lausanne. She lived in an apartment not far from the Philharmonie, where the great von Bülow directed his wonderful orchestra.

One of the daughters of this household was a demure young person with plenty of latent fire which she always kept under perfect control. She was engaged to a young man who did not live in Berlin, and she spent the major portion of every Sunday afternoon writing him long letters. Her sister, however, was a regular hoyden, a bundle of mischief, and delighted in letting the world know it. She had been off to school somewhere and boasted that she and the other girls in her set smoked whenever they liked. I did not believe her. At that time I had never heard of girls from respectable families smoking. I had never seen a woman smoking, not to mention a girl, and I had not yet heard that many women in Europe had acquired the habit.

But this young German girl had heard that all American girls smoked, and she believed I was misrepresenting the facts, to say the least, when I denied that allegation. But in this case there was no use trying to "defy the alligator," for she firmly believed that American girls committed indiscretions of every kind without even attracting attention.

After I had lived in Berlin a while it was easy to understand why and how this estimate was placed upon American girls. Freed from the restraint of home, a goodly number of them studying abroad had violated the proprieties, perhaps without any evil intent. Many Germans, therefore, judged American girls as a whole by the indiscreet few whom they saw in their country or about whose behavior they had heard. It was interesting as well as painful to me to see that American girls are the victims of the same kind of blanket accusations made by the Germans as those of which colored people are the victims in the United States.

In Frau Oberprediger's home I spoke German all the time and was never tempted to lapse into English. I enjoyed the mischief and fun of the younger daughter, but the bond of union between us would have been much closer if she had not hated the Jews so fiercely and bitterly. She was poking fun at them all the time. According to her, everything they did was wrong. She reeled off story after story at their expense. It amazed me to see how a girl so young could hate so deeply a race, no representative of which had ever done either her or any member of her family any harm. Her attitude toward the Jews irritated and annoyed me greatly. I would never laugh at her stories in which the Jews were made the butt of ridicule, no matter how funny they were. And she had a remarkable sheaf of them, to be sure! I could not help thinking how the race with which I myself am identified is misrepresented, ridiculed, and slandered by people who feel the same animosity against it as the young German girl manifested toward the Jews.

After she had criticized and ridiculed the Jews one day, I said, "Fräulein, I am a member of a race whose faults and mistakes are exaggerated by its enemies and detractors just as you are exaggerating those of the Jews, and if you should come to the United States, many would make out as bad a case against us as you have made against the Jews. The people who see little or no good in my racial group delight in telling the world about its vices and defects just as you have enjoyed regaling me with those you claim are characteristic of Jews. There are good and bad in all races, and the Jews are no exception to a general rule."

I told her also that if she lived in a certain section of the United States, she would not eat at the same table with me, would not even allow me to sit beside her in the streetcar or in the railway coaches, and that her mother would not give me room and board in her home.

But my young German friend did not understand this at all. She was sure I was exaggerating the facts. She could not believe that any human being could object to another solely on·account of the color of his skin. If a race had all the vices and defects which she insisted were characteristic of the Jew, she could understand why people would not want to come into close contact with such a group, but for the life of her she could not comprehend why anybody would object to another human being because he happened to be a few shades darker than himself. It is always difficult for one prejudice-ridden human being to understand why his brother should be obsessed by a prejudice which differs from his own.

My young German friend admired my type very much. She had never seen a colored woman before. She used to pat my cheek and say, "You are so schön schwarz (so beautifully dark) and your hair curls so prettily."

After steeping myself in German literature, music, and the drama, taking lessons every day from a very capable teacher and going to the opera at night, I left Berlin for Italy one bitter cold day, when the ground was white with snow.

CHAPTER 10

I LEAVE BERLIN AND GO TO FLORENCE

THE PARTING between Herr von D. and myself affected us both considerably, I must confess. After the theater party we occasionally met, sometimes going with Frau General von Wenckstern, sometimes sightseeing, and sometimes taking long walks together. He said he had never before been closely associated with a young woman who had taken a college course and could discuss subjects pertaining to it with him. Through our Spanish friend there is no doubt that he had learned all about the race prejudice of which I was the victim in my own land. His admiration and his sympathy with me soon ripened into affection and he asked me to marry him.

One day he asked me casually where my father lived and how I wrote such an address in English. Thinking he was prompted solely by curiosity in seeking this information, I showed him how to write my father's address. About a week afterward he told me he had written to my father telling him that he loved me and asking his consent to our marriage. At that time he had not told me how serious his intentions were, and I upbraided him for having written to my father before getting my views on the subject. But he said no gentleman would pay serious attention to a young woman without first gaining her father's consent. Since I had been reared in the United States and had always seen young men win the girl before they consulted her parents in the matter, I was not exactly prepared for this explanation and reply.

I was very sorry Herr von D. had written to my father for several reasons. I knew father's views on intermarriage of the races and was certain he would not consent, however much I might urge him to do so. Moreover, I feared he might insist upon my coming home immediately. But he knew that I intended to leave Berlin in a short time and, much to my joy, he did not even suggest that I should come home. However, he wrote Herr von D. in no uncertain terms that he would never consent to his daughter's marrying a foreigner and living abroad.

When I bade Herr von D. good-bye at the station I knew full well that I would never see him again. If I had been white, I might have married him. I admired him very much. He was a man of high intellectual attainments, had lofty ideals, was good-looking and agreeable, and seemed genuinely fond of me. Now that Hitler has risen to power and has launched a savage attack against both non-white people and the Jews, I wonder what my fate would have been if I had married my German friend. Where would I be today? Would I have been forced to leave Germany? If there had been any children, what would be their status now? I thank a beneficent Providence that I was spared the painful ordeal through which I would have been obliged to pass if I had married Herr von D. I had made up my mind definitely that I would not marry a white man if I lived in the United States, and I feared I would not be happy as an exile in a foreign land.

While I was a student at Oberlin College my attention was first attracted to the intermarriage of the races, when Frederick Douglass married Miss Helen Pitts, a white woman living in Anacostia, D. C. I used to go into the little reading room of Ladies Hall, where I boarded, so as to read the editorial comments of the newspapers and the magazines. I was then and there convinced that no sound argument could be produced to prove that there is anything inherently wrong in the intermarriage of the races. I realized that a great hue and cry had been raised against it in this country, simply because it outraged custom and tradition.

I was greatly surprised and pained at the attitude assumed by many colored people, who criticized Mr. Douglass savagely because he had married a white woman. And these very people were continuously clamoring for equality—absolute equality along all lines—equality of opportunity, equality in the courts, educational, political, and social equality, world without end, amen. And yet, when a representative of their race actually practices equality by choosing as his mate an individual classified as white, these very advocates of equality pound down upon him hard and condemn him for practicing what they themselves have preached long and loud, more insistently than anybody else.

While I have no patience with people who assume such an attitude as that, as soon as I read the comments made upon Mr. Douglass' marriage, I decided that under no circumstances would I marry a white man in the United States. I have always felt very keenly the indignities heaped upon my race, ever since I realized how many and how big they are. And I knew I would be unhappy if I were the wife of a man belonging to the group which sanctioned or condoned these injustices and perpetrated these wrongs. At an early age I reached the conclusion that under existing conditions in this country marriage between the races here could bring very little happiness to either one of the parties to the contract.

Not including the blind musician, three white men have proposed marriage to me. One was the German baron to whom I have already referred and the other two were Americans whom I met abroad. One of them was a student whom I saw frequently, because we were pursuing the same studies and were interested in the same things. He had no race prejudice whatever and had great strength of character. He said he was eager to defy the customs and traditions of this country which ostracizes everybody of African descent, no matter what their attainments or virtues may be. But I was not willing to assist him in this effort, however worthy it might be. He thought I was a great coward and told me so.

The other American was a prosperous business man to whom I was introduced on the steamer, when I was returning from Europe with my father and his family. I told him that neither one of us would be happy in the United States on account of the conditions which obtain in practically every section of the country. But he answered these objections by saying we would go to Mexico, where comparatively little race prejudice exists. "You look like a Mexican," he argued, "and we would have no trouble about difference in race."

I have dwelt upon these episodes in my life at greater length than I would if I were a white woman because I wish to cite my case as proof of the fact that some colored people are not so eager to marry white people as many in that group suppose. From private conversations with my white friends, and I am glad to say I have many of them, from the questions often asked me when I have addressed forums in the East and elsewhere, I am persuaded that the average Caucasian in this country believes that there is nothing which colored people desire so much as to marry into their group. It seems to me it is my duty to inform those who entertain this opinion that at least one colored woman voluntarily rejected such a proposition three times.

On my way to Florence from Berlin I had several experiences which made this trip memorable. At one of the stations, where I had changed cars late in the afternoon, I had gone into a compartment set aside exclusively for women. I was obliged to travel all night and I felt perfectly safe taking a compartment for women. I knew I could stretch out on the long seat and have a good rest. About two or three o'clock in the morning I heard the door of the compartment open, and, when I looked up half asleep to see who had entered, I saw it was a man. Then I heard the guard slam the door and I realized I was all alone, locked in the compartment with a stranger. Since I knew it was against the rules to allow men to enter a compartment at night set aside exclusively for women, I felt very uncomfortable indeed.

As soon as the stranger started the conversation, I knew he was German and he knew I was American. In replying to his question as to what I was doing in Europe, I told him I had come abroad to study and was on my way to Florence, where I intended to study Italian and visit the wonderful galleries. Although I was indignant at his intrusion, I tried to exercise sufficient self-control to conceal it. I have traveled alone ever since I was a little girl, and I have talked with women who have done the same thing, and I believe that, as a general rule, if a woman deports herself correctly she need have little fear that men whom she casually meets on a journey will not do the same thing. At any rate, this stranger, whose presence in the compartment I resented so much, knew Florence by heart, advised me what to see and how to see it, and gave me some very valuable information.

Several times since then I have read about murders which were committed in broad daylight in the compartments of English and European trains, and a shiver runs down my spine when I think of my experience en route to Florence: how I was awakened at night out of a sound sleep in a foreign land, finding myself confronted by a strange man and knowing I was locked alone in a compartment with him on a train which was speeding along in the dark.

Still another incident fraught with danger occurred on this trip. Baedeker's guidebook advised those who wished to get an unusually fine view of Genoa to arise very early in the morning and go to the top of a certain church. The directions were explicit and clear. One had to ascend the narrow, steep stairway in the back of the church and keep climbing till he reached the spot from which the superb view could be obtained. The morning after I reached Genoa I arose very early, full of enthusiasm, and made my way to this church.

I had climbed about halfway up the steep, narrow stairway when I heard a noise behind me. Turning around quickly, I saw in the dark the form of a man following me. My heart beat fast, but there was nothing to do but continue the ascent. Come what might, I certainly could not turn back. When I reached the top of the stairway and stepped out on the tower, I waited breathlessly to see who had been coming up behind me. He was the sexton of the church, and although he was evidently surprised to meet a young woman all alone so early in the morning, he congratulated me upon coming at the best time to get the view.

After I left the church the beautiful blue Mediterranean beckoned me on. It was the first time I had seen it, and I wanted to dip my hand into the water and gaze on it to my heart's content. While I was standing on the shore two men who had a small boat in which they rowed strangers out to sea asked me if I did not want to take a short ride. After settling upon the price they would charge, I was soon being rowed rapidly along. My mind was so occupied with the scene and the sentiment it occasioned that the men had gone a long distance before I observed how far from shore we were.

When I asked them to return, they did not comply at first and I had to insist several times that I did not want to row any farther before they returned toward the shore. Some of my friends declared I ran a risk when I went alone with Italian boatmen and allowed them to row me so early in the morning a long distance from the shore. And several of them have told me blood-curdling stories of robberies in which foreigners who allowed themselves to be taken alone at a distance from traffic not only lost all they carried, but sometimes lost their lives. But at that time and for many years afterward I scarcely knew the meaning of fear. There were few things I hesitated to do when I was in the twenties and thirties, simply because there was a certain element of danger in them. There are scores of things which I would not dare to do today that I undertook without fear when I was young. If I reached a city at midnight or after, it never occurred to me that there was the slightest danger in taking a conveyance and going to a hotel alone. After I grew older, however, I lost much of the fearlessness I formerly possessed.

Before I had been in Florence six weeks I could not only make my wants known, but could state in understandable Italian anything which I cared to express. I lived with an Italian widow who had a son about twelve years old who was one of the most mischievous children imaginable. With my landlady and some of her friends I attended the Artists' Ball, which was a gay and unique affair indeed. The costumes of some of the participants were bizarre, not to say risqué, and the favors which were presented to the guests were grotesque and queer.

In the treasure-filled art galleries of Florence I literally entered a new world. Before the marvelous canvases of the old masters I stood long hours with no thought of getting tired. I was greatly encouraged when I had learned the touch and characteristics of certain artists so well that I recognized their pictures the minute I glanced at them.

I found an edition de luxe of George Eliot's *Romola* in two volumes bound in white and trimmed in red. Unmounted photographs of the places and pictures mentioned by the author were pasted in the book opposite the pages in which they were described. It was a delightful experience to take this book, visit the places, and look at the pictures to which George Eliot referred.

The monasteries and the nunneries were a never-failing source of interest to me. I never tired of seeing the monks themselves and the great stone structures in which they lived, moved, and had their being. I acquired the habit of going into beautiful old Catholic churches several times a day. The architecture, the pictures, and the very atmosphere of those grand old structures lifted me out of myself and filled me with noble aspirations for a while at least.

One morning about two o'clock while I was still in Florence I received a cablegram from my father, telling me he would leave Memphis on a certain date to take a steamer in New York and spend the summer with me in Europe. He brought his whole family with him—his wife; Robert, who was four years old, and little Annette, who was only two. I took charge of the little sister immediately and let Father do the honors for the small brother. I had mapped out a delightful itinerary of several months, not knowing the children would be members of the party. And it was surprising what a small portion of my program had to be revised or eliminated altogether and how much of it was carried out as originally planned, in spite of the presence of two little children.

We went to Heidelberg, not only to see that famous university and the wonderful old castle, but to take a package to a daughter of a neighbor who had lived next door to us in Memphis for years and who belonged to one of the old, aristocratic slaveholding families of the South. In the palmy days of slavery, if anyone had told the father of this woman that less than forty years from that day a man then held in slavery would be taking a tour through Europe with his family and would be politely requested by his daughter to deliver a package to his granddaughter in Heidelberg, he would either have laughed inordinately at the man who could imagine such a preposterous situation, or he would have suggested that a lunatic like that should be slapped into an insane asylum right away.

Reams upon top of reams I might write if I tried to tell the innumerable acts of kindness shown me by the people through whose countries I traveled or among whom I lived. The unpleasant incidents or those fraught with danger to which I have referred were the notable exceptions which proved the general rule. Everywhere I went in Europe I received a cordial reception and made a host of friends. My nerves were not on edge, neither was my heart in my mouth because I feared I would be persona non grata to people I met abroad, if perchance they happened to discover I was of African descent.

I did not attempt deliberately to deceive these new friends concerning my racial identity. To be sure I did not wear a placard on my back announcing in big black letters, "I am a colored woman from the United States, BEWARE!" But after our relations of friendship were close enough to justify it, I told some of those belonging to the social circle in which I moved that I had African blood in my veins.

At what I considered the opportune time I always told people with whom I boarded how I am classified in the United States, and interested them in the marvelous progress which we have made as a race. I never failed to reveal my racial identity to my foreign teachers, who invariably plied me with questions and manifested genuine interest in our group. I felt that I could not be loyal to my race if I did not pursue such a course.

But now the time had come for me to return to my native land, and my heart ached when I thought about it. Life had been so pleasant and profitable abroad, where I could take advantage of any opportunity I desired without wondering whether a colored girl would be allowed to enjoy it or not, and where I could secure accommodations in any hotel, boarding house, or private home in which I cared to live. I knew that when I returned home I would face again the humiliations, discriminations, and hardships to which colored people are subjected all over the United States.

Nevertheless, I loved the country in which I was born. There was no doubt about that. I had indisputable proof of that fact over and over again. Even though one's mother has been unkind to her at times, one loves her just the same. But the first time I realized I was genuinely, deeply patriotic was when I saw an American flag in Berlin.

I was walking along the street on which the American consulate was located, without knowing it, and suddenly looked up to see my country's flag proudly waving in the breeze. Instantly my eyes grew moist and a big lump came into my throat. I had to exercise self-control to suppress the tears. "Truly this is patriotism," I said, "and I am patriotic, after all. If my rights were infringed upon over here in Germany, or if I got into trouble of any kind," I soliloquized, "that flag would protect me just the same as it would do if I were white." "That is more than it would do for you at home," whispered an unpleasant little voice.

Then, involuntarily, I thought of the rights, privileges, and immunities cold-bloodedly withheld from colored people in the

United States which practically everybody else is allowed to enjoy. I thought how they are disfranchised in that section where the majority live in spite of the fourteenth and fifteenth amendments, while the whole country looks on with utter indifference at this flagrant violation of the Constitution and thus, by reprehensible silence and connivance, actually gives its consent. The injustices and discriminations of many kinds rushed through my mind like a flood. I thought of the many fine women and men who, solely on account of their race, are debarred from certain pursuits and vocations in which they would like to engage, for which they are splendidly fitted by education and native ability, and in which they would achieve brilliant success, if they only had a chance.

Then I turned around and looked again at the flag waving over the American consulate in Berlin, and for a second I was transfixed to the spot. "It's my country," I said indignantly. "I have a perfect right to love it and I will. My African ancestors helped to build and enrich it with their unrequited labor for nearly three hundred years, while they were shackled body and soul in the most cruel bondage the world has ever seen. My African ancestors suffered and died for it as slaves and they have fought, bled, and died for it as soldiers in every war which it has waged. It has been cruel to us in the past and it is often unjust to us now, but it is my country after all," I said aloud, "and with all its faults I love it still."

The day I was to take the steamer home I saw a colored woman who had married an Englishman who belonged to a good family and was well-to-do. She had been living happily near London with a devoted husband and several children for years. Would such an existence appeal to me? I was perfectly certain it would not. I knew I would be much happier trying to promote the welfare of my race in my native land, working under certain hard conditions, than I would be living in a foreign land where I could enjoy freedom from prejudice, but where I would make no effort to do the work which I then believed it was my duty to do. I doubted that I could respect myself if I shirked my responsibility and was recreant to my trust. After mature deliberation I decided then and there that I would be happier living in the United States of America than I could be anywhere else on earth. So I was glad when the steamer began to plough the sea to bring me home.

CHAPTER 11

I RETURN TO THE UNITED STATES

AFTER I landed in New York, I spent a few days with Mother and then we both went to Marietta, Ohio, where my brother, Thomas Ayres Church, had been attending college and was about to graduate. From the Commencement exercises Mother and Brother returned to New York and I proceeded to Memphis. But trying to get there was a thrilling experience sure enough.

In purchasing my ticket to Memphis I explained that I wanted a through sleeper, and the agent sold me both the railroad ticket and the Pullman. I left Marietta at night and when I asked the porter to make up my berth after he had finished with several others, he said it would be hardly worth while for me to go to bed, because I would have to get off at Louisville, Kentucky, at midnight and wait till the next morning for the train going to Memphis. I was very much surprised and agitated, and insisted that I be allowed to remain on that sleeper, since my Pullman ticket entitled me to a berth from Marietta to Memphis. I was all the more wrought up because I suspected that I was being ejected from the Pullman car on account of my race. Several of my personal friends had been ejected a short while previous to this incident, and one had been seriously injured by a mob who had pulled him off the train. So I felt that my own doom had come.

Then the conductor was called and he frankly admitted that my Pullman ticket did entitle me to a berth from Marietta to Memphis, but that the agent had sold me a Pullman ticket over one road and the railroad ticket over another. He said the agent knew better and had evidently done it deliberately. There was nothing for me to do, he said, but get off at Louisville, remain there all night, and take the train in the morning for Memphis over the route for which my railroad ticket called. If I did not care to do that, he said, I would have to buy another railroad ticket from Louisville to Memphis over the road on which my Pullman ticket was sold. I was in great distress.

I knew I could not secure accommodations at a hotel in Louisville. Telephones were not common. And even if a friend had had a phone, I did not care to ask anybody to take me in at midnight. I greatly preferred buying another railroad ticket, so that I might continue my journey in my Pullman berth for which I had already paid. But I had brought only ten dollars with me, and that was not enough to get a railroad ticket from Louisville to Memphis. Hearing the conductor explain the situation to me, several passengers came over to my berth to see if they could help me.

Then a gentleman in a berth a few seats in front of me, who lived in Memphis and was well acquainted with my father, suspected that I was his daughter and came to ask me my name. He offered to lend me enough to buy a ticket to Memphis. He said he knew it would be all right with my father and that he would trust him for any amount.

When the matter was investigated, it was discovered that the agent in Marietta received a commission for the tickets sold over the route on which he sent me. But that road did not have a through sleeper to Memphis. So he deliberately sold me a Pullman ticket from Marietta to Memphis, knowing that the railroad ticket called for a different route and that I would be obliged to change cars in Louisville a few hours after I boarded the train. Such tricks are often played upon colored people traveling through the South. The railroad company wrote Father that the agent had been discharged.

Shortly after I returned from Europe I received a letter from Mr. Robert Heberton Terrell urging me to come to Washington immediately to notify Mr. George F. T. Cook, superintendent of colored schools, that I would resume my position as teacher in the high school. I had secured a leave of absence for one year, then had had it renewed, but I had failed to notify the superintendent when I would return. I followed Mr. Terrell's suggestion and was reappointed.

My work in the school that year consisted mainly in teaching Latin and German. At the end of the spring term the senior class presented a play in German which was creditable both to the pupils and to the teacher. I had taught them by what is now called the "natural method," which had not been previously used in the school, and the ability of my pupils both to express themselves and to pronounce the language correctly surprised even me.

I had urged my pupils to get a book which I had seen by chance in a book store and which taught them by easy methods to express themselves in German without using English to translate the meaning of words. Seeing this book used in my class one day, a teacher who had been long in the service asked me by what authority I had introduced it into the schools, since it was not included in the curriculum. I had not intended to violate the rule, but it had never occurred to me to ask permission to use anything in the classroom which would help my pupils to do their work well. I was told, however, that this was considered quite a lawless thing for a teacher to do.

Mr. Terrell came to see me regularly and was very attentive. The course of true love did not always run perfectly smooth, but it always became calm and peaceful after any little turbulent eddies that caused it to flow in the wrong direction, and we became engaged. He was the head of the Latin department, as he had been during the first year I taught in Washington, and I was his assistant. In explaining my decision to link my destiny with his, I used to say that I enjoyed assisting him in the Latin department so much, I made up my mind to assist him in all departments for the rest of my natural life. And this I certainly tried to do.

Mr. Terrell and I were very remote and circumspect during school hours. Occasionally, however, some of our pupils would see us attending a meeting or walking on the street together, so that it soon became known that we were interested in each other and they enjoyed our romance immensely. Now and then when I entered my room, I would see something like this written on the blackboard: "Mr. Terrell is certainly getting good. He used to go to dances, but now he goes to Church." My maiden name lent itself admirably to puns and there were many of them, of course.

Several months before the summer vacation began I received a letter from Mrs. A. A. F. Johnston, the dean of women, inviting me to become registrar of Oberlin College. I wondered whether the letter was genuine when I read it. I had never dreamed of securing such a position in an institution of Oberlin's standing. It had never occurred to me that any colored woman, however great her attainments might be, would be considered in the search for officers or instructors in a college for white youth in the United States.

Although I had promised definitely to marry the following October, it was a great temptation to postpone my wedding and go to Oberlin as registrar. I thought seriously about the matter, reviewing the arguments pro and con, over and over again. There were many reasons why I wanted to accept the position. But, after mature deliberation, plus much agony of soul, I decided not to change my plans. Among other things, it seemed to me that I would be taking the position under false pretenses, if I knew, when I accepted it, I would keep it only a year, for I did not think it would be right to postpone my wedding any longer than that. Under the circumstances I feared it might not be dealing honorably with Oberlin College if I promised to go.

The day I wrote Mrs. Johnston declining the position I was very unhappy indeed. If I had accepted I would have been a member of the faculty of Oberlin College, for Mrs. Johnston had definitely stated that in her letter.

It is quite possible I made a mistake in not becoming registrar of an institution which was attended mainly by white students and in which each member of the faculty was white. It may have been my duty to establish such a precedent in a white college of Oberlin's standing as that undoubtedly would have been. It might have encouraged other institutions to recognize their colored alumnae. If I acted unwisely, I am sorry, although regrets do no good now. In declining to become registrar of Oberlin College, whether I made a mistake or not, I certainly deprived myself of the distinction and honor of being the first and only colored woman in the United States to whom such a position has ever been offered, so far as I am able to ascertain.

During the summer before our marriage I remained in New York with my mother, getting my trousseau, for which my father gave me the money. My wedding dress was white faille silk trimmed with a white chiffon embroidered scalloped edging instead of lace. There was a wide flounce of it across the bottom of the front gore, and a narrower width formed a bertha on the long-sleeved waist. The dress second in importance to the wedding gown was a yellow faille trimmed in white lace. I had a red cashmere dress and a maroon broadcloth made quite plain and tailored. Blue has always been my favorite color, because I thought it was more becoming than any other. I cannot understand now why I did not have a blue dress in my trousseau.

My mother insisted that I should have a maroon velvet hat to go with the broadcloth dress of that shade, and I agreed with her. But I could not find one anywhere. Finally my mother went with me. She found one that suited her on Fifth Avenue and paid twenty dollars for it. I was horrified and wretched. I had never paid that much for a hat in my life and I did not think it was right for a woman in moderate circumstances to put so much money into one. Especially did I object to the price paid for that particular specimen, for it was a little affair shaped something like a bonnet and made of velvet with two ball-shaped gilt ornaments stuck on each side of the front. I have never paid so much for a hat since then and I have not even been tempted to do so. Early in life I learned that paying a large sum for a hat or a frock was no guarantee that it would be becoming.

We were married at six o'clock in the evening. I was ready about five minutes before the hour. For years afterward, whenever he had to wait for me to get ready to go anywhere, Mr. Terrell reminded me that at least on one occasion in our lives I took good pains to be ready in ample time.

My father insisted upon having a regular feast—anything I might say to the contrary notwithstanding. He served turkey, roast pig, several kinds of salad, ice cream, and wine to a large number of guests. "As they discussed the elaborate menu," said the *Memphis Commercial Appeal,* one of the largest newspapers of the South, "and drank the excellent champagne of the host, the guests were regaled with the sensuous strains of Joe Hall's orchestra, which, hidden in an alcove, made the air sweet with its beautiful music."

About ten o'clock the same evening we took the train for New York to go to see my mother. She told me that she dressed herself exactly as she would have done if she had actually attended the wedding, and at the hour she knew her daughter was being married she imagined she was listening to the ceremony and taking part in it. From New York we went to Boston, remained there a short while, and then returned to Washington, where Mr. Terrell resumed his duties as chief of the division in the Fourth Auditor's office in the Treasury Department.

From every section of the United States friends of both races sent us presents. I do not agree with those who say that one cannot love an inanimate object, for I have a real affection for every wedding present I possess. As I looked over them not long ago it occurred to me that for entirely different reasons two of them were very interesting indeed. One of them is a sterling silver cream pitcher which was presented to us by the grandson of Thomas Jefferson, the third president of the United States. T. Jefferson Coolidge, the donor, was one of my husband's classmates whom he held in the highest esteem.

The other present consists of a half-dozen sterling silver oyster forks and recalls an awful tragedy, the brutal murder of the donor, Tom Moss, one of my best friends. We were children together and he was always invited to the parties which my parents gave me. For many years he was a letter-carrier, but he saved his money and with several other colored men opened a store in the suburbs of Memphis. Then the colored people who came from the country stopped trading at a store kept by a white man across the street, and began to patronize Tom Moss, because the supplies he sold were more reasonable and were exactly what they were represented to be, while the patrons themselves were treated right.

So angry did the white storekeeper and some of his friends in the neighborhood become that they decided to break up Tom Moss's store, and deliberately started a row to do so. They called in the police, who placed the owners of the colored store in jail, and the next night all three were taken out by a mob and shot to death. Thus Tom Moss, who left a wife and several children, and two others were murdered, because they were succeeding too well. They were guilty of no crime but that.

I had read of such lynchings before and had been deeply stirred by them. A normal human being is always shocked when he reads that a man or a woman has been burned at the stake or shot to death, whether he is acquainted with the victim or not. But when a woman has been closely associated with the victim of the mob from childhood and knows him to be above reproach, the horror and anguish which rend her heart are indescribable.

For a time it came near upsetting my faith in the Christian religion. I could not see how a crime like that could be perpetrated in a Christian country, while thousands of Christians sinfully winked at it by making no protest loud enough to be heard nor exerting any earnest effort to redress this terrible wrong. I thoroughly understood Abraham Lincoln's state of mind when he refused to join a church in Springfield, Illinois, because only three out of twenty ministers in the whole city stood with him in his effort to free the slave.

No one can be more grateful to the church for the assistance it has rendered the colored American than I am. Nothing but ignorance or malice could prompt one to disparage the efforts put forth by the churches in the colored man's behalf. However unfortunate may have been the attitude of many of the churches on the question of slavery before the Civil War, from the moment the shackles fell from the black man's limbs till today, the American church has been most kind and generous in its treatment of the maligned and struggling race. But in the face of so much lawlessness today, surely there is a role for the church militant to play. When one reflects upon the large number of colored Americans who have been victims of mob violence, one can not help realizing that as a nation we have fallen upon very grave times indeed. Surely it is time for the ministers in their pulpits and the Christians in their pews to pray for deliverance from this awful tide of barbarism which threatens the whole land. The colored man's loyalty to the Christian religion in spite of the outrages and crimes perpetrated upon him by people who call themselves Christians is one of the most striking and beautiful exhibitions of faith which it is possible to cite.

The summer after my marriage I was desperately ill and my life was despaired of. My recovery was nothing short of a miracle, and my case is recorded in medical history. In five years we lost three babies, one after another, shortly after birth. This was a great blow to Mr. Terrell and to me. The maternal instinct was always abnormally developed in me. As far back as I can remember I have always been very fond of children. I cannot recall that I have ever seen a baby, no matter what its class, color, or condition in life, no matter whether it was homely or beautiful according to recognized standards, no matter whether it was clad in rags or wore dainty raiment, that did not seem dear and cunning to me.

When my third baby died two days after birth, I literally sank down into the very depths of despair. For months I could not divert my thoughts from the tragedy, however hard I tried. It was impossible for me to read understandingly or to fix my mind on anything I saw in print. When I reached the bottom of a page in a book, I knew no more about its contents than did someone who had never seen it.

Right after its birth the baby had been placed in an improvised incubator, and I was tormented by the thought that if the genuine article had been used, its little life might have been spared. I could not help feeling that some of the methods employed in caring for my baby had caused its untimely end.

A few of my friends could not understand how a woman could grieve so deeply as I did over the death of a baby that had lived only a few days. But I sometimes think a woman suffers as much when she loses a baby at birth as does a mother who loses a baby who has been with her much longer. There is the bitter disappointment of never having enjoyed the infant at all to whose coming the mother has looked forward so long and upon whom she has built such fond hopes.

Acting upon my physician's advice, my husband insisted upon my leaving home, where everything reminded me of my sorrow, and I went to visit my dear, sunny mother in New York. She would not allow me to talk about my baby's death and scouted the idea that its life might have been saved. This short visit to my mother with her cheerful disposition and her infectious laugh did much for me physically, mentally, and spiritually. Many a human being has lost his reason because he has brooded over his trouble indefinitely, when a slight change of scene and companionship might have saved it. I do not like to think what might have happened to me if I had not left home and gone to see my mother at that crucial time in my life.

A few months after my baby's death a thought which came to me one day, while I was in a paroxysm of grief, helped to reconcile me to my loss. While I was happily expecting his arrival, the lynching of Tom Moss, to which I have already referred, occurred. The mob's murder of this friend affected me deeply, and for a long time I could think of nothing else.

As I was grieving over the loss of my baby boy one day, it occurred to me that under the circumstances it might be a blessed dispensation of Providence that his precious life was not spared. The horror and resentment felt by the mother, coupled with the bitterness which filled her soul, might have seriously affected the unborn child. Who can tell how many desperadoes and murderers have been born to colored mothers who had been shocked and distracted before the birth of their babies by the news that some relative or friend had been burned alive or shot to death by a mob?

I was greatly impressed by a statement made by one of my white friends who met me on the street one day shortly after I was bereaved. "I do not see," she said, "how any colored woman can make up her mind to become a mother under the existing conditions in the United States. Under the circumstances," she continued, "I should think a colored woman would feel that she was perpetrating a great injustice upon any helpless infant she would bring into the world." I had never heard that point of view so frankly and strongly expressed before, and while I could not agree with it entirely, it caused me much serious reflection. The more I thought how my depression which was caused by the lynching of Tom Moss and the horror of this awful crime might have injuriously affected my unborn child, if he had lived, the more I became reconciled to what had at first seemed a cruel fate.

Years afterwards I marched through the streets of Washington in a silent parade staged by colored people as a protest against continued lynching of members of our race. This was an effort to influence Congress to pass the Dyer anti-lynching bill. Not a band played. Not a sound of music was heard. As I walked in silence up Pennsylvania Avenue, I thought of the fine boy whom I knew as a girl, who had been brutally lynched when he became a man. And I said to myself, there is at least one person in this protest parade who understands personally exactly what it means.

CHAPTER 12

WITH FREDERICK DOUGLASS AND PAUL DUNBAR
AT THE WORLD'S FAIR

THE YEAR FOLLOWING THE CRIT-
ICAL ILLNESS during which I lost my first baby and came near
losing my life, my father invited me to visit the World's Fair
while he and his family were there, and generously paid the expense of the trip. The Midway Plaisance with all its original
denizens and dancers was something new under the sun, and
many perfect ladies who went there to see them perform came
away shocked. Compared with what one commonly sees on the
stage today, however, and what one beheld at the second World's
Fair, those exotic ladies knew nothing but the A B C of sending
thrills down the spines of American sightseers by their terpsi-
chorean stunts.

The first World's Fair was held in 1893 to celebrate the
four hundredth anniversary of the discovery of America by
Columbus, a year later than it should have been, when Chicago
was only an overgrown village and was not the stirring, milling,
mammoth metropolis of the West that it now is.

When my friends saw me walking up and down the endless
aisles of the long buildings filled with exhibits from nearly
every civilized country in the world, they marveled at my power
of endurance. The men, as well as the women, would stop
completely exhausted, while I went joyfully on my way leaving
them to "rest." My power of endurance has always been a
great asset. Even if I get tired I can work an incredibly long
time. There are few young woman who can walk farther, stick
to a job longer, or dance longer than I can even today.

But there are two impressions of the World's Fair which

have left a more delightful flavor in my memory than anything else. One was the great honor paid to Frederick Douglass by people of the dominant race as well as by those in his own group. The other was meeting Paul Dunbar just as he was starting his career as a poet.

Mr. Douglass was the commissioner in charge of the exhibit from Haiti at the Fair, and he employed Paul Dunbar to assist him. Mr. Douglass was accustomed to entertain his friends there by taking them to see the exhibits which he especially liked. Following this custom, he invited me to go with him one afternoon to take in some of the sights. As we walked along, either through the grounds or in the buildings, Mr. Douglass was continually halted by admiring people who begged the privilege of shaking hands with him. A mother would stop him and say, "You are Frederick Douglass, aren't you? Please shake hands with my little son [or maybe a little daughter], because when he grows up I want him to say that he has shaken hands with the great Frederick Douglass."

"Let's get on the scenic railway," suggested Mr. Douglass, "so that we may have a chance to talk a little. Nobody can get us there." But he had reckoned without his host, for we had no sooner settled ourselves on that little railroad than a man reached over two seats to touch him on the shoulder and greet him. "Well, we'll go up on the Eiffel Tower," chuckled Mr. Douglass. "I know nobody can interrupt us when we are in one of those cages." But just as we started to ascend, a man in another cage shouted, "Hello, Mr. Douglass, the last time I saw you was in Rochester."

The great man had become deeply interested in Paul Dunbar, because his struggle for existence and recognition had been so desperate. The fact that Mr. Douglass was the first person I ever heard mention Paul Dunbar's name is a recollection that I cherish. By appointment I had gone to see him in his home in Anacostia, across the Potomac River from Washington. After we had finished the business I had gone to transact, the "Sage of Anacostia" inquired, "Have you ever heard of Paul Dunbar?" I told him I had not. Then Mr. Douglass rehearsed the facts in the young man's life.

"He is very young, but there is no doubt that he is a poet," he said. "He is working under the most discouraging circumstances in his home, Dayton, Ohio. He is an elevator boy, and on his meager wage of four dollars a week he is trying to support himself and mother. Let me read you one of his poems," said Mr. Douglass. And then he arose to get it. I can see his fine face and his majestic form now, as he left the room. He soon returned with a newspaper clipping and began to read "The Drowsy Day." When Mr. Douglass had read several stanzas, his voice faltered a bit and his eyes grew moist. "What a tragedy it is," he said, "that a young man with such talent as he undoubtedly possesses should be so terribly handicapped as he is."

Fate decreed that I should be with both these renowned men shortly before they passed away. I was with Mr. Douglass just a few hours before he died suddenly at his home. A little before noon he had attended a meeting of the National Council of Women. As soon as one of the officers spied him entering the door, she announced from the platform that Frederick Douglass was in the house. A committee was immediately appointed to escort him to the platform, and when he reached it the audience gave him the Chautauqua salute.

When the meeting adjourned and the admiring women had ceased paying homage to Mr. Douglass, which I enjoyed at a distance, I came forward and greeted him. He and I left what is now called the Columbia Theatre and walked together to the corner. There he stopped and asked me to have lunch with him. But I was not feeling very well and declined the invitation, alas! Lifting the large, light sombrero which he often wore, he bade me good-bye. About seven o'clock that evening a friend came by our house to tell us that Frederick Douglass had just died suddenly, while he was at the table describing to his wife the ovation tendered him in the forenoon by the members and officers of the National Council of Women. How deeply I regretted then that I had been unable to spend another hour in the company of that great man whom I would never see again!

When Paul Dunbar married he brought his wife and his mother to live in my father's house, which was next door to ours. Precious memories rush over me like a flood every time I pass that house. I can see Paul Dunbar beckoning me, as I walked by, when he wanted to read me a poem which he had just written or when he wished to discuss a word or a subject on which he had not fully decided. Paul often came to see me to read his poems or his prose articles before he sent them to magazines.

Sometimes he would tauntingly wave back and forth a check which he had just received and say, "Wouldn't you like to see that?" Then, after he thought he had aroused my curiosity sufficiently, he would show it me and say, "Now, look quick. Don't keep it long. Give it back to me right away."

The Ohio State Federation of Colored Women's Clubs invited me to deliver an address when it met in Dayton, Ohio. Paul had been critically ill for a long time, but when he heard I was coming he wrote me a letter inviting me to stop with him. Knowing that his mother had the burden of the house resting on her shoulders in addition to the mental and physical strain of nursing her son, whose life had been despaired of even then, I declined. Almost by return mail Paul wrote again, urging me to stop with his mother and himself, saying it would do him so much good to talk over the good old times. I could not resist that and I went to his house.

When I saw him then, he was wasted and worn by disease and he was coughing his precious young life away. He was cheerful, however, when not actually racked with pain. And he was perfectly resigned to his fate.

Some beautiful young girls of the dominant race once called, while I was with Paul, to chat with him a while and pay their respects. When they had gone, in a nervous effort to relieve the tension of my own feelings, I turned to him and said, "Sometimes I am tempted to believe you are not half so ill as you pretend to be. I believe you are just playing the role of interesting invalid, so as to receive the sympathy and homage of those beautiful girls."

"Sometimes I think I'm just loafing myself," he laughingly replied. How well he remembered this was shown a short while after I returned home, not long before he passed away. He sent me a copy of his *Lyrics of Sunshine and Shadow*, which at that time was his latest book. On the flyleaf he had written with his own hand (a feat which, during the last year of his illness, was often difficult for him to perform) the following lines:

"Look hyeah, Molly,
Ain't it jolly
Jes a loafin round?
Tell the Jedge
Not to hedge,
For I am still in town."

CHAPTER 13

BUYING A HOME UNDER DIFFICULTIES

For SEVERAL YEARS AFTER OUR MARRIAGE we lived in a two-room apartment in a desirable section of the National Capital, and then we decided we would start to buy a home. But deciding to do so was much easier than carrying out our plans. Washington is like most cities in our country. Colored people have to overcome difficulties when they try to buy homes. How huge they are I did not know until I tackled them myself. It was easy to find houses where self-respecting people of any color would not care to live. But finding the kind we wanted which either the owners themselves or their agents would sell us was a horse of quite another color.

We looked with longing eyes upon many a dear little house which was just exactly what we wanted in every respect, but we were frankly told we could not buy it, because we were colored. Finally I selected one, only one house removed from Howard Town, which was almost exclusively inhabited by colored people. It was named for General Howard, under whose supervision a camp for refugees was established there during the Civil War. The little house was an English basement with six rooms, a hall room, and a bath. It was several blocks from Howard University, one of the finest institutions for colored youth in the United States. This institution was also named for General Howard, who was deeply interested in the education of colored people and was the leading spirit in founding the university, over which he presided for four years.

Although the house was near the settlement occupied by colored people, it was located in Le Droit Park, a section in which nobody but white people lived excepting one colored family.

It is said that the white people used to build a fence to separate their bailiwick from Howard Town, so their colored neighbors could not walk through Le Droit Park on their way to the city. Every night this fence was kicked down by colored people, according to the story related to me by Major Fleetwood, a colored man who was awarded a medal by Congress for distinguished bravery during the Civil War. And every day it was rebuilt by the whites, who were determined to keep colored people out.

Be that as it may, when the woman who owned the house which we had selected learned that colored people wanted it, she refused to sell it to us. Since it was so near a settlement of colored people, I had no idea there would be the slightest objection to selling it to us. I had been searching continuously and diligently for several months, and this was the only desirable house I had seen which I thought I would like to buy.

It reached the ears of an old, well-established real estate firm that we wanted this piece of property. Both father and son came to see us one evening. After I had given a detailed account of the prolonged strenuous efforts I had made to find a house, the elder of the two men said, "Do you want that house in Le Droit Park?" I assured him that I wanted it very much. "Well, you shall have it," he declared. "I'll be damned if you shan't."

He fulfilled his promise to get it for me to the letter. He induced a wealthy man who had a colored secretary (which was indeed a rare thing in Washington) to buy the house for us, and then he sold it to us immediately.

It was in this house, soon after we lost our second baby at birth, that University Park Temple was organized. For several years afterward the services of this church were held in a little mission near Howard University which had been conducted by the First Congregational Church, of which President and Mrs. Coolidge were members during their residence in the White House. Later this church, founded in our home, merged with the Lincoln Memorial Congregational Church, and the union of the two is now known as Lincoln Congregational Temple.

From the English basement we moved into another house in Le Droit Park, which my father gave me. Here we remained fifteen years. When I started to furnish the first house we bought, I discovered that our exchequer was a bit low and economy must be used. Then I acquired the habit of going to a well-known auction and discovered that I could find furniture there which I could not afford to pay for new, but which I could buy at a reasonable price second hand. I took great pride in some of the wonderful bargains I got in this auction room in those early days.

Mother died in the second house into which we moved. After that so many things reminded me of her I decided it was my duty to myself to make a change. She had lived with me continuously for fifteen years. It was the first time I had been with my mother longer than a few months at a time since I was a small child. In reviewing the period she spent with me, after she had passed away, it seemed to me that each of us had tried to make up for lost time by concentrating into those fifteen years all the devotion we could have shown each other during the time we had been separated. She was a great comfort, and in spite of physical affliction she was an unalloyed joy to us all. Mr. Terrell and she always combined against me in an argument. Mr. Terrell used to assure his friends that they did not know what real life was until they lived with their mother-in-law.

When I started in quest of a house for the second time and asked several real estate firms to show me what they had on their list, I discovered they took me to see nothing but residences which had been discarded by discriminating people, because they were old-fashioned and devoid of modern improvements. Then it dawned upon me that, as a colored woman, I would be unable even to SEE the kind of house I desired. I decided to devise some sort of scheme by which I would be able to look at desirable houses with modern improvements without benefit of real estate agents.

I felt then, as I feel now, that people who are discriminated against solely on account of race, color, or creed are justified in resorting to any subterfuge, using any disguise, or playing any trick, provided they do not actually break the law, if it will enable them to secure the advantages and obtain the rights to which they are entitled by outwitting their prejudice-ridden foes.

As I motored through a street one day, I saw a "For Sale" sign on a house which, judging from the exterior, I thought I would like. My daughter Mary and I went to see it next day, and the caretaker who was showing it was eager to have me take it. It was new, and the man told me that the purchaser would be allowed to paper it and select the fixtures to suit his taste. Then I went to a real estate agent who had been highly recommended to me by a friend. "He sold me my house in this fine neighborhood," she said, "and I feel sure he would sell you one. I have had no trouble at all. After my neighbors saw I had neither hoofs nor claws, they almost embarrassed me with their attention."

I went to this agent and threw my cards on the table at once. I asked him frankly whether he would object to selling a house to me in the neighborhood designated. I would not bother him further, I stated, if he had any scruples whatever on the subject. Referring to the record in the city which my husband and I had made, the real estate agent declared that "anybody would be glad to live next to Judge Terrell and his wife." But, knowing my city as well I did, I took this assertion with several grains of salt.

It was a reflection upon my intelligence and my knowledge of conditions on general principles for the gentleman to deliver himself of any such speech as that and expect me to believe it. If our dear Lord and Saviour should come to this country in the form of a colored man, He would be obliged to say again, "The Son of man hath not where to lay his head," unless He was accommodated by colored people or was willing to take anything He could get. There are exceptions to all general rules, and there is no doubt that there are a goodly number who would give shelter to a colored man or woman, just as Robert G. Ingersoll opened his house to Frederick Douglass in Peoria, Illinois, when he had been refused accommodations at all the hotels.

The agent appeared perfectly willing to negotiate the purchase of the house, and I commissioned him to do it. I gave him the required deposit and urged him to close the deal as soon as he could. He promised to let me hear from him in a short while. I grew apprehensive about getting the house, but my daughter, who had heard the agent give me positive assurance that there would be no trouble about buying it for me, read me delightful little lectures about worrying unnecessarily. "You just like to borrow trouble, Mother," she would say, "and you dearly love to worry. Mr. L. said he would get that house for you, and of course he will keep his word." My dear little girl was filled with the faith of youth, because she had had no experience battling with the Race Problem, as her mother had had.

So much confidence did she repose in the agent's promise that she planned a house party for the Christmas holidays and assigned each of the prospective guests to her respective room. Not only did she complete all her plans for the housewarming, but she wrote her name with the new address upon newspapers, paper bags, and anything else she dared inscribe that she happened to come upon, when she had a lead pencil in her hand.

Several times I 'phoned the agent, urging him to complete the transaction as soon as he could, so that we might move into our new home before the opening of the fall term, which was not far away. He would tell me that I would have to wait a little longer, but that everything was going all right. Finally, I went to his office just before school opened to get a definite reply. He then returned my deposit and frankly admitted that he could not sell me the house, because the owner had discovered that a colored family wanted it and refused to let us have it. It is quite probable that after having promised to negotiate the purchase of the property the agent had had an attack of cold feet and changed his mind.

"It is well for you," said the agent, returning my deposit, "that you did not succeed in getting that house. If you had, you would have been boycotted by everybody upon whom you would have had to depend for supplies. Neither the milkman nor the iceman would have served you. And every time you or the other members of your family appeared on the street, the boys in the neighborhood would have pelted you with bricks and stones."

"Such a fearsome prospect as that would not have frightened me a bit," I replied, "if I could have gained possession of that house. There is always a cure for violence like that due to race prejudice, if one goes about it in the right way."

After that dismal failure I decided that never again would

I attempt to buy a house in Washington. To that decision I adhered a long time, and we lived in a rented house. But the times change and we all change with them. Circumstances seemed to demand that we should get a house of our own after a while, and I started on a wild-goose chase of house-hunting again.

We had no car at that time, so I trudged many weary miles before I finally found a residence which appealed to all our family as desirable. I had decided definitely not to buy a house that had a kitchen in the basement. I had had enough of that arrangement in the second house to last me for the rest of my natural life. No more basements for me, running up and down the steps to answer the doorbell when I was busy in the kitchen and there was no one to help me!

The house which I finally selected had the kitchen on the first floor and was bright with sunshine the greater part of the day. A colored real estate agent had shown us this house and he assured me he could get it for me. There was absolutely no doubt about that, he said, so I gave him the deposit. After he had kept it for several months and had been unable to complete the deal, the deposit was returned. He had failed. But I could not bear to give the house up. It had taken me a long time to find it, and the thought of being obliged to go through another ordeal of house-hunting was nerve-racking.

I 'phoned the real estate agent who had it for sale and urged him to sell it to us. Without mincing matters at all, he told me right off the reel that he would not sell that house to colored people, no matter who they were. "But a colored family already lives next door to the house I want to buy," I said, "and there are several others on the same side of the street." "But they do not own their homes," he replied. "They rent them." This statement did not tally with the facts. I knew that one of the teachers in the colored high school, who lived four or five doors below the coveted house, had bought his home. I was at my wits' end. There seemed nothing more that I could do. Wherever I turned, disappointment stared me in the face.

As a last resort I called up a colored man who was in the District tax office, whom I had known from girlhood, and asked him to ascertain the name of the owner of the house which I wanted so much to buy. I explained the situation fully. He promised he would help me get the house if he possibly could.

A few days afterward a white agent came to see me to inquire whether I would like to purchase the house in question, and to assure me he could make arrangements to get it for me. I called his attention to the fact that there were several colored families living in the block on the same side of the street, and a colored family lived next door to the one I wanted to buy. The agent kept his word. I had to pay several thousand dollars more for the house than the price at which it was originally offered, and I was obliged to make a much larger deposit than the one which was at first required. But I was glad to be relieved of all the worry and trouble incident to hunting another house, and I cheerfully accepted the terms.

And so, after many troubles and trials, we finally obtained possession of the house which we now call home, which, by the way, is on the same street, several blocks away, on which both President Wilson and President Hoover once lived.

It is not because colored people are so obsessed with the desire to live among white people that they try to buy property in a white neighborhood. They do so because the houses there are modern, as a rule, and are better in every way than are those which have been discarded and turned over to their own group. If colored people could find houses on a street restricted to themselves which were as well built and as up to date as are those in white districts, they would make no effort to thrust themselves upon their fair-skinned brothers and sisters who object to having them in close proximity.

When we were obliged to pay several thousand dollars more for our house than the price which was first quoted, we were not being subjected to a hardship from which other colored people are generally exempt. It is well known that from $8 to $10 more rent per month is demanded from colored people than white people have to pay for the same kind of house. As a rule, they also have to pay much more for the property they buy than do others. For instance, the price charged us for the house in which we are now living was at least $2,000 more than a white purchaser would have been obliged to pay.

African blood is truly a luxury in the United States for which those who show it or acknowledge it pay dearly indeed.

CHAPTER 14

LEARNING TO COOK AND ENTERTAINING GUESTS

W HEN I STARTED HOUSEKEEP-
ING my father said I did not know how to boil water. I had been
sent away to school when I was six years old and was considered
a visitor when I spent the summer vacation at home. I had never
learned to cook, because when I went into the kitchen, the presiding genius of that sanctuary would run me out. She didn't
want to bother with me.

While I was in college I made up my mind I would do
nothing which would reflect upon college-bred women. At that
time comparatively few women, even of the dominant race,
had received the A.B. degree, and only two colored women
before our Commencement. College-bred women had a bad
reputation for neatness both as to personal appearance and in
the home. Words simply failed the public when it talked about
them as housekeepers! It was enough to make angels weep to
behold the awful homes kept by women with college degrees,
people declared. The comedians on the stage always represented
them as wearing bad-looking, unbecoming hats, long dresses
with the hem ripped half out, and shoes run down at the heel.

And as for cooking! Of course college-bred women knew
nothing whatever about that! Women who had studied the
higher mathematics, the sciences, and Greek had so violated
the laws of nature that it was never possible for them to learn
afterwards to do well the work which the Creator had ordained
they should do.

I resolved, therefore, that I would prove all those charges
against college-bred women were false, so far as I myself was

concerned. In the first place, I would dress as well as I could. I would not wear shoes run down at the heel. I would not walk around the streets with a portion of the hem of my skirt ripped, and I would try to select becoming hats. All this I promised myself solemnly to do.

Then, too, I would learn to cook. I would be a very good cook and put to shame women who had not graduated from college, just to prove that the foul aspersions cast upon their sisters who had were not justified by the facts.

We had been in our new home to start housekeeping for the first time about two weeks when Thanksgiving rolled around. That surely was the time to make a big reputation as a cook, I thought. I would set such a dinner before my husband as no experienced cook could surpass. I was full of enthusiasm and started to prepare the turkey right after breakfast.

The bird was lying on one side of the kitchen and the cookbook on which I had to depend for success lay open on the other side. I feared I might soil it if it were in too close proximity to the turkey, and I wanted to keep the precious volume clean. In making the dressing, when the recipe called for a teaspoonful of salt, I would painstakingly measure that, put it into a bowl near the turkey, and return to the cookbook on the other side of the kitchen to see what else was needed. I did not trust myself to gather two ingredients at a time, so eager was I to do everything exactly right.

After the turkey was ready to put into the oven I started to make the Queen of All Puddings, the recipe for which was found in a little paper-back book given away by the Crisco Company, which was just beginning to distribute its products. By the time I had corralled all the ingredients for the turkey and the pudding, I am sure I had walked at least ten miles. I have always regretted that I did not have a pedometer that day, so as to prove I walked that distance.

In the afternoon my husband attended the football game and returned about six expecting to find the dinner ready. He was disappointed. The oven was refractory and did not seem to want to bake things. Mr. Terrell went off and returned later, but still the Queen of All Puddings was not done. I tried to keep up appearances and look unconcerned, but my morale was completely destroyed. Finally, about nine o'clock two of our friends—a husband and wife—called to see us. Although it was very humiliating to me, I frankly told them what had happened. None of my dishes I had tried to cook in the oven was done. The good woman said she would look at the stove and see what was the matter. When she did so she discovered that the section under the oven was just as full of ashes as it could possibly be. Nothing in the world could cook in that oven, she declared. And, as if that were not bad enough, I had turned the damper the wrong way. It was cooling the oven off all the time instead of heating it. About ten o'clock Thanksgiving night we sat down to dinner. A more wretched, tired, disgusted woman than I was could not have been found in the United States. I just did manage to restrain the tears, and that was all. I certainly could not have been described as "cheerful" at that meal. My husband enjoyed joking about my mistakes in cooking, and for a long time he talked about "that wonderful Thanksgiving dinner" which it took me twelve hours to cook; and he often referred to me as "The Queen of All Puddings" for years.

Both my mother and my father were hospitable, and I inherited that trait from them. But I dreaded having company for dinner like a toothache, because something was always sure to go wrong, no matter how hard I tried to have everything right. Once I invited four young men to dinner, a few years after we had gone to housekeeping. Two of them were sons of caterers and one of them was the son of a man who had kept one of the best hotels in Boston, so they all knew what a good dinner was. I tried to make the meal absolutely perfect, and I thought I had succeeded.

I had made some delicious ice cream myself. My father, who was a connoisseur and hard to please, said I excelled in that. I was answering a question, so I did not begin to eat the ice cream as soon as my husband and the guests did. I was greatly chagrined when I observed that the young men simply tasted it and let it go at that. When I took the first spoonful I discovered it was full of coal oil. The young woman who had frozen the cream confessed that she had poured coal oil into the little hole at the top of the freezer cover to lubricate it. She had done this, she said, because she thought the job would be easier for her, but had no idea that the coal oil would get into the freezer and spoil the ice cream.

When I invited Samuel Coleridge-Taylor, the great composer, to a home dinner, another tragedy occurred. He said he liked oysters and was especially fond of oyster soup, so I decided to have some. In those halcyon days it was possible for me to have a real, sure enough cook, for they did not receive so much for their services as they do now. I am glad they are getting a living wage, even though I cannot now afford such a luxury. This particular cook was an expert at making oyster soup, so I thought it was unnecessary to give her any directions or to hold any conference with her on the subject. I would scarcely have dared to be so presumptuous. But when that soup reached the table it was so badly curdled it looked for all the world like dishwater—dirty dishwater at that! The cook was never able to explain exactly what happened. She thought she had made a mistake about putting in the salt, she said. She had never failed before and she never failed afterwards. But she certainly embarrassed me when she placed that curdled soup before the distinguished British composer.

Mr. Terrell invited a friend to dinner once and said he would send home some nice lamb chops. The butcher from whom we were accustomed to get them had always sent us good ones, so my husband simply ordered them, as he usually did. That afternoon I was obliged to be away from home and returned just in time for dinner. When the chops were brought into the dining room they were as tough as leather, and we could scarcely eat them.

Just one other incident to show why I dreaded to invite guests to a meal. A very distinguished woman once came to Washington, and I invited her to stop with me. Assisting me at that time was a young woman from South Carolina whom I had sent through the high school and who was about to complete her course in the normal school. She was absolutely dependable in every way and quite a good cook.

I explained to her that I was especially anxious to have everything pass off well while this friend was my guest, because she had treated me so handsomely when I was in her home. My dearly beloved Eula promised me she would do her best. I bought a chicken from a dealer who assured me that it was as tender as a broiler. It did not exactly look the part, and when I applied certain tests I had my doubts. But the man assured me it was all right. However, I wrote a note to Eula before I left home to attend a very important meeting, in which I advised her to parboil the chicken if she had the slightest suspicion that it was not tender enough to roast as it was. I also suggested that she should get some ice cream, so that she would not be bothered with making any dessert when she came home from school.

When my friend and I sat down to dinner, the chicken was so tough we could not eat it. Eula had not parboiled it, as I had advised her to do. Naturally, I expected her to have ice cream for dessert, but instead of ice cream Eula brought us something, the like of which I had never seen before and have never beheld since. She had decided to make a certain kind of tapioca pudding in which she was an expert, because she added some sort of a demisemiquaver to it which made it particularly good. But the concoction which she set before us looked like a piece of brown parchment, and it tasted like that, too. My guest and I could not eat that either. Eula afterward explained that she had tried to make the pudding particularly good and had injected into it more of something than she usually did, and had thus spoiled it completely.

When I first went to housekeeping, I enjoyed it. I studied all the new notions, attended Mrs. Rorer's lectures on cooking, and made a business of keeping up with the housekeeping times. I realized that I was seriously handicapped, because I had to teach myself to cook and had never been in the kitchen with a woman who was efficient and willing to show me just how certain things should be done. I followed the cookbook slavishly and did not dare to add to or subtract from a recipe, as some of my friends who had enjoyed such training either in their own homes or in somebody else's kitchen were able to do.

I balked at nothing which had to be done in the home. Once I gave each of four rooms originally finished in oak four coats of ivory paint. When anything needed a coat of varnish or the floors had to be stained, I did that.

The parlor furniture which we bought when we went to housekeeping began finally to show wear and needed recovering.

But when I got an estimate for the job it was more than I felt I could afford, so I decided to do it myself. With the assistance of a seamstress I upholstered those five pieces of furniture. My father declared that it looked like the work of an expert. I learned to tie up the springs in sofas and chairs when they sagged, and could do odd jobs in carpentering as well. I sewed for my mother and the girls and myself with the aid of a seamstress when I could get her. I generally used a gold thimble which my mother gave me when I was twelve years old. I have it yet. But the gold thimble was occasionally misplaced, and then the whole family had to help me find it. My husband often threatened to hide it, so that I could not use it and worry myself and the whole family when it was misplaced.

I liked to can and preserve fruit, and I put up large quantities every fall for many years. My jellies were considered especially good. My mother was very proud of my work and was boasting of my skill in doing various housekeeping stunts to Mr. Lewis Douglass, son of Frederick Douglass, whom she met on a street car one day. But the manner in which Mr. Douglass received this information took Mother back considerably. Instead of enthusing over the fact that I spent so much time and strength in doing such work, Mr. Douglass, who was one of my best friends, stated in no uncertain terms that he thought I was making a great mistake. He thought it was a pity, he said, that I could not devote more of my time and strength to the work for which I had been trained and which I seemed to enjoy.

Public work of various kinds was my forte, he said. There were comparatively few colored women at that time who could discharge those duties, he declared, and if the few who could were going to use themselves up in drudgery, the race would be the loser and the sufferer in the end. "Try to persuade your daughter to use her head," he said, "and let others whose brains have not been trained use their hands."

Mother was very much impressed with Mr. Douglass's advice, for she had often expressed an opinion similar to his herself. But the duties which pressed in my home had to be done, and often there was nobody to do them but myself. Even though I had a helper in the kitchen for a long time after we went to housekeeping, there were numerous things about the home which, like other women, I had to attend to myself. After my dear mother came to live with me, I was relieved of much responsibility and I was able to leave home to fill lecture engagements occasionally, which I could never have done with a clear conscience but for her presence in the home. But Mother was not well and it was difficult for her to walk, so that I could not allow her to do any manual labor if I could prevent it.

CHAPTER 15

THE COMMISSIONERS OF THE NATIONAL CAPITAL APPOINT ME A MEMBER OF THE SCHOOL BOARD

SHORTLY BEFORE MY THIRD BABY WAS BORN and lost, I had received a great honor. Congress had empowered the Commissioners of the District of Columbia to appoint three women to serve on the Board of Education. Since colored people at that time comprised about one-third of the population of the District of Columbia, many felt that a colored woman should be appointed. But it was currently reported that even if white men could be found who would be willing to work with a colored woman, it would be hard, if not altogether impossible, to find a white woman who would agree to do so.

Dr. C. B. Purvis, son of the well-known abolitionist who lived for years in Philadelphia, suggested to Mr. Terrell that I be a candidate, because, he said, I was well qualified by education and training to represent the colored people of the District. But as I was then expecting to become a mother, the idea did not appeal to me at all. However, I thought it was my duty to cast about for a colored woman who would be a worthy representative and then suggest her to the authorities. Therefore I went to see Commissioner Ross, who had charge of the educational affairs of the District, to recommend a woman who I believed would fill this important position admirably.

I began by saying, "Commissioner Ross, I have come here to implore you not to appoint a colored woman who will not worthily represent the colored people of the city. Without intending to do so, white people who have the power of placing colored people in responsible positions often appoint individuals who misrepresent their race instead of representing it well, because they are not well enough acquainted with colored people to know whom to select. Please don't make this mistake in this case." And then I proceeded to name the candidate for the position and present her qualifications.

When I had finished, Commissioner Ross began to ask me questions about myself. Where had I been educated? He was interested to know I had studied abroad several years, and asked my opinion about four or five matters affecting the public schools. "Have you any letters from your former teachers at Oberlin?" he inquired. "I wish you would let me have them immediately," he said. "I want to show them to the two commissioners who will meet with me this afternoon. Can you bring them to me by two o'clock?" I was not at all sure I could find those letters, and it was then nearly noon. However, I promised Commissioner Ross I would search for them carefully and would bring them to him if I succeeded in finding them. I found them, and when I brought them to his room, his secretary told me that the Commissioner had instructed him to tell me to wait a few minutes if I came. In a few minutes Mr. Ross called me into the conference room and presented me to his colleagues.

When Mr. Terrell came home to dinner that night, I told him what I had said to Commissioner Ross about the mistakes which white people sometimes make in appointing misrepresentative colored people to responsible positions. My husband was greatly amused at this frank statement and laughingly replied, "Well, it's a good thing you yourself are not a candidate for the position, for, after reading such a lecture to a man in authority, you wouldn't have a ghost of a chance to get it."

Shortly after midnight our doorbell rang and a reporter was ushered in, bringing the news that I had been appointed a member of the Board of Education that afternoon and asking for a sketch of my life as well as my photo. All the direful predictions made by doubting Thomases that white women would not work on a board of education with a colored woman were false. There was no friction whatever between us on account of race. Nobody patronized me and nobody seemed to object to any opinion I expressed because it came from a colored woman. I realized what a tremendous responsibility was resting upon me and what it would mean to my race if I made a serious mistake. There were very few cities in which white women were members of the board of education then, and I was the first colored woman to be appointed to such a position in the United States.

It happened that I was the only member of the Board, white or colored, who had ever taught in the public schools of the District of Columbia. There were four white and two colored men and two white women and one colored woman on the Board. I was often requested to describe conditions which obtained in the schools and to answer questions which were asked.

It finally occurred to me, however, that reference was too often made to the fact that I was more thoroughly acquainted with conditions in the schools than the other members of the Board. It began to embarrass me considerably. One day after there had been a lengthy discussion in the Board meeting about something affecting the teachers and I had been asked as a former teacher to express an opinion, I requested General Harries, president of the Board, to let me speak to him a few minutes when the meeting adjourned.

"I would rather not be asked so often to express an opinion because I have been a teacher in the schools," I said. "If you think there is any information I can give you, because I have taught here, I'll be glad to let you have it either before or after the meeting. But please don't ask me to do so during the session." I decided to take this stand because I have often observed that no matter how broad and liberal white people are, as a rule they do not like to have it appear that colored people know more about anything in the world than they do. It seems to be "human nature" for people recognized as belonging to a "superior" group not to want to be enlightened by those classified as "inferior."

I had scarcely been appointed before people came running to me to tell me about the shortcomings and the evil deeds of some of the teachers. I was shocked to see how eager some people are to cause others to lose their positions. Both men and women would come to my house to tell me some scandal about a teacher, generally a woman, and urge me to have her removed. At first I did not know how to handle such a situation. In some instances I was well acquainted with the teacher and did not believe a word I heard. I could not help feeling that the people who came to relate the various scandals did so because they thought a woman would lend a willing ear to it.

I wanted to impress upon those who came bringing evil reports that while my own standards were high and personally I wanted nobody in the schools whose standards were low, I would never make a move against a teacher solely on hearsay evidence. A very bad case was reported to me and I was urged to have the teacher removed immediately. I explained that I could not do that single-handed and alone, even if I wished to. But my informant was not satisfied with that statement and hinted rather broadly that my own standards were not as high as they should be if I did not take drastic action upon the facts she had presented right away.

She was unwilling to relate what she stated to a small committee consisting of two Board members besides myself. She did not want me to jot down any of the facts she presented so that I might place them before the proper authorities. Under no circumstances must I mention her name. She expected me to have the teacher dismissed on hearsay evidence of a woman who cared so little for the schools that she was not willing to help in any way to have the unworthy teacher removed. I tried to show her that it was a very serious thing to have a teacher lose her position in the public schools on account of improper or immoral conduct and that I would not be justified in trying to do so on the unsupported testimony of one person.

After this experience I knew exactly how to handle each similar case. I always had paper and pencil ready, and as soon as I was aware that somebody had come to tell me about the misdeeds of a teacher I began to take copious notes. As a rule, the informer would ask immediately why and what I was writing. When I informed him or her that I would use the notes in presenting the facts to the proper authorities, invariably the visitor would become greatly agitated and declare excitedly that his or her name could not be mentioned under any circumstances to anybody connected with the Board or to any other human being. There were few exceptions to this rule. Other members of the Board told me they had practically the same experience.

After a lapse of years it is a great comfort to reflect that with three exceptions I never cast a vote to remove a colored teacher from the public schools. I would have been derelict in my duty and recreant to my trust if I had not pursued the course I did with reference to the cases mentioned. Over and over again I fought desperately to save a teacher against whom charges were preferred, if I believed he or she was innocent.

While I was on the School Board, several times I stood alone in casting my vote to decide some mooted point. Perhaps the most conspicuous case was the one in which it was decided to remove from the white schools a beautiful little girl whose mother was white and whose father was practically white also with about a teaspoonful of African blood in his veins.

The little girl's parents lived in the suburbs of Washington, where the child, who was about nine years old, had always attended the public school for white children. Some one in that suburb had discovered that her father was supposed to have a few drops of African blood in his veins and reported the matter to the school officials. Then the "leading citizens" of that suburb had insisted that the child be forced to attend the public school for colored children.

While the matter was being discussed by the Board of Education, the little girl was brought to a meeting one afternoon, so that the members might see her. And a truly lovely picture they saw! The child had long, golden curls, blue eyes and was unusually fair and strikingly beautiful. One seldom sees such a vision of loveliness as that child presented.

Those who wanted to exclude her from the white schools argued that the fact that her father was known to have even the slightest infusion of African blood was sufficient reason for taking this step. I contended that during slavery it was customary in some southern states for the child to follow the condition of the mother, and, since the mother was white, the child should be allowed to attend the white schools and not be forced to go to the colored schools against the wishes of her parents.

Both the white and the colored members of the Board declared that I was reflecting upon the colored schools when I plead to have the child remain in the white schools. But I insisted that the comparative merits of the two schools were not involved at all. In a city where there are separate schools, as there are in Washington, if a white woman wants her child to attend a white school, she has a right to insist upon that privilege. Years before this occurred the children of a white woman and a well-known colored physician had actually attended the white schools here without any question, trouble, or friction whatsoever.

I was eager to have the beautiful little girl admitted to the white schools, because I knew in a prejudice-ridden city she would have many more advantages if she were classified as white than she could enjoy if she were classified as colored, and that she would be spared many of the hardships, humiliations and injustices of which she would be the helpless victim if she were forced to cast her lot among colored children. But my plea in the little girl's behalf was all in vain. Every member of the Board of Education in the National Capital, including the two colored men, voted to exclude the child from the white schools except myself.

A few years after this happened, my doorbell rang one day and a white woman was admitted to my home. As soon as she saw me, she told me she was the mother of the little girl for whom I had made such a hard fight. She had come to say that they had left the suburb in which they formerly lived and had moved to another section of Washington, and her daughter was attending the white school near her home under an assumed name. And later on that little girl was one of the best actresses on the American stage, till she passed away a few years ago.

Rather an amusing incident occurred once, when I decided to do everything in my power to have a director of music for the colored schools. After discussing the matter with the colored superintendent, I learned that there was no salary available for that position. When I presented the matter to the Board, all the members agreed that such a position was needed in the colored schools and promised to vote to create it. But where was the salary to be found? That was indeed the question!

I was informed there was a salary for a teacher in the sixth grade which might be used for the position. A teacher in the fifth grade was about to be promoted to the sixth and that salary would have to go to her, unless she agreed to teach the rest of the year on the stipend she was then receiving in the fifth grade. When I explained the dilemma to the teacher, she readily consented to the arrangement, and thus was the position of director of music for the colored schools created.

Shortly after that a certain man about town who was a "conscientious objector" to almost everything proposed by the school officials threatened to sue me for using the money designated for a teacher of the sixth grade as a salary for the director of music in the colored schools. But when he discovered there was nothing illegal about the transaction, he let the matter drop.

My attention was called to the fact that there was no Easter holiday for the pupils and teachers of the public schools in the District of Columbia. Some of the teachers in both the colored and the white schools helped me to get the data from other school systems showing that both pupils and teachers needed the rest just at that time of the year and that the benefit from the Easter holiday was strikingly apparent in the work done afterward both by the instructors and by the children. After marshaling the facts before the Board, it was not difficult to induce the trustees to give the public schools a short vacation at Easter.

After Frederick Douglass died it occurred to me that a day should be set apart in his honor. In my opinion, by all odds Frederick Douglass is the greatest man whom this country has produced. If it were customary to judge human beings by "points," I am sure it could be proved mathematically that Mr. Douglass possessed as many of the points, mentally, morally, and spiritually, which are necessary to make a great man as any man born in the United States, if not in the whole world. In reading history I cannot recall a man who was born into such depths of poverty and degradation, who was reared in such a quagmire of handicaps and ignorance, and who largely by his own efforts was able to rise to such lofty heights as Frederick Douglass did.

In referring to the resolution which I introduced at the meeting of the Board in its issue of February 18, 1897, the Washington correspondent of the *New York Age* commented as follows:

"About a month ago Mrs. Mary Church Terrell conceived

the idea that the colored children of this community ought to celebrate in a fitting manner the day on which Frederick Douglass was said to be born. In her capacity as a member of the Board of Education she introduced a resolution to this effect at its regular meeting, which resolution was unanimously adopted. Through her efforts, therefore, and by virtue of her foresight, the 14th of February will hereafter be known in our school system as 'Douglass Day.' On this day songs of freedom will be sung, essays will be read, declamations given by the pupils and orations delivered by distinguished men and women touching the career of Frederick Douglass."

Colored children need to be taught self-respect and pride in their own group. Nothing can do this more quickly and more surely than teaching them that certain representatives of their race have accomplished something worth while and have reached lofty heights in spite of the fearful disadvantages under which they have labored. I was sure that Douglass Day would be instrumental of much good. It was the first time that a Board of Education in any city set aside a day on which colored children should learn about the career and services of a distinguished man of their own group. Perhaps Douglass Day inspired Dr. Carter Woodson to establish Negro History Week many years afterward.

I failed to introduce "Animal Day" into the public school system, although I tried hard to do so. I urged the school board to set aside a day in which special efforts should be made to teach children to be kind to animals. A long time after this plea was made the idea was carried out in another way.

But I did introduce a measure which completely revolutionized the methods previously used for admitting pupils into the normal school. Before this measure was adopted, pupils who wished to enter the normal school were required to take an examination and submit to a physical test after graduating from the high school. For many years there had been a great deal of dissatisfaction. Criticism of school authorities and charges of unfairness as a result of this method were commonly heard. It was often asserted by disgruntled parents and pupils who failed to pass that a great deal of favoritism had been shown in an oral test which counted 25 per cent in the final mark the pupil received. This caused much bitterness, of course.

When, therefore, my resolution to allow all graduates from the high school to enter the normal school was passed, there was great rejoicing in the land. Then everybody had a chance to make a good teacher. It often happened that the pupils whose marks were the lowest in the high school stood at the head of the class when they graduated from the normal school. These facts seemed to me to justify the strenuous efforts exerted to do away with the examination for admission into the normal school and allow everybody who graduated from the high school to enter, if he wished to do so.

Many incidents occurred to prove that the teachers in the white schools disregarded my race entirely when they wished me to serve them or their schools in any way. They often came to my house to prefer requests of various kinds, to discuss propositions in which they were interested, and to ask me to vote for any measure they wished to have passed. One of the cherished mementos of my service on the school board is the following letter from the white teachers of the Eighth Division. It read:

> "DEAR MADAM: The teachers of the Eighth Division at a regular meeting called for the transaction of official business by Mr. Isaac Fairbrother, Supervising Principal, took advantage of the opportunity to propose and unanimously approve a resolution to convey to you, through a committee, their sincere congratulations upon your appointment as a member of the Board of Education. Your past services in behalf of the public schools of the District of Columbia have been of incalculable benefit. Therefore, the teachers of the Eighth Division congratulate you and send renewed assurance of their continued confidence and loyalty.
>
>   "Yours very respectfully,
>   "ELIZABETH RILEY.
>   "ANNIE VAN HORN.
>   "CHARLES A. JOHNSON.
> "Approved, I. FAIRBROTHER."

A school has been named for Mr. Fairbrother, who has passed away. I had served as a member of the Board five or six years when this letter was sent me by the Eighth Division, and had just been reappointed for another term of three years.

The nearest approach to "friction" of a serious nature occurred when I tried to assist one of the finest white instructors in the corps to get permission to have an entertainment so as to raise money to buy a victrola for her school, when victrolas were decidedly a rarity under the sun. Miss Westcott was principal of the Western High School and wanted to use a victrola to instruct her pupils in a variety of ways. She told me she wished to have them hear the best speakers in the country, and the great singers whom the average pupil could not afford to hear, and to receive information of many kinds through what was then an entirely new medium of rendering such service to her pupils.

But the Board of Education voted against granting this progressive high-school principal this permission. Then she came to me and urged me to do what I could to persuade the Board of Education to rescind its vote. She cited the many advantages which would accrue to the pupils from having a victrola in her school and declared it was a means of education which nothing that she was able to get could surpass. I was greatly impressed with her statement and thoroughly convinced she was right. But I told her frankly that I was very dubious about persuading the Board to rescind its vote, because the victrola's most aggressive opponent was a woman whose opinion it was extremely difficult, if not impossible, to change, once it had been formed and forcibly, publicly expressed.

However, feeling as Don Quixote must have felt, I promised Miss Westcott I would do what I could to help her get the much-coveted victrola. We decided that each one of us would go to see the members of the Board privately, present the case to busy men who had not had time to reason things out for themselves before they had cast their ballots against it, argue our point diplomatically with them, and try to secure their respective votes to open the subject again.

We succeeded. At the next regular meeting of the Board the motion denying the principal of the Western High School permission to give an entertainment for the purpose of raising money to purchase a victrola was rescinded. Then another motion granting permission to do so was made and carried with only one dissenting vote—the vote of the lady who would not be convinced that a victrola in a schoolroom was a good thing. Thus I lost that good lady's friendship forever. I was compensated, however, by the gratitude and appreciation expressed by the teachers and pupils of the school, who believed they would be greatly benefited by it.

Shortly afterward Miss Westcott invited me to come to the Western High School to hear a speech on peace which was made to the teachers and pupils in the assembly room. She had me sit on the platform during the exercises, then took me through her beautiful building and introduced me in a very complimentary manner to her teachers, who received me most cordially. I would be derelict in my duty if I did not refer in detail to this incident. It is well known that the city of Washington is Southern both in sentiment and in tradition. It is only fair to cite this proof of freedom from prejudice on the part of the outstanding white teachers and officers of the public schools toward a colored member of the Board of Education of whose services they approved.

The officers and teachers in my own group also expressed confidence in my efforts to do my duty toward them. Once when I attended a Board meeting I found a basket of beautiful flowers in front of my seat. It was a gift of the teachers of the Tenth, Eleventh, and Twelfth Divisions, who placed on a card a very complimentary reference to the work I had done.

After I had served the Board of Education nearly six years I resigned. One of the reasons which caused me to do so was the decision to make my husband principal of the high school; I did not want to be a member of the Board which voted to give him this position. I received many letters from officers and teachers in both the colored and white schools expressing regret at my action and thanking me for the efforts I had made in their behalf.

A few years after I resigned, Congress decided to abolish the Board of Education which was functioning at that time, remove the power of appointing members from the District Commissioners, and place it in the hands of the judges of the District Supreme Court. When this duty was assigned to them, the first thing those gentlemen did was to declare that they would appoint on their new Board nobody who had previously served in that capacity in the District of Columbia. And I was the only person who had previously served whom the judges placed on the first Board they formed. I felt that in this way the District of Columbia placed its seal of approval upon the efforts I had exerted to do my duty to the public schools during my first term.

Some people explained what they called my "influence" on the Board by saying that I was a "politician." By that they meant that I accomplished what I did by being mysterious, "keepin' 'em guessin'," and working in the dark. This picture they painted of me amused me very much. Nothing could have been farther from the facts. I did nothing in secret or on the sly. I threw my cards on the table from the very start. If a teacher asked me to vote to give him a certain position and I had decided to support another, I told him frankly that I could not comply with his request. But I always reminded him that I had only one vote on the Board and assured him that if he could get the requisite number of votes to elect him to the position, I would do nothing to oppose him. I worked hard to place teachers for whose character and scholarship I had a high regard at the heads of departments or in responsible positions. I did not always win, but the instances in which my candidate lost or the measures I advocated failed were comparatively rare.

Among the white members of the Board it was a sort of unwritten law that they would vote for no colored candidate unless the three colored members agreed upon him or her, and they would vote for no proposition especially affecting the colored schools unless the three colored members favored it. And yet I succeeded in having two men appointed to important positions who were opposed by the two colored men on the Board. After carefully considering the qualifications of my candidates on the two occasions mentioned and after mature deliberation, the white members of the Board decided to vote for them, not to favor or please me personally, but because they honestly believed they were the best teachers for the place.

During my first term of office each of the "trustees" had a special division whose affairs he administered with the approval of the Board as a whole. I had the Tenth Division, and it was my duty with the advice of the Superintendent and Supervising Principal to appoint the regular teachers in the grades according to their rating when they graduated from the normal school, promote them when a vacancy occurred, appoint special teachers as well as janitors, and help adjust complicated, mooted points of any kind.

On one occasion I was advised by the proper officer to promote a teacher from the fourth to the fifth grade on the ground that she deserved it. But another teacher heard what was in the air and came to me posthaste to inquire why I had made the recommendation and to prove that she herself deserved it according to the rule generally observed. She showed me to my entire satisfaction that both because of excellence of record and because of length of service the promotion rightfully belonged to her.

I was at the breakfast table when I received this information, and I had already directed the Superintendent to promote the teacher who had been recommended by the Supervising Principal, but who, I had been convinced later, did not deserve it. It was just a few minutes before nine o'clock. School was about to begin and I had no telephone. Few private individuals had a telephone then, and there was no time for me to reach the Superintendent to instruct him to change the recommendation I had already sent in. But it occurred to me that there was a telephone at Freedmen's Hospital, which was about four blocks from my residence. Grabbing my coat and hat, I ran nearly every step of the way to the hospital, rushed to the telephone breathless, and reached the Superintendent just as he was sending a messenger to notify the teacher who did not deserve it that she had been promoted. It goes without saying that the teacher whose excellence of record and length of service entitled her to the promotion received it.

Another interesting case also occurred in my division. At that time it was a violation of the rules for a woman teacher to marry and retain her position in the schools. Marriage of a woman teacher automatically severed her connection with the school system. One day a colored friend who had taught in a white school in a Western city and who wanted to get into our schools came to tell me that a certain teacher in my division was married. She presented me facts which convinced me she was telling the truth. She had gone to Baltimore, where the license had been secured, and had seen the record of it.

I urged her not to make the matter public until I had a chance to talk to the teacher. At first the married teacher denied it, but she finally admitted it. I promised to let her remain in the schools till the end of the month if she would resign then. She kept her word, resigned, and had a wedding. Unless she herself had told it, nobody ever knew that she was secretly married before she had her wedding. It seemed to me it was much better to handle the matter quietly in this way than to expose the teacher and reflect discredit upon the public schools. I have never been able to understand why those in authority should insist upon creating a sensation and making a scandal by publishing broadcast an unfortunate incident which had happened in the schools, when the matter might have been adjusted quietly without injuring the reputation or the interests of anybody concerned.

Among my activities on the School Board I sometimes went to Congress to urge members of the Appropriation Committee to give the public schools the funds needed for buildings, teachers' salaries or for anything we lacked. It sometimes happened that the appropriation which the Board of Education asked for the colored schools was cut and then I was sure to make a pilgrimage to Congress in their behalf. I once asked a Congressman to use his influence to secure for one of the colored officers of the schools the same salary proposed for the white officer holding a similar position. "How much is that salary?" he inquired. "Four thousand dollars," I replied. "Four thousand dollars," he exclaimed. "Why, no colored man in the world is worth that much."

Since the citizens of the District of Columbia are all disfranchised, black, white, grizzle and gray, men and women, sane and insane, there is nobody for us to look to in time of trouble except the Congressmen upon whose political doorstep we have been laid. And some of these gentlemen are so busy looking after the interests of their own constituents they have very few minutes in which to study the needs of their stepchild or to minister to its wants.

As I look back upon my record on the School Board, I am happy in the belief that I did everything in my power to promote the welfare of the pupils, facilitate the work of the teachers and raise the standards, so far as I could. While I had charge of the Tenth Division, I visited the schools often, and made strenuous efforts to become personally acquainted with the teachers, so that I might have first-hand knowledge of their temperament, their methods of teaching, their attitude toward their pupils, and might help them in every way I could. When I served on the Board of Education the members were not paid, as they were later on, but I gave both time and strength for eleven years without money and without price.

It sometimes happened that hostile forces worked against a good teacher vigorously, either because there was personal animosity or because the other fellow wanted the job for himself or for one of his friends. In such an emergency the individual who is being fought must have a friend at court to present his side of the case, if he is to be saved. I tried conscientiously to be that friend when I felt that by so doing I could thwart an attempt at injustice either to the teacher or to the schools.

It was indeed a joy to work with the teachers, both colored and white, in the public schools of Washington. Take them by and large, a finer group of human beings can not be found anywhere in the world. They are a picked lot. This is especially noticeable when one visits the colored schools. And there is a reason. Among colored people school teaching offers one of the most desirable vocations which well-educated representatives of the race can enter. Particularly is this true of the women. Consequently, those best equipped mentally and spiritually are eager to secure positions as teachers either in the public schools or in the colleges for colored youth. In the colored high school of Washington, as well as in the grades, may be found colored men and women who have graduated with honor and wear Phi Beta Kappa pins from the best universities and colleges in the country. It is quite common to meet a colored teacher in Washington who has traveled extensively in Europe and has studied abroad several years.

Shortly after I resigned from the School Board the citizens of Washington gave me a testimonial. Among those who were present at this meeting and who spoke were the President of the

Board of Education and several judges of the District Supreme Court by whom I had been appointed after Congress had delegated to them the selection of members of the School Board. A bronze statuette of the Venus de Milo was presented to me and a beautiful bouquet of flowers was given me by the children of the public schools as a token of their appreciation of the efforts I had exerted in their behalf.

CHAPTER 16

THE NATIONAL AMERICAN WOMAN SUFFRAGE
ASSOCIATION INVITES ME TO SPEAK

AFTER I CAME TO WASHINGTON I became deeply interested in club work among women. Before the nineteenth amendment granting suffrage to women was passed, the National American Woman Suffrage Association used to hold its meetings in Washington every two years, and there were few sessions which I did not attend. On one occasion when the members of the Association were registering their protest against a certain injustice, I arose and said, "As a colored woman, I hope this Association will include in the resolution the injustices of various kinds of which colored people are the victims."

"Are you a member of this Association?" Miss Susan B. Anthony asked. "No, I am not," I replied, "but I thought you might be willing to listen to a plea for justice by an outsider." Then Miss Anthony invited me to come forward, write out the resolution which I wished incorporated with the others, and hand it to the Committee on Resolutions. And thus began a delightful, helpful friendship with Miss Anthony which lasted till she passed away.

Shortly after I met Miss Anthony she sent me the *History of Woman Suffrage* and several valuable brochures. In each of them she had written with her own hand her name and mine and a little sentiment besides. On the cover of one of the paperback books she wrote: "Mrs. Mary Church Terrell, from her sincere friend and co-worker, Susan B. Anthony, Rochester, N. Y. February 15, 1898."

The first large suffrage meeting which I attended was the one in Washington at which women who were interested in the subject were present from all over the world. Among the women sitting on the platform at that meeting were Elizabeth Cady Stanton and Lucretia Mott, two of the pioneers of the suffrage cause. Of course, Miss Anthony was there. At the close of one of the meetings the presiding officer requested all those to rise who believed that women should have the franchise. Although the theatre was well filled at the time, comparatively few rose. I was among the number who did. I forced myself to stand up, although it was hard for me to do so. In the early 1890's it required a great deal of courage for a woman publicly to acknowledge before an audience that she believed in suffrage for her sex when she knew the majority did not. I can not recall a period in my life, since I heard the subject discussed for the first time as a very young girl, that I did not believe in woman suffrage with all my heart. When I was a freshman in college I wrote an essay entitled, "Resolved, There Should Be a Sixteenth Amendment to the Constitution Granting Suffrage to Women." Nevertheless, it was not easy for me publicly to commit myself to woman suffrage in that large gathering.

This happened before Mr. Terrell had proposed to me. When I told him that I had stood up in Albaugh's Theatre and had publicly taken a stand for woman suffrage, he laughingly replied that I had ruined my chances for getting a husband. I told him that I would never be silly enough to marry a man who did not believe a woman had a right to help administer the affairs of the Government under which she lived. Mr. Terrell, however, believed ardently in woman suffrage when few men took that stand. Nothing amused him more than to hear a self-sufficient, important young man argue against suffrage with a woman who had the points in its favor at her tongue's end and could deliver her verbal blows with telling effect. "Just listen to that woman wipe the floor up with that narrow-minded, conceited, young coxcomb," he would chuckle. "There won't be a greasespot left, when she gets through with him."

I am glad I always believed in this great cause, not only because it gives me satisfaction to know that I was on the right side of the question when it was most unpopular to advocate it, but because it was the means of bringing me into direct, personal contact with some of the brainiest and finest women in the country.

I was well acquainted with Mrs. May Wright Sewall, at one time President of the National Council of Women, and heard her outline plans for this organization, before it was formed. I was also well acquainted with Rev. Anna Howard Shaw, one of the first regularly ordained woman ministers and also one of Miss Anthony's co-workers; with Alice Stone Blackwell and with Henry Blackwell, her father, who was the husband of Lucy Stone, one of the first women to receive a degree at Oberlin College, and among the first to retain her maiden name instead of using her husband's after marriage. For years I have enjoyed the friendship of Harriet Stanton Blatch, Elizabeth Cady Stanton's daughter, who has extended me numerous social courtesies in this country and once when we were abroad. It was rare to find any of the original suffragists or their immediate families who were badly afflicted with race prejudice. Mrs. Carrie Chapman Catt, one of the twelve foremost women in the United States, has demonstrated her freedom from race prejudice and her friendship for me over and over again, ever since I met her at least thirty years ago. For the June, 1936, issue of the *Oberlin Alumni Magazine* Mrs. Catt wrote an article entitled "Mary Church Terrell, An Appreciation," in which she reviewed and praised the work I have tried to do.

Miss Anthony once invited me to speak in Rochester, New York, where she and her sister Mary lived, and entertained me in her home. If my espousal of the cause of suffrage in the early days had done nothing but make such a rare and delightful experience possible and bring me into intimate relationship with Susan B. Anthony, I would have felt that I had been more than fully repaid for taking an unpopular stand. During this visit, Miss Anthony sent her biography which had been written by Mrs. Ida Husted Harper to my little daughter, Phyllis, in which she had also written a sentiment expressing the hope that the little girl would follow in the footsteps of her mother.

The first complimentary notice given me in the press because of a public speech was received when I addressed the National American Woman Suffrage Association, which held a biennial session in Washington in what was then called Columbia Theatre in 1898. I had been invited to deliver an address upon "The

Progress and Problems of Colored Women" and was allotted twenty minutes. The audience received my message enthusiastically. Miss Anthony presided and when she arose to introduce the next speaker, she said, "I am sure you have all been thrilled by what you have heard."

A few years after that I received another invitation to address the National American Woman Suffrage Association at its biennial session, which was held in the Universalist Church. The letter sent me by the program committee stated that the first time I had been invited to appear before the organization I had been requested to speak as a colored woman about colored women and had been allotted twenty minutes, but at the approaching biennial session, the committee wished me to speak as a woman without regard to race on "The Justice of Woman Suffrage," and I would be allotted thirty minutes. Some members of the Association declared that in assigning me that subject the program committee had asked me to make the key speech of the entire session.

I worked very hard on that speech. I spoke without a manuscript, although I had carefully written every word, and I poured my very soul into everything I said. The audience gave me an ovation which more than repaid me for the time and pains I had expended on it.

In its issue of February 10, 1900, the *Boston Transcript* had an article with the conspicuous headline, "Mrs. Mary C. Terrell's Address Able and Brilliant," and commented as follows: "The Friday evening session of the Suffrage convention brought before a very large audience a woman of whom few present had heard, but whose address was one of the ablest and most brilliant to which a Washington audience may listen. The woman was Mrs. Mary Church Terrell, a member of the School Board of the District of Columbia, a graduate of Oberlin College, and president of the National Association of Colored Women. Her topic was 'The Justice of Woman Suffrage,' and she combated the old objections with earnest argument, biting sarcasm and delightful raillery. At her close the applause lasted several minutes."

In an editorial February 19, 1900, the *Boston Transcript* reviewed the work I had done for my race in a most complimentary way and referred to my speech again as follows:

"Perhaps the most striking and concise statement of the whole session was uttered when she declared during her impressive address on 'The Justice of Woman Suffrage' "—and then the editor devoted considerable space to quoting passages from my address which caused him to bestow so much praise upon it.

Several days after I delivered this address Mrs. Isabella Beecher Hooker, who had heard about the impression I had made upon the Biennial, sent me a bust of her sister, Harriet Beecher Stowe. It was a copy of the bust that had been carved by the sculptor, Anne Whitney, of Boston, and had been exhibited in the World's Fair in Chicago in 1893. Mrs. Hooker asked her friend, Mrs. Howell, of New York, to present the bust to me during the session, and she complied with this request.

CHAPTER 17

CLUB WORK

HAVING OBSERVED from attending the Woman Suffrage meetings how much may be accomplished through organization, I entered enthusiastically into club work among the women of my own group. For many years colored women had been binding themselves together in the interest of the church and had done very effective work in many ways. But secular organizations among them were comparatively rare. As soon as the idea of uniting their forces outside the church dawned upon them, it took definite, tangible form quickly, and women of all classes and conditions seized upon it with enthusiasm.

In Washington, where there were probably more colored women who had enjoyed educational advantages than in any other city of the country, this was especially true. A goodly number of these women decided to band together to raise the standard of their group, and the Colored Women's League was formed in 1892. Among other things, the League established a sort of night school on a small scale. Classes in various subjects were offered. As Chairman of the Educational Committee, I gave my services gratuitously to teach a class in English Literature and one in German several nights a week.

Meantime in Boston, a club of progressive colored women was formed whose purposes and aims were similar to those of the League. Each one of these organizations grew apace and enlarged its sphere of usefulness more and more. In the summer of 1895 women from several states met in Boston at the call of Mrs. Josephine St. Pierre Ruffin, and the Federation of

Afro-American Women was formed. There were then two national organizations of colored women, for clubs outside of Washington had already become affiliated with the League.

A dispute soon arose as to which was the first to become actually national in scope and later on the question was raised as to which had more clubs affiliated with it than the other. The Colored Women's League declared it was the first to *suggest* that there should be a national organization. An article which I wrote and which appeared on page 73 in the May and June, 1893, issue of *Ringwood's Afro-American Journal of Fashion,* Vol. 11, No. 7, proves beyond a doubt that this contention is correct. The title of the article is:

"WHAT THE COLORED WOMEN'S LEAGUE WILL DO

"A national organization of colored women could accomplish so much in a variety of ways that thoughtful, provident women are strenuously urging their sisters all over the country to cooperate with them in this important matter. In unity there is strength, and in unity of purpose there is inspiration.

"The Colored Women's League, recently organized in Washington, has cordially invited women in all parts of the country to unite with it, so that we may have a national organization similar to the Federation of clubs of the women of the other race. . . . There is every reason for all who have the interests of the race at heart to associate themselves with the League, so that there may be a vast chain of organizations extending the length and breadth of the land devising ways and means to advance our cause. We have always been equal to the highest emergencies in the past and it remains for us now to prove to the world that we are a unit in all matters pertaining to the education and elevation of our race."

So far as I know, this is the first article which appeared in any magazine announcing that a national organization of colored women had been formed, and I have preserved a copy of it. But the Federation of Afro-American Women, whose president was Mrs. Booker T. Washington, declared that even if the

League were the first to *suggest* that there should be a national organization, the Federation was the first actually to *become national* in scope. Among some of the close friends of the officers and members of these two bodies this dispute created no little bitterness of feeling.

In some respects it resembles the controversy between the Wright brothers and the Smithsonian Institution which caused the former to decide to send to England the first plane in which they flew. To quote the late Will Rogers, "The trustees of the Smithsonian Institute decided that Langley's machine COULD have flown, but didn't. I could have flown to France ahead of Lindbergh, but I just neglected doing it. I had a lot of other things on my mind at the time."

It would appear, therefore, that while the Colored Women's League of Washington was the first to "resolve that colored women of the United States associate ourselves together to collect all facts obtainable to show the moral, intellectual, industrial and social growth and attainments of our people, to foster unity of purpose, to consider and determine methods which will promote the interests of colored people in any direction that suggests itself," the group which assembled in Boston in 1895 at the call of Mrs. Ruffin was the first secular, national gathering of colored women in the United States which actually met with the intention of becoming a permanent organization. Thus was the National Federation of Afro-American Women formed.

Its second convention was held in Washington a few days after the League had held its first in the same city, and then a remarkable thing was done. It was decided to merge the two organizations into one. For it was apparent to the thoughtful women in our group that there would be little likelihood of two national organizations achieving success at that stage of their development. It was the consensus of opinion among those women that only one organization was needed.

A committee of seven was appointed from the League and seven from the Federation, of which I was one, to effect the union of the two organizations on the first day the Afro-American Federation's second convention met. This joint committee selected me chairman and proceeded to discuss the terms on which we could unite with justice to each organization.

Considering the difficulties encountered, this was accomplished with comparatively little friction.

It was not easy to name this baby, but it was finally decided to call it the National Association of Colored Women. Then the most difficult task of all confronted us! Who should be the first president of the new Association? That was indeed the question! It is safe to assert that while we were in the throes of electing the president, the name of no colored woman who had achieved success or prominence anywhere in the United States failed to be presented for consideration. To begin with, the name of every member of the Joint Committee was mentioned, not once but several times during the day. When a member of this committee was nominated, the result of the poll showed that every woman on her half of the joint committee voted for her, while every woman on the other half voted for somebody else. Over and over again the tellers would report that Miss A had 7 votes and Miss B had 7. And this went on indefinitely, so that most of us had little hope that anybody either in the United States or out of it could ever be elected.

Several times during the committee meeting prayers were offered by the members who sought divine guidance in accomplishing the task they were trying to perform. Like the other members of the committee, I had been nominated early in the day and had met the same fate as the others. Finally I was nominated the second time, the deadlock was broken, I received a majority of the votes cast and was elected the first president of the National Association of Colored Women. It was nearly six o'clock when this occurred. The Joint Committee had been in session all day long and had to return to the church for the evening session at eight o'clock, although each and every one of us was worn to a frazzle. I shall never forget the sensations I experienced while presiding over that Joint Committee. It was the hardest day's work I have ever done.

The meeting was held in July and at the time I was expecting a little stranger who would arrive, I hoped, the last of September. He came but did not tarry long with me. It was a bitter, grievous disappointment to Mr. Terrell and myself, but like other mothers who have passed through this Gethsemane, I pulled myself together as best I could and went on with my work. I had to go on with it. The teachers, the parents of children and others who wanted to talk with the only colored woman who was a member of the Board of Education insisted on seeing me and presenting their respective cases, anything my nurse might say to the contrary notwithstanding. And they rendered me a great service for which I am grateful today. Obliged to be interested in the troubles and trials of others, I had little time to think of my own aching heart.

Naturally, I felt it was a great honor to be elected president of the National Association of Colored Women and I was especially gratified because the members of the committee who finally broke the deadlock declared they had done so because my fairness as Chairman of the Joint Committee convinced them I was the right woman for the place. It was a great undertaking for a young woman with little experience and it required prodigious effort, not to mention patience, to establish the organization on a firm foundation, so that the superstructure would be secure.

I presided over three conventions—one in Nashville in 1897, the year after the Association was formed; the next one in Chicago in 1899, and the third in Buffalo, New York, in 1901. Each of them was successful from every point of view. The one in Chicago, however, overtopped them all. There were one hundred forty-five delegates, which was a large number for that time. There was an unusually interesting program. The most distinguished colored women in the country participated in the meetings. The biggest and best dailies in Chicago gave the Association more publicity than it has ever received since then from the press of any city in which we have met. Column after column, giving detailed accounts of the proceedings, appeared in all the big dailies, while the editorials in several leading newspapers bestowed unstinted praise upon the meetings, the officers and the delegates.

"Of all the conventions that have met in this country this summer," said the *Daily News*, "there is none that has taken hold of the business in hand with more good sense and judgment than the National Association of Colored Women, now assembled in this city. The subjects brought up, the manner of their treatment and the decisions reached exhibit wide and appreciative knowledge of conditions confronting colored people."

In commenting upon the delegates, the *Times-Herald*

frankly admits "these women were a continual revelation, not only as to personal appearance, but as to intelligence and culture. If by a bit of magic the color of their skin could be changed white, one would have witnessed a convention of wide-awake women, which in almost every particular would compare favorably with a convention of white-skinned women."

There were crowded houses day and night. Long before it was time to call the meetings to order, there was hardly standing room in Quinn Chapel, which was one of the largest churches in Chicago.

I believed it was the duty of colored women to do everything in their power to save the children during the early, impressionable period of their life. So I tried to raise a fund with which to establish kindergartens, wherever it was possible to do so. In order to do this I had printed in pamphlet form the address on "The Progress of Colored Women" which I had delivered before the Thirtieth Annual Convention of the National American Woman Suffrage Association in Washington, and sold it to the delegates and visitors to the convention. I charged only twenty-five cents for it, but some in the audience were so interested in this effort they paid a dollar for it, and even more. Quite a neat little sum was raised, and during the next two years it was a great privilege to use it to assist in establishing and maintaining the kindergartens which appealed to the Association for aid. It is gratifying to recall that the first fund started by the organization was raised to help the children.

Establishing Schools of Domestic Science, the Labor Question, the Convict Lease System, the Necessity for an Equal Moral Standard for Men and Women, and the Jim Crow Car Laws were ably treated by women who had made a special study of these important subjects.

Miss Jane Addams of Hull House invited several of the officers to lunch with her. In commenting upon this the *Times-Herald* said: "The color line was given another good rub yesterday by Miss Jane Addams of Hull House, who entertained at luncheon a party of colored women. . . . They were shown all about by the residents, evincing great interest in every department. 'We were impressed,' said one of the residents later in the afternoon, 'with the intelligence of these colored women. They inspected the settlement understandingly and poured in upon us as many interested questions as we could answer.' This is the first time," continued the *Herald*, "that colored women have been given recognition in a social way by a woman of lighter skin."

"When Miss Addams invited the delegates of the National Association of Colored Women to lunch with her," said one of the papers, "it was the whitest thing she ever did."

The *Chicago Tribune* said in an editorial: "That within a single generation since the war which gave freedom to the race such a gathering as this should be possible means a great deal. Could Abraham Lincoln have looked in upon the nearly two thousand people crowded into Quinn Chapel the other evening and have seen the representatives of the race he emancipated and listened to the addresses said to have been so admirably spoken by the president of the convention, Mrs. Terrell, and others, and observed their essential dignity, evident refinement of manner and noted the breadth of their outlook for their race and country, it is not difficult to imagine some of the emotions which would have stirred him, especially in view of their so clear apprehension of the real conditions of the problems before them."

"After watching these capable colored women three days," said one distinguished white woman, "I never want to hear another word about there being no hope for the Negro. Another thing, if the Lord helps him who helps himself, these colored women will have a good, long pull with Providence."

At the Chicago Biennial I was reelected president by an overwhelming majority. I had declared repeatedly that I did not desire to be reelected. So anxious was I to impress upon the delegates my reluctance to assume the presidency again that I went so far as to say that I would not accept a reelection, unless it were unanimous (which from the nature of the case I knew could never happen). And, even if it were, I stated, I greatly preferred not to serve again. Before I left home my father came from Memphis to Washington to urge me not to accept the presidency again under any circumstances. And my husband's opposition to it was as strong as my father's. For this reason I felt I dared not take the office again, and thus turn a deaf ear to the advice and requests of the men in my family.

Most of the delegates supposed that the constitution prohibited the reelection of officers who had served the past two years. Indeed, this had been positively stated as a fact. Especially did the women who wished to become president themselves insist upon this interpretation of the law. On the morning of the election of officers, after the names of five or six candidates for the presidency had been mentioned, one of the delegates announced to the convention that there was no reason why all the officers could not be reelected if the women wanted to retain them.

"The constitution," she explained, "forbids an officer from serving more than two consecutive terms. As it was adopted just two years ago at Nashville, and as our present officers have served only one term since it was adopted, they are all eligible for reelection." I still stoutly maintained I did not want to serve again. But some of the officers on the platform persuaded me to go before the women and promise to accept the presidency if I received a two-thirds vote of the convention. I did as I was requested. Many of the delegates had urged me to remain in office two years longer, so that the Association might be established on a firmer foundation, and they convinced me that it would be an injustice if I did not comply with their request.

Naturally, two or three women who wanted to be elected themselves were not pleased with this turn in affairs. One of them moved that as the name of each delegate was called, she should come forward and deposit her ballot on a table in front of the pulpit in the presence of the whole convention. This was done exactly as prescribed and the vote showed that Mary Church Terrell had received 106 ballots out of a possible 145.

In other words, there were thirty-nine votes distributed among the five other candidates whose names were before the convention. There was a great demonstration when the result of the poll was announced. Some of the women wept and rushed upon the platform to embrace me. Such a spontaneous outburst of confidence in me more than repaid me for all the strenuous efforts I had exerted to make the Association as a whole and the convention in particular a success.

At the close of the convention in Buffalo, when I had served two terms, the delegates unanimously voted to make me honorary president for life and presented me with a silver loving cup on an ebony stand.

During the term I was president, both before the adoption of the constitution and throughout the two terms I served afterward, I strove to place the National Association of Colored Women on a solid foundation and to make its ideals high. In the first years of its existence there were comparatively few women who had had any experience in club work and upon whom I could call for assistance. But the cooperation I received from those who were able to assist was hearty, genuine and valuable to the highest degree. Without the help given me by those loyal co-workers, the National Association of Colored Women could not have been brought up to the high standard during the first five years of its existence to which it undoubtedly attained.

CHAPTER 18

ON THE LECTURE PLATFORM

MY APPEARANCE on the lecture platform happened more by accident than by design. I really didn't mean to do it. If I had been questioned about it a month before I was swept into it by an unexpected and unforeseen event, I should have expressed a very strong opinion against doing such a thing.

I was invited to speak to the Congregational Association of Maryland and the District of Columbia, which was holding a meeting in the First Congregational Church (of which President and Mrs. Coolidge were members while they occupied the White House). Contrary to a custom observed all my life when speaking in public, I used a manuscript and spoke on "The Progress of Colored Women." After the meeting Mr. Robert Nourse, a well-known lecturer who lived in Falls Church, Virginia, told me he would like to talk with me about something very important. As soon as he was free to have a private conference, he unburdened his mind. He told me he had had years of experience on the lecture platform, that he knew the material out of which a good lecturer was built when he saw and heard one, and he was certain I possessed all the qualities which would insure success. Dr. Nourse left nothing unsaid to me which one human being could say to another, so as to encourage him to undertake an enterprise or engage in a pursuit in which he had previously had no experience.

The suggestion was literally like a thunderclap out of a clear sky to me, for it had never occurred to me to go on the lecture platform. When I enumerated the obstacles which would prevent me from attempting it, Dr. Nourse waved them all aside and assured me that when I talked to my husband and my mother about it, they would do the same thing. And this they certainly did.

Judge Terrell agreed with Dr. Nourse and reminded me that through the medium of the lecture platform I would have a better chance of engaging in the work I had always wanted to do than by employing any other method. For years I had been wishing that the opportunity of creating sentiment in favor of our group would be presented to me in some way, and it seemed that going on the lecture platform would give the longed-for chance.

Some of my husband's friends, however, warned him gravely against allowing his wife to wade too deeply into public affairs. They conceded it was a great honor for me to be appointed a member of the Board of Education. But there was no telling what dire evils would result therefrom. When, however, my husband consented to let me go on the lecture platform, some of his friends were so shocked and horrified that words simply failed them as they attempted to express their disapprobation and to show him what an irreparable mistake he was making. When a woman became deeply interested in civic affairs and started on a public career, they said, that was the beginning of a disastrous end. Under such circumstances a happy home was impossible.

It is no wonder that these friends entertained such an opinion at that time. Comparatively few white women either were on the lecture platform or engaged actively in public work. But during his Harvard course my husband had been closely associated with both the men and the women who believed in woman suffrage, and he had been thoroughly converted to their point of view. He was not influenced, therefore, by the dire predictions made by the prophets of evil who tried to persuade him to confine me within the four walls of our home. In fact, it was he who encouraged, almost forced me to accept the first invitations extended to me to make public addresses. Among these was one which came from the National American Woman Suffrage Association, which asked me to speak on the Progress of Colored Women, and another from the Whittier Historical and Literary Association of Memphis, Tennessee, which wanted me to deliver an address on Harriet Beecher Stowe.

I hesitated to accept either one of them. This irritated my husband considerably. When so few colored women had been fortunate enough to complete a college course, he said, it was a shame for any of them to refuse to render any service which it was in their power to give. I used to tell him he was largely responsible for my being on the lecture platform.

An offer was made by the Slayton Lyceum Bureau which I accepted with the understanding that I would never be obliged to remain away from home longer than three weeks at a time. Mother declared that she could easily look after affairs in the home during that length of time and urged me to embrace the opportunity which had been presented to me so miraculously.

I did not have the confidence in my ability which Dr. Nourse and Judge Terrell possessed. With fear and trembling, misgivings and doubts I made the decision to appear before the public as a lecturer. "But, Dr. Nourse," I remarked one day while we were all discussing the subject in our family, "I may not be able to say anything which will either interest or enlighten the public." "Oh, never mind about that," he replied seriously. "Maybe you won't. But people never go to hear what a woman says anyhow. They simply go to see how she looks."

Mr. Charles Wagner, who was then an agent in the Slayton Lyceum Bureau, was the first to book me. From the press notices of the addresses which I had previously delivered on various occasions, he got up a very good circular for me. Neither Mr. Wagner nor any other official of the Slayton Bureau had ever seen me or heard me speak when they consented to offer me as one of their attractions for the Chautauqua that summer. So great was their confidence in Dr. Nourse's ability to "pick 'em" that they took me on his recommendation alone. It was said that up to that time the Bureau had never promised to back a speaker whom none of its officials had heard till Dr. Nourse persuaded them to try me "sight unseen," so to speak.

Mr. Charles Wagner, who has since then so successfully managed John McCormack, the famous tenor, and other celebrities, secured for me some very fine engagements at the leading Chautauquas of the West. At that time he was booking Maud Ballington Booth, William Jennings Bryan and other well-known lecturers, so that my name often appeared on the same program with theirs. On several occasions I spoke to the same audience which Tom Dixon addressed—the same Tom Dixon who wrote *The Clansman,* which, as a novel, a movie and a talkie, has done a great deal of harm. It has been an instrument of evil, appealing to race prejudice, inciting to riot and arousing the murderous passions of the mob.

I offered the Chautauquas the following four subjects: "The Progress of Colored Women," "The Bright Side of a Dark Subject," "Uncle Sam and the Sons of Ham," and "Harriet Beecher Stowe."

In my address on our women I gave specific instances of the marvelous success achieved by colored women as teachers, founders of schools and charitable institutions of different kinds, such as old folks' homes and orphan asylums. I referred to the public work done by colored women through the medium of the National Association of Colored Women and through the clubs in churches as well as in their numerous beneficial organizations.

I emphasized their intellectual and cultural advancement by citing the splendid records which colored women have made in some of the best institutions of the land. I discovered that very few white people had ever heard of Phyllis Wheatley, the African poetess, so I related a few facts about this remarkable woman whose career reads more like fiction than fact. I referred to colored women who have shown decided literary ability from time to time.

Naturally, I referred to the huge obstacles which block the colored woman's path to success in many pursuits in which she would like to engage. I always ended with an appeal to the white man's sense of justice, especially in behalf of the children and youth of the race. People interested in interracial relations felt that the address on "The Progress of Colored Women" did some good, because it opened the eyes of many to the difficulties which confronted colored women about which they had never heard before. It was also a revelation to many who had never heard about the success which colored women have achieved in certain pursuits and vocations which they have been allowed to enter.

"The Bright Side of a Dark Subject" was an appeal to consider the creditable things which colored people have accomplished and to talk about that phase of the subject instead of dwelling continually upon their backwardness, their defects and their crimes. I referred to the brilliant success achieved by colored students of Harvard University, Yale and other institutions of the North, East and West. I gave a brief résumé of the marvellous military record of colored soldiers who have fought courageously in all the wars which this country has waged. The first blood spilled for it was shed by a colored man. It was Crispus Attucks, a colored man, who first led the American soldiers against the British troops and who fought desperately for the independence of this country until he was killed. The emotions which surged through me when for the first time I beheld the statue of Crispus Attucks on the Boston Common would be hard for me to analyze and describe.

I rejoiced in the financial progress of the Colored-American and stated that while he had been storing his mind with useful knowledge he had been filling his pockets as well—for the most part filling them honestly, too.

I referred especially to the charges against the Colored-American that he is innately dishonest and proved that it is not founded in fact. From conversations which I heard in my childhood and youth I got the impression that practically all colored people would steal if they got a chance. Those who held this view declared that this tendency was easy to explain. Before the birth of their children slave women had to steal the food that appealed to their appetites when they longed for choice tidbits which they saw, but could not get, it was said. Since this went on for nearly three hundred years, this tendency to steal was inherited, near-students of the problem declared. I was wretched. I did not want to steal, but I feared that I was doomed, since it was in every colored person's blood according to the theory just set forth.

But after I went to Oberlin I ceased to worry on that score. During my college course I heard several missionaries state that in Africa theft is practically unknown, and that the natives do not learn to steal until they have come into close contact with other races. It was a great comfort to know that I would not be forced to steal, whether I wanted to or not, just because there was African blood in my veins. It was a relief to be informed that I had inherited the strictest honesty from my African forebears, and if I developed a penchant for laying heavy hands on my neighbor's property, it would be an acquired rather than an inherited taste.

In the address entitled "Uncle Sam and the Sons of Ham" I dwelt upon the Government's relation to the race. I presented some shocking facts concerning the Convict Lease System and the wholesale disfranchisement of colored people in that section where the majority live. But even in this address I took occasion to refer briefly to the progress which the race has made. No matter what my subject was, whether I talked about the odontopteris-toliapicus, or the ramphorincus philurus, I never let an opportunity of presenting facts creditable to us as a group pass. I believe it is the duty of every speaker who makes a specialty of discussing the Race Problem to emphasize the fact that in spite of almost insuperable obstacles colored people have taken long strides ahead. As soon as I was fairly launched on the lecture bureau, I decided never to crack a joke at the group's expense. Nothing displeases and disgusts me more than to hear a colored speaker relate stories or crack jokes which make his race appear ridiculous, cowardly or light-fingered. Nobody could be more fed up on the chicken and watermelon stealing jokes than I am.

The address on Harriet Beecher Stowe was truly a labor of love. I enjoyed nothing more than to deliver it to audiences who wanted to hear it. There were cordial expressions of appreciation from those who heard it. I poured out my soul when I delivered it.

The press comments which appeared in the leading papers in the places where I spoke were all that anybody could ask. There were headlines announcing my appearance and my subject and big ones after I delivered my address. I marveled at the space devoted to a résumé of my talks even when I had to compete with that. most beautiful woman and that incomparable orator, Maud Ballington Booth.

Although I was warned by some of my friends not to present certain facts showing the injustice and brutality to which colored people are sometimes subjected, for fear it would militate against my success as a speaker, I felt that I could not be true to myself or to my race, if I did not touch upon this phase of the subject. I never failed, therefore, to tell the truth about the barbarities perpetrated upon representatives of the race when I discussed the problem. For that reason the following comment upon my address pleased me greatly: "Saturday's Assembly closed with an address by the colored orator, Mary Church Terrell, of Washington, on 'The Bright Side of a Dark Subject.' She fired no pyrotechnics. She touched lightly on southern bonfires lit with living, human flesh. She only incidentally hinted at the flaying of live negroes and other holiday sports whereby the 'superior race' whiles away the festive hour. The whole discourse was lacking in all efforts at blood-curdling and blood-boiling effects."

I was glad to see that it is possible to present the facts concerning the injustice and brutality of which colored people are often the victims without being misrepresented and denounced by the press. I did not have the knack (or whatever it is) of inducing newspaper men to give me write-ups of any kind. Whatever favorable or complimentary notices were received were given me gratuitously. I was grateful, for I knew that such publicity helped a great deal.

CHAPTER 19

NOTABLE LECTURE ENGAGEMENTS

M Y EXPERIENCE in the Ford Hall meeting in Boston was something new under the sun, so it stands out conspicuously in my mind. I had been invited by Mr. George Coleman, who was then president of the organization, to address a Sunday evening meeting. I had met him and Mrs. Coleman in Atlanta, Georgia, when I delivered an address at the celebration of the twenty-fifth anniversary of Spelman Seminary, in which they were both deeply interested and which is the largest school for colored girls not only in the United States but in the whole world. John D. Rockefeller, Senior, was one of the principal patrons of the school because he had been interested in the founders and it bears the family name of his wife.

When I went to fill the Ford Hall engagement Mrs. Coleman invited some of her friends to dine with us Sunday afternoon. During the conversation at the table one of the guests asked me if I felt equal to answering all the questions the audience would ask me that night. Although I had often heard about the Sunday evening meetings which were held in Ford Hall, for some reason I did not know that people in the audience were accustomed to ask the speaker to answer questions which they wished to pose. When I learned that was the custom at that dinner table, if I had been given to fainting, I should certainly have fallen out in a fit then and there. No human being could have possibly dreaded an ordeal more than that to which I knew I should be subjected within a few hours, unless it be one condemned to be electrocuted or hanged at the expiration of that time. If I could have run away somewhere and broken the engagement without being disgraced myself and disgracing the race in the bargain, I should have done so.

But like most ordeals in this world to which we look forward with fear, it was not nearly so terrible as I had anticipated. To tell the truth, I enjoyed it immensely. Most of the questions were so simple that any colored person who had thought seriously about the problem at all could have answered them with ease.

I had not realized till then how little even intelligent white people know about conditions which confront our colored group. The experience at Ford Hall was duplicated every time I addressed a Forum audience, when the speaker was requested to answer questions which the audience propounded. It mattered not whether I spoke in Massachusetts, Rhode Island, Connecticut or New York, the questions asked were practically the same, and the evidence that those intelligent people possessed comparatively little knowledge about the race problem was equally convincing.

At every meeting, invariably somebody asked me what I thought about intermarriage of the races. That seemed to agitate the minds of the audience—particularly the men—more than anything else. "Do you think it is right or wise for white people to marry colored people?" was asked me every time I spoke and was expected to reply to questions put to me by those who heard my address. From these experiences I became convinced that many white people believe that colored men lie awake nights trying to devise ways and means of marrying white women. I was fully persuaded that this fear of the intermarriage of the races is really the root of much, if not all, of the evil encountered by those who are trying to solve the race problem according to the dictates of justice and fair play. I did my level best to convince my audiences that white people are evidently thinking more about intermarriage than colored people are.

When I was in England I had a talk with Lord Kinnaird, who was then connected with the Bank of England in an important capacity. After asking me a few questions about the relations which existed between the two races in the United States, he said rather abruptly, "I understand why there is friction between the two races in your country. It is because colored men want to marry white women and white men won't tolerate it." "But colored men marry English women," I replied. "Yes," he admitted, "they do sometimes, but the best English people object to it." Then I reminded him that only a short while before our conversation an English girl from one of the best families had married an East Indian. "He certainly is a colored man," I said. "Yes," agreed Lord Kinnaird, "but he was immensely rich. Even though he was very wealthy, there were many people in England who protested against that intermarriage. White men object to having their women marry colored men."

Before slavery was abolished, those who favored the iniquitous institution used to ask abolitionists, "Would you want your daughter to marry a nigger?" This was considered a poser both by slaveholders and their sympathizers, and when they had propounded that question they felt they had played a trump card. But after the Emancipation Proclamation was signed, there was no epidemic of intermarriage between the two races. None of the dire predictions made by the prophets of evil along this line was fulfilled.

If I were a white woman, I should vigorously resent the low estimate placed upon my judgment and good taste by the men of my group when they show plainly by the statements they make and by the laws they enact that they believe if white women were not forcibly restrained from marrying colored men, they would rush pell-mell into matrimony with dark-skinned suitors every time they got a chance. Nothing could be more ridiculous than that. It has always seemed strange to me that white women did not rise up to a woman and resent the implication that the masses of them have no better sense and no better taste than to marry men of another race who are reputed to be both inferior to their own and objectionable from every point of view.

It also became clear to me from the information gained by addressing Forums in New England that many northern white people know practically nothing about the wholesale disfranchisement of colored citizens in the South. Whenever I made a reference to this condition in my speech, the questions showed that many of my auditors either had never heard of it or doubted that it was true, if they had.

A conversation with several young Bostonians who were Harvard graduates well illustrates this point. The daughter of Thomas Wentworth Higginson invited me to dine at her home one evening when I had spoken in Boston, and among the guests were two fine young men. One of them remarked casually that he would like very much to go to Congress. But, he said, in addition to the red tape and trouble it would involve, it would cost a great deal of money to gratify this ambition. Jokingly, I told him I could give him a recipe for getting into Congress with very little trouble and at comparatively little expense.

"All you have to do," I said, "is to go to Mississippi, for instance, become a citizen of the State, advertise yourself as an honest-to-goodness Democrat, then announce yourself as a candidate for Congress. And, presto, you will be elected and rushed off to Washington so fast, it will make your head swim. You will need only a few votes, comparatively speaking. The Democratic candidate always wins in the South. Not long ago John Sharp Williams, for instance, was sent by Mississippi to the Senate on only a couple of thousand votes. If he had lived in Illinois or Massachusetts, he would have had to poll many thousand ballots to get to Congress."

When he asked me to explain what I meant and I informed him he would need only a few thousand votes to get elected to Congress from Mississippi, because colored men were disfranchised in that State, he did not believe me. "What has become of the fourteenth amendment?" he asked with a fine show of indignation. When I told him that the fourteenth amendment had been null and void, not only in Mississippi, but in the other southern States for years, he replied, "Walk softly, Mrs. Terrell, walk softly, when you declare that an amendment to the Constitution is so flagrantly violated as you claim it is." Even after I gave him definite facts and figures, showing that the vote of one man in certain southern States counts for as much as does that of 8, 10, or even 12 men in some northern States during a national election, he showed plainly that he thought I was either greatly exaggerating the facts or was not telling the truth.

While I was filling lecture engagements, incident after incident occurred to prove to me conclusively that there are thousands upon thousands of good citizens in the North, East and West who have no idea how flagrantly in a large section of the country the law is violated which confers upon colored men and women the right of citizenship, and who know practically nothing about the unfortunate and deplorable conditions under which colored people are obliged to live in some parts of the United States.

A striking illustration of this fact occurred while I was addressing the Baptist Women's Missionary Society in Beverly, Massachusetts. I had been invited to speak on the Progress and Problems of Colored Women. During this talk I referred to the Convict Lease System, stating that colored women have often been placed in dark, damp, disease-breeding cells, whose cubic contents are less than those of a good-sized grave, and that they had given birth to children who had breathed the polluted atmosphere of those dens of vice and woe from the moment they had uttered their first cry into the world until they had been relieved from their suffering by death.

Mrs. George W. Coleman, the president of the Association, interrupted me to ask me to explain what I meant by the Convict Lease System. I told Mrs. Coleman that I had only a half hour in which to discuss the big subject assigned me and that there were so many things I wanted the audience to know that I wouldn't be able to describe the Convict Lease System. "Wait a minute," said the president stepping to the front of the platform. "How many in this audience," she asked, "know anything about the Convict Lease System to which the speaker has just referred? If anybody knows anything about it please raise your hand. I won't ask you to give us any information, but I should like to see how many in this audience think they know anything about the Convict Lease System."

Not a hand was raised, although this audience was largely composed of women who had graduated from some of the best institutions of New England. After waiting a second or two, the president of the Association turned to me and said, "We'll extend your time ten minutes if you will tell us as much about the Convict Lease System as you can in that length of time." This was another revelation to me about the limited knowledge possessed by many white people who are not only well educated, but who are working to promote the welfare of less favored people and who for that reason would be supposed to have some information about the abominable conditions in their own country.

One of the most delightful experiences on the lecture platform I ever had was an engagement in Rochester, New York, made for me by Susan B. Anthony, to which I have already referred. I was invited to speak for the Political Equality Club, of which Miss Anthony was a member, and was entertained in her home. Mary Anthony took charge of the household affairs and relieved her famous sister of many burdens which she would otherwise have had to bear. It was a joy to spend several days in this well-managed household in which every thing moved like clock work and which was presided over by one of the greatest women whom this or any other country has ever produced.

When, as a young woman in college, I had read about Susan B. Anthony and had allied myself to her very unpopular cause, I little dreamed that Fate would ever be kind enough so to order my life as to cause her to invite me to be a guest in her home. During my visit Miss Anthony tendered me a reception at which I met many of her personal friends. She was genuinely interested in my efforts on the lecture platform and encouraged me in every way.

An honor which I greatly appreciated was an invitation to represent Frederick Douglass at the sixtieth anniversary celebration of the first Woman's Rights Convention in the history of the world, which was held in Seneca Falls, New York, in 1848. The pioneers in the cause were represented by members of their respective families on May 27, 1908. Harriet Stanton Blatch represented her mother, Elizabeth Cady Stanton, who worked so hard and so faithfully with Miss Anthony to convert the public to their righteous cause. Mrs. Henry Villard, the daughter of the great abolitionist, William Lloyd Garrison, represented Lucretia Mott. Mrs. Eliza Wright Osborne, the daughter of Martha Wright, one of the four promoters of the original Woman's Rights Convention, could not be present, but her paper was read by a friend. Mrs. Alice Hooker Day, the daughter of Isabella Hooker and the niece of Harriet Beecher Stowe, related the efforts made by her father and mother to secure suffrage for women by petitioning the legislature of Connecticut to give them the ballot, for which they were severely criticized.

It was a great privilege to be invited to represent Frederick Douglass in a company like that. And there is certainly a very good reason why Frederick Douglass should always be represented at an anniversary celebration which woman suffragists hold. When Elizabeth Cady Stanton presented a resolution demanding equal political rights for women at that Seneca Falls meeting in 1848, the members of the convention could not have been more shocked at her temerity than if she had thrown a bomb into their midst. Her friends rushed to her and begged her to withdraw it. Even dear, brave Lucretia Mott, who for years so courageously championed the cause of woman suffrage, implored Mrs. Stanton not to present the resolution. "Elizabeth," she plead, "thee will make us all ridiculous, if thee insist upon pressing this resolution through the meeting."

But Mrs. Stanton did insist upon demanding equal political equality for her sex just the same. The resolution was in imminent danger of defeat, because there was not a man or a woman in the convention willing to second it. But there was present at that meeting a single, solitary man through whose veins the blood of Africa flowed. He was the incomparable Frederick Douglass, a run away slave, upon whose head his former master had set a price. It was he who arose and seconded Mrs. Stanton's resolution. And it was largely due to Frederick Douglass' masterful arguments and matchless eloquence that the resolution passed in spite of the determined opposition of its powerful foes.

In addition to representing Frederick Douglass on this memorable occasion I was invited to speak at the unveiling of a bronze tablet which was placed on the wall of the opera house now occupying the site on which stood the Methodist Church in which the first Woman Suffrage Convention was held. This tablet shows in relief the figure of a woman supporting a shield on which was inscribed "On this spot stood the Wesleyan Chapel where the first Woman's Rights Convention in the world's history was held July 19 and 20, 1848." Elizabeth Cady Stanton moved this resolution, which was seconded by Frederick Douglass: "That it is the duty of the women of this country to secure to themselves their sacred right to the elective franchise."

Therefore, whenever the women of this country pause long enough to think about the hard fight which had to be waged so as to enable them to enjoy their rights as citizens in this Republic, they should remember the great debt of gratitude they owe a colored man for the courage he displayed on a crucial occasion in their behalf, when no other man was willing to come to their aid.

In the book containing the addresses made at this sixtieth anniversary celebration which was published by the Seneca Falls Historical Society my address on Woman Suffrage and the one on Frederick Douglass are included.

On that occasion I was entertained by Mrs. Elizabeth Smith Miller, the daughter of Gerritt Smith, the noted abolitionist. Mrs. Miller and her daughter together with seven servants lived in an elegant country estate consisting of broad, green acres not far from Geneva, New York, and they related many interesting facts about Gerritt Smith.

Few addresses I have delivered received more publicity than the second one I made for the American Missionary Society at an annual meeting held in Cleveland, Ohio. In my address entitled "The Strongest for the Weakest" I emphasized the fact that the North was losing interest in the Colored American and leaving him to get along the best he could. I accounted for this lack of interest by referring to the pernicious propaganda which had been waged against him for a long time and which had poisoned the mind of the North. "By a continual exaggeration of the colored man's vices," I said, "by a studied suppression of the proofs of his marvellous advancement, by a malicious use of epithets, such as the scarecrow of social equality, the bugaboo of Negro domination and others which mislead and poison the public mind, the North has been persuaded by the colored man's detractors that they are martyrs and that he is a brute."

I referred to the colored man's progress along all lines and declared that he had even transcended the expectations of his best friends, but that in spite of this fact the interest once manifested in the colored man by the North was growing painfully less and that I sometimes feared it was reaching the vanishing point as fast as it could.

There were many strong comments on this speech made by the newspapers of the North. Justice Brewer, who was then a member of the United States Supreme Court, presided at the meeting the morning I spoke and in the afternoon he referred to my speech and made a stirring appeal for justice to the Colored-American. "Many of the vast multitudes pouring into this country are racially cold-blooded and selfish," he said. "Not a few come tainted with anarchy and are willing to destroy all social order in the hope of personal gain out of the wreck.

[171]

Colored people are firm believers in the social order," he said. "You will find no Johann Most, Emma Goldman, Czolgosz or Guiteau among them. In the struggle which may be expected to come between order and anarchy may it not be that these people grateful to the nation for their liberty and to the good people of the land for their uplift in knowledge, purity and social standing prove themselves a mighty force, upholding law, order and the supremacy of the nation? Stranger things have happened than that these people crushed and wronged for generations should become at last strong defenders of the nation and the community at whose hands they have hitherto received mainly injustice." There were many who believed that Justice Brewer's remarks in the afternoon had greatly heightened the effect of the appeal for justice that had been made at the morning session.

One morning the door bell rang, and I was informed that General Tremain of New York City wished to see me. For years General Tremain, who had an honorable record in the War of the Rebellion, had been deeply interested in the Race Problem and had taken a definite stand in behalf of justice and opportunity for the struggling race. He had come to Washington to invite me to speak at a mass meeting to be held in Cooper Union and he wanted me to talk on "Lynching," allotting me half an hour. Although there was only a short time in which to prepare my address and General Tremain told me some of the most distinguished men in the country would appear, I screwed my courage to the sticking point and accepted the invitation.

Every opportunity to address schools, colleges or universities was eagerly seized. I believed then as I do now that the only way to "solve the problem" is to appeal to the sense of justice in the white youth of the United States. This view came to me forcibly and suddenly as the result of an experience that I had in the middle West.

I had been invited to address the National Purity Congress which met in LaCrosse, Wisconsin, and some engagements had been made for me en route so as to help defray my expenses there. One of these was in Milwaukee, and I arrived there a little before noon. Just as soon as I left the train a little woman approached me and said, "This is Mrs. Terrell, isn't it?" I agreed with her on the point. "Well, Mrs. Terrell," said she,

"I have come to take you to address the pupils of the Normal School here. We shall have to hurry a bit for they will assemble at one o'clock."

I was speechless with surprise, and a kind of stage fright took possession of me. I told the principal that as much as I should like to comply with her request it was impossible for me to do so, because I was so tired from traveling and speaking, had to fill an engagement in Milwaukee that night and felt that duty both to myself and to my audience demanded that I should go to my stopping place and rest till it was time to deliver my address. I explained also that I was not accustomed to addressing audiences composed exclusively of young people and feared that I could not interest them. But she was a typical western woman, determined and bound to have her way. She would not take No for an answer. "The very idea of your telling me you cannot address my pupils," she remonstrated, "when they have all been assembled from different sections of the city and are expecting you to talk to them!" I was completely subdued. There was no such thing as refusing to do what she had planned. "I should like to refresh myself and change my dress," I pleaded meekly. But she told me positively that there was not time enough for me to do that and I looked well enough. There was nothing to do but surrender again to that personification of determination. "Please be kind enough not to talk to me," I begged. "While we are on the street car going to the building, I'll try to think what I had better say on the Race Problem to a group of young white people who know very little about it, I assume." As I rode along to this engagement which I dreaded more than any I had ever filled before, it occurred to me that the best thing for me to do would be to relate briefly to the pupils the progress which colored people have made—particularly the women—and then appeal to their sense of justice.

As I concluded my talk to about four hundred of these Normal School pupils, I told them I was not asking them to embrace a colored person every time they saw one. "You may have an insuperable aversion to people whose skins are dark. If that is true," I declared, "I do not blame you at all. I pity you. It is your misfortune, not your fault, to dislike human beings whom our Creator has made, simply because their complexion is darker than yours. But even though you may dislike to be near a swarthy individual, you can be just to him and treat him like a human being and give him a chance." I told them that there are thousands of colored boys and girls who have good minds and whose aspirations are high, but who have to knock their heads against a stone wall of race prejudice every time they try to enter certain trades and occupations and professions from which they are barred solely on account of their race and color, although they are fitted by native ability and training to engage in them as well as the youth of other races. I implored them to decide then and there that when they grew to be men and women they would throw the weight of their influence on the side of justice, opportunity of all kinds and fair play in behalf of their brothers and sisters of a darker hue.

Letters which came to me later from some of the pupils of that Normal School proved conclusively that the lesson I tried to teach had been well learned. Some of them wrote me that they had never thought about the difficulties which confront colored boys and girls in their effort to earn a living. But since they realized what a hard row they had to hoe, they pledged themselves to do everything in their power to remove these disabilities and improve conditions for their handicapped brothers and sisters when they grew to manhood and womanhood. Having discovered that it was possible to interest white youth in the Race Problem, thereafter I accepted every invitation to address pupils in the public schools, or students in colleges and universities, which was received.

Oberlin College, my alma mater, invited me to deliver the Thursday lecture. It happened, however, that I did not speak Thursday, the day of the week on which lectures to students were generally delivered, but on Wednesday. This caused Professor Charles Martin, one of the professors who had known me well in my youth, to remark facetiously that "Mollie Church was the only person in the world who could deliver a Thursday lecture on Wednesday."

The impression which my talk made on some surprised me greatly. The dean of women, Mrs. A. A. F. Johnston, who had been very fond of me while I was a student and who had written the letter inviting me to become registrar, expressed deep regret that her former pupil had grown so "bitter." I had presented practically the same facts in about the same way to audiences in many southern cities in which there was usually a fair sprinkling of white people, and never once did a white southerner suggest that he took exception to anything I said and not one of them gave me any reason to believe he thought I was bitter. On the contrary, some of the finest commendations I have received as a public speaker have come unsolicited from white southerners, and I have made it a rule to which there has never been an exception to use the same arguments in the South and in the same way that I do in the North.

Mr. J. W. Spencer, who was president of the Farmers and Mechanics Bank of Fort Worth, Texas, urged me to talk to the white people of the South and declared he thought it was my duty to do so. He had heard me speak to my own group and felt that the points I made would give white people something to think about. When I stated that I feared the white people of the South would not give me an opportunity of talking to them about the Race Problem, he cheerfully promised to do everything he could to make it possible. Entirely unsolicited he sent me a letter of commendation which ended by saying that my lecture was "wholly devoid of bitterness."

After the same speech delivered at Fort Worth was pronounced "bitter" by a northern woman, my eyes were opened to a fact which I had never known before. Colored people so seldom tell certain truths about conditions which confront their race that, when they do, even white people who are interested in them feel that they must be "bitter." In this case truth is confounded with bitterness.

Nothing delighted my heart more than to receive invitations to deliver addresses in the South. The response from my own group in that section was always cordial and the satisfaction of trying to inspire young and old was great. Without exception the white people who came to hear me acknowledged that I presented nothing but facts, although some of them were frank enough to admit they did not derive any great amount of pleasure from hearing them. They agreed, however, that the disagreeable facts should be told in an effort to remedy some of the evils which are a blight upon this country and a disgrace.

Many amusing incidents occurred during my tours in the South, but none surpassed this one which happened in a small town in Texas. The address was delivered in the Court House and the white janitor elected to come to hear me. Custom and tradition in that section demand that there shall be a definite and distinct separation of the races at a public meeting. This problem was easily solved by the janitor. He sat on the platform in the seat of honor, while the distinguished colored people of the town who had invited me to speak sat humbly at his feet in the audience.

During that same lecture tour I had a memorable experience indeed, while I was riding on a Jim Crow car. I am sure the conductor thought I was a prisoner being taken to a Convict Lease Camp or to some other place to be incarcerated. A sheriff had brought a group of prisoners into this car and gave a bunch of tickets to the conductor. I sat in a seat in front of the prisoners. The conductor looked at me, evidently took it for granted that I belonged to the crowd in charge of the sheriff and passed by without asking me for my railroad ticket. For a long time I preserved that ticket as a rare souvenir of an experience which is guaranteed to give a thrill that comes only once in a life time.

My engagement at Wellesley was delightful, and one of the teachers wrote me it was productive of much good. I was assigned a room in the dormitory which was occupied by a senior from Mississippi. She had requested that she be allowed to show me this hospitality. She greeted me most cordially when I arrived, showed me where I could find the articles which she thought I might need, and expressed genuine pleasure that she had the "honor" of entertaining me in her room.

The occasion on which I accepted an invitation extended me by the Principal of the Randolph-Macon Institute for girls in Danville, Virginia, stands out distinctly in my mind. I spoke to the pupils at a morning session, feeling that it was a rare opportunity to present to the girls from the best families of the South the subject in which I wished to interest them in their youth. They listened with close attention, and, while I was speaking, behaved exactly as they would have done if a woman of their own group were addressing them. Then something happened which had not been prepared for the program. When the school sang at the close of the exercises, the principal stepped to my side, offered me his hymn book and we sang out of it together. Some of the small girls who sat in the front seat tried hard to conceal their surprise, but in spite of their fine self-control, I could easily see they were shocked.

I believe that if certain facts were presented to the young white men and women in the various universities and colleges of the country, the status of colored people in the next thirty or forty years would be greatly improved. Both Mr. Moorfield Storey and Mr. John Milholland agreed with me on this point and opened up opportunities for me to render this service whenever they could. Because I believed that if young white people were enlightened concerning the struggles which colored people are making to forge ahead—particularly the women—they would be more interested in them and more willing to work for their welfare, I sent a year's subscription of the *Crisis*, the official organ of the National Association for the Advancement of Colored People, to Bryn Mawr, Mount Holyoke, Smith, Vassar and Wellesley Colleges. Letters from all the librarians expressed appreciation. They all thought it was a good thing to have the *Crisis* in the magazine room with the other periodicals. One of them regretted that the college could not subscribe for it another year, stated that they had enjoyed having it on their shelves and would like to have the subscription continued.

I met Mr. Francis Garrison at Houghton Mifflin's Publishing House in Boston, where he was an important official for many years. It was largely through the influence of this son of William Lloyd Garrison that I was invited to address the students of Radcliffe College. He was very much pleased when I told him I had read every word of the four thick volumes about the life of his father which are entitled *The Story of His Life Told by His Children*. "You are the first person I have ever met who had done so," he said. Perhaps that is the reason he invited me to dine with him and to spend the night in his home in Lexington, Massachusetts, a few miles from Boston, where I met Mrs. Garrison and their young son.

Mrs. Henry Villard, the daughter of the great abolitionist, honored me with her friendship and was a patron at a meeting in New York City given under the auspices of the National Association for the Advancement of Colored People and wrote a letter of commendation which is highly prized.

Mr. Moorfield Storey, who was president of the National Association for the Advancement of Colored People till he passed away, secured for me the opportunity of addressing the girls in the English High School in Boston.

Dean Briggs came to hear me when I talked at Radcliffe College and wrote Mr. Francis Garrison a letter about the impression I made upon the young women.

Professor Jenks of Cornell University invited me to address the students of the Sociological Department, of which he was head. I referred to the record of the colored soldiers. One of the young men was so impressed with the service they have rendered their country he decided to take their record as the subject of his thesis.

At a tea given for me by Mrs. Andrew D. White, wife of the former Ambassador to Germany, who was once president of Cornell University, I met some very interesting women of the "university set." I was also invited to meet the young women of Sage College and had an informal tea with them. The pastor of the Ithaca Unitarian Church asked me to speak at the Sunday morning service and felt that the message delivered did the cause I represented some good.

The girls at Mount Holyoke seemed deeply interested in the struggle colored girls were making to reach high standards and showed by the questions which some of them asked that they had studied the subject seriously.

The invitation extended me by the Liberal Club of Harvard stands out very distinctly in my public career as a speaker, because it is the only one ever given me by a group composed exclusively of college men. It was a glorious opportunity to tell the plain, unvarnished truth and to call a spade a spade in the presence of broad-minded young men who were open to conviction and among whom one felt that making a plea for a less favored and proscribed group would be energy and time well spent.

It was customary for the Liberal Club to invite a speaker to take lunch with its members, who sit eight at a table, and then, after a certain time has elapsed, to ask him or her to begin the talk. The young men enter the dining room and leave, when they have finished their lunch, if they must, while the guest is speaking. When the time allotted for the talk has expired, the young men ask questions. It was then that I felt a long-wished-for chance to sow seeds had arrived, and I hope they fell into good ground.

The Women's Henry George League of New York City once invited me to deliver an address on Lincoln's Birthday. I spoke in Brooklyn when the eighty-fifth birthday of Susan B. Anthony was celebrated.

Fisk University in Nashville, Tennessee, paid me the compliment of allowing me to be the first woman Commencement speaker in the history of that splendid institution. Since then I have delivered many Commencement addresses, for I always accept them cheerfully when an invitation is extended. It gives me a new lease on life to visit the universities and colleges attended by our youth, where I see the aspiring young men and women of a handicapped race striving to cultivate their minds and develop their characters, so as to equip themselves for their life work as well as they can. It renews both my faith and my hope to see how conscientiously and strenuously the teachers work to encourage their students to reach the highest standards which they can attain. The teachers of colored youth in the South are obliged to work for a small salary, as a rule, and they deserve unstinted praise for the invaluable service they render their race.

The opportunities to speak to the pupils and students in our schools from the primary grade on up were always hailed with delight. I am glad Howard University is located in the city in which I live. I have often been invited by the presidents and other officials of that institution to address the students. My husband was a professor in the law school. I have kept in close touch with it and have been personally acquainted with the presidents for nearly fifty years; I have watched its gratifying development and growth with the keenest interest and joy. In fact, I was once a member of the Howard University faculty. For I was appointed to teach conversational French to the students who might be called to go to France in the first World War.

Some of the happiest recollections of my life are centered around the occasions on which I delivered addresses for the State Federations of the National Association of Colored Women, where I met wide-awake progressive women who were striving to accomplish something worth while. In many cases they were trying to raise money to establish or maintain something which would contribute to the uplift of their group.

For two seasons I addressed the Brooklyn Institute of Arts and Sciences in Brooklyn, New York. I spoke in the afternoon, and my audiences were never large. The following letter dated December 20, 1911, from the director, Franklin W. Hooper, gives such a clear and such an unusual statement of the public's attitude toward lectures that I shall quote it in full.

"My Dear Mrs. Terrell:

"On behalf of the Board of Trustees and Council of the Institute I thank you most heartily for your series of five lectures on the 'Negro in the United States.' The subject matter of these lectures, I am assured by my officers and members of the Institute, has been excellent and the matter admirably presented.

"I regret exceedingly that I was not able to hear any part of any of your lectures. I needed to hear them. The lectures deserved to have a very large attendance. I believe the attendance should have been larger because of their great value. We have to take into account, however, that the great body of people in any community go to hear lectures only on those subjects in which they are especially interested, or go to hear lectures from which they derive personal benefit or enjoyment. In other words, people do not go to lectures in order that they may help along a good cause, or in order that they may find what they themselves ought to do in the interest of a good cause. We can give a lecture on Goethe's Faust and have a thousand come to hear it, although they may have been hearing lectures on Faust, reading Faust, seeing the play and hearing the opera for a quarter of a century. All this is well, but I fear this continual hearing of lectures, witnessing the drama and hearing the opera contains an element of selfishness among the well-to-do. We none of us have any right to spend our time and money in a selfish way, but only in the interest of the public good. We are glad to have the opportunity to offer lectures such as those that have been given by you, because they are a protest against the selfishness and indulgence to be found in members of any community. Personally, also, I thank you for coming to us. It has been a privilege to make your acquaintance and I trust we may have you with us in future years.

"Very sincerely yours,

"FRANKLIN W. HOOPER."

That wish was gratified, for the next year I was invited to deliver three lectures on the "Race Problem" and accepted. The audiences did not increase in size, but the spirit in which my views were received compensated for the small number which came to hear me.

The Sunday I spoke at the morning service of the Ethical Culture Society in New York City a large crowd greeted me. Later on Dr. Felix Adler, its leading spirit, took the pains to write me a letter to tell me he agreed with my opinion on the Race Problem, commended my manner of expressing it and believed I had made a distinct contribution to its solution.

At a meeting of the National Negro Conference which was held in the Berkely Theater in New York I spoke one evening with three distinguished men—Professor Albert Bushnell Hart of Harvard University, Professor Boas of Columbia University, and a Mr. Crosby, a graduate of West Point, a southern aristocrat, as colored people call his type. The subject of my address was "The Effect of the Disfranchisement of Colored Men upon Colored Women in the South." Naturally, I traced a great many disadvantages under which colored women labor in that section to the inability of their men to protect them and their families by means of the ballot.

Mr. Crosby told the audience that white men in the South would receive colored men on terms of equality, if they would only let their women alone. This was hotly resented by some of the colored men, who referred to the manner in which their women had been treated by white men for nearly three hundred years and who declared they would marry whom they pleased.

Several nights before that gathering the late Clarence Darrow delivered one of the strongest appeals for justice to colored people that I have ever heard. It was too strong for some who were considered quite broad on the subject.

The National Afro-American Council appointed me Director of the Anti-Lynching Bureau. A great mass meeting was held at Cooper Union at its ninth annual session to discuss lynching and its remedy and I was invited to speak on that subject. After I reached New York and learned that I had to appear on the program with such men as Honorable John Milholland, ex-Governor Pinchback, Honorable J. C. Napier, once Register of the Treasury, and others I went to that meeting with my heart in my mouth.

Shortly after Susan B. Anthony died, a meeting was held in the Hudson Theater in honor of her memory and I was asked to come to New York to express the appreciation and gratitude of colored people for the services she had rendered as an abolitionist in their behalf. At a time when Miss Anthony was working hard for the enfranchisement of women, she stopped in the midst of her efforts to promote this movement, so that she might labor for the emancipation of slaves.

Dr. C. H. Parkhurst, pastor of the Madison Avenue Presbyterian Church, invited me to speak for him soon after there had been a disturbance between white and colored people in New York in which several colored people had been injured. While I was talking one of the colored men who had been a victim of the interracial strife walked in with his head bandaged. It was a striking object lesson of the conditions which sometimes obtain in the North. A short time before I filled this engagement at his church Dr. Parkhurst had created quite a sensation in New York by exposing the vice of the city. He had gone to some of the notorious resorts himself and had entered into the activities, so as to secure the desired information first hand.

There was a great reunion of Oberlin Alumni at the sixty-seventh annual Commencement of the college, which was held in June, 1900, and I took part in the program. The exercises were held in a tent and the following account of what happened when I finished speaking appeared in the *Oberlin News*: "Her classmates perched upon the elevated seats at the west end of the tent gave the salute 'What's the matter with Mollie Church?' with the usual changes." My classmates thus gave indisputable proof of the fact that their attitude on the race question had not changed since they had gone out into the cold world. They received me with the same warmth and heartiness that they would have given one of their own group.

Whenever I appeared before the Colored State Teachers Associations, notably those of Kentucky and Tennessee, I felt that I was meeting some of the real heroes and heroines of our group. The duties and responsibilities which confront a large number of them living in the South are truly staggering, and they are meeting them exceedingly well.

The Twentieth Century Club of Boston invited me to speak on "The Colored People of Washington." I was introduced by Mr. Robert Treat Paine, a descendant of one of the signers of the Declaration of Independence. I told the Twentieth Century Club of Pittsburgh about conditions which confront colored women and I used the same subject when I appeared before the Calhoun Club of Boston. I talked to the Woman's Club of Fall River, Massachusetts, about Harriet Beecher Stowe. The invitation was extended by one of my college friends, Mrs. Clarence Swift, wife of the pastor of the Central Congregational Church, whom I knew in the Oberlin public schools. After a friendship of fifty years, Mrs. Swift has recently helped me in several important matters which concerned me greatly by her good judgment, active cooperation, sympathetic interest and excellent advice.

I was seldom misrepresented, unduly criticized or ridiculed by the press, although I did not always escape. A report of the speech which I delivered before the International Purity Congress, which held a meeting at Battle Creek, Michigan, was full of wild, sweeping statements about the colored domestic problem in the South which it never occurred to me to make. In great headlines some of the newspapers announced that I had delivered a "Bitter, Furious Invective against the People of the South." In fact this interpretation of my speech was sent by the Associated Press and appeared in nearly every newspaper in the United States.

"White Women of the South Raked by Colored Woman. Southerners Denounced. Colored Girls Their Prey. So says Purity Congress Speaker Arraigning White Men. Grows Bitter against South. No Colored Servant Girl Safe in White Family, Says Mrs. Terrell."

It is significant that no newspaper in Battle Creek attributed such statements to me. I have never made wild, sweeping statements about any phase of the Race Problem and have never delivered a "bitter, furious invective against the people of the South." My mission on the lecture platform has been to tell the truth and to appeal to the sense of justice of broad-minded, generous-hearted people of the country, both North and South, not to disseminate falsehoods, nor to stir up dissension and strife. I have had common sense enough to know that there is no better way of hurting a good cause than by indulging in wholesale abuse, or making blanket accusations against any race, class or group.

Through the press I denied that I had ever made the statements attributed to me. Many of the southern newspapers published my reply. Not only did the Charleston, South Carolina, *News and Courier* publish it on the editorial page, but the editor called special attention to it by a kindly reference.

Not a few colored people publicly disapproved of my Battle Creek speech. Among this number were some clergymen who were attending the Tennessee Conference of the A. M. E. Church at Nashville. Those who gave interviews to the press disagreed with me in toto, if I had been correctly reported, but some of them were charitable enough to refrain from condemning me, until they knew just exactly what I had said.

Considerable dissatisfaction was also expressed by a few colored people in Washington about certain statements I made in the speech before the American Missionary Association in Cleveland, Ohio. In the main, however, representatives of my group agreed with my views, and urged me to continue to express them, whenever I had a chance.

Sometimes I am asked what was the largest sum for an address which I ever received. I usually reply "about $400." It is interesting to watch the look of incredulity which spreads over the inquirer's face. After allowing that statement to sink into his consciousness for a second, I explain by saying that the Woman's Congress of Missions invited me to represent colored women at a meeting which they held at San Francisco during the Panama-Pacific Exposition in 1915, and it cost them that much to transport me bag and baggage from the Atlantic to the Pacific and return and pay all the other expenses incident to a long jaunt across the continent twice.

[184]

For the first time in my life I was referred to as an "alien" by the chairman who introduced me at the San Francisco meeting. I had never thought of myself as an "alien," and I was greatly shocked and pained. As I arose to speak, I remarked that even if I were technically an alien in the United States, I certainly did not feel like one. It occurred to me afterwards that everybody in this country is an alien except the Indians.

Because I accepted the invitation to address the Woman's Congress of Missions in San Francisco I was unable to be present at the Commencement of St. Johnsbury Academy in Vermont when my daughter, Phyllis, graduated.

Doubtless, some believed I was fairly coining money on the lecture platform. The truth of the matter is that I made very little compared with what I might have earned. The lecture bureau paid me $25 a lecture and all expenses as a rule. When I started, however, I received only $15. Once I received $100 for delivering three lectures at the same Chautauqua, speaking in the morning, in the afternoon and the next evening.

Sometimes I was compensated when I spoke for my own group and sometimes I was not. On one occasion after I had taken a long journey to reach the town in which I was to speak, the man who had engaged me handed me $3, saying that was all he had. The railroad fare alone had cost me $20. But when a colored woman's club invited me to speak for it and agreed to pay me a certain sum, I was always certain that the members would fulfill their contract to the letter. And seldom was I disappointed.

I was not on the lecture platform to make money, but to create sentiment in behalf of my race and to acquaint the public with facts which it did not know then and does not know today. I needed money, of course, and was glad to get it, but I never decided to accept or to refuse a date solely on account of the compensation I would receive. I discovered, however, very early in my lecture career that when I promised to speak for nothing the audience was invariably small. Nobody felt any particular responsibility about working the meeting up. It was poorly advertised, as a rule, so few people came. If I wanted to have an audience it was clear I would have to charge something for my services, no matter how little. On more than one occasion the admittance fee to my lecture was only ten cents.

There is no doubt whatever that if I had talked about the shortcomings, vices and defects of the race more than I did; if I had advised my group to think of nothing but their duties and let their rights take care of themselves; if I had urged them to fasten their eyes upon the ground and never lift them up to the ethereal blue of the Heavens, I would have made much more money on the lecture platform than I did. Also, if I had played the clown, and talked "natural," as one manager advised me to do, my bank account today would be much bigger than it is.

It is impossible for me to decide which were the most notable engagements I filled during the time I was on the lecture platform, which covered a period of thirty years. Nor can I tell which addresses delivered for organizations formed for widely different purposes by people of different nationalities enabled me to deal the most effective blows in behalf of the cause I tried so hard to advance.

Because I practically never used a manuscript when I delivered an address, many thought I spoke extemporaneously. But this was not the case, and I attempted to disabuse people's minds of this impression. As a rule, I decided not only what arguments I would make and what facts I would present, but I spent considerable time choosing the language in which my thought should be couched. I took myself very seriously indeed as a public speaker. It always amazed me to hear an individual who had been especially invited to address an audience say nonchalantly, as he arose, "I don't know what I shall talk about tonight. I haven't decided what my subject shall be. Perhaps I had better talk about this"—naming the theme he had chosen. I always felt that either the speaker had prepared himself and wished the audience to believe he was such a genius that he could make a fine speech without doing so, or, that he had done the people who came to hear him a great injustice, if he had not.

I had many experiences while traveling which seem amusing now, but which did not appear funny at the time they occurred. Once when I was to deliver a commencement address at a college in North Carolina I forgot to bring with me a white silk slip which had to be worn under a white net dress. I had brought no other which was suitable for the occasion. Fortunately I discovered my mistake in the morning several hours before I spoke in the afternoon. I told my tale of woe to one of the teachers, who scurried around, found a slip which could be used, fitted it to me around the waist and thus a near tragedy was prevented.

On another occasion when I went to put on a dress I found the hooks and eyes had been sewed on the wrong side. When it was the style to wear puffs I used sometimes to lose them on the train. The first time this happened I was panic stricken, for the lost puffs were absolutely essential to my coiffure. A friend to whom I told my dilemma suggested that she had seen puffs in the 5 and 10-cent store. She did not know whether I would be willing to use them, or whether I could find the proper shade, but she would take me to the store if I wanted to go. Of course I wanted to go! I went and found just the shade I needed. After that, losing puffs on the train had no terrors for me at all. Although I did not use a manuscript when I spoke, I always carried my speeches with me when I had three or four engagements to fill. It was well for me that I did not have to depend upon them, for several times I have left them behind and they have been gone a whole week.

I left Washington one morning in March to go to New York to address the West Side Branch of the Y. M. C. A. with only twenty-five cents in my purse. Judge Terrell sent his clerk to the train to give me some money, but the clerk was late and I had to leave without it. On the train I bought a sandwich for ten cents, paid five cents car fare to cross Twenty-third street, got a transfer to go to the hotel and spent the remaining ten cents for a sandwich and a cup of coffee. But when I reached the hotel I found a telegram from my husband saying he had sent me the money by special delivery and it reached me that night at 9.30.

One of the most thrilling experiences of my life occurred comparatively recently. I had been invited to deliver an address at Greenwich, Connecticut, to commemorate the signing of the Emancipation Proclamation, and had gone to Boston afterwards. I registered at a hotel and retired. Suddenly I woke out of a deep sleep and thought I heard somebody in the room. I tried to make myself believe that I was not fully awake and that I was mistaken. But I heard a human being breathing in the dark room. There was no doubt about that. I knew I had locked the door before I jumped into bed. I tried not to breathe and decided to be as quiet as I could. It occurred to me that I was in the end room on the fifth floor. If I screamed, nobody would hear me on the street, even though the window was open. Nobody could hear me across the hall and it was not likely anybody would hear me in the next room. Besides, I was sure I would be choked if I dared to scream.

After waiting what seemed to be an interminable time I said as calmly as I could—"Who is in this room?" Immediately the light was switched on near the door and I saw a young white man standing there looking at me. "Why did you come into this room?" I asked. "Please leave." For a second or two the man stood perfectly still looking at me without saying a word. Then he opened the door and left. I called up the clerk as soon as I could muster courage enough to go to the phone and I told him what had happened. He said that it was 2:30 and that he would investigate the matter immediately. It was impossible to go to sleep again.

The next day, after repeated efforts, I saw the proprietor of the hotel and related my nerve-racking experience to him. He said he knew exactly who the young man was who had entered the room. He was one of a set of twins. The two young men drank heavily and became intoxicated occasionally. They had been in the habit of putting up at the hotel, he said, and presumably kept the keys to several rooms. The young man whom I saw had probably stayed there recently, had kept the key to the room, thought nobody was occupying it, was half intoxicated and entered it. He had given the strictest orders that the young men should never be accommodated at his hotel again, he said.

It has always been a mystery to me how it was possible for the young man to enter my room by unlocking the door, since I had locked it on the inside, had turned the night latch above it and the key was still in the keyhole on the inside. But I had to accept the proprietor's explanation and let it go at that. I did not stay another night at that hotel, however.

CHAPTER 20

PRINCE HENRY OF PRUSSIA, DR. BOOKER T. WASHING-
TON AND TUSKEGEE

W HEN PRINCE HENRY OF PRUS-
SIA, the brother of Wilhelm, then Emperor of Germany, visited
the United States, I had the pleasure of meeting him through the
courtesy of Booker T. Washington. I happened to be in New
York at the time on my way home from New England, where
I had been filling some lecture engagements for the Forums and
other organizations. As I was passing through the lobby of the
Grand Union Hotel, where I was stopping, I suddenly spied Mr.
Washington, who invited me to meet Prince Henry the next day.
Since neither one of us knew the other was in the city, I felt
that this chance meeting with the only man in New York with
whom I was acquainted who could make it possible for me to
meet this much-talked of man was most fortunate.

Prince Henry had invited the Hampton singers and Booker
T. Washington to meet him on his yacht. But a case of scarlet
fever on the *Hohenzollern* disarranged this plan at the last minute. It was then decided to have the meeting take place at the
Waldorf Astoria, which has since then been torn down. The
Hampton singers filed into an indescribably beautiful room in
that palatial hotel, which was then comparatively new, and took
seats provided for them. A profound silence fell upon those
of us who were awaiting the Prince, as this courtly gentleman
and his escort filed in and seated themselves. When the singing
began, Prince Henry listened with rapt attention and evident
enjoyment. He was so pleased with one of the songs that he
asked to have it repeated. Suddenly Admiral Evans limped

across the room from the Prince's side and approached Mr. Washington.

"Mr. Washington," said he, "His Royal Highness, Prince Henry of Prussia, asks to have you presented to him." With dignity and perfect composure Mr. Washington arose and crossed the room with Admiral Evans, who presented him to the brother of that Emperor of Germany who has since been sent to Holland in exile. Prince Henry arose and shook hands cordially with Dr. Washington and then the two men sat side by side on a sofa. The distinguished visitor exhibited the liveliest animation while he was talking to the founder of Tuskegee. The Prince gestured and smiled as though he was enjoying the conversation immensely. This grandson of Queen Victoria, who was the son of her eldest daughter, spoke English fluently, of course. He expressed a wish to have a copy of the jubilee songs and a copy of Dr. Washington's *Up from Slavery*. When Dr. Washington told him he would be glad to give him both books, the Prince asked him for his note book, so that he might write therein his name and address. Thus it was that Dr. Washington secured Prince Henry's autograph, which thousands of Americans at that time would have been glad to possess.

At the close of the concert Prince Henry came forward to the singers, and in a speech characterized by simplicity of language and genuineness of feeling spoke as follows: "My dear young friends, you have been very kind to come here and sing for me today and I have enjoyed your songs very much. God has put music into the hearts of men to bind them together. Your songs are beautiful and I hope you will see that they are perpetuated. Again, I thank you." What a contrast between the views expressed by Prince Henry and those with which Hitler is corrupting and disgusting the world today!

After Dr. Washington had presented a few people to Prince Henry, and I was among that number, he left with his suite to go immediately to a luncheon given him by one of New York's society queens, Mrs. Cornelius Vanderbilt. That very morning the great grandson of John Jay and the granddaughter of Cornelius Vanderbilt had entertained Booker Washington at breakfast. Thus did an ex-slave and one of his friends touch elbows and clasp hands with royalty, as represented by a monarchical government of Europe, and sit at the table of royalty, as represented by Republican America. As I thought about the significance of these events, I felt I had grown an inch taller, believed that the recognition of our group coming from such a source would add a few years to my life and, like the fortunate people in the story books, I would live happy ever afterward.

This was only one of several delightful experiences for which I was indebted to Booker T. Washington. He had a heart full of generous impulses and enjoyed giving pleasure to his friends. He knew full well that I did not agree with some of his views, although I admired him greatly for the work he was doing in his effort to educate and uplift those representatives of his race who had so few and such meagre opportunities to develop themselves.

During the time when colored people engaged in such heated discussions about industrial training and the higher education, Dr. W. E. B. Dubois was the High Priest of higher education and Dr. Booker T. Washington was the recognized champion and spokesman for industrial training. I appreciated Dr. Washington's effort to train the masses to earn a living because I knew that no race can hope to stand on a firm financial basis without a well-trained laboring class. But I felt that he emphasized industrial training to the exclusion of everything else when he first started his crusade in its behalf. Moreover, it seemed to me that he sometimes tried to make colored people who had acquired the higher education appear as ridiculous as he could, which I considered both unwise and unfair. I was known as a disciple of the higher education, but I never failed to put myself on record as advocating industrial training also.

Dr. Dubois is now teaching in the South and his views on important phases of the Race Problem have changed considerably from what they once were.

I visited Tuskegee for the first time when I accepted an invitation which Dr. Washington extended me by wire. Dr. W. E. B. Dubois, who was then a teacher in Atlanta University and held annual conferences on some phases of race work, invited me to address the eighth conference on "The Negro Woman and the Church." This talk required a great deal of research. While I was getting the necessary information, I discovered this is one of the many subjects pertaining to the work well done by a single group in the race about which practically nothing has been written and about which the public will continue to remain in ignorance until the interesting facts are published. I felt repaid for my research. I marveled at the prodigious amount of work which colored women did for the church in the early days of this country's history, long, long before the emancipation of slavery.

While I was in Atlanta filling the engagement for Dr. Dubois, I received a telegram from Dr. Booker T. Washington, saying he wanted me to come to the Tuskegee Commencement and remain two days. He would defray my railroad expenses from Atlanta and return, he said. His invitation to visit Tuskegee, concerning which I had heard so much good, bad and indifferent, seemed providential and I accepted it with the keenest anticipation of pleasure. At last I would see for myself what this much-discussed school was like.

I had never seen a Commencement like Tuskegee's before. On the stage before our very eyes students actually performed the work which they had learned to do in school as a part of the exercises. They showed us how to build houses, how to paint them, how to estimate the cost of the necessary material and so on down the line. I was completely taken off my feet. I was a convert with all my heart. Here was a school giving just the kind of instruction that the majority attending it needed.

Owing to the lessons (or the lack of them) inculcated during slavery, neither the white nor the colored people of the South know any more than they should about injecting system into their work or making accurate calculations. I was sure these students would get a good start in the right direction and might be expected to be the little leaven which would eventually leaven the whole lump.

After I had seen Tuskegee with my own eyes I had a higher regard and a greater admiration for its founder than I had ever entertained before. I realized what a splendid work he was doing to promote the welfare of the race, and that he was literally fulfilling "a long-felt want." From that day forth, whenever those friends tried to engage me in conversation about Tuskegee who knew that 'way down deep in my heart I was a stickler for the higher education, and that if it came to a show down I would always vote on that side, I would simply say, "Have you seen Tuskegee? Have you been there? If you have not seen it for yourself, I will not discuss it with you till you do." I felt that it was a waste of time and energy to enter into a discussion with anybody who had not been to the school, but had formed his opinion from hearsay.

Mr. Scott Bone, who was then managing editor of the *Washington Post* and later became governor of Alaska, asked me to write an article about the Tuskegee Commencement when I returned home. I told him that I had also attended the Commencement of Atlanta University, a college for colored youth which had a scientific and an academic course and awarded the A.B. degree to those who completed it, and that I should like to write an article about that also. He refused to commission me to write this article for the *Post* on the ground that there was nothing new or distinctive about such a commencement, that it was like all the rest and for that reason the readers of his paper would not be interested in it at all. I was greatly embarrassed and disturbed by this decision. Disliking to write an article which described the Tuskegee Commencement and ignored completely the one which represented the higher education of colored youth, I made several references to Atlanta anyway. They were ruthlessly cut out of the article. Later on I learned from a reliable source that I was severely criticized by some of Atlanta's friends for failing to say a single word about it in my release for the *Post*. But an obdurate editor's blunt refusal to publish an article and his hard-hearted blue pencil (which invariably eliminates one's most precious thoughts and most brilliant phrases) have caused many another poor, helpless writer to be pilloried by the public and misunderstood.

By some I was severely criticized because I joined the National Association for the Advancement of Colored People, because it was supposed to have been founded to counteract the influence of Booker T. Washington and to discredit him. President Theodore Roosevelt admired the founder of Tuskegee very much and it was generally known that Dr. Washington used the influence he possessed at the White House to have the President appoint my husband to the judgeship. Both Mr. Terrell and myself were very grateful to him for this service which he rendered. But it goes without saying, that Mr. Washington's influence alone would not have been sufficiently strong to secure the judgeship for Mr. Terrell. If the leading citizens of the National

Capital had not wanted my husband to occupy that position, he would never have been appointed by the President. Nevertheless, Mr. Terrell enjoyed nothing more than expressing his gratitude to Mr. Washington for the efforts he exerted in his behalf.

When I joined the National Association for the Advancement of Colored People, my husband was warned that this action on his wife's part would alienate Dr. Washington from him and would finally lead to his political ruin. But Judge Terrell answered that prediction and warning with the statement that nobody but Dr. Washington's most bitter enemy would declare that an organization working to secure for the Colored-American all the rights to which he was entitled was formed to oppose or discredit him. The people who took it for granted that Dr. Washington was antagonistic to the principles enunciated by the National Association for the Advancement of Colored People, said my husband, evidently believed he was in favor of having the rights, privileges and opportunities which other citizens enjoy withheld from his own heavily-handicapped group. To accuse Dr. Washington of assuming such a reprehensible attitude toward his race, said Judge Terrell, is one of the most serious charges which could be preferred against him. Then, when the knowing ones continued to shake their heads at him in warning, my husband said that if he had to lose his position because his wife lived up to the light she had and joined an organization which she believed would promote the welfare of the race, he was perfectly willing to lose it.

I was a charter member of the National Association for the Advancement of Colored People. I traveled a thousand miles to attend its first meeting in New York City. I was filling some lecture engagements in the South and a telegram was sent to New Orleans where I had spoken, urging me to come to New York immediately for the important meeting which was to be held in a few days. Eagerly did I respond to that call. Such an organization was sorely needed at that time and it was my duty, as it certainly was my pleasure, to render any assistance in my power. There is no doubt that when the Association was formed there were many colored people who believed in the principles for which it stood, who hesitated or refused to join it because they feared membership in it would cause them to lose their jobs or hurt their influence in the communities in which they lived. It required a bit of courage for many colored people to join the National Association for the Advancement of Colored People when it was first organized. But fortunately that day has passed. It has done much to stiffen the backbone, elevate the standards and advance the interests of the race.

The colored people of this country owe a debt of gratitude to Mr. Moorfield Storey which they could never repay. As president of the Association, he rendered a service, the magnitude and importance of which it is impossible to estimate or express. Although he was president of the Bar Association of the United States, counselor for two railroads and the head of a large law firm in Boston, he found time on many occasions gratuitously to give us the benefit of his legal advice. Before the Supreme Court he argued the case against the city of Louisville, Kentucky, for passing an ordinance to segregate the race and won it. He filed a brief against the State of Oklahoma for passing a Grandfather Clause and the Supreme Court declared it unconstitutional. In a short statement it is impossible to enumerate the services which Mr. Moorfield Storey rendered the colored people of the United States for many years.

No one who was present could forget the "Amenia Conference" called by Mr. Joel Spingarn, the treasurer of the N.A.A.C.P. until he passed away recently, who courageously, splendidly championed the Colored-American's cause. This conference was held on his beautiful estate at Troutbrook, New York in the summer of 1916. It was an effort to induce colored people of all shades and varieties of opinion to thrash out their differences and unite on some definite program of work. There were sixty leaders, men and women from as many different camps. Before they left that Amenia Conference, however, "they had arrived at virtual unanimity of opinion in regard to certain principles," as the resolution expressed it. That was the first time that so many colored people who differed so widely in their views concerning their problems as they did, had come together since the Emancipation Proclamation had been signed. "That Amenia Conference," said one, "marked an end of old ways of attacking the race problem and the beginning of the new." All of us who participated in that meeting felt that Mr.

and Mrs. Spingarn deserved the gratitude of the group they were trying to assist for having accomplished so much.

It was also largely through the instrumentality of Mr. Spingarn that an officers' training camp for colored men was established in Des Moines, Iowa, during the World War. If this had not been done, not a colored man who went across the sea to fight to "make the world safe for Democracy" would have received an officer's commission, but all our fine, highly educated young men would have been doomed to remain in the ranks as privates.

Mr. Oswald Garrison Villard, the grandson of William Lloyd Garrison, has also upheld the tradition of his forebears by the attitude he has assumed toward the Race Problem. As one of the officers and leading spirits in the N.A.A.C.P. he has been a strong champion and a valiant contender for justice and right.

CHAPTER 21

IN BERLIN, GERMANY

IT WILL SURPRISE no one if I frankly admit that the April morning I received a letter from Berlin, Germany, inviting me to deliver an address at the International Congress of Women which would meet in Berlin in June was truly a red-letter day in my life. It took my breath away for a second, for I had no idea that such an invitation would be extended me. I wanted very much to accept the invitation, of course. But how could I go?

In the first place, the financial aspect of the case had to be considered. Decidedly so! What about the money necessary to make the trip? Where was it coming from? My husband's salary was not very large and our living expenses by no means small. But even if I could scrape together the money, how could I summon courage enough to leave my family? Especially my small daughter! But like most difficulties which seem impossible to smooth out when they first appear, those which confronted me the morning I read that memorable letter soon dwindled in size and finally disappeared. Both my husband and my mother were eager to have me go to Berlin. Mother would and could take care of my little daughter just as well as I could, she said, so there was no reason in the world why I should decline such a wonderful invitation.

Then I wrote to my father about the matter and asked him to tell me what to do. Father was also eager to have me go and promised to send me $300 to help me finance the trip. Whenever my courage seemed to be oozing away and the horror of leaving my family seemed greater than I could endure, I would think of the opportunity which had been miraculously afforded me of presenting the facts creditable to colored women of the United States, and my spirit would immediately revive.

After I had definitely decided to go abroad there was very little time in which to make a reservation on a steamer which would reach Berlin in time for me to deliver my address Monday evening, June 13, 1904, when I was scheduled to appear. I went to several steamship companies in Washington before I realized that it would not be easy for a colored woman to secure accommodations such as I desired for the price I was able to pay. Then I went directly to the Nord Deutscher Lloyd office in Baltimore. There one of the officers consented to let me have his room on a one class steamer for $80, so that the problem which at one time had assumed threatening proportions was thus easily solved.

A short time before the steamer sailed from Baltimore my little daughter, Phyllis, who had gone there with her father to see me off, begged me to take her with me. I was never more tempted to do anything in my life than I was to grant her request. But my husband argued me out of it by showing how impossible it would be for me properly to attend to the business for which I was making the voyage and to care for a little girl among strangers at one and the same time.

As soon as I reached Berlin some of the German women who discovered that I spoke German began to ask me about "die Negerin" (the Negress) from the United States whom they were expecting. At first I thought they knew I was that individual, and this was the German way of telling me so. But I soon learned that I was mistaken, and that they had no idea they were talking to this very unusual anthropological specimen whom they were seeking. The newspaper reporters were especially anxious to lay eyes upon this rare, colored bird, so that they might interview her, and each one wanted to publish this interview in his or her particular paper first.

"When will die Negerin arrive?" some one would ask me. "Haven't you seen her yet?" I would reply. "She is already here, I think. Why don't you ask some of the other delegates from the United States? Perhaps they can tell you where die Negerin is." "But the women from the United States whom we have approached don't speak German well enough for us to talk to them," they would usually complain. Finally, a dear, little newspaper woman came to me and implored me to let her know the minute die Negerin arrived, so that she might have the first interview with her. I could not resist the temptation then and there to confess on the spot that I was the individual she sought. Her joy was great indeed, but her surprise was greater. In relating this phase of my experience when I first reached Berlin, I have sometimes told my friends that the natives who were so eager to see what manner of person a Negro woman would be evidently surmised that she had rings in her nose as well as in her ears, that she would both look and act entirely differently from other women and that she would probably be "coonjining" or "cakewalking" about the streets.

I had hardly reached Berlin before the German women began to complain because both the British and American delegates addressed the Congress in English. "Five years ago," they would say, "the Quinquennial was held in London. The women from the United States and England knew when that meeting adjourned that the next one would be held in Berlin. They have had plenty of time, therefore, to prepare their papers, so that they might be translated into German and read here by some one familiar with the language if they could not read them themselves. We German women would not think of going to the United States and perpetrating long discourses in German upon an American audience on hot nights. If we could not speak English well enough to express our thoughts ourselves, we would have our papers translated into English and get somebody to read them for us. And that is the way English and American women should treat us. Many of us can speak English well enough to carry on an ordinary conversation, to be sure, but we don't know the language well enough to understand a speaker who delivers a formal discourse, speaking rapidly at a distance from us, so that we cannot see the motion of his lips."

This criticism of English-speaking women seemed just to me. I was very sorry, therefore, I had not decided to write my address in German, before I left home. I had thought of doing so, but when I broached the subject to my husband, he was decidedly opposed to the idea, and he had a good reason for the faith that was in him. "Everybody speaks best in his own mother tongue," he would argue, "and you are no exception to a general rule. What you want to do in Berlin, both for your own sake and for the sake of the women you represent, is to do the best you can. And you certainly can do your best in the English language."

I was very much impressed with this argument. It appealed to my intelligence, and I decided, not without misgivings, I must confess, to take his advice. I gave up the notion of trying to deliver my address in German. But now that I was in Berlin and heard the Germans criticizing the Americans and English for perpetrating discourses upon them on hot nights in a foreign language, I realized what a terrible blunder I had made. Two days before I delivered my address, it was borne in upon me with tremendous force that much I wanted the foreign women to know concerning colored women in the United States would be lost to them if I did not speak in German. In my perplexity I asked some American women for their advice. They urged me not to attempt to write a new address and try to speak in German at that late hour. They showed me what a prodigious amount of labor it would involve, how much time it would consume and what a nervous strain it would be for me to write what would practically be a new address in a foreign tongue just two days before I was to appear. They reminded me also that I had to speak twice the same day, once in the morning on the status of wage-earning colored women in the United States, and again in the evening on an entirely different theme. I appreciated this advice because I knew the women who gave it to me were good friends and wanted me to do as well as I could when I addressed that vast assembly.

But the more I thought of speaking in English to an audience, the great majority of whom would not be able to understand a word I said, the less inclined I was to do so. I was convinced that I would not be able to do the very thing I had crossed the sea to accomplish if I did not convey my thoughts through the medium of the language spoken in the country in which the Congress was held and which the majority who would hear me could understand. Finally, I asked the opinion of Mrs. Ida Husted Harper, a well-known newspaper correspondent, who has since written a fine biography of Susan B. Anthony. She was greatly surprised to learn that I thought I could speak German well enough to attempt to make a public address in it. But she declared without the slightest hesitation and with considerable emphasis that if it were possible for me to do so, she would advise me strongly to do it. From several other friends I received the same advice. Finally, one woman declared emphatically, "Well, Mary Church Terrell, if you can deliver an address before this Congress in German and don't do it, I think you are a fool in 57 varieties of languages." She laid great emphasis upon the word YOU, as she expressed this opinion, and I understood exactly what she meant. I decided right then and there that I would deliver my address in German in spite of the effort and the trouble it would cost.

This conversation took place Saturday morning, and the following Monday I was scheduled to speak. I hurried home and tried to write my address in German. Having done the best I could I took it to a translator for correction. Then I rushed home and began to read it over and over again, so as to familiarize myself with it. Perhaps it is well to state here that as soon as I went aboard the Nord Deutscher Lloyd steamer in Baltimore, I began to speak German to the crew. The waitresses, the stewardesses and the stewards were all pleased to speak their mother tongue with the passengers who wished them to do so. Moreover, I drew from the library a most interesting love story—a thick volume, a blood and thunder love story, which I read from cover to cover. Having thus steeped myself continuously in German for nearly two weeks on a slow sailing vessel, I discovered when I landed in Bremen that I could both speak and understand it as well as I had ever done, though I had neither spoken nor read the language for fifteen years. While languages seem to be ingrates of the deepest dye because one forgets them so soon if one does not speak them continuously, still, it is remarkable how quickly and easily it is possible to relearn them when one tries to renew acquaintance with them after a long period.

When I first reached Berlin I had gone to one of the hotels recommended to the delegates. I had been there but a single day, however, before the Committee on Entertainment informed me that I had been invited to stay with Herr and Frau Dr. Ginsberg. At first, I demurred a bit because, all things considered, I thought it would be better for me to remain at the hotel. But the good lady who notified me of the arrangements which had already been made insisted upon my accepting the hospitality provided for me, and told me that the host and hostess would be very much disappointed if I declined.

The wealthiest and best people of Berlin were deeply interested in the Congress and proved the extent of their interest in the most substantial way. In some of the elegant homes placed at the service of the committee, delegates and speakers were entertained and in others regal receptions were held.

My host's residence was located in one of the most desirable sections of that beautiful German city and the appointments were the very last word in elegance and taste. Moreover, my gracious hostess gave me a suite of rooms consisting of a bed room, a sitting room and a private bath, while she assigned me a maid whose duty it was to assist me in any way she could.

As soon as I came home Saturday afternoon with the determination to write and deliver my address in German, I told the little maid not to admit anybody to my apartment, no matter who it might be, because I would be too busy to see visitors. I left the sitting room but a few minutes Sunday evening, and when I returned I found a man who looked as though he might be an anarchist. As soon as I recovered my speech, I remonstrated with the little maid for admitting this stranger. She was very much agitated and explained most apologetically that she had tried her best to keep the man out when he had asked to see me, but that he had pushed past her and entered the room in spite of her efforts to restrain him.

The man, whose hair stood up straight all over his head, explained that he was a reporter from Austria and wanted to interview me. As I was telling him I was too busy to talk with him, his eye fell upon my manuscript in German lying on the table. "Was ist das?" he inquired, picking up the paper and reading it. "Ah," said he gloatingly, "you are going to deliver your address in German." The cat was out of the bag. There was no use denying it. I have rarely been provoked with any human being more than I was with that man. I had intended to keep it a secret from everybody. I enjoyed anticipating how surprised the audience would be to hear me deliver my speech in German. But now this stranger had the evidence in his hands with his eyes glued upon it.

"No matter how well you speak German," he said, "you have made some mistakes, I am sure. I am going over this manuscript with you right now." There was no use objecting to it. He was the kind that is built to have his way. He went over the manuscript carefully, making suggestions here and there which he said would improve it. Several times he cut a long sentence into two, saying that the very long German sentence was passé, quite out of style now. Again he would substitute a word which he preferred to the one I had used. "That is not conversational enough," he would comment. "It is too formal." And so, when he had finished I knew that my German speech was letter perfect, which was a great relief to my mind. Then I started to learn it as fast as I could.

During each of the two nights preceding the eventful evening I slept just three hours by the clock. But I felt then, as I feel now, no amount of trouble and toil is too great to be undertaken and endured in behalf of a cause to which one has dedicated her ability and consecrated her powers, and which one wishes to represent well.

When I discovered that practically nobody realized that I was "die Negerin" in whose appearance so many were interested, I decided to say something in the very beginning of my discourse which would impress that fact upon my audience. I wanted to be sure that they knew I was of African descent. As soon as I arose, therefore I said,

"If it had not been for the War of the Rebellion which resulted in victory for the Union Army in 1865, instead of addressing you as a free woman tonight, in all human probability I should be on some plantation in one of the southern states of my country manacled body and soul in the fetters of a slave."

As soon as these words were uttered, one of the reporters who sat at a very long table in front of and near the platform half arose from his seat, stamped his foot and exclaimed: "Die Schame!" (What a shame!)

"In all this great world gathering of women," I continued, "I believe I am unique in two respects. In the first place, I am the only woman participating in these exercises who represents a race which has been free so short a time as forty years. In the second place, I am the only woman speaking from this platform whose parents were actually held as chattels and who but for the kindly intervention of a beneficent Providence would have been a slave herself. As you fasten your eyes upon me, therefore, you are truly beholding a rare bird."

The audience was amused at this, for "rare bird" is translated into German as "ein weisser Rabe," which literally means "a white robin."

"And so, as I stand here tonight," I continued, "my happiness is two-fold, rejoicing as I do, not only in the emancipation of my race, but in the almost universal elevation of my sex. If any one had had the courage fifty years ago to predict that a woman with African blood in her veins would journey from the United States to Germany to address the International Congress of Women in 1904, he would either have been laughed out of Court, or adjudged insane."

This address was delivered in the Philharmonie and consumed thirty minutes. When I finished the audience applauded tumultuously. There was a perfect Babel of tongues ringing in my ears. Women of different nationalities who sat on the platform near me were congratulating me, I presume. I did not know what they were saying. After the applause had continued several minutes somebody suggested that I arise and bow. This I did mechanically, for I was bewildered by the unexpectedly hearty reception which had been given the address. The presiding officer tried to call the audience to order. Instead of using a gavel for that purpose the Germans ring what looks and sounds like a dinner bell. But the applause continued in spite of the bell, until I had arisen from my seat and bowed, like a prima donna, three times.

I had scarcely looked at my manuscript, while I was speaking, for I had read and studied it so thoroughly it had become a part of me. I had only one thought in mind. I wanted to place the colored women of the United States in the most favorable light possible. I represented, not only the colored women of my own country but, since I was the only woman taking part in the International Congress who had a drop of African blood in her veins, I represented the whole continent of Africa as well. I felt, therefore, that a tremendous responsibility was resting upon me, and the nervous strain was great. I have always believed that the ovation I received from that Berlin audience was largely due to the fact that a descendant of recently emancipated slaves spoke a foreign language well enough to deliver an address in it.

The *Washington Post* commented upon my address as follows: "The *Post's* correspondent" (Mrs. Ida Husted Harper) "related that the hit of the congress on the part of the American delegates was made by Mrs. Mary Church Terrell, of Washington, who 'delivered one speech in German and another in equally good French.' Mrs. Terrell is a colored woman, and appears to have been, beyond every other of our delegates, prominent for her ability to make addresses in other than her own language."

So great was the interest aroused in the Race Problem of the United States that requests for articles on the subject came from newspapers and magazines in Germany, France, Austria, Norway and other lands.

It was agreed among all the delegates that the Berlin Congress had set a pace which it seemed impossible to surpass anywhere if, indeed, it could ever be equaled. The opening of the Congress was preceded Sunday evening by a concert, such as one can hear only in Germany. The orchestra was composed of one hundred young women perfectly trained by a woman leader. It was given in the Philharmonie Hall and was followed by a banquet for 2,000 guests, before whom the delicacies of the season were spread as well as the choicest wines. It would be impossible to mention all the social functions so admirably planned which were given in honor of the delegates to the International Congress. An elegant garden party was given by Count von Bülow, Minister of Foreign Affairs, who lived in the mansion formerly occupied by the great Bismarck, and another by von Posodonsky, the Minister of the Interior, so that the delegates were thus afforded an opportunity of meeting those distinguished German statesmen and their wives as well as having the pleasure of seeing those historic mansions in the very heart of Berlin. There are few cities, if any, in which private mansions are surrounded by such grounds as were those in Berlin. The trees showing growth of half a century or more, the indescribable luxuriance of vines and shrubs, the long stretch of green turf made us feel that we were walking through a veritable paradise on earth.

But even these were surpassed by magnificent country estates, whose gardens were terraced down to the shores of a river or lake. At least half a dozen parties were given at these wonderful places. The guests went out from Berlin by train, and in several instances the Government helped the hostesses entertain by placing at their disposal its pretty boats for little trips on the water. Five invitations for one afternoon were not unusual. Every delegate and speaker was invited to attend a performance at any theater to which she cared to go free of charge. At many of the receptions the most renowned singers and artists of that day had been secured for the entertainment of guests.

At the close of the session the City of Berlin gave a banquet which seemed less like reality than a dream when I looked at the hall of almost barbaric splendor in which the delicious feast was spread, beheld the artistic decorations, listened to the heavenly music and drank in the scene as a whole.

In marveling at the magnificent scale on which we had been entertained, a woman who occupied a conspicuous position in one of the largest organizations in this country confessed to me that if she ever heard the International Congress was to meet in the United States, she would pack up bag and baggage before it convened and leave for parts unknown. Nothing which could possibly contribute to the success of the meeting was left undone. No expense was spared. Everything which could add to the pleasure or comfort of the guests was carefully arranged.

When we compare the status to which German women have been relegated by the Hitler regime with that which they enjoyed in 1904 we cannot help deploring the conditions under which they are living today.

The aftermath of my address had one amusing feature, at least. During the first meal I took as a guest of my hostess the problems confronting several lands were discussed. References to the disabilities of the Jews in Germany were made several times. My hosts told me of the injustices of many kinds to which Jews in Germany were subjected. Naturally, I expressed great sympathy with the oppressed group. Then somebody at the table asked me quite naively whether I thought the Negroes in the United States were capable of being well educated and of reaching a high degree of culture. I thought it was quite a leading question for a man who considered himself highly cultured and well educated to ask me, but I assured him quite calmly, though emphatically, that they could be and proved it by citing the splendid records made by individuals over and over again. Then somebody else reminded me of the terrible crimes committed by Negroes and rather sympathized with the people who took the law into their own hands and lynched the brutes.

Again I defended the maligned group by stating that many of the stories they had heard and read were absolutely false and gave a few statistics to prove what I said. In trying to explain the situation, I said that just as the Jews are misrepresented and disliked in Germany, so Negroes were victims of falsehood and hatred in the United States. I could not help wondering why my hosts discussed so nonchalantly and frankly the vices and defects charged against the Negro, and expressed such uncomplimentary opinions about him in my presence. But I did not allow myself to become peeved in the least.

The day after I addressed the Congress Herr Doctor and Frau Doctor Ginsberg were very much embarrassed indeed. They told me they had no idea I was called a "Negerin" in the United States. They knew, they said, that a "Negerin" was going to deliver an address before the Congress, but they had not remembered the name and did not dream I was the individual. They expressed deep regret over the questions they had asked about the Negro and assured me they would never have done so if they had known I was identified with the race.

In the meantime, I had heard by the merest accident that my host and hostess were Jews. I had not had the slightest suspicion that they were. There was nothing either in their physical appearance or anything else to indicate to me that they were Hebrews. So I, too, had a few compunctions of conscience about certain questions I had asked concerning Jews. And while I had said nothing uncomplimentary about them, I certainly would not have illustrated several points by alluding to their status in Germany and comparing it with that of colored people in the United States if I had known my host and hostess were Hebrews.

The situation had its humorous side without doubt. Here were Jews entertaining a Negro unawares, while said Negro had no idea she was the guest of Jews. I had no cause to suspect that my hosts would have objected to entertaining me, even if they had known with what racial group I was identified before they opened their beautiful, hospitable home to me. On the contrary, they assured me they were glad I had been assigned to them. They extended me every courtesy imaginable, and since actions speak louder than words, I believe them.

CHAPTER 22

DISTINGUISHED PEOPLE I MET ABROAD

FROM BERLIN I went directly to Paris a few days after the International Congress of Women adjourned and remained there about ten days. What joy, what rapture to return to my old French camping grounds after an absence of fifteen years! How I love France and the French people! To be sure, they have faults like other groups, but with all their faults I love them still. Goethe says that everybody has a fatherland and a motherland. The country in which I was born and reared and have lived is my fatherland, of course, and I love it genuinely, but my motherland is dear, broadminded France in which people with dark complexions are not discriminated against on account of their color.

In Paris I met Jean Finot, who was then editor of *La Revue de la Revue*. He was deeply interested in the Race Problem in the United States. Indeed he was deeply interested in the dark races all over the world. Since then he has published *Le Préjugé des Races*, in which he ridicules the claim made by certain races that they are innately superior to others and exposes the fallacy of many views entertained by scientists concerning the physical and mental characteristics of the various divisions of the human family. In this book, which has been translated into English, Monsieur Finot does me the honor of referring in complimentary terms to my work and myself.

A striking and a pleasant illustration of the proverbial affability of the French was given me in Paris. I wanted very much to see a picture painted by H. O. Tanner, a colored man from the United States. His "Raising of Lazarus" had been awarded the first prize, had been purchased by the French government and had been hung in the Luxembourg gallery with others painted by renowned artists from all over the world. Imagine therefore, how bitter and keen was my disappointment when, on reaching the Luxembourg gallery with a heart full of joyous expectancy, I learned that the picture painted by the great colored artist was no longer there. This gallery is by no means small, but it is not large enough to hold the pictures which are painted and accepted by the French Government every year. In order to do justice to everybody concerned, therefore, the pictures from artists from one country are exhibited one year, those painted by artists from another country the next year and so on down the line. As ill luck would have it, the pictures of American artists were not on exhibition this year, so that Mr. Tanner's had been removed. I approached one of the guards and almost tearfully told him how disappointed I was. I besought him to secure permission for me to see Mr. Tanner's picture if such a thing could possibly be done. I admitted that I was not personally acquainted with the artist, but I declared that I knew his father, his mother, his sisters, his brothers, and when I finished I am sure the guard thought that there must be a mistake somewhere if I did not belong to the family myself. I told him I could not return to my country with my head erect and I certainly could not die happy if I did not see the picture painted by that great American artist.

When I finished, the kind-hearted guard gave a delightful shrug to his expressive shoulders, which was a cross between encouragement and doubt, and promised to do everything he could to obtain my heart's desire. He then gave me the name of Monsieur Bénédit, the superintendent of the Luxembourg, and advised me to write to him. I rushed home as fast as I could and wrote Monsieur Bénédit a letter, each and every word of which was a prayer or a tear. Almost by return mail I received a reply from this obliging and courteous French official, stating that he would be very happy to comply with my request. He told me that the permission which he was about to give me was rarely granted, but that if I presented his letter to one of the Luxembourg guards, Mr. Tanner's painting would be immediately unfolded to my view. Armed with this precious letter, I betook myself again to the Luxembourg and gave it to one of the guards.

After consulting with those in authority for a short time,

he returned and told me that Mr. Tanner's picture was no longer in the gallery, but that it had been taken to the Louvre. I was spared any anxiety which I might otherwise have had, however, by being informed that one of the guards would be immediately sent to the Louvre with me to show me the painting which I so much desired to see. Thus it was that I had the rare privilege and the great pleasure of feasting my eyes upon the masterpiece of a colored man, which will bear witness for many years to come to the artistic talent of the race to which he belongs.

In London I met Mr. W. T. Stead, who gave me his interesting book, *The Americanization of the World,* which was greatly prized, not only because of its literary value, but because it contained an inscription written by the author's own hand. Although Mr. Stead was well past middle age when I met him, he had the enthusiasm and the exuberance of youth. He had read the newspaper comments upon my address before the International Congress of Women in Berlin and was enthusiastic about the reception accorded to me.

We had talked only a few minutes when he exclaimed: "I have a dear friend you must meet, an American, John Milholland. Are you acquainted with him?" I told him I was not. "That won't do at all," frowned Mr. Stead. "He should know you and you should know him." Mr. Stead was pacing back and forth like a lion in a cage all the while he was talking He was too restless to keep still. His complexion was florid and his hair was snow white. Suddenly he paused and his face lit up with a smile, as though he had an inspiration. "I can arrange that nicely right away," he said beaming. "Mr. Milholland invited me to dine with him today, and I have an important engagement which will prevent me from accepting. You just go right along in my place and tell John Milholland that I sent you. He will be very glad to see you, I know."

I was surprised, not to say shocked, at such a suggestion. But Mr. Stead was so pleased with his clever idea I did not have the heart to tell him I would not carry it out. He plead with me to go, assuring me that knowing John and Mrs. Milholland as well as he did, he was certain that nothing would afford them greater pleasure than to have me dine with them.

Then and there he gave me a letter of introduction to his friends and sent them a telegram stating that I was coming in the bargain. I wrote to Mr. Milholland that afternoon and inclosed the letter of introduction from Mr. Stead. By return mail Mr. Milholland invited me to tea with his family the next afternoon. It would have been hard to find a more interesting family than Mr. Milholland's that July afternoon. His daughter, Inez, who later became such a conspicuous and forceful leader in the cause of woman suffrage and who died in its interest in the beauty and bloom of youth, was then a strikingly handsome girl, just budding into womanhood. She gave promise even then of doing much which, as Inez Milholland Boissevain, she accomplished before she was suddenly snatched from her family and friends, while she was speaking on the Pacific coast in behalf of the cause of suffrage, which was so dear to her young heart.

I once marched in a parade in Washington which was arranged by women who thus expressed their desire and their determination to secure suffrage. At the head of the procession on a snow white horse rode Inez Milholland, a vision of loveliness, an example and an inspiration to the young womanhood of the United States. When some of the suffragists objected to having the colored girls of Howard University march in the parade, it was Inez Milholland who insisted that they be given a place with the pupils of the other schools.

This chance meeting with Mr. Milholland in London was the beginning of a friendship with a man who spent much of his time, energy and money trying to improve the conditions under which colored people live in the United States. He had the determination, courage and zeal which characterized the leaders of the abolition movement, and he never stopped working for what he called the complete emancipation, till he died. It was largely through his suggestion and efforts that the Constitution League was formed. He invited me to come to New York, and allowed me to be the first to sign the papers incorporating the Constitution League. This was done in the office of General Clarkson, another good friend of our group.

Mr. Milholland was present at a drive for the Washington branch of the National Association for the Advancement of Colored People and in his speech he said that "Mrs. Terrell, Dubois and I formed the Constitution League in Cooper Union in New York fifteen years ago, February 3rd, 1906, and I am prouder of the National Association for the Advancement of

Colored People than of any organization that has grown out of that meeting."

Mr. Stead, Mr. Milholland and I had several interesting conferences while I was in London. Mr. Stead urged me to write stories on the Race Problem, but he warned me to use a nom de plume, so that the editors would not know I am colored. He suggested that I write an article for the *Contemporary Review* and gave me a letter of introduction to the editor, Mr. Bunting, which read as follows: "Permit me to introduce to you the ablest colored lady I ever met, Mrs. M. C. Terrell. Her article about the truth about 'Lynching' in the June number of the *North American Review* was the most convincing piece of writing on that subject I have ever read. She was one of the lionesses at the International Congress of Women at Berlin and was the only American delegate who addressed the Congress in German. If you want an article on the Colored People of the South, especially from a woman's point of view, you will have to go far afield to find a more competent contributor. I am yours truly, W. T. Stead."

Accompanying this letter of introduction to the editor there was a personal inclosure from Mr. Stead to me in which he expressed himself as follows:

"My dear Friend and Comrade: Herewith a letter of introduction to Mr. Bunting. I hope it will help you. You deserve help and will command it. It was a sincere pleasure to meet you yesterday. I hope we may meet again. And what is perhaps even better, I feel confident that the words few and inadequate though they were which I was privileged to address to you will dwell in your heart as a glowing flame of hope and courage to warm and cheer you and inspirit you in dark days or darker nights. May God bless you and make us both to be his junior partners in the cause of his Priestess, Woman.

"I am gratefully yours,

"W. T. STEAD."

Mr. Stead was one of the most democratic men, one of the most brilliant conversationalists, one of the most original thinkers and one of the most whole-souled men it is possible to imagine. The advice he gave, the courage and inspiration received from him during the visits we had together will abide with me like a precious treasure as long as I live. The colored people of the United States had few friends who championed their cause so loyally, so fearlessly and so eloquently as did Mr. Stead.

The Countess of Warwick was another interesting and distinguished individual whom I met in London that season. She and I were invited to address the International Congress of Women in the section devoted to the discussion of Wage-Earning Women. The Countess was to talk about the English women who earned their living at farming and I was to describe the conditions under which colored domestics in the United States work. The Countess was ill, however, and could not come. She had a baby just three months old. From the program the Countess learned that a colored woman from the United States was to speak the morning on which she was to deliver her address, and when she heard that this colored woman would be in London before she returned to the United States, she cordially invited her to come to see her. Naturally, I was glad to make the acquaintance of this far-famed English beauty, the active, generous philanthropist and the acknowledged society queen all in one. She had done many things which appealed strongly to me. For instance, she had established an Agricultural College for women because at that time no provision had been made in England whereby gentlewomen who were reduced in circumstances or those who were obliged to support themselves were taught to earn a living, and the Countess thought it would be a step in the right direction to teach them to farm on scientific principles. I felt that such a woman was worth going miles to see.

The Countess' London residence was in St. James Square, just a minute's walk from Buckingham Palace, where the King and Queen of England reside. When I reached the house the door was opened by a tall, well-proportioned man whom anybody would call handsome. He went ahead and asked me to ascend a broad stairway which was carpeted in red velvet. When the top of the stairway was reached, I was ushered into what must have been Lady Warwick's private library. Here and there books were lying around as though they had just slipped from the hands of their fair mistress. When I looked at the pretty little desk there was something about it which impressed me with the fact that it was frequently used.

The room was a veritable bower of flowers. It looked like a bit of fairyland let down into a dwelling of mortals. There must have been at least ten vases filled with the choicest and most beautiful flowers imaginable. And they peeped at one from corners and angles where the effect was most artistic. I had just time enough to look around at the dainty French furniture, when the soft rustling of garments announced the approach of the lady I had come to see. Her beauty fairly stunned me and she was the very quintessence of grace.

As the Countess of Warwick advanced toward me, she extended her hand and gave me a most cordial welcome. "How kind and good you are to come to see me," she said. "I was greatly disappointed in not being able to keep my first engagement with you, but I was suddenly called away and I was obliged to go." The Countess had sent me a telegram stating she could not see me the day on which she first invited me to call.

Before I reached the Countess' residence I had prepared a few remarks which might do to start the conversation with the distinguished lady. I knew it was proper to address her as "Your Ladyship," and I had promised myself solemnly to do so. I had drilled myself thoroughly in this respect, but I was so overcome by the Countess' assertion that I had displayed an excess of kindness and goodness in calling on her that I forgot completely the neat little speech I had so carefully planned to make. In my confusion I fear that instead of addressing the Countess as "Your Ladyship," I used the good, old informal "You." But after the first embarrassment passed, I succeeded in displaying my knowledge of the proper English form.

The Countess had no sooner seated herself upon a white satin lounge which here and there had a touch of pink, than she arose and walked toward the door, explaining as she did so, that she had left her little dog outside. Since I am so fond of animals myself, my admiration for the beautiful woman was greatly increased. When the door was opened in ran the smallest canine I have even seen. As soon as the Countess seated herself on the divan again, Tiddledy Winks (for that was his Dogship's name) curled himself up snugly in a small round ball, laid himself upon the train of his mistress' elegant robe and then went fast asleep.

The Countess of Warwick was as willowy as a girl sixteen, as fair as a lily and as beautiful as her pictures represent her to be, although at that time she was the mother of fo ir children—a son who was a war correspondent in the Russian army, a daughter who had married Lord Helmsly, a small son six years old and a baby girl just three months old. She showed me the photos of each of the children except the baby girl, and each had inherited comeliness from their beautiful and charming mother. As I beheld her clad in a gown of some filmy material, the yoke and sleeves of which were real lace, wearing a large picture hat with a delicate pink rose in front, around which a very pale blue filmy veil was drawn and tied in a loop on her bosom, I wondered how it was possible for a woman to approach more nearly the ideal of perfect beauty than she did.

The Countess assured me she was deeply interested in the work I was trying to do for the women of my race and asked me many questions concerning it. She confessed that she was unable to grasp many phases of the Race Problem in the United States. She could not understand the prejudice against well-educated, cultivated men and women of color. The more the Countess discussed this aspect of the problem, the more evident it became that she was hopelessly groping in the dark. In trying to get light on the Theodore Roosevelt-Booker T. Washington luncheon, which had created a big sensation in the United States, she said she had conversed with some Americans in the hope of discovering the reason for the criticism, abuse and censure with which the President of the United States had been flooded on this account. "But," she said, and she paused a moment as though the mystery in which the subject was shrouded had deprived her of the power of speech, "I have never been able to comprehend it all."

The Countess had heard Englishmen discuss my article on Lynching, she said, but she had never read it herself. It was difficult to converse on this painful subject with the Countess, for she could hardly believe that colored men and women and even children were still being hanged, burned and shot to death in a country so highly civilized as the United States. She was sorry that colored men seemed to precipitate the trouble, she told me. It was quite evident she believed the statement circulated by the enemies and detractors of the race both at home and abroad that there is "one particular crime" for which colored men are usually lynched. I felt it my duty, therefore, to tell her Ladyship the truth—that out of every hundred colored men who are lynched in this country, from seventy-five to eighty-five are not even accused by the South of what is so maliciously and falsely called "the usual crime."

To an Englishman the lawlessness in the United States must be very hard to understand. No one can travel far in England without being impressed with the Englishman's reverence for law. From the lowest and roughest specimens to the King, there are a reverence and a veneration for law which are ingrained in the very marrow of their bones. It was very unpleasant trying to describe the Contract Labor System and the Convict Lease System and attempting to explain how such cruelty and oppression happen to be tolerated without strong and vigorous protests from the North. I felt so depressed and discouraged I turned the conversation into more agreeable channels, so that the pleasure of my visit should not be destroyed. No one enjoys expatiating upon the wickedness and weakness of his country when he is in a foreign land, however much he may feel it is his duty to do so at home. No matter what evils are rife in it, when separated from it by the ocean one feels that they should not be discussed, when it is possible to avoid doing so without misrepresenting the facts. I took special pains to emphasize the loyalty of the colored people to the country in which they and their parents had been born, and this seemed to please her Ladyship very much.

But I was eager to have the Countess tell me about her work and she graciously complied with my request. "You know I am a Socialist," she began. That was precisely what I did not know, and I almost gasped for breath. Remembering that well-bred people always suppress their emotions, I tried to look natural and to hide my surprise. "I'm a Socialist," continued the Countess, "because, after a long and careful study of conditions in England, I am convinced that Socialism is the only thing which can help poor people here to help themselves. I did not reach this conclusion hastily, and now that I am fully persuaded, it would be difficult for me to change my mind."

"Is the Earl of Warwick a Socialist?" I ventured to ask. "No, I am the only one in my family who believes in Socialism," she frankly replied. "But I am trying to convert my sister, the Duchess of Sutherland, and I should not be surprised if I succeed." "What do Your Ladyship's family and friends think of your Socialism?" I asked. The Countess laughed as heartily and as genuinely as a school girl. "Many of them think I'm going straight to the bad," she replied. "I dare say there are many good people who do not approve of it at all." The Countess' face was wreathed in smiles, as she talked about the disapprobation of those who disagreed with her on Socialism. I felt certain she did not lie awake nights worrying about it. Neither the Countess nor any of her family suffered in the slightest degree because she had espoused an unpopular cause. The Countess herself belongs to an old and well-known family and she married into one of the greatest and most powerful families in Great Britain. Even if people did not approve of her views, therefore, they were obliged to treat her with courtesy and respect.

"Will you be here next Monday?" the Countess inquired. "I shall leave London early Wednesday morning, as I sail from Liverpool for home Wednesday afternoon," I replied. "I am very sorry," said the Countess, "for we shall have the closing exercises of the Agricultural College Wednesday. There will be speaking and several interesting exercises which you would enjoy, I am sure. I shall go to the school Tuesday and spend the night there. I wish you could go, too. You would enjoy a visit to Warwick Castle, I know. Everything in the United States is so new," continued her Ladyship, "that I am sure you would be interested in the ancient, and Warwick Castle is a magnificent old pile. You will be in England again some day, will you not?" I expressed the hope that I would. "If you ever come again," said the Countess, "write me a short while before you sail, and we shall plan some delightful excursions together."

But nobody I met in London was more wonderful and more interesting than Samuel Coleridge-Taylor, the great composer, whose father was a full-blooded African and whose mother was pure English. The afternoon and evening I spent with this renowned musician and his charming English wife stand out conspicuously in my mind as being among the most delightful experiences of my trip. Samuel Coleridge-Taylor was a great musician, to be sure. He knew all about harmony, sharps and flats, but he knew many other things besides. He was a cultured gentleman who conversed well on any subject. He was the worthy son of his African father, who was a noted physician in one of the largest hospitals in England when he died.

Mrs. Coleridge-Taylor had a voice which was sonorous, rich and sweet. As her gifted husband accompanied her, while she sang with so much feeling and art a dainty little lyric which he had composed, I thought it would be a long time before I would see a more beautiful picture of domestic harmony and bliss than the one on which I was then feasting my eyes. With great anticipation of pleasure Mr. Coleridge-Taylor was then looking forward to his first visit to the United States.

At the dinner table the conversation turned naturally and imperceptibly upon the manifestations of race prejudice in this country. I listened with breathless interest as the noted Anglo-African composer related experiences through which he himself had passed in England. In the most humorous way he would recount stories in which he himself was the victim of Anglo-Saxon prejudice without feeling any resentment at all, as though he were talking about the ordeals which had overtaken an acquaintance and not himself. The revelations of prejudice on the Caucasian's part seemed to amuse him rather than rile him. They had never touched him at all. He did say, however, that he had once caned a boy, because the youngster had called him "Blackie" practically every time they met in the street.

In the evening we attended a concert at which the famous musician conducted an orchestra composed of some of the prettiest English girls I have ever seen. As I looked at the great composer's face light up with fire and enthusiasm for his art, I raised my heart to God in gratitude and praise that this gifted son of the muses dwelt in a land in which his transcendent genius was neither crippled nor crushed by a blighting prejudice and a cruel oppression based on the color of his skin.

Before I left England Mr. Coleridge-Taylor gave me an autographed photo of both himself and his little son, Hiawatha. Later on, the composer came to Washington to conduct a large chorus of colored people which sang his trilogy of "Hiawatha," and I had the pleasure of entertaining him a few days in our home. It has always been a source of deep regret that I did not make notes of some of the stories Mr. Coleridge-Taylor told, while he was our guest. I cannot recall anybody who was a more entertaining conversationalist than he was.

As one of my friends expressed it, I had a wealth of identity at the International Congress of Women on account of my African blood, so that from the nature of the case I met many distinguished people, both titled and untitled, those with pedigrees dating back to the flood and those who scarcely knew who their parents were.

Among the princesses to whom I was presented none appealed to me more strongly than did the Princess Maria Rohan, whose head was as full of excellent ideas as her heart was filled with the desire to do good in the world. The photo which she sent me after I reached home served to remind me of many a pleasant conversation we had together in Berlin.

Throughout my trip to Europe on this occasion it was very heartening to see how all without exception were genuinely interested in the colored people of the United States, sympathized with them, regretted the obstacles interposed by race prejudice and hoped they would gloriously surmount them in the end.

CHAPTER 23

MY EFFORTS TO SUCCEED AS A WRITER

THE FIRST TIME I saw my name in print I stood speechless with joy as I gazed upon it on a page of *St. Nicholas*, the well-known children's magazine. I must have been nine or ten years old. I had answered a puzzle correctly and my name with those of the other successful ones appeared in the back of the book. There it was! Mary E. Church—actually in print in a real, sure-enough book! I could scarcely believe my eyes. It seemed too good to be true. No amount of money could have bought that book from me. It was so precious to me I did not know where to put it for safe keeping. If anybody had tried to take it from me forcibly, I would have fought to retain it till the last ounce of strength had gone.

I cannot recall what the puzzle was all about, but the solution of it was one of Tennyson's poems which I had to search long and hard to find. The first time I saw my name in print as a writer was when I beheld it in the *Oberlin Review*, the Oberlin College paper, edited and manned by the students. Under the heading "Editorial Board," the name of Mary E. Church appeared as one of the editors representing her society, "Aelioian." I wrote several editorials for the *Review* which received favorable comment.

If ever a human being wrote with fear and trembling, it was surely I. I penned my thoughts painfully in longhand, of course, for the typewriter had not yet appeared. I interlined, changed and rechanged, crossed out, reinserted and made composition a difficult task for myself indeed.

No human being in the wide world but me could have deciphered my manuscript when I had finished writing an essay, and it was not an easy job for me. No matter how much pains I took with an essay or an oration, I was never satisfied with it. Writing a "composition" was a grueling, painful, heart-breaking task for me.

After my marriage I was invited by Mrs. Josephine St. Pierre Ruffin to write the Washington news for the *New Era,* a magazine which she established and published in Boston. Later on, Mr. Cooper, the editor of the *Colored American,* a newspaper published in Washington, invited me to write a column for women entitled "Women's World" and I wrote under the nom de plume of Euphemia Kirk.

Then Mr. T. Thomas Fortune, a pioneer in the newspaper field of our group, asked me to write for the *New York Age,* of which he was the brilliant editor for many years. My short articles appeared with the name of the writer on the editorial page. I believe Mr. Fortune paid me $4 a week for these contributions.

From that time on, I have written for a goodly number of magazines published either by or in the interest of colored people. Among these may be mentioned the A. M. E. *Church Review,* published in Philadelphia; the *Southern Workman,* published in Hampton, Virginia; the Indianapolis *Freeman,* the *Afro-American* of Baltimore, the *Washington Tribune* and others. For a while I wrote a column both for the *Chicago Defender* and for the *Norfolk* (Virginia) *Journal and Guide,* in which I commented upon current events.

I contributed several articles to the *Howard Magazine,* which was published by my brother, Thomas Ayres Church, who for forty years was a clerk in the Magistrate's Court in New York City. For quite a while I wrote for the *Voice of the Negro,* published in Atlanta, Georgia, and edited by Max Barber, who has done so much since then to perpetuate the memory of John Brown.

I thoroughly enjoyed writing for the *Voice,* although the remuneration I received was small. At that, it was more than was usually given me for an article. When I wrote for our newspapers I did not expect to be recompensed, for few of them at that time were financially able to pay much for their contributions, and I was glad to assist in any way I could. So far as I can recall, the *Colored American* was the first newspaper to pay me anything. Not long ago I came across a letter which had "inclosed a check for one dollar for your article of one column" in a certain issue.

Among my articles which appeared in the *Voice* I especially enjoyed writing one entitled "Christmas in the White House." When Mr. Barber asked me to write this article I feared to attempt it, for the task of going to the White House several months before Christmas to learn what was going to happen then, and to get enough information about the manner in which it would be celebrated to make an acceptable article seemed prodigious indeed. But when I tell you that the Theodore Roosevelt children lived in the White House at that time, you will not be surprised that the job of finding out what was going to happen there was far from dull. In this article for the *Voice of the Negro* I related with a great deal of pleasure that among the gifts for the President, Mrs. Roosevelt and their children Santa Claus always left some for two little colored boys whose father was the White House steward at that time.

Colored newspapers literally fill a long felt want in the life of our group. I am indebted to them for knowledge concerning the achievements, the progress and the efforts of colored people in and out of the United States which I could not possibly have obtained from any other source. For a long time white newspapers featured only the crimes and misdeeds of the race, but they are much more liberal now and are opening up their columns more and more to news reflecting credit rather than discredit upon the race.

Among the white newspapers for which I have written I want especially to mention the *Washington Evening Star* and the *Washington Post*, each of which has accepted quite a number of my articles for both the Sunday and other editions. I have often contributed also to the *Sunday Boston Globe*.

A very large and well-known newspaper in the East rejected an article on a prominent colored scientist which had been featured in the Sunday edition of the *Washington Post*. Shortly afterward I met a friend who told me he had seen an excellent article on this same scientist in this large newspaper. At my urgent request he promised to send it to me. He did so, and when I read it I saw that it was a reproduction of certain parts of my rejected article word for word without change of a "the" or an "and." When I wrote the managing editor of this paper requesting that he kindly give me some sort of compensation for my article which had appeared in spite of the fact it had been rejected, he sent me a check for $10 in a note which I still preserve. The *Washington Post* is the only newspaper in which one of my stories appeared. When reading the life of some well-known novelist I have often been awed to learn that the very first story he or she ever wrote was accepted. Well, I can say the same thing, although I can not lay claim to being a well-known or any other kind of a novelist.

The very first story I ever wrote, which was entitled "Venus and the Night Doctors," was accepted by the *Washington Post*. But the comparison between the writers whose first story was accepted and me ends right there. For those whose names shine bright in the galaxy of letters kept on producing stories which were accepted, while my very first was also my last which managed to burst into print. All of my stories were based on the Race Problem. Several reputable critics to whom I submitted them averred they passed muster quite nicely, but the editors of the magazines to whom they were sent thought otherwise and returned them post-haste.

I soon discovered that there are few things more difficult than inducing an editor of the average magazine to publish an article on the Race Problem, unless it sets forth the point of view which is popularly and generally accepted. Nobody wants to know a colored woman's opinion about her own status or that of her group. When she dares express it, no matter how mild or tactful it may be, it is called "propaganda," or is labeled "controversial." Those two words have come to have a very ominous sound to me. I can not escape them; they confront me everywhere I go.

When my manuscripts were rejected at first, I took it for granted they were returned to me because they fell too far below the required standard to be accepted. But after I had been laboring under that impression a long time, something happened which proved that there was nothing wrong with my manuscripts except the facts presented and the opinions expressed.

In the 1904 January number of the *North American Review*

Thomas Nelson Page had an article on Lynching which was one of the most scurrilous attacks upon the colored men of this country which has ever appeared in print. It was full of misleading statements from beginning to end. When I read it I thought I could not survive if something were not done to correct the impressions that Mr. Page's article had made.

I wrote to Mr. Munro, editor of the *North American Review*, a Scotchman, and told him I thought it was unworthy a great magazine like his to kick people who were already down by presenting only one side of the story which depicted them as brutes without allowing the other side to be shown. I urged him to have some outstanding colored man write the story of lynching from his point of view, so that the truth might be told. I wish I had all the money I spent on stationery and postage stamps in sending such letters to Mr. Munro. After writing at intervals for several months without receiving a reply, I finally wrote to Mr. William Dean Howells and asked him if he could not induce the editor of the *North American Review* to allow the other side of the story to be shown. Almost by return mail I received a letter from Mr. Howells saying that he agreed with me perfectly, that while he was simply a contributor to the Harper Publications and had no great influence, he would do what he could to have the colored man's side presented.

Shortly after that I received a letter from Mr. Munro, saying that he would like to have me write the article suggested, but that he did not want me to consider I had been commissioned to write it. He told me plainly that if he wanted to publish it, he would; and if he didn't, he wouldn't.

I wrote the article, which was one of the easiest tasks in that line I ever attempted. For several years I had been keeping a scrap book, and all I had to do was to turn to it and find concrete examples proving that the statements that innocent Negroes had never been lynched and that the Negro was practically the only rapist in the country were absolutely false.

This article, entitled "Lynching from a Negro's Point of View," was published in the 1904 number of the *North American Review* almost exactly as I sent it to the editor. The joy of seeing my article in the magazine was greatly enhanced because of the circumstances under which I beheld it for the first time. I went to the post office in Berlin, Germany, to get my letters from home which had been sent *poste restante,* and in the mail was a copy of the *Review* which my husband had sent me as soon as it reached him. For me it was truly a thrill which comes once in a lifetime.

When I returned from Europe, I called on Mr. Münro in New York and outlined another article which I wanted to write for the *North American Review.* "A Plea for the White South by a Colored Woman" was to be its title. As I gave him the points which I intended to make, Mr. Munro seemed very much pleased and thought there would be no doubt it would be accepted. When he received it, however, he sent it back to me by return mail. In the letter accompanying the manuscript Mr. Munro advised me to send it to the *Nineteenth Century and After.* This proved conclusively that the article was not rejected by the *Review* because it was too poorly written. If this had been the case Mr. Munro would never have suggested that I should send it to the *Nineteenth Century and After.*

He did advise me, however, to "blue-pencil" some of the statements I made on the ground that the relations "between the United States and England were very cordial indeed." Since I knew Mr. Munro would never have advised me to send a poorly written article to an English magazine noted for its high literary standard, it dawned upon me then and there that my manuscript had been rejected by the *North American Review,* not because of its mediocrity or inferiority, but because of the indisputable facts presented by it which the magazine would not print.

As I read and reread it carefully and prayerfully before sending it to the *Nineteenth Century and After,* I could find nothing which veracity, diplomacy or good taste would prompt me to change. So I forwarded it exactly as it was. It was accepted and published in a very short time as it had been originally written, and I was perfectly satisfied with the size of the check which I received. I considered that acceptance by the *Nineteenth Century* sufficient proof that my article came up to the required literary standard.

I had still another striking proof of the same fact. Having learned from an experience which occurred during an address that I delivered before the Baptist Woman's Home Missionary Society in Beverly, Massachusetts, that even well-educated people who kept abreast of the times knew nothing whatever, or very little, about the Convict Lease System, I decided to write an article on the subject. Accordingly, I went to the Congressional Library and spent six weeks looking over old files of the *Atlanta Constitution* and other newspapers published in the South. I knew that a few years previously the Governor of Georgia had been so shocked by some of the revelations which reached his ears about the barbarity of the Convict Lease System in his State that he decided to probe it to its depths. This he did, and the testimony of the eye witnesses to the murder and the unspeakable cruelties practiced upon the helpless prisoners, most of whom were Negroes, was published in the *Atlanta Constitution*.

Having armed myself with facts gleaned nearly first hand, I wrote my article, making it as readable and as interesting as I could. I was very careful not to "tear passion to tatters," and I made it a point to state nothing which could not be proved by what a southern white man had either spoken or written. Then I sent my manuscript to practically every magazine in the United States which would be likely to publish such an article. It was promptly turned down by every single one of them. Remembering that Mr. Munro had advised me to send an article rejected by the *North American Review* to the *Nineteenth Century and After,* I resolved to follow his counsel in this case, and I did so. A few months afterward, while I was talking to my brother in New York one day, he said, "Sis, somebody else has that old Convict Lease System bee in his bonnet as well as yourself." In explaining this remark he said that in several New York dailies he had recently seen excerpts from an article on the Convict Lease System which had appeared "in some English magazine." My heart beat fast. I wondered whether they had been taken from mine. Without telling my brother that I had submitted a manuscript to an English publication, I rushed to the City Library as fast as I could to see whether the one I had sent had been accepted. Sure enough! There it was in the *Nineteenth Century and After.*

I realized then more clearly than ever before that the reason my manuscripts had been rejected by American magazines was because the editors objected to having certain conditions which obtain in the United States broadcast to the world. I was thoroughly convinced that it would be difficult for me to write an article on the Race Problem which would be accepted by any publication in the country. I became discouraged and I did not try again to induce an editor in the United States to accept an article on the Race Problem for many years.

My article on "How, Why, When and Where Black Becomes White" was accepted by the Sunday editor of the *Chicago Tribune* and was kept in the office for a year before it was released. When I wrote to the editor requesting him to return it, and stating that I intended to send it to another paper, he asked Mr. Raymond Patterson, who was for many years the *Tribune's* Washington correspondent, to tell me that he intended to publish it eventually, since it was one of the most striking articles he had read for a long time. He would have to wait a bit, however, he said, till the psychological moment arrived because the paper had a large southern clientele which he did not want to offend. The *Boston Herald* accepted and released the article as soon as the editor received it, and the *Chicago Tribune* also finally decided to publish it.

Just one more incident to illustrate the difficulty experienced by a white woman who wished to present facts favorable to her colored sisters in the magazines to whose editors she submitted them.

A very successful writer in New York asked me one day why I did not write an article on "The Progress of Colored Women." She told me occasionally she was paid a neat little sum just for suggesting a subject or presenting an idea to an editor about something which appealed to him. "Don't you think I have already done so?" I replied, answering her question "Yankee fashion" by asking another. Then I related the efforts I had made to induce the editors of several magazines to accept an article on Colored Women, which had been rejected by all of them. On one occasion I had actually been commissioned to write the article, I told my friend, but it also had failed of acceptance. Miss X felt she understood perfectly why my manuscript had been rejected. I had felt too tense, she said, and "injected too much feeling into the matter."

"All right," I replied. "You write the article yourself. Some time when you are planning a trip to Washington, let me know beforehand and come to my house for lunch. Spend the day with me. I'll give you my manuscript, and let you browse to your heart's content through my scrap book, which contains a great deal of information concerning the work colored women have actually done."

She accepted the invitation and came. True to my word, I gave her my manuscript and helped her to take notes for the article which she intended to write immediately. She promised to apprise me of the result. I waited in vain to hear from her. About a year afterward I happened to be in New York, called her up, and she arranged to meet me. Then she told me she had written the article on "The Progress of Colored Women" and had offered it to every magazine likely to publish it, and every one of them had rejected it.

She also related the comments on the article made by some of the editors who were frank enough to express their opinions. One of them declared that in the heyday of Booker T. Washington's glory his magazine had not published a word about him. He would not think of publishing an article showing the progress of colored women because colored people on general principles were "too cocky" as it was, he said. Thus it happened that the article on "The Progress of Colored Women" written by a well-known contributor to the best magazines has never appeared. My own article was more fortunate, however. After it had been offered to various newspapers and magazines for a period of many years, each of which had promptly rejected it, I submitted my "Progress of Colored Women" to the editor of the *Boston Transcript,* who accepted it and gave it a prominent place in the Saturday evening issue. The reputation of the newspaper in which it finally appeared compensated me for the number of times it had been rejected.

My article on "Being a Colored Woman in the United States" was once read by a reader in a first-class publishing house, and he was so favorably impressed with it that, without my knowledge, he sent it to the editor of a leading magazine, feeling certain that he would accept it. The fact that a man whose business it was to read manuscripts for a large publishing house thought well enough of the article to submit it to one of the oldest magazines in the country was proof positive that there was no glaring defect in the style, and there was no evidence of bad taste. But the article was rejected.

In returning my manuscripts editors have praised them on

several occasions and have suggested that if I would submit something on any subject except the Race Problem, it might stand a pretty good chance of being accepted, but they gave me distinctly to understand they drew the line on that. Those who advised me to write about something else evidently thought that all I had to do was to select any subject which might tickle the fancy of an editor, then proceed to produce an article on it. They believed I could direct my thoughts and my interests to any other subject that occurred to me and produce a good article just as one turns the faucet to get water in a sink. But my whole being was centered on the conditions confronting my race, and I poured my very heart's blood into efforts to promote its welfare. It was impossible for me to write on anything which did not concern the race.

And it seemed to me that the only kind of article which found favor with the editors was one that emphasized the Colored-American's vices and defects, or held him up to ridicule and scorn. Stories which represented him as being a crap-shooter, a murderer, a bum or a buffoon were considered fine examples of literary art, and appeared in reputable magazines from time to time. But those which related his struggles to accomplish something worth while against fearful odds were labeled "controversial" and never saw the light of day. Those who wrote them were accused of trying to "spread propaganda" through the country, which was a case of literary treason on the high seas.

More than once my articles have made friends for me among literary people who have stimulated and encouraged me greatly. Through my article on Lynching I met Mrs. Van Renssalaer Cruger, a novelist of distinction, who wrote to congratulate me upon it, declaring that few of her friends were capable of making a literary effort comparable with mine. Mrs. Cruger lived in an old-fashioned house in Georgetown, D. C., and often invited me to take tea with her. Those were rare treats indeed. Mrs. Cruger had lived abroad for years, had been intimately associated with distinguished people all over the world, and was an exceptionally fine conversationalist.

She always wore a picture hat, when we sipped tea together, and looked like a genuine grand dame. When my literary friend came to my house to take tea with me, I omitted my chapeau, although on general principles I am quite imitative, like the rest of my group. I missed her very much when she married her second husband. Mrs. Chance left Washington and did not reside here any more.

Mrs. Mary Roberts Rinehart, the well-known playwright and author, manifested her friendship toward me in many ways. She declared that she had received more information from my articles on Lynching, on the Convict Lease System, and from my Plea for the White South by a Colored Woman than from any articles she had read in twenty years. I doubt that the one on Lynching would ever have seen the light of day in an American magazine if William Dean Howells had not used his personal, powerful influence in its behalf.

And yet, when Colonel Harvey, who differed with me on several points, reviewed it in *Harper's Weekly*, he began by saying: "It is in respect to diction a remarkable article on 'Lynching from a Negro's Point of View' which is contributed in the June number of the *North American Review* by Mrs. Mary Church Terrell, and scarcely less striking in form." At the risk of appearing conceited, I quote this defense of my articles from two outstanding writers of this generation. The other two articles would have been resting peacefully in my desk, where manuscripts like them have been hidden away in the dark, lo, these many years, if they had not been accepted by an English magazine.

Mrs. Rinehart encouraged me to write and was willing to assist me to get entree into the magazines which had not opened their columns to me. I often called on her and invariably came away from her presence encouraged and inspired. I miss her since she left Washington to live in New York. It is impossible for anybody to entertain broader views on the position which intelligent colored people should occupy in the United States than she does. She has no patience with that narrow, petty prejudice which excludes colored people of education and character from the advantages and privileges which other people enjoy. It grieved her that I did not receive the consideration which would have been shown me if I had been white and which had been accorded me in every country which I visited abroad.

When Mrs. Ella Wheeler Wilcox, the well-known poet and newspaper correspondent, was at the height of her popularity she manifested her friendship toward me in a variety of ways. In the *New York Journal and American,* for which she was writing, she devoted considerable space to approving the efforts I was making in behalf of my race.

She once gave a reception at the Willard Hotel which was largely attended by people well known in the political, literary and artistic life of the National Capital. In the invitation which she sent me came a little personal note, stating that she would like to have me come early and stay till the other guests had gone, so that she might talk to me a few minutes and give me her photograph. I hesitated a bit to comply with this request because I feared it would display bad taste on my part to do so. I reached the reception when it was about half over, was introduced to the distinguished guests and had a good time. I wondered whether this was Mrs. Wilcox's way of showing how she felt about extending a courtesy to a colored woman she chose to number among her friends. I have preserved the photo she gave me as a memento of that occasion.

I have already mentioned the friendship entertained for me by Mr. William T. Stead after we met in London. When he and Mrs. Stead visited Washington years afterward, he permitted nobody to interview him for the press but myself. My interview with him in the *Washington Evening Star,* therefore, was the only one which appeared in any daily while he was in the National Capital.

I was once invited to a luncheon in New York given by the widow of Colonel Robert G. Ingersoll, who was one of the best friends the colored people of this country ever had. I owe a debt of gratitude to him personally because of a great service he rendered my brother. When Thomas A. Church graduated with honor from Columbia Law School, he had to serve an apprenticeship in a reputable law firm before being admitted to practice in New York. Every one of the lawyers he requested to accept him as a clerk refused.

Finally, in despair, he went to Colonel Ingersoll. "Sometimes my friends ask me to take their sons into my office," he replied, "but I refuse, as a rule, because clerks are often greater hindrances than helps." "It is comparatively easy for the sons of your friends to find lawyers who will take them into their offices as clerks," said my brother, "but it is very hard for me."

Mr. Ingersoll looked pained, said Brother, and was silent for a while. Then he said, "Mr. Church, come back next Thursday at two o'clock, and I'll let you know definitely what I can do."

When my brother returned at the appointed time, he was told that Mr. Ingersoll was not in the office. "But Mr. Ingersoll promised to give me his decision about an important matter at two o'clock today," said Brother. "Oh yes," said the clerk. "Colonel Ingersoll told me to tell Mr. Church to look on a desk at the right in the next room and he will find the decision there." "T. A. Church's Desk" was written on a paper on the top. And so my brother had the privilege, the advantage and the honor of being admitted to the bar of New York frcm Colonel Robert G. Ingersoll's office. "People were always running to Colonel Ingersoll for help," said Brother. He was charitable and generous to everybody without regard to race, color or creed.

Ray Stannard Baker, who was then one of the editors of the *American Magazine,* was one of Mrs. Ingersoll's guests at this luncheon. I asked him if he thought that his or any other publication would accept a modern version of *Uncle Tom's Cabin* if Harriet Beecher Stowe were still alive and depicted the injustice commonly perpetrated upon colored people all over the United States and showed the towering obstacles erected by a cruel race prejudice which they have had to surmount in order to accomplish something worth while ever since they have been emancipated, as the original *Uncle Tom's Cabin* exposed the cruelties and barbarities of slavery. In short, would an American magazine publish a novel showing the shackles by which colored people are bound today, though nominally free, as the original *Uncle Tom's Cabin* bared the cruelties perpetrated upon them, when they were legally enslaved.

Both Mr. Baker and Mr. Philip Boyden, who was also on the staff of the *American Magazine,* debated the question for a while and finally admitted that, in their opinion, no periodical in the country would publish any such story at that time. That confirmed my own views on the subject and sounded my literary death knell. I knew full well that the kind of story I would be able to write would not appeal to the average editor of an American magazine. I was sure it would be interpreted as "propaganda" of the deepest dye and would be voted controversial and "inartistic" to the nth degree. Right there I gave up my literary ghost.

It has been a bitter disappointment to me that I did not succeed as a story writer. I have thought for years that the Race Problem could be solved more swiftly and more surely through the instrumentality of the short story or novel than in any other way. In this position I was more strongly confirmed than ever when I learned that at least one other person agreed with me.

After my article on Lynching appeared, Mr. Bruce Porter, of San Francisco, wrote me a letter which greatly whetted my desire to attempt a book such as I had long wanted to write:

"My Dear Mrs. Terrell:

"I have read with deep interest and impotent shame that every true American suffers in the face of fact your direct and fearless article in the current number of the *North American Review*. My regret is that in this standard publication the circle of your readers is necessarily limited. I would suggest—if you feel it to be within your power—that you embody these truths (with moderation and justice) in form of a novel. You possess the fervor of conviction (which is of first value in such an effort) and that can easily carry your work above the difficulty of literary expression. There has lately been published a book written so—and with justice—upon the case of the Jews in Austria—'Idylls of the Gass'—a story of wrong—written about the life of a child. With the primariness of the question of the Negro with us all—I believe a book of that sort would have a wide influence upon the mind of the public.

"Very faithfully yours,
"Bruce Porter."

Here then was a disinterested man who believed that people of this country could not only be educated and aroused on the subject of Lynching, but sentiment against it could be created by a novel. I shall never cease to regret that I did not take Mr. Porter's advice and attempt to write the novel he suggested. But I had no faith in my ability to write such a story, although my very soul yearned to do it, and I could not generate courage enough to attempt it. But even if I had possessed both the ability and the courage, I should have had to surmount many obstacles to find the time, the opportunity for concentration and the peace of mind necessary to write such a book. I had to discharge my duty to my family, to the public schools in my capacity as a member of the Board of Education, and not infrequently I filled lecture engagements.

I was often invited to deliver addresses on special occasions for churches or secular organizations of different kinds. This meant that I had to make special preparation by first writing my thoughts in long hand and then typing them myself. After carefully preparing my speech I would go over it so many times and get the points so definitely fixed in my mind that I practically committed it to memory. I never depended upon "the inspiration of the moment" to receive the message which was to be delivered to the audience. Every now and then I accepted an invitation to write a special article for a paper published by my own group. All this consumed a great deal of time and there were innumerable interruptions in the home.

Just as I would get seated at my desk, after I was already tired from doing a day's work, the doorbell would ring and I would be obliged to talk to somebody who "wanted to see me on business," or with a man who had brought something to the house which had to be adjusted in some way and needed my attention. Leaving him, I would try to refocus my thoughts on my subject, but I would scarcely write a sentence before the bell would ring again and some parent would appear to see me about "a little unpleasantness" his child had had in school, perhaps. My statement that, as a member of the Board of Education, I had nothing to do with the discipline meted out to children made no difference to the parent at all. The child's mother or guardian insisted upon telling me the circumstances and presenting his side of the case anyhow, so that I "might be fully acquainted with the facts."

The mother of a teacher who thought her daughter should have been promoted, but wasn't, would lay her case before me, or the teacher herself who *knew* she had been marked unfairly would review her case from A to Z. Sometimes the ashman had to be "seen" about taking out the ashes, or a bundle from the store would arrive and have to be taken in, or the laundry man would come, either to get the laundry or to return it, and so on down the line ad infinitum. After I had answered the bell three or four times in the morning and talked with several visitors on "business" (their business, not mine), the minutes at my disposal for literary composition had been consumed, to say nothing of my patience, strength and inspiration. It is quite possible for a woman to succeed as a writer, if she has nothing to do but look after her children and her home. But when exacting public work is added to her other cares, it is very difficult, if not impossible, to do so.

People conceived the idea that I had a great deal of influence with the Powers That Be, which I did not possess, and they often wanted me to "go with them to see somebody" by whom they wished to be employed. If I told them truthfully I could do them no good, they did not believe me. Sometimes I felt I would actually hurt the individual instead of helping him. There is no doubt, however, that I might have protected myself better than I did. Nobody is to blame but myself. I have always enjoyed the reputation of possessing a strong will, and about most things I really have, I think. But I dreaded doing anything which might make people believe I was disobliging and mean, so I often allowed my time to be wasted which I should have reserved for myself to accomplish those things which I had planned and wanted very much to do. It was an exhibition of unpardonable weakness to allow myself to be spread over too wide a surface, and to try so hard to be all things to all men.

Moreover, I tried hard to discharge my duties as a citizen and I would respond to almost any call. For instance, I was once asked to take charge of a drive among colored people for the Instructive Visiting Nurse Society. Before I finished with it, at least three months of my time had been consumed, attending and holding meetings and getting all the returns from a group of efficient, faithful women who helped me. It was a great joy to render this service, and I did not regret the effort. It was the duty of the colored people of the District to make as large a contribution as possible to an organization that had rendered such signal service to them as the Instructive Visiting

Nurse Society had, and we all rejoiced that the sum of $4,000 was raised.

On another occasion I helped the Columbia Hospital in a drive for funds and had the satisfaction of bringing in the second largest sum collected by the captains, who were all representatives of the dominant race and well-known society leaders except myself.

But throughout my life, no matter what I was doing, I kept dreaming of the day I would have the leisure and the mental peace to write some of the things I longed to say. But that day never came. In every diary that I have kept, the yearning to express my thoughts on the printed page and the poignant regret that I could not do so run like a Jeremiad from the first day of the year to the last. "I am always getting ready to write something," I lament in one place, "but I am never prepared to begin. I am more like George Eliot's Casaubon than anybody either in fiction or out of it with whom I can be compared."

If I had lived in a literary atmosphere, or if my time had not been so completely occupied with public work of many varieties, I might have gratified my desire to "tell the world" a few things I wanted it to know. I do not regret the time and energy consumed in serving others. I can not help wondering, however, whether I might not have succeeded as a short-story writer, or a novelist, or an essayist, if the conditions under which I lived had been more conducive to the kind of literary work I so longed to do.

CHAPTER 24

MY CHILDREN AND I

W HEN THE YOUNGER of my two daughters was about three years old, she came very near being burned to death. As soon as she fell asleep, she would snort and snore so loud she would wake up immediately. I had never seen a child or anybody else so affected, and I did not know what the trouble was. Neither she nor anybody in the room with her could sleep. Several doctors had prescribed for her, but her condition had not improved, and we were in despair.

I read an advertisement in a newspaper about a preparation whose fumes were guaranteed to correct this trouble. I tried it. But in some way which I have never been able to explain, the fumes suddenly burst into flames. I ran around the foot of our bed, which was beside her little crib, and lifted her out of the flames before they had ignited the bed covers or her night clothes. It was a narrow escape for her, and a harrowing experience from which I did not recover for a long time. Shortly afterwards a colored physician from Harrisburg, Pennsylvania, called on me and inquired about my baby's health. When I described her condition to him, he said at once: "She has an adenoid growth which must be removed." It was the first time I had ever heard the word, and he explained what he meant. His diagnosis was correct, and there was no more trouble when the adenoids were removed. Since then, I have seen hundreds of children so affected—mouth breathers—whose growth is often retarded, whose physical condition is seriously impaired and whose record in school is indifferent, simply because their adenoids are not removed.

I enjoyed my children thoroughly, while they were growing up, and spent as much time with them as I possibly could. We went on long hikes together. Occasionally I took them to the theatre, to the movies and to the operas which they could understand. If we had put a placard on our backs announcing that we were of African descent I could not have taken them to a single white theatre in the National Capital, unless we were willing to be Jim-Crowed, and I made up my mind definitely that I would never allow them to be humiliated if there was any way in the world to avoid it.

We spent nearly every summer vacation away from Washington. After a lecture bureau booked me for Chautauquas in the West I made an arrangement, already mentioned, by which I would never be obliged to remain away from home more than three consecutive weeks. For several summers we went to Harpers Ferry, the scene of John Brown's raid and execution. We had quarters in Storer College, a splendid school for colored youth, whose lawn was an ideal playground for children.

Several vacations were spent in Opequon, a small country resort about seven miles from Winchester, Virginia. Twice we went to Oak Bluffs, Massachusetts, and the girls had a good visit in New York City, when they returned home.

Shortly after we went to housekeeping in our little English basement, Major Charles Douglass, the son of Frederick Douglass, invited us to Highland Beach, which is about five miles from the Naval Academy in Annapolis, Maryland, to look at a tract of land he had bought on Chesapeake Bay. He intended to convert it into a summer resort for our group, he said, and he wanted us to buy a lot there. It was in the country, and no human being ever disliked the country more than my husband. He had remained in the country till he was ten years old, he used to say, and he had got plenty during that period; enough to last him for the rest of his natural life.

I was delighted with the place and decided to use the money I had earned by substituting in the high school during Miss Patterson's illness to buy the lot. The Honorable Frederick Douglass selected a corner lot, facing Chesapeake Bay, and asked us to take the one next to his. Our neighbor on the left, therefore, was Mr. Douglass, and on the right a short distance away Paul Dunbar bought a lot. Never have I seen a finer combination of the country and the seashore than Highland Beach affords. The girls and I planned a house. We had just one clear idea about it, and that was that it should have "a great, big porch" and as large a living room as possible. We succeeded so well in carrying out this plan that, while he was building the front and side porches, the head carpenter used to tell everybody passing by that he was fencing in Anne Arundel County, in which our little summer resort is located. A sprint down the steps, a bound across the road in front of our house, and then a hop, skip and jump over a sandy beach and presto! we are in the Bay. This summer home has been a great blessing. I attribute much of the good health which my daughters and I enjoy to the swimming and outdoor life we have been able to lead down there. I regret that we have not spent more time in the beneficial surroundings which it so generously affords. What was a settlement of only a few houses when we purchased our lot has developed into quite a summer resort which literally fills a long-felt want for colored people in and near the National Capital, who are excluded from all the others.

One of the most perilous adventures I ever had occurred when we were at Harpers Ferry one summer. Among the mothers who had brought their children to the Ferry, I was the only one who liked to take long walks. On a glorious summer day several of the older girls, who were between 12 and 14 years, begged me to take a group of them to the top of the mountain near by. Nobody could enjoy mountain climbing more than I do. I consented to do so, and a party of young people, ranging in age from eight to fourteen years, started off gaily to negotiate the mountain. Fortunately, I left the younger of my two daughters at the dormitory.

We reached the top of the mountain after the usual struggles which such an effort entails. When we started to return several of the older girls insisted upon taking a different route from the one we had used in the ascent. I objected strenuously to doing so. I feared to try a new route, knowing how poor is my sense of direction and how easy it is for me to lose my bearings. But the girls assured me they knew the way down the mountain and were so eager to go another way that I could not bear to oppose them. And so, after many serious misgivings, I finally granted their request.

All of a sudden, as we were walking along the new path, we reached a point where we could not go a step further. In front of us was a steep precipice, so sheer and deep it made us dizzy to try to look down to the bottom of it. It was growing late, for we had taken our time in the ascent, but there seemed to be nothing to do but retrace our steps and try to find the path we had followed when we were climbing to the top. The girls said they were too tired to go back. Moreover, neither I nor anybody else was at all sure we could find this path, even if we tried to retrace our steps.

After searching for a long time, one of the girls discovered a precipitous path, so narrow that it was hardly possible for one person to walk on it, even if one dared. But she said it led down to another by which she thought we could descend the mountain. We decided there was only one way to get down the narrow path with the sheer drop of many feet on one side. We would have to lie down on our abdomens and slide down, holding on to the edge to keep from falling over the side.

While we were discussing this we heard voices of men who were approaching us. When they came near enough to talk to us they said they had been lost in the mountain for at least two hours, and they did not know how to get down. They refused to try to slide down that narrow defile and strongly advised us against trying to do so. But the children begged me to let them attempt it, and I finally was forced to yield to their entreaties. I did not know what else to do.

The eldest girl went first. I scarcely dared to look at her, for fear I would see her fall down that steep cliff. When the smallest child and my daughter, Mary, started down, my heart literally stood still, and I was in an agony of suspense and fear. I was the last one to try to slide down that dangerous path. I remained back, so that I might look after any child who at the last minute might lose her nerve and fear to make the attempt. By the time I had seen each of the children risk her life, I was so nerve-racked that I could scarcely summon the courage to start. Nothing but my duty to the children and the horror of spending the night alone on that mountain forced me to make the effort.

It was quite dark when we finally reached home. Naturally, everybody was greatly alarmed and several of the mothers were on the verge of hysterics. I dreaded to see them, and I asked the children to tell them what had happened. Those who lived at Harpers Ferry and knew the mountain we ascended declared that it was full of venomous rattlesnakes. They considered it a miracle that, as we ploughed through the leaves which were ankle deep even for me in many places, not one of us had been stung by those poisonous reptiles which would have meant certain death for the victim, as far removed as we were from medical aid. Since then I have never taken other women's children any place about which I knew so little that I was not sure I could return them safe and sound to their homes.

Whenever it was possible for me to take my children on a trip I was sure to do so. I enjoyed watching their reactions when they saw or heard anything new. Having been invited to deliver an address at the Lancaster, Ohio, Chautauqua, I made up my mind to take my small daughter Phyllis with me. She was about four years old. My husband and mother advised me strongly not to do so. It would be very easy to arrange to have her cared for while I was speaking, I thought, and she would enjoy the trip so much. Sure enough, several young women volunteered to look after my little girl while I was filling an afternoon engagement, and I left her in their care.

I had been speaking about fifteen minutes when I spied her walking rapidly—almost running—down the aisle from the back of the big tent. In the twinkling of an eye she darted up the steps to the platform and stood as close to me as she could, looking out upon the large audience without any embarrassment whatever and remaining perfectly still. I was speaking without a manuscript, so I placed my right hand on her shoulder and went on with my address without stopping. In a short while one of the officials of the Chautauqua came upon the platform, took the child in his arms, and she went out of the tent with him without making any effort to remain. It was a tense moment for me, and I realized that when a mother has a lecture engagement to fill and brings a young child with her she takes a desperate chance.

The next day when I was sitting at my hotel window I heard the hoofs of a horse clattering down the road very fast. I looked up just in time to see a girl about fourteen years old riding horseback at a breakneck speed with my little daughter sitting behind her, holding on to her waist, while her long curls were lifted up by the wind straight out from her head.

It was also while I was at Lancaster that I discovered what a daring little lady my young daughter was. A gentleman who had brought his family to the Chautauqua told me he intended to take his children and several others out rowing and asked me to let my little girl go along with them. I consented, of course. Several hours afterwards he brought his guest back to her mother. "Your little girl is game, all right," he said. "The children in the boat were talking about swimming, and two of them claimed they could swim. 'Can you swim?' one of the children asked your daughter. She said she could. 'Oh, you can't swim. You're too little,' said one of the party. And then, before anybody could stop her, she jumped into the river, clothes, shoes, curls and all, to prove that she could swim. But before she had a chance to display her skill as a swimmer, we fished her out." Although the daring and courage of my little girl amused the gentleman who brought the news, they did not amuse her mother quite so much.

My two daughters were sent to the public schools for colored youth in the National Capital, and both of them took piano lessons also. After the older graduated from the high school and the younger had finished the first year, I took them to Oberlin. I decided to do this because I thought it would be wrong to bring them up having contact with nobody but their own racial group. I felt it was my duty to give them the same chance of measuring arms with white youth that I myself had had. I remained in Oberlin with my daughters about five months and enjoyed revisiting the beautiful, little town where I had spent so many pleasant and profitable years in my youth. The thought of leaving the house in Washington in which we had lived so long did not sadden me as much as it might have, because my mother had died there, and so many things constantly reminded me of her I felt a change of scene would do me good. When I decided the time had come to take the girls away I did not have the courage to broach the matter to my husband, but delegated the girls to break the news to him to see what his reaction would be. After he recovered from the shock, he agreed with me and cheerfully consented.

Mary, the older of the two girls, entered the freshman

class. Phyllis, the younger, matriculated for two subjects in the Academy and took violin and piano in the Conservatory of Music. She had started the violin shortly after she had begun to take piano lessons. When she completed the eighth grade she played a violin solo at the closing exercises of the school, and I accompanied her on the piano. The girls remained in Oberlin a year. The older returned to Washington, studied a year in Howard University, entered the Normal School, graduated, and was appointed to teach in the public schools.

The younger daughter went to St. Johnsbury Academy in Vermont, graduated, returned to Washington, entered the Conservatory of Music of Howard University, graduated and was appointed to teach music in the public schools. My husband was relieved of the responsibility of defraying the expenses incident to sending both girls to Oberlin and one to Saint Johnsbury later on, because I used the income from the property left me by my father to do this.

One of my daughters married a physician, who taught in Rush Medical College, in Chicago, and recently passed away at the height of his career. The husband of the other daughter is the principal of one of the Washington schools.

The year one of my daughters was in St. Johnsbury and the other at Howard University is indelibly impressed upon my mind because of two incidents which occurred. For several years I had known that my health was such that it would be necessary for me to undergo a surgical operation or become an invalid for the rest of my life. I said nothing to my husband about it or to anybody else. It was never pleasant for me to discuss my physical ailments with anybody, unless it was absolutely necessary. With each daughter living in the dormitory of the institution she was attending, it was easy for me to arrange to go to the hospital in Rochester, Minnesota, over which Dr. Will Mayo, one of the greatest surgeons in the world, presided.

When I reached the hospital and requested that this far-famed physician should perform the operation, I was told that, as he advanced in years, he was doing as little work as possible, and preferred to have younger men, who were as skillful as himself, operate in his stead. This was very bad news for me. I had set my heart on having the famous surgeon, about whom

I had been reading so long, take my case, and this message was conveyed to him. Immediately he sent me word that if a woman had come alone 1,000 miles to have an operation performed and wanted him to do it, he would certainly comply with that request. And he did. I remained at that hospital two months, and I think of it today as I probably would if I had been permitted to remain that long in Heaven, even though I was placed on the operating table three times. I feel also that I could never pay in dollars and cents for the attention I received there.

The other incident to which I referred occurred while I was at the hospital. When I returned home I learned that there had been a fire in the building where our furniture and household goods had been stored when we broke up housekeeping and took our daughters to Oberlin. Almost everything we possessed had been destroyed. Practically all the furniture from a ten-room house, pictures and china, including many of our wedding presents, went up in flames. Most of the silverware was saved, as were also pieces of a Limoges china set which my mother had given me and which I was able to match when I tried to replace the lost pieces. The beautiful sealskin ulster which my mother had made for herself in London from selected skins, and the one which she gave me, were so badly damaged by chemicals they were completely ruined.

The three volumes on the *History of Woman Suffrage* and other books given me by Susan B. Anthony were burnt up, together with other literary treasures which I greatly prized. Among these were the autographed copies of books given me by the great temperance advocate, Frances Willard; W. T. Stead, for many years editor of the *Review of Reviews;* Mrs. Van Rensselaer Cruger, and several other well-known authors and publicists.

Ten days before the fire broke out in the storage rooms the agent of the company with which we were insured notified Judge Terrell that the storage house was unsafe and refused to renew the policy on our belongings, until they were removed. But the invincible optimism of my husband led him to believe that nothing would happen if he took his time in moving them, so he let them remain where they were. This is a splendid illustration of my husband's cheerful outlook on life. He believed in looking at the bright side of everything. It seemed never to occur to him that any bad luck would overtake him, and, truth to tell, it rarely did. But when we lost everything which we possessed, it was the one exception which proved the rule.

I taught my daughters they were doing their Heavenly Father a service when they prevented anybody from treating His children with injustice, scorn or contempt solely on account of color or race. I taught them also they were justified in using any scheme, not actually criminal or illegal, to secure for themselves what representatives of other racial groups enjoyed, but of which they would be deprived on account of their African descent. I impressed upon them that they would perpetrate a great injustice upon themselves if they failed to take advantage of any good thing which they had a right to enjoy, simply because certain people had the power to deprive them of it by making arbitrary and unjust laws.

I missed pictures and plays to which I should have enjoyed taking my children because the idea of trying to hoodwink even those who imposed unjust restrictions upon us was very distasteful to me. Inwardly I rebelled against being obliged to play such a disagreeable role with all the self-respect which a woman who was trying to reach high ideals would naturally have. And I hated to teach my children to use such an unpleasant subterfuge. But what was I to do? Moreover, every time I availed myself of the opportunity of seeing what I wanted to see and of going where I had a right to go I ran the risk of getting a disagreeable notoriety which would have been painful both to Judge Terrell and to me. It certainly would not have helped to advance the interests of a colored man who wanted to be reappointed to the judgeship of the Municipal Court in the National Capital every four years, and confirmed by the Senate, some of whose members used all the power and influence they possessed to defeat him every time the President sent in his name.

Uncle Tom's Cabin was to be played at one of the theatres. I wanted my girls to see it, and they were eager to see it also. But it was produced at a second-rate theatre whose accommodations for white people were none too good and whose arrangements for colored people were simply out of the question. That was the first time I had to explain to them that we would have to be very careful indeed because colored people were not allowed to sit in the good seats in the desirable part of the theatre where I hoped to buy tickets for them. There are few things more heart-breaking for a colored mother than to be obliged to explain to her children that they can not go where children of other racial groups may go, and they can not see what those favored children may see.

After she understood the situation, one of my daughters invariably took some friend with her when she went to a white movie. This friend was usually darker in complexion than my daughter. In fact, some of the friends she took with her were so dark in complexion I marveled that she succeeded in getting them by the eagle eye of the ticket taker. "Well," my daughter would explain, "I would tell Susie, or Jane or Madge that if she wanted very much to see the picture and had the nerve to go with me, I certainly had the nerve to go ahead, get her ticket, give it to the ticket taker, lock arms with her and walk in boldly with her if she would come along with me." I do not recall that she failed to carry out her contract or that she had any trouble in any of these risky escapades.

But these young folks were more fortunate than some of their elders were on a certain occasion. Bob Cole, the comedian, and Rosamond Johnson, the musician, were to appear at a theatre in Washington some years ago. I wanted very much to go, because I enjoyed Bob Cole more than any comedian I have ever seen. The press comments about this well-known colored team were very complimentary and about six of us women decided we would go to see them and take a chance, no matter what happened. Two of these were fair enough to pass into the theatre unobserved, two not quite so fair, one medium and the other showing her racial characteristics more distinctly than the others.

We decided to go in one at a time at intervals, except in the case of the fairest one, who bought the ticket for the darkest one, and they went in together. The rest walked the plank alone. We felt that our scheme to enable us to see the colored men had been crowned with success. But suddenly, just before the curtain went up, I felt, rather than saw, the usher come up behind us, put his hand on the shoulder of the darkest woman and say something to her. I sat next to her, but I could not hear what he said. My heart was in my mouth, and I was both indignant and embarrassed. Then I witnessed an illustration of courage, resourcefulness and determination not to be outdone such as one seldom sees.

My friend turned to the usher and said in broken English—very broken indeed—"What you say to me? I buy my ticket, I come to the theatre, I take my seat" (with a distinctive rising inflection characteristic of the French), "and now—what you saying to me?" Then she turned completely around to look the usher squarely in the eye, as though she could not understand what was the matter and why he should speak to her. She won her case hands down. "Oh, pardon me, madam," said the young man in the most apologetic manner imaginable, and departed posthaste.

Of course we were all greatly relieved that nothing more serious had happened. We were glad that she had not been picked up bodily from her seat and dragged out of the theatre, if she refused to go. That has happened in Washington more than once. We were also proud of our brave, clever friend. But it was very hard for us to keep our faces straight the rest of the evening.

On several occas s when Roland Hayes, the world-famous tenor, has sung in Washington colored people could not go to hear him, unless they were willing to be relegated to a part of the auditorium where they could scarcely see or hear him. For that reason the radio has been a great boon and blessing to colored people living in those sections where they are excluded from theatres, movies and auditoriums, unless they are willing to be segregated and seated in the sections which, in most instances, are the most undesirable parts of the house. Now, thanks to the radio, colored people, especially the youth of the group, can hear the best artists, actors, lecturers of the day, derive great benefit and inspiration therefrom and still maintain their self-respect.

It is not hard to understand why some colored people succeed in gaining admittance to movies and theatres from which their group is excluded. There are many dark-skinned people in Washington and everywhere else, for that matter, who are considered white and are granted all the rights, privileges and immunities which the dominant race enjoys. For instance, there are the East Indians, some of whom are almost black; the Indians, indigeous to our own soil, whose land we have benevolently appropriated; the Mexicans; the dark-skinned sons and daughters of Italy, France and Spain, many of whom are much darker in complexion than hundreds of colored people are.

As a general rule, all these dark people are allowed to enter theatres, movies, restaurants and other public places from which the colored people of the United States are excluded. Naturally, the managers of these places do not want to get into trouble because their employees make the mistake of denying admittance to these swarthy folks who are considered white. Consequently, they are probably cautioned against refusing admittance to anybody except those who are unmistakably colored. The employees are not always wise and clever enough to draw a line between those who, though colored are white, and others who, though white are black. Not many years ago the Supreme Court of Louisiana decided that a man who looks like white shall not be subject to conditions imposed upon Negroes.

Because a conductor on a southern train in a certain southern State thought he knew colored people when he saw them, the road which employed him had to pay $20,000 to a woman who was forced to leave the white coach and ride in the Jim Crow car. When she reached her destination, her husband, who was a well-known white man, came to meet her and was restrained with difficulty from murdering the conductor who had dared to say his wife was colored and had forced her to ride in the Jim Crow car. It was currently reported that a fair colored woman had ridden on the same train in the white coach. The wise conductor who had boasted that no colored person, however fair, could escape detection by his eagle eye had failed to classify her correctly.

CHAPTER 25

MY EXPERIENCE AS A CLERK IN A GOVERNMENT DEPARTMENT

DURING THE WORLD WAR almost everybody in Washington who knew how to write and spell was taking an examination of some kind, so as to get a job in one of the Government departments. The officials were calling loudly for assistance, as the volume of business incident to the war continued to increase, and they were urging citizens all over the country to take an examination for the various clerkships, so that they might have the extra help required to do the work. Accordingly, I decided to take an examination as typist and presented myself with my machine at the building designated for that date.

I knew I had passed, but I took it for granted that it would be a long time before I would be called if, indeed, I ever received an appointment. So I thought very little about it. Ten days after I took the examination our doorbell jangled one morning between two and three o'clock and a telegram addressed to me was handed to me. "Come immediately to the Aetna Building, Room 305," it read, and was signed by General Crozier.

At first I was speechless with surprise, for I did not connect the telegram with the examination I had taken. It came at such an unearthly hour in the morning I thought it must be very urgent indeed. I asked my husband whether it was not my duty to answer the summons immediately, as I was requested to do. He laughed heartily at the idea, saying that even if I went to the Aetna Building at three o'clock in the morning, nobody would be there to receive me.

About nine o'clock, therefore, I presented myself at Room

305 and handed the telegram to General Crozier's secretary. The young man soon ushered me into his presence, and I found him reading a paper. It was my questionnaire at which he was looking, for everybody who took an examination for Government service was required to answer certain questions showing what his preparation and record were.

When General Crozier first saw me, he merely glanced at me but greeted me very cordially, nevertheless. His eyes were fastened upon my questionnaire, which showed that I had received the A.B. and A.M. degrees from Oberlin College, that I had traveled abroad, that I could speak, read and write both German and French and that I had once spoken Italian quite well. Perhaps I should state here that, in replying to the question concerning race, I simply wrote "American," without specifying what particular kind of an American I am.

After the General had carefully read my record, he laid it on the table and looked at me squarely for the first time. "You have had very fine training indeed," he said. "We need the services of those who understand German and French." Then he studied me intently for a second and a shadow passed over his countenance. He began to appear puzzled and then displeased, as he looked at me. The longer he looked, the more puzzled and displeased he became. A light of some kind seemed to be dawning upon him. The General picked up my questionnaire and looked at it again. "I see you have taught in a high school here," he said, eyeing me closely. "Which one was it?" he inquired. "I taught in the M Street High School." Instantly an expression of pronounced displeasure swept over the General's face, and I knew my doom was sealed. He tossed the paper aside immediately.

"Mrs. Terrell," he inquired, "have you ever had any office experience?" His tone was that of a man about to offer a criticism of some kind. "I have had none, General," I replied. "I have stated that in my questionnaire." "Well, I'm sorry you haven't had any office experience. I hoped you had." As he said this, he flicked my questionnaire farther away from him. "I do not see how anyone who summoned me here could have hoped I had had any office experience, unless he thought I would tell a falsehood," I ventured, "for in answer to the question 'Have you had any experience in office?' I stated on my questionnaire 'Absolutely none.' " "So you have," agreed the General, picking up my questionnaire again. "Good morning." I knew then that my name would be among the uncalled.

By those in a position to know I have been informed that at that time college graduates were being eagerly sought, especially those who could speak and translate both German and French. Had I been a white woman there is no doubt I would have secured a responsible and lucrative position in the Government service at that time.

Shortly after that I was summoned to the War Risk Insurance Bureau and appointed to a clerkship. The man before whom I then appeared did not consume enough time in giving me the "once over" to note any peculiarity in my complexion which would suggest to him that I was "different from the rest." That little oversight on his part undoubtedly accounts for the fact that I was placed in the room with white women. After I had been appointed and assigned to this room, I learned that the women who were known to be colored had been placed in a section to themselves.

In the division to which I was assigned it was the duty of the clerks to send in the records of the soldiers who were ill or insane. One of the young women in the room was designated to give me the necessary instructions and did so cheerfully. All the clerks in the room were very cordial and pleasant indeed, and I entered upon my duties with enthusiasm and zest.

I had been working about two months in this section when, suddenly, I received a letter saying I had been suspended from duty from October 15 up to and including October 20, during which time I was requested to prepare my defense in answer to the following charges preferred against me: "It has been reported that you have taken action on cases contrary to the rules and regulations of the Bureau and contrary to the regulations of the chief medical adviser. It has been found that you have made numerous mistakes, and when these mistakes were called to your attention you cause considerable disturbance and tend to deny responsibility. You do not want to understand or can not understand the requests of your superiors in the matter of properly performing duties assigned to you."

There was not a scintilla of truth in any of these charges. It was a case of "framing" a colored woman, so as to remove her from a room in which she had been placed by mistake where they did not want one of her race to work. If I had really "taken action contrary to the rules and regulations of the Bureau and of the chief medical adviser," those responsible for the proper conduct of the office would have called me to account the very first time they learned I was guilty of the infraction of the rules. If they allowed me to persist in such a disobedient, inefficient course, they themselves were derelict in their duty, and deserved to be punished as well as the offending clerk.

But I had never seen any rules and regulations in print, nor had anybody stated any to me which I had violated in any way, shape or form. As careful as any colored woman would be in an office in which she knew her slightest mistake or dereliction of duty would be greatly exaggerated and summarily punished, it is inconceivable that she would fail to obey to the letter every rule or regulation enforced. I realized that I was treading on thin ice all the time, and I was very careful to do the work exactly as I was instructed. Several times I observed (for I kept my eyes and ears open every second to catch anything new floating around in the air) that a change in the manner of making out certain records had been ordered by those higher up without notifying me as they had the other clerks in the room. As soon as I was aware of this, and it was easy for me to discover it by constant vigilance, I would ask a young woman from the far West, who was very cordial, to show me how to do the work, and she always complied with my request cheerfully. On several occasions, without being asked to do so, she slipped me papers showing the new way of filling out certain records, as soon as she herself had been instructed, for she knew that I would not be notified.

Nobody who understands conditions in the National Capital would believe that a colored woman working in one of the Government departments in a room with white women "would cause considerable disturbance" when mistakes were called to her attention if she were sane and wished to retain her job. Colored women know all too well if they make themselves conspicuous or objectionable, either to their fellow clerks or to their superior officers, they are courting disaster and ruin. The few colored women who are assigned to rooms in which white women work are constantly in a state of suspense and apprehension, not knowing the day or the hour when the awful summons of removal or dismissal will come. They know they are there either by mistake or suffrance, and they would as soon think of "creating a disturbance" as they would plot to dynamite the White House. All they ask is to be let alone and be allowed to do their work in peace.

Young women with only a high school education were able to perform the duties in the room to which I was assigned. It could scarcely be possible, therefore, that a woman who had graduated with a good record from a reputable college, who had studied all her life and had taught school, could not surmount the difficulties which these girls could master with ease.

If any woman known to be colored who was working in a Government department during the World War had been "either unable or unwilling to understand requests of her superior officers," she would not have been allowed to retain her job a single week.

A very interesting episode happened once when I was told by a substitute to change the wording of a printed slip during the absence of the woman who had charge of the room. I thanked the substitute for the information she gave me, but I stated at the same time that the director in charge had instructed the clerks to make the slip out as I had done. The clerk who sat next to me overheard the conversation and volunteered to corroborate what I said. Each and every clerk in the room did the same thing. During the conversation between the clerks and the substitute I preserved the silence which is always golden for a colored woman similarly situated.

Very much irritated at the unanimous decision against her, the substitute went to consult the doctor in charge of the section and returned to the room saying she, and not we, was right. When this incident was related to the regular director on her return to the room, she calmly remarked that so many changes were being constantly made in methods of doing the work that nobody could tell one day what would be done the next. I saw to it, therefore, that I kept up with the newest methods of doing the work, for I knew that the slightest error on my part meant embarrassment and loss of my job. There is no doubt that it irritated some of the higher ups, who were hungry for reasons to dismiss me, that I was constantly on the alert and kept abreast of the times.

My relations with both the officer in charge of the room and with the clerks were most cordial. For instance, whenever the clerks brought candy to the room, they always passed me some, and if I refused to take it, they insisted upon giving me a piece anyway. One afternoon, just before I left the building, the director asked me if I would help her inspect some of the files the next day because she had a great deal to do and no one to assist her. I readily consented. But the next morning she requested some one else to help her and ignored me completely. She showed plainly that she was embarrassed. Undoubtedly she had been warned by somebody higher up not to allow me to assist her in inspecting the files. She would never have requested me to help her in the first place if she had not believed I understood the work very well.

The truth of the matter is that when some of the superior officers of the Bureau saw that a colored woman was working in that particular room, they decided to remove her at all hazards. The easiest way to do this was to prefer charges against the colored woman, and they decided to resort to this method to get rid of me.

I am certain I know by whom the agitation to remove me was started. A doctor, who hailed from the South and who had charge of the section in which I worked, walked into the room one day and saw me at my desk. He stood looking intently at me for several seconds and then left abruptly without transacting the business to which he came presumably to attend. Either he had been informed that a colored woman was working in that room and he entered to see whether it was true, or he came on a tour of inspection and observed for the first time that was the case. It was shortly after this doctor's visit that the notice of charges preferred against me was received.

Colonel Wainer, who wrote the letter containing the charges, was a Jew. When I urged him to give me a square deal, presented facts to show that the charges were trumped up, and requested him to get my record directly from the woman in charge of the room, he turned a deaf ear to my appeal. I did not want to allow myself to be dismissed from that clerkship without waging a hard fight against such cruel injustice. It was one of the most galling experiences of my life. If my husband had not occupied such a prominent position in the city, I should never have submitted to that outrage without waging a righteous war against it. I knew that any contest on my part would embarrass him and might easily hurt his standing as a judge in the Municipal Court. I have always believed that a wife has no right to injure her husband's career by what she says or does.

Shortly after this experience I was appointed by the Census Bureau. Here I was placed in a section, one portion of which was set aside exclusively for colored clerks, although white clerks sat in another part of the same large room. From the building on Pennsylvania Avenue, which was once occupied by the Census Bureau and in which I worked when I was first appointed, all of the colored clerks were transferred to one of the temporary structures erected in another section of the National Capital during the World War. Here they were herded together in a room with a colored man as director who was very efficient and whom it was a pleasure to assist.

One day a clerk sitting near me wrote me a note telling me to stop work a second and look ahead. Then I saw a woman, who I knew had been working in another section of the Bureau, come into our large room carrying her hat, her umbrella and her purse. The white man who accompanied her then left and she was given a seat by the colored director of our division. In a few minutes another woman was ushered into our room and given a seat. And this was repeated half a dozen times. Then it suddenly dawned upon me what the advent of these newcomers signified.

They were colored women so fair that they had been assigned to sections set aside exclusively for white women. By fair means or foul their racial identity had been disclosed to somebody "higher up," who was opposed to allowing the women of two races to work in the same room together. Suddenly on that beautiful spring afternoon somebody pounced upon those fair colored women, snatched them from the places to which both their ability and their personal appearance had caused them to be assigned, and removed them to the room to which "they belonged."

It was doubtless a very depressing and humiliating experience to these victims of race prejudice to be forced publicly to leave their desks at which they had been happily doing their duty and marched like culprits into strange surroundings, the cynosure of all eyes. They themselves had done nothing to justify this humiliation to which they had been subjected. They had not tried to deceive anybody. They had simply neglected to place a placard on their backs notifying the world that they belonged to a socially ostracized race in the United States.

One of these women who had to "walk the plank" came from Florida. She told me she was summoned to the office of the man in charge of her section and subjected to a searching examination about the racial affiliation of her parents. "As a matter of fact," probed this inquisitor, "aren't you a colored woman?" "Yes, I am," she replied. "I have never denied it. It was not my fault that I was placed in a section with white women. I made no request to be assigned there, but I have been very happy attending to my duties where the authorities placed me."

"Didn't you know it was not customary to put white and colored people together here in Washington?" she was asked. "No, I was not aware that was the case," she said. "Before I came here, I heard that in some of the departments the two races sat together, so I did not know that by remaining in the room to which I was assigned I was violating any hard and fast rule. Now that I know there is a new rule in force, I shall be much happier in a room set aside exclusively for colored people than I would be working where they are excluded. But I am sorry I had to be publicly humiliated to learn this fact."

A short while after that drastic separation of the two races occurred, one of the young women came to tell me that an order had been promulgated whereby the colored women clerks in our section would no longer be allowed to enter the lavatory which they had used up to that time because it had just been set aside for the women of the other group. Then and there I made up my mind I would do everything in my power to prevent that order from being executed. I knew it was just another device to humiliate colored women. There was no earthly reason for excluding colored women from a room they had been using ever since they had been working in that building.

After a painstaking investigation I learned that the colored clerks had done nothing to cause them to be embarrassed by being subjected to such treatment. First, I went to the colored supervisor of the section. He stated that the order advising him to notify his women clerks not to use the lavatory to which they had been accustomed to go had been sent to him, but, since it was not signed, he did not intend to pay any attention to it. Soon after that conversation with him, however, he told me that the order had been signed by the proper authorities, and that he intended to talk with them about it before issuing it.

The next day some of the women came to me to ask me if I would not go to see the man who issued the order because our own supervisor had been unsuccessful in persuading him to withdraw it. I complied with their request. Even if it were possible to give a verbatim interview with two of the men I tried to induce to spare the colored women clerks an unnecessary humiliation, I should not do so. Although one of the men was reasonable and courteous, he gave me no assurance that the objectionable order would be withdrawn. Then I decided to resign and sent in my resignation immediately. As my reason, I stated that I was unwilling to remain in a Government department in which colored women were subjected to such an indignity as we had been.

A few minutes after the author of the order had received my resignation he sent for me to come to see him immediately. "Why are you resigning?" he inquired. I told him that the reason assigned in my resignation was the correct one. Under the circumstances, I declared, there was only one thing for me to do to maintain my self-respect. After a long conference with him in which I had a splendid opportunity to reveal to him a colored woman's point of view, I agreed to modify the reason of my resignation if he would rescind the objectionable order which he had issued. This he agreed to do. After weighing the matter as carefully as I could in the short time given for my decision, I felt it would be foolish to stick to the original statement when, by making a slight compromise, I could relieve the women of my group from embarrassment and humiliation without sacrificing my self-respect.

The head of the division in which I worked urged me to remain in the Bureau, but I decided to resign. The work was enjoyable and I needed the money, to be sure. But the idea of remaining in a section over which were placed men who had no regard whatever for the feelings of colored women was abhorrent to me. I simply could not stay even for the sake of the salary which would have filled a long felt want.

During the World War when so many were taking examinations for positions under the Government it was very hard for colored women who showed plainly to what race they belonged to secure the positions to which they were entitled by their records. Some of the teachers in our public schools who made high marks failed to receive an appointment. Several told me they had been marked as high as 95 per cent, but had not been given jobs. On the other hand, young colored women who were fair enough to "pass" secured positions without any difficulty whatever, even though their examination papers were marked comparatively low.

Several of these fair colored women came to ask my advice as to what they should do about accepting positions offered them, knowing as they did they would never have received them if the appointing power had been aware they were colored. I could see no good reason why these women should refuse to take positions which they had earned and for which they would be paid, because those in authority did not know they had a few drops of African blood coursing through their veins. Some of them who received these good positions under "false pretenses," so to speak, held them for four or five years, and a few have retained them up to the present time.

CHAPTER 26

EFFORTS IN SENATE TO PREVENT JUDGE TERRELL'S CONFIRMATION

EVERY TIME HE WAS CHOSEN by a President of the United States to preside as judge over the Municipal Court of the District of Columbia my husband had great difficulty in being confirmed by the Senate. This exhibition of race prejudice directed against Judge Terrell caused me great anguish. He was first appointed by President Theodore Roosevelt and reappointed by him, then by President Taft, by President Wilson twice and finally by President Harding. Each time the appointment was for four years. So every four years he had to pass through the same humiliating ordeal of having his confirmation held up by Senators who were hungry for charges against him and who were determined to defeat him at all hazards. He was vigorously opposed by men like James K. Vardaman, so long as he was Senator from Mississippi, by Reed of Missouri, by Ben Tillman of South Carolina, by Hoke Smith of Georgia, and by others from the South. These men literally fought him tooth and nail. They would hold his feet (and consequently my own) to the fire for several months at a time.

To tell the truth, I suffered much more than my husband, for, as I have already indicated, he was an optimist from the crown of his head to the soles of his feet. I have never seen a more wonderful exhibition of calm, cool-headed courage, of a faith that amounted to a conviction that somehow or other justice would prevail in the end than that displayed by Judge Terrell. Even when people who knew the ins and outs of matters pertaining to the Government and whose predictions usually came true, when a confirmation was withheld for a long time, would shake their heads doubtfully and tell my husband that things looked very dubious for him, he would smile blandly and say that even if their prophecy were fulfilled, he could not help matters by worrying about it, that he was doing all he could to present his unblemished record to justice-loving, open-minded Senators and there he would rest his case.

But, as for myself, I literally descended into the very depths of despair every time Judge Terrell was the victim of race prejudice. It provoked me to see him so cheerful, cool and calm. I wanted him to suffer a little as I did, and not be so sure he would eventually be confirmed.

If Mr. Terrell had failed to make good in his position, I could have borne the attacks leveled at him by the prejudice-ridden Senators with fairly good grace, I think. But here was a colored man whose record in his Court had been so brilliant that even in a southern community he had been able to overcome the prejudice against him, win the respect and secure the cooperation of the citizens, both black and white.

For instance, when the terms of six judges expired on one occasion, he was the only one of them reappointed. *The Bulletin*, a news sheet which appeared twice daily in Washington and which is posted in hotels and business places, came out in large headlines demanding the reappointment of Judge Terrell. "We are interested in having only one judge reappointed," said the *Bulletin*, "and that is Judge Robert Heberton Terrell." The five who failed of reappointment were all white men. The Bar Association of the District of Columbia, which was then, as it is now, composed exclusively of white men, urged President Wilson to reappoint Judge Terrell on the ground that he was by far the best judge that ever sat in the Municipal Court. Attorney General McReynolds, now a member of the United States Supreme Court, who a few years ago appeared conspicuously in the headlines of the press, because he was one of the four judges who opposed abrogating the gold clause, also strongly favored the reappointment of Judge Terrell. Like President Wilson he was also a southern man. The New York *Sun* quoted Attorney General McReynolds as telling the Judiciary Committee that "Terrell was undoubtedly the best Municipal Judge that Washington has ever had."

Once when the opposition to Judge Terrell was especially

bitter and prolonged, the most powerful man in the Senate came to his defense and threatened to allow no more business to be transacted until he was confirmed. Some of his strongest champions had been born in the South, but had so far overcome the prejudice against his race that they were willing to deal justly by a man who had so signally proved his worth.

It was harder for me to bear this ordeal because I knew that the very men who were fighting my husband so viciously solely on account of his race owed their political preferment to the fact that their respective states had trampled upon the Colored-American's rights as a citizen and had robbed him of his vote. These were the very men who left no stone unturned to defeat Mr. Terrell. They resorted to all kinds of schemes which would tend to influence the public mind against him.

For instance, in a number of southern papers there appeared a cartoon representing Judge Terrell as a large, black, repulsive-looking man with very thick lips and a broad, flat nose, sitting on a dais thundering threateningly to a long line of white people standing beneath him, some of whom were women, trembling with fear as they gazed upon this frightful, black terror filling a judge's chair. Under this forbidding picture were the following words which this black horror was represented as hurling at his white victims, while he glared at them like an ogre: "You white folks come up here and git yo sentence."

In his paper, *Vardaman's Weekly*, a scurrilous attack upon Judge Terrell written by the editor, James K. Vardaman, appeared. He referred contemptuously to my husband as "a saddle-colored gentleman," with an interrogation point after "gentleman." "I sought an interview with the President of the United States," said Vardaman, "and undertook to convince him of the unwisdom of appointing any negro to office." Then Vardaman proceeded to argue that political recognition of a Negro (and he always used a small n) resulted in rapes upon white women. In fact, the article against Judge Terrell's appointment began with an account of a rape which was said to have been committed upon a white woman by a Negro.

"No decent white man," he declared, "could read the account of the crime without experiencing an almost uncontrollable impulse to destroy the species capable of producing such a beast." And then he gave a lurid account of the effort he had made to dissuade President Wilson from appointing my husband to the judgeship. "But that conversation," complained Vardaman, "did not have much weight with Wilson. He went ahead in his diabolical course and with the assistance of Republican Senators and the treachery of Democrats succeeded in the confirmation of this man Terrell, the son-in-law of the infamous Bob Church of Tennessee. As long as the white men of the country submit to such things," continued Vardaman, "we are going to have rape and murder and race riots and turmoil throughout the South. The work being done by the Superintendent of Mississippi and the Welfare Workers, will also bring their bitter fruit in due time. If you give a negro an inch he will take an ell and he will take the country to hell with him."

This is a sample of the attacks made upon my husband by men representing some of the southern states. But President Wilson also came in for his share of denunciation from the same source. The people of that section declared they were shocked beyond expression that a son of the South should so outrage the customs and traditions under which he had been reared as to appoint a "nigger" a judge. President Wilson defended himself by saying "my campaign managers promised to give the Negro as much political recognition as my predecessors, Taft and Roosevelt did, and I feel in honor bound to do it." He also declared that the popular clamor for Mr. Terrell's reappointment was so great that he was forced to name him, whether he wished to do so or not.

Every four years for twenty years I went through these harrowing experiences every time Judge Terrell's term of office expired. Each and every time I was overwhelmed with discouragement and despair. Instead of becoming accustomed to the awful ordeal I felt it more and more as the years rolled by. With all my soul I hated that type of diabolical injustice which inspired prejudice-ridden men to try to ruin my husband's career for which he had shown such signal fitness. However much I might rage inwardly, I knew I was helpless to change or remove conditions against which I rebelled. Nevertheless, I did what I could. I did not sit supinely by and bemoan my cruel fate.

While Judge Terrell's confirmation was hanging fire, I would sometimes go to the Senate and talk with the Senators who, I was sure, believed in a square deal. Without exception, they always received me cordially and pledged me their support. Once, when the odds against my husband seemed more threatening and terrible than usual, I urged Senator Theodore Burton of Ohio personally to take up the cudgel in his defense and lead the fight for his confirmation. On the principle that what is everybody's business is nobody's business I was eager to enlist a dependable, powerful man in his cause whom I could trust to go ahead and expedite matters.

I felt freer to appeal to Senator Burton to do me this favor than to anybody else because he was an Oberlin man. Without the slightest hesitation he promised to take charge of my husband's case and right royally did he do so. I am inserting the letter written to Senator Burton at the time because it expresses better than anything I can write now exactly how the fear that Judge Terrell would be defeated affected me then.

"March 29, 1914.

"My dear Senator Burton:

"It is a great relief to my heavily burdened mind and heart to know that a man of your courage and ability is interested in my husband's cause. The ordeal through which we are now passing is truly a trying one. I presume I feel as near like a victim of the Spanish inquisition as one not subjected to such physical torture as they endured could feel. It is very disheartening to see a man like Judge Terrell, who has so admirably filled the office which he has held for twelve years that the best white people of this southern city are insisting upon his retention, threatened with failure of confirmation by the United States Senate, solely because he has the demisemi quaver of a thousandth part of a drop of African blood in his veins.

"Such an ordeal as this is enough to crush every vestige of hope in the human heart. The conditions which confront a colored man of ability and character in this country are really too terrible to be described. If the just and generous white people of this country only knew the hundredth part of the trials and tribulations of various kinds which able, aspiring colored people have to bear, I verily believe that many of them would start a vigorous crusade against the unchristian and inhuman conditions which make them possible.

"The fight waged against my husband in the Senate today is based solely on the slight infusion of African blood thought to be lurking somewhere in his anatomy. Although my husband is bearing up under the trial as bravely as any man could, I fear that he will gradually go to pieces under this latest fierce and bitter attack upon him. It is the first time I have had reason to suspect that his courage and his patience are reaching the breaking point.

"After struggling for years to excel in his chosen profession, after receiving indisputable proof of the fact that he has achieved brilliant success, he now feels the ground slipping from under his feet and sees failure staring him in the face. It is a great wonder that a man in his predicament does not lose his mind. He is being reviled and persecuted for nothing which he himself has done, but solely because he happens to be identified with an oppressed and ostracized race.

"Busy as you are, it is wrong to inflict such a long letter upon you. As kind as you are, it is inconsiderate, perhaps, to tell you such a tale of woe. I feel, however, that it is my duty to let you see the chamber of horrors and injustices through the eyes of one of the victims. I am sure you will do everything in your power to see that my husband is confirmed. A great principle is at stake. It does not seem possible that the Senate of the United States intends to serve notice on colored people that no matter how able, worthy or successful one of their representatives may be, he shall receive no recognition at their hands, but shall be driven from any position of honor or trust that he may hold.

"With renewed gratitude for the consideration and kindness which prompted you to see me and the hope that something may speedily be done in behalf of justice, I am yours with the highest esteem,
"MARY CHURCH TERRELL."

I must not forget to mention the assistance which some of the newspaper men gave me. I refer to those who sit in the press gallery and from long experience know about how much time it takes to confirm a man to whom a strong majority objects. The truth of the Biblical injunction to cast thy bread upon the waters with the promise that it will return to thee after many days was well illustrated in my own case one day when I was walking through the corridors of the Senate.

"Is this Mrs. Terrell?" inquired a man whom I did not recognize at first, but whom I knew I had previously met when I looked at him a second. He had started his newspaper work on one of the dailies of Washington, he said, and used to report the meetings of the Board of Education for the *Washington Post,* when I was a member. He told me I had done him several favors by giving him the information he needed and that he had never ceased to be grateful to me for helping him when he was a "cub reporter." Now that he was in a position to assist me, he intended to do so to the extent of his ability. At that time he was sending out news from the press gallery of the Senate. He knew all about the fight being waged against my husband and told me that Judge Terrell would not be confirmed for two months at least, and that under certain conditions it might take longer than that.

"It will be a tough battle," he predicted, "but I believe there will finally be enough votes to confirm him." He then promised to let me know anything of importance in my husband's case which he learned. And he kept his promise. I happened to mention the names of a few men who seemed more determined than others to defeat Judge Terrell's confirmation. He greatly surprised me by saying that Senator Reed of Missouri was as bad as Vardaman of Mississippi ever dared to be.

Several important decisions which were rendered by this judge who had a few drops of African blood in his veins displayed his knowledge of the law and proved that he had the courage of his convictions as well. One of his decisions which had been reversed by the Court of Appeals in the District of Columbia was afterward sustained by the United States Supreme Court. The Ball Rent Act was enacted as a war-time measure to prevent rent profiteering and ejectment of tenants who either refused to pay exorbitant rentals or who could find no other dwelling except the one which they occupied. When a case based on this law was tried in Judge Terrell's Court, he declared it was constitutional and rendered his decision accordingly. The case was afterward carried to the District Court of Appeals which reversed Judge Terrell's decision and declared the Ball Rent Act was unconstitutional. When this case was finally carried to the United States Supreme Court, the judges of that tribunal sustained the decision originally rendered by Judge Terrell in the Municipal Court.

It is a matter of record that very few decisions rendered by Judge Terrell were reversed by the higher courts. Without making invidious comparisons I hope I will be excused for saying that in this respect Judge Terrell had no equal on the bench.

I took pride in the brilliant success which my husband achieved as a judge. From my point of view his duties were far more difficult to perform than were those which any other colored man in the National Capital had ever before been asked to discharge. He presided over a Court in which debts had to be settled and sums as high as one thousand dollars were involved. Here was a colored man sitting on the pocketbooks of white people in a southern city and putting over this delicate and difficult job triumphantly.

His reputation for justice was so well established that it was no uncommon occurrence for litigants to wait till their cases could be tried in Judge Terrell's Court. No better proof of the confidence reposed in him could be cited than the fact that a lawyer against whom Judge Terrell had rendered thirteen decisions out of fourteen cases which had been tried in his Court started a petition to have him reappointed when one of his terms expired.

CHAPTER 27

THE SECRETARY OF WAR SUSPENDS ORDER DISMISSING COLORED SOLDIERS AT MY REQUEST

JUST AS I LEFT THE FALL RIVER BOAT from New York one morning to take the train for Boston I read the glaring headlines of a newspaper which stated that President Theodore Roosevelt had dismissed without honor three companies of colored soldiers who had been accused of shooting up Brownsville, Texas, where they were stationed. I could scarcely believe my eyes. Although rumors had been floating around Washington several days before I left home that the President might take such drastic action, few believed he would do so. If my heart had been weak, I should have had an attack of heart failure right then and there.

When I reached Boston I got in touch with Colonel Thomas Wentworth Higginson immediately and went to see him. He had commanded the soldiers of the First South Carolina Volunteers in the Civil War and was a well known champion of the race. Colonel Higginson regretted that such terrible punishment had been inflicted upon the soldiers, but he was quite irritated with me because I did not see in this incident indisputable evidence of the marvelous progress the race had made. The fact that the colored soldiers refused to tattle on each other, even if they knew who the culprits were, convinced Colonel Higginson that they had greatly improved since the Civil War. "When I commanded them in the South," he said, "I feared that colored men would never learn to stick together and be loyal to each other because they were so treacherous to representatives of their own race. But if the colored soldiers really shot up Brownsville and they can neither be forced nor bribed to tell who did it, they have taken a long step forward. I am so glad to see the progress they have made in this respect, I do not worry very much about the drastic order the President has issued." "The Conspiracy of Silence" for which the colored soldiers at Brownsville were so severely condemned by many, therefore, was not charged against them as a crime by Colonel Higginson.

Shortly after I reached home from Boston the telephone rang one morning about ten o'clock. It had just been installed, after we had urged the telephone company for several months to give us service. It startled me for I did not know the workmen had finished the job. "Is this Mary Church Terrell?" a voice inquired. "Yes," I replied. "Well, this is John Milholland of New York City. The colored soldiers of Brownsville, Texas, have just been dismissed without honor and I want you to go to see Secretary Taft right away to urge him to suspend the order till an investigation can be made." I could scarcely believe my ears. "Is this Mr. Milholland of New York City?" I asked incredulously. "Certainly it is," he replied impatiently, "and I want you to go to the War Department right away as a representative of the Constitution League."

My throat had gone on a strike and I could scarcely speak above a whisper, but I decided to obey orders from so courageous and fine a chief as John Milholland. When I reached the State, War and Navy Building, Mr. Carpenter, Mr. Taft's secretary, told me it would be utterly impossible for me to see him. The Secretary of War had just returned from a tour of inspection of the posts out West, he said, and he would leave the next day for the East. A man who was about to sail for Spain that day had tried to see the Secretary of War on business, I was told, but he had been obliged to leave without doing so, because Mr. Taft was so busy.

"Why do you want to see the Secretary of War?" inquired Mr. Carpenter. I knew if I explained my mission I would have no chance of seeing Mr. Taft at all. I knew also that if I did not give some reason for insisting upon having an interview with him, my chances of getting one would be equally slim. "I want to say a few words to Secretary Taft about the colored soldiers who have just been dismissed," I finally mustered up courage enough to state. A look which plainly showed how he felt spread over the secretary's face. He went to report to the

Secretary of War and remained closeted with him for quite a while.

Finally, he returned, saying "the Secretary is still too busy to see you and he doubts that he can see you any time today." "I'll wait here just the same," I replied. "I have already been here several hours and I might as well remain longer." Nothing but desperate illness could have induced me to leave that office, so long as I knew Mr. Taft was still in it. About an hour later I was told that the Secretary of War was willing to see me. "What do you want to say to me?" inquired Mr. Taft, as soon as I entered his office. "I have come to see you about the colored soldiers who have been dismissed without honor in Brownsville, Texas," I said. "What do you want me to do about it?" he inquired, "President Roosevelt has already dismissed them, and he has gone to Panama. There is nothing I can do."

"All I want you to do, Mr. Secretary," I said, "is to suspend the order dismissing the soldiers without honor, until an investigation can be made." "Is that ALL you want me to do?" inquired Mr. Taft with good natured sarcasm, as he emphasized the word "ALL" and then smiled. "ALL you want me to do," he continued in the same vein, "is to suspend an order issued by the President of the United States during his absence from the country."

"But, Mr. Secretary," I pleaded, "as colored people we take great pride in our soldiers. They have always had an unblemished record and they have fought bravely in every war this country has waged. It seems more than we can bear to have three companies of our soldiers summarily dismissed without honor, at least until a thorough investigation has been made." The smile left Mr. Taft's face. He became serious and remained silent for several seconds. Then he said with an intensity and a sympathy I can never forget: "I do not wonder that you are proud of the record of your soldiers. They have served their country well."

Less than half an hour after I had left Secretary Taft he had cabled President Roosevelt, who was on his way to Panama, that he would withhold the execution of the order to dismiss without honor the three companies of the Twenty-fifth Infantry until he heard from him—or words to that effect. In spite of my keen disappointment that the order to discharge the colored soldiers without honor was not rescinded, I was very grateful to Mr. Taft for the effort he made in their behalf.

When he withheld the execution of the President's order thirty-six hours in response to my plea for the discharged soldiers, he did what no other cabinet officer has ever done since the Declaration of Independence was signed. So far as I have been able to ascertain, no other cabinet officer has withheld the execution of a Presidential order thirty-six seconds. There was nobody in Secretary Taft's office but himself and myself. The interest he manifested in the colored soldiers and the tribute he paid them were not the flowery words of a politician, uttered to serve personal ends, but they were the genuine expressions of an honest, generous-hearted man, who meant what he said and who intended to do what he could in their behalf. The effort he made was commendable and it required great courage, too.

Although Mr. Taft's attitude toward some matters affecting colored people was deeply resented by many of them later on, I shall never cease to thank him for trying to save those three companies of colored soldiers from dishonor and disgrace.

The morning after I had seen Secretary Taft the newspapers featured the interview with striking headlines, some of which read as follows: "Appeal for Black Troops—Mrs. Mary Church Terrell Asks Suspension of the Order." "Secretary Taft at Her Request Cables President for Authority to Stop Soldiers Dismissal." The *Washington Post* contained the following account: "Mrs. Mary Church Terrell, a colored member of the Board of Education, saw Secretary Taft yesterday, as the representative of the Constitution League of New York, of which she is a member, in the interest of the negro soldiers of Companies B, C, and D, Twenty-fifth Infantry, recently dismissed without honor by the President. She asked that the Secretary suspend the operation of that order until representatives of the League and others interested in the colored soldiers could have an opportunity to see the President upon his return from Panama, and ask a rehearing of the case. At her request Secretary Taft last night cabled the President in regard to the matter."

The *Washington Evening Star* had practically the same account, adding however, that "Mrs. Terrell stated her case with precision and effect, pleading that the colored troops be given another opportunity to defend themselves and asserting that they had not yet had their side of the case properly presented. Secretary Taft listened with consideration and interest to Mrs. Terrell's plea. He pointed out that the action complained of was not his own, having been taken in his absence from Washington, and also that it was a presidential order."

Nearly all the newspapers in the United States had an account of my plea for the colored soldiers and every one of them gave me credit for persuading the Secretary of War to suspend the order which had been issued by the President of the United States. The *St. Louis Globe Democrat* featured the story with the headline: "Taft Intervenes for Woman in Dismissal of Negro Troops."

The suspension of that order for only a few days enabled Gilchrist Stewart of New York City to go to Brownsville, Texas, before the soldiers had left. Therefore, they could tell him their own story in their own way. If all of them had been scattered before they had a chance to relate the events which preceded and immediately followed the violent outbreak, many facts in their favor which greatly helped their case would in all probability never have been brought to light.

When President Roosevelt returned from Panama Mr. Stewart and I went to see him, as representatives of the Constitution League, formally to present the case of the colored soldiers. The President simply stated that the evidence in the case would be sent to the War Department and that it would be given due consideration. He also promised us that the soldiers would be allowed to re-enlist if they furnished sufficient evidence to convince the War Department of their innocence.

The case of Mingo Saunders touched me deeply. The reason for my attitude towards him is so clearly stated in an interview which appeared in the *Washington Evening Star* I shall quote it. "Sergeant Mingo Saunders and Private Brown, two of the colored soldiers recently discharged by order of President Roosevelt called upon Mrs. Mary Church Terrell and talked about the circumstances relative to their dismissal from the army. Both declared they did not know who of their battalion 'shot up' Brownsville.

"Speaking of the matter to a *Star* reporter Mrs. Terrell declared both of the former soldiers stated to her they did not believe any members of the battalion were connected with the disorder at Brownsville. She also cited the fact that Saunders had been in the army for more than twenty years and had served his country in both Cuba and the Philippines. 'During his long service,' said Mrs. Terrell, 'his record was a good one, and now he is dismissed summarily while declaring his innocence and his belief that the other members of the battalion are not guilty as charged.'

"Mrs. Terrell said she was much impressed with the demeanor of both the men and during the conversation asked them to explain why empty cartridges, such as are used in the army, were found in Brownsville after the trouble. To this both Saunders and Brown replied that it was an easy matter for cartridges belonging to the military stores to be procured by outsiders. Mrs. Terrell said she assured Saunders and Brown that the Constitution League of New York, of which she is a member, will do all in its power to see that they are given a hearing in an effort to secure reinstatement.

"Mrs. Terrell commented on the fact that the men seemed to have no resentment toward any one who had been connected in any way to the investigation which led to their summary dismissal from the army. On the contrary, they said they hoped and believed they would be given justice in the end. It is probable Mrs. Terrell will communicate with other members of the Constitution League within a few days with a view of aiding the former soldiers."

Nothing happened during President Theodore Roosevelt's entire administration which stirred up the War Department to such a pitch as did the dismissal without honor of three companies of colored soldiers. Protests were received from every part of the country against the injustice of punishing innocent men and soldiers with splendid records for the misdeeds of a few, when no misdeed had been proved against even the few. Many army officers who dared not express their opinions openly for fear of being court-martialed did not hesitate to say in private conversation that President Roosevelt's impetuosity had caused him to make a serious blunder.

The tragedy which overtook the colored soldiers affected nobody more than Brigadier General A. S. Burt, who had retired. He had commanded the colored soldiers in the Philippines and never grew weary of recounting their marvelous deeds of valor.

I was presented to him one day in the office of Raymond Patterson, who was special Washington correspondent of the *Chicago Tribune* and one of the General's best friends. There was one story about his soldiers which the General enjoyed relating more than anything else.

When he was taking them to Cuba during the Spanish-American War he was asked several times by southerners who came to the station to see them, as they passed through the towns en route to Cuba, "whether those 'niggers' would really fight." When he told what he replied the old General's face would flush a bright red, and he would jump quickly from his chair like a sixteen year old. "Will our colored men fight?" you ask. "FIGHT, did you say? Why they would charge into hell, fight their way out and drag the devil out by his tail." The General was so afraid I might forget his exact words that he took the pains to write them out on his card in his own hand, and that card is lying on my desk today.

General Burt declared that the colored soldiers were the first to fight both in the Philippines and in Cuba. They could not be surpassed, he declared, and they had few equals.

In discussing the terrible punishment inflicted upon the colored soldiers by President Roosevelt, people talked about the evidently unconstitutional part of the sentence of dismissal which carried with it the prohibition of the right to hold civil office under the United States, which meant that none of the soldiers could become messengers, letter carriers or hold any office under the Federal Government, in spite of the fact that civil service rules give an honorably discharged soldier or sailor many preferences over civilians.

President Roosevelt made the wholesale discharge of three companies of colored men, privates and non-commissioned officers, some of whom had served the United States for more than a quarter of a century and were nearly eligible for retirement, absolutely without consulting the Secretary of War, who is charged with personal supervision of the army. At the time this was done Secretary Taft was in the West. The order was issued in his absence without waiting for his return, although the soldiers had been removed to Fort Reno and there was plenty of time for further investigation into their conduct if such a thing were necessary. President Roosevelt probably consulted

Assistant Secretary Oliver, who was in charge of the War Department during Secretary Taft's absence. The old heads of the department and many older army officers themselves said that it was unprecedented for such a radical order to be issued merely upon the advice of an under secretary without full consultation with the chief of the department.

Every effort was made to have it appear that the race question had nothing to do with the terrible punishment meted out to the soldiers. But those who tried to accept that point of view could not help remembering that it was Lieutenant Colonel Garlington, a native of South Carolina, who had been sent to investigate and who recommended the summary dismissal of all three companies to which President Roosevelt subscribed. It was the consensus of opinion among a large number of people that Colonel Garlington's service in the army had not relieved him of his sectional prejudice against colored people.

The majority of the three companies was in barracks when the disturbance occurred and had no knowledge at first hand who the participants were, even if they were soldiers, because there was always a squad loose in town. Some of the soldiers were sick in the hospital, one man was on sick leave in Washington; several were at their homes on furlough, and yet they were all punished alike by President Roosevelt's order of dismissal without honor. Many of the men thrown out of the army were too old to go into business and their training as soldiers had unfitted them for ordinary work.

A number had had medals of honor granted them by the War Department, but this did not protect them in any way from the harsh sentence. A wave of public sentiment swept over the country as a result of it, and the War Department was swamped with protests against the idea of punishing innocent men for the misdeeds of a guilty few. A case somewhat similar to the Brownsville affair had occurred fifteen years previously.

In what was known as the Walla Walla case in 1891 the Court of Inquiry recommended that four troops of the Fourth Cavalry should be disbanded and the men discharged if the officers and men did not turn over the soldiers who had been guilty of taking the guns from the barracks. But President Harrison declined to take such action. No innocent men were then punished and the army did not seem to be any worse because of the lenient action of the President.

If the soldiers in the Brownsville affair had been white, it is hardly possible that they would have been dismissed by President Roosevelt, even if he had insisted upon such drastic action himself. The people of the country would have raised such a storm of protest, it is quite likely he would have respected their wishes and refrained. This opinion was expressed in an editorial of one of the largest and best dailies in the country.

With impassioned eloquence Senator Foraker of Ohio pleaded the colored soldiers' cause. Crowds flocked to the Senate to hear him. With the ticket given me by this fearless champion of a righteous cause I arrived every morning early and stood in line several hours before the Senate was open to the public, so as to be sure to get a seat. As I listened to that courageous man plead for justice to the colored soldiers and present fact after fact to prove their innocence, I thought of Charles Sumner, who had stood in that same Senate 50 years previously and had been beaten into insensibility because he had raised his voice in behalf of the slave. But Senator Foraker's efforts to save the doomed men, condemned on circumstantial evidence alone, were all in vain.

A reward of $10,000 was offered to anybody who would give any information leading to the identity of the men who shot up Brownsville. It is very significant that nobody came forward with any facts to claim that reward. Certainly $10,000 was a large sum to renounce if a soldier or any other human being had been able to present sufficient evidence to prove the culprits' guilt. Nearly forty years have passed since those three companies of colored soldiers were dishonorably discharged. And, although those who were hungry for facts on which to convict them overturned Heaven and earth to find them, they have failed of success even unto this day.

Two years after Mr. Taft withheld the execution of the order to discharge the soldiers he was Republican candidate for the presidency. Mr. William Hayes Ward, who was for many years editor of the *Independent*, wrote me a letter in which he stated that he had read in the press that the Secretary of War had done this because I had requested him to do so. "Since this will have no little effect upon the approaching presidential election," he said, "I should like to have you send me a statement for publication in the *Independent*." I complied with his request and my article appeared in that magazine on page 189, July 23, 1908, under the title "Taft and the Negro Soldiers, by Mary Church Terrell," followed by a statement concerning the college from which I had graduated and the work in which I was engaged.

I have related the details of the result accomplished by my plea to Secretary Taft in behalf of the colored soldiers because in a book published several years ago which referred to the matter I was not given credit for it.

By nature, preference, education and cultivation I have been a hero worshipper all my life. Theodore Roosevelt had been one of my idols. In my opinion he could do no wrong. When he made what others called mistakes, I forgave him freely because I believed that his heart was in the right place. He seemed really to love his fellow man, whether he was white or black, high or low, rich or poor. I was personally acquainted with him and he knew my brother in New York City well. The morning I presented him a letter from my brother, Thomas A. Church, introducing me to him, he received me immediately and left some waiting who had come before me till he had talked to me. He was Assistant Secretary of the Navy at the time. When he was President he appointed my husband Justice of the Peace and later Judge of the Municipal Court. When he learned that the War Camp Community Service was thinking about making me its special representative to work among colored women Colonel Roosevelt wrote a very complimentary letter about me which I still prize highly. He was no longer President then, but was a private citizen writing special articles for the *Kansas City Star*. I am grateful to him for all the favors he bestowed upon my family and myself.

But after he had meted out such terrible punishment upon many innocent men over whom he had the power of life and death, I could never respect and admire him as I did before. I have sometimes wondered whether President Roosevelt was influenced to take this step in order to appease the South. After he had invited Booker T. Washington to lunch with him at the White House, he had been caricatured, vilified and abused by the press of the South, as no President had ever been criticized before. He might have thought by discharging three companies of colored soldiers without honor he would prove to the South he was not such a negrophile as he had appeared to be. Whatever may have been the reasons and the motives by which he was actuated, it was an ugly blemish upon an otherwise spotless career.

CHAPTER 28

HARRIET BEECHER STOWE CENTENARY AND MY
SALLY INTO SPIRITUALISM

THE EFFORT I MADE to work up an appropriate celebration of the one hundredth anniversary of the birth of Harriet Beecher Stowe was truly a labor of love. The *Washington Star* and the *Washington Post* came out in striking headlines to announce it. The colored newspapers featured it and people from all over the country most heartily approved of the idea. Since I had begun to call the attention of the public to my plans a year before the Centenary, I hoped it would be celebrated generally throughout the country. But I was doomed to disappointment in this, for there were comparatively few observances of the occasion.

In Washington, however, Mrs. Stowe's Centenary was most appropriately and most delightfully celebrated June 14, 1911. I invited Lyman Beecher Stowe to deliver the principal address on the life of his famous grandmother and he accepted. His references to *Uncle Tom's Cabin* were replete with information and interest to the large audience which gathered in the Lincoln Congregational Temple to participate in the celebration. There was not a foot of standing room when the exercises began. Brigadier General Burt was one of the speakers and a violin solo was rendered by Joseph Douglass, grandson of Frederick Douglass, one of Mrs. Stowe's personal friends.

I felt it was my duty to do everything in my power to call the attention of the American people on general principles and of my own group in particular to the marvellous contribution made by Harriet Beecher Stowe to the abolition of slavery. In recount-

ing the incidents and stating the reasons which led to the abolition of slavery it would be difficult to exaggerate the role played
by *Uncle Tom's Cabin*. After she had written this powerful book,
Mrs. Stowe called on President Lincoln at the White House one
day. When he saw her approaching he seized her hand and
exclaimed "Are you the little woman who made the great war?"
President Lincoln's estimate of the influence in behalf of emancipation which *Uncle Tom's Cabin* exerted is not exaggerated.
There is no doubt that many of the men who fought in the Union
Army had been induced to enter it because eleven years before
the conflict, when they were boys, they had either read *Uncle
Tom's Cabin* themselves, or had heard it read aloud by their
mothers to the family group. They were fighting, not only to
preserve the Union, but also to deliver the slaves from the cruel
bondage which Harriet Beecher Stowe had so graphically described in her book.

Before the celebration of the Centenary I wrote a short
Appreciation of Harriet Beecher Stowe, so that it might be
available to as many as possible. It pained and shocked me to
see how few, comparatively speaking, especially among young
people, knew anything about the great service which had been
rendered by Mrs. Stowe. My little paper bound book was 5 x 7½
inches, consisted of 23 pages and sold for twenty-five cents. I
did not sell enough, however, to pay for the expense of printing
it. The failure to do so may have been due to my inexperience.
I tried to dispose of the little books myself and did not know how
to do it. I have never taken a prize in "salesmanship."

I intended to write a Child's Life of Mrs. Stowe and consulted several authorities about the advisability of doing so.
Mrs. Charles Dudley Warner of Hartford, Connecticut, widow
of the well-known essayist, novelist and editor, was very much
interested in my plan, and after discussing the matter with me,
she gave me Reverend Charles Stowe's life of his mother. Dr.
Edward Hooker, Mrs. Stowe's nephew, also encouraged me to
write the book. Hanging in Dr. Hooker's residence were two
beautiful paintings of flowers made by Mrs. Stowe which he
showed me, as he told me how fond his distinguished aunt was of
children, music and flowers.

That celebration of her Centenary in the National Capital
would have greatly rejoiced the heart of the author of *Uncle*

Tom's Cabin because it was under the auspices of the College Alumnae Club, which was then composed of twenty-two colored women who held diplomas from some of the largest and best institutions in the land. There were several from Cornell, one of whom wore a Phi Beta Kappa key, together with representatives from Ann Arbor, Michigan, the University of Vermont, the Ohio State University, Smith, Wellesley, Oberlin and such splendid institutions for the higher education of colored youth as Fisk University of Nashville, Tennessee, and Howard University of Washington, D. C.

If Mrs. Stowe had been alive on that occasion, less than sixty years after her book appeared which described the evils and horrors of slavery, she might have seen descendants of the bondmen for whom she had made such an effective plea standing on an educational equality with their former masters. The College Alumnae Club was formed in my house on March 5, 1910. A few women who were eager to have such an organization urged me to be president and I agreed to serve.

A dramatic and a reading club were formed for pupils in the public schools by some of the members. An effort was made to ascertain what becomes of the boys and girls who graduate from the colored high schools of the District of Columbia. It was decided to give a reception to the graduating classes of the high schools, the normal schools and the college classes of Howard University. Therefore, when I issued a call for the appropriate celebration of the Centenary of Harriet Beecher Stowe, this College Alumnae Club volunteered to assist in making the Washington meeting a success. Some of the most distinguished women in the nation accepted the invitation to become patronesses of the Centenary. Among that number may be mention Mrs. Sherman, wife of the Vice President of the United States; Mrs. Murray Crane, wife of the Senator from Massachusetts; and Mrs. Hay, widow of John Hay, who studied law in Abraham Lincoln's office, was private secretary when Mr. Lincoln became President and was Secretary of State when he died.

Since no fitting monument had been erected to Mrs. Stowe, I urged the National Association of Colored Women to raise funds with which to establish a Harriet Beecher Stowe scholarship in some good institution in the East for a colored girl who wished to follow a literary career and gave evidence of possessing ability in that direction. I wish the colored women of the country would show their gratitude and appreciation of the efforts made by Harriet Beecher Stowe in some substantial, outstanding way, for no author has ever done more with the pen for the cause of human liberty than she did.

Mrs. Isabella Beecher Hooker, who gave me a bust of her half sister, to which I have already referred, when I delivered an address before the National American Woman Suffrage Association, invited me always to visit her whenever I had engagements in New England, and I often accepted her invitation. One of the visits was especially enjoyable, both because I met the twin daughters of Mrs. Stowe, who had come to see their aunt, and because Mrs. Hooker presented me with a copy of *Uncle Tom's Cabin*.

Mrs. Hooker was very much interested in Spiritualism. It was her custom to communicate with spirits every morning. A relative stayed with her and assisted her in writing the messages which the spirits conveyed, while Mrs. Hooker sat up in bed. Questions would be asked by the living woman and answered by her relatives or friends long since dead.

I happened to be in Mrs. Hooker's home shortly after there had been a terrible volcanic eruption in the West Indies. She told me that she had asked the spirit with whom she had been talking at the time if he had noticed an unusually large number of spirits flocking from the earth to his abode. "What did the spirit say, Mrs. Hooker?" I inquired. "He told me," she replied, "that it was such a common occurrence to see spirits continually arriving there from the earth that he had paid no particular attention to the group to which I referred."

For many years I preserved the slips of paper on which the messages from the spirit land to Mrs. Hooker were written. They were unintelligible to me, but since she gave them to me, I prized them for her sake. And I still cherish a lock of her snowy, silken hair.

Harriet Beecher Stowe believed in Spiritualism also and she has related several remarkable incidents to prove she had a good reason for the faith that was in her. Whenever I have been asked whether I believed in Spiritualism, I have always stated that I knew too little about the subject to give an intelligent answer. The first time I had any experience concerning the matter I was urged by a friend to go with her to a medium about whom she had heard wonderful tales, after she had lost a beautiful cape during the inaugural festivities in Washington. "If this woman is as remarkable as people claim she is," said my friend, "she might be able to locate my cape." In the spirit of fun, rather than because we expected to get the desired information, we sallied forth on a lark to see this medium one day. My friend went into the presence first and then I took my turn.

"Your name is Mary," said the medium, as soon as she saw me. "And there are three little spirits flying around your head. Look over there," she continued, pointing to my right. "There is a spirit near you who is angry with you. He committed suicide on account of something you did to him. Then there is another spirit near you. She is a member of your family and her name is Emmeline."

Right there I stopped her, stating positively that no member of my family had ever borne that name. But the medium paid no attention whatever to this contradiction of her statement. She insisted that the spirit she saw near me was a relative and that her name was Emmeline. "Perhaps you have never met her in the flesh," she explained, "but there she stands just the same."

When the medium stated, as soon as I entered the room, that she saw three little spirits flying around my head, I remembered, of course, that I had lost three babies in five years, practically at birth. When she referred to the spirit who was angry with me and had committed suicide on my account I laughed at her and assured her that nothing like that had ever occurred in my life. But she insisted that she knew what she was talking about and my denials did not move her an inch. She saw this angry spirit standing right there in the room, she declared, and what her spiritual eyes saw she was bound to believe.

After leaving the medium I thought of a man who was very fond of me when I was a mere child and had asked me to marry him later on. He graduated from West Point and served as a Lieutenant in the Army for quite a while. Then he was appointed to drill the students in a college for colored youth and died one day while sitting in a barber's chair. If the medium really possessed the power she claimed and saw this man's spirit, she knew that a tragedy of some kind had occurred in his life.

She interpreted it to mean that he had committed suicide, and since his spirit was near me, she inferred that some act of mine might have caused him to take his life.

But her surmise had no foundation in fact, for this man and I had been fond of each other from childhood and remained the best of friends till the end. His relations with my husband were most cordial. Whenever he came to Washington he was a welcome guest in our home after we married, and he told Mr. Terrell that the reason he had chosen a feather fan for my wedding present was because he wanted to give me something he could not use. Everybody considered this a good joke and my husband complimented him upon being clever enough to select something which really shut him out.

Therefore, if this was the spirit of a former admirer and it was angry, this resentment toward me must have developed after he passed into the other world. That naturally brings up a most interesting question. Do people change their point of view when they enter the spirit world?

When we left the medium's house my friend told me that she had had precisely the same experience that I did. "Your name is Josephine," said the woman to my friend, whom she had never seen or heard of before. "Your sister's name is Victoria." Then she proceeded to tell my friend about some things concerning her husband, who was in public life, which had actually taken place, but she had to confess she could not tell where the cape might be found.

My friend declared emphatically that she had not told the medium what my name was and had not given her the slightest inkling concerning my husband or my children. In fact, she said she had not referred to me at all. This medium, therefore, guessed our names correctly and those of members of our families without getting information from either one of us.

Since she had insisted so strongly that a member of my family was named Emmeline, I wrote to my father to inquire whether that was true. I had not yet received the letter from the man who gave me the facts about my grandmother. Father replied that it certainly was true, because that was the name of his own mother, who died when he was a child.

Fearing that I might become too deeply interested in Spiritualism, I did not attempt to investigate it any further after that experience. Particularly did I fight shy of it because the medium assured me that I had great psychic power and might easily become a medium myself. I did not want to achieve that distinction, so I decided that the only safe course for me to pursue, in order to avoid being tempted to develop my power in that direction, was to keep away from Spiritualism altogether. I feel as Joseph Cook, a well-known preacher and lecturer some years ago, is said to have expressed himself when he was reproved by some members of his congregation for referring in respectful terms to Spiritualism. They thought he should have ridiculed the spiritualists or at least should have put his seal of disapproval upon them. "I have learned never to ridicule anything which I cannot explain," he is said to have replied.

All my life I have been conscious of something within me which enables me to feel things which were coming to pass. At times, without knowing why, I have been very wretched, and after a while I would discover that something deleterious to my family or to myself had occurred during that period. Once when I was a girl about thirteen years old I cried all day one Saturday without knowing why. No girl in town was gayer than I, as a rule. I ran and played and climbed trees and sang whenever I had a chance. On this particular Saturday I had intended to spend the afternoon with one of my friends. But I felt too unhappy to go anywhere. Some time afterward I learned that my dear mother had been in serious trouble and had been treated very badly that day.

I do not pretend to be able to diagnose my case, psychically speaking, but I know I have had peculiar "manifestations" several times. I was very ill a few years after my marriage and I was advised to go to a hospital for surgical treatment. I was with my mother, who was living in New York City at that time. The surgeon told me frankly I was taking a chance, and he could not tell what the result of the operation would be. Neither my husband nor my mother wanted me to run the risk. But I felt I would rather die trying to regain my health than drag out a weary, useless existence as an invalid.

I was lying in the bed of the private hospital to which I had gone, waiting to be taken to the operating room. I was praying fervently to live. I did not want to die. I promised God that if my life was spared I would devote it to the service of those who needed it most. Suddenly I felt a presence near my bed. I opened my eyes and literally saw the Saviour standing beside it, separated from me only by a small table at the head. I looked at Him just as I would have looked at a human being. It seemed perfectly natural for Him to be standing there. He assured me that all would be well with me. He smiled at me as a father would smile at a child in the grip of a terrible fear whose terror he wished to dispel. From that moment I felt perfectly sure I would recover from the operation and get well. I had absolutely no fear. The spirit, or whatever one chooses to call it, vanished immediately, and I have never seen anything like it since. Many years afterward I heard an author and a psychologist on the faculty of Harvard University say that under certain circumstances it is possible for a human being to see God.

CHAPTER 29

TRYING TO GET A COLORED GIRL INTO AN ACADEMY IN THE NORTH

A YOUNG GIRL OF WHOM I was very fond and with whose family I had been closely associated for years decided to prepare herself for college in a large fitting school in the West—quite near Chicago, to be exact. But there followed such a series of cold rebuffs and positive refusals from the principal to whom the application was sent that even those of us who thoroughly understand prejudice against colored people in the United States, and who have ourselves tasted its bitterness to the very dregs, were shocked.

The young woman to whom I shall refer as Ruth lived in a southern city in which there was no high school for colored youth at that time. At a family council, therefore, it was decided to make the necessary sacrifice to enable Ruth to go to the fitting school. A letter was written to the principal and a favorable reply was received. "We have a room large enough for two girls which we can allow Miss R to occupy alone at the rate of $115 a quarter," read the letter. "We can hold the room till you have time to reply. I very much hope that you will decide to send Miss R to us, and I am sure we will do our best to justify any confidence you may place in us. I will hope to hear from you very early next week."

While the letter was being written in which to send the required deposit, it occurred to us that it might be wise to say that Ruth had a drop of African blood in her veins. Some of us did not think it necessary to supply that information, since the young woman was to room alone. We insisted upon that arrangement and were perfectly willing to pay for the privilege.

At that time we took it for granted that all first class institutions in the North admitted colored students. My own husband had prepared for college at Groton Academy in Massachusetts. It did not occur to us, therefore, that high grade academies for girls would be an exception to this rule. In referring to Ruth's nationality it was explicitly stated that, although she had a speck of African blood in her veins, she was so fair that nobody unaware of the fact could possibly suspect or detect it. Stating that a colored person was fair, so as to induce those with power to grant him the privilege to which he was entitled, has always seemed to me an unfortunate concession to race prejudice.

Replying to this letter the principal wrote:

"My dear Madam: I am in receipt of yours of December 3 and we make no objection to receiving Miss R and on receipt of the deposit required in all cases we will hold a room for her. I do not anticipate any difficulty and we will do our best to make Miss R's stay with us a pleasant one."

Upon reading this reassuring letter, we sent the deposit, and Ruth's trunk was packed right away. But within forty-eight hours the following letter was received:

"My dear Madam: I regret exceedingly that a close study of the situation here makes it clear to us that we cannot be sure that Miss R could be comfortable here, and I therefore feel that it is better that the engagement of the room be canceled. I return herewith the deposit and hope the delay may cause you no inconvenience."

This letter greatly shocked us all. Ruth had set her heart on going to this particular school, had told her friends about her plans, and now her application for admission was rejected because she was colored. I resolved to save the girl from this bitter disappointment and keen humiliation if I could. So I wrote the principal a courteous letter, telling him how much his decision embarrassed us, how it wounded Ruth's feelings, appealed to his sense of justice, implored him to reconsider his action and admit her to his school. He replied:

"My dear Madam: I regret exceedingly that my first decision was made without sufficient study of the situation. I can only say, however, that I must repeat what I said in my first letter. I would add, however, this—that the University of Chicago is in no way responsible for my decision."

The principal probably felt it his duty to exonerate the University of Chicago because his fitting school made a specialty of preparing girls to enter that institution. When Ruth was finally told she had been denied admission to the school a look of despair and pain came into the girl's face which I cannot forget.

Then Ruth's family, determined to carry out its plans, looked toward the East and made arrangements for Ruth to attend a fitting school near Philadelphia. Remembering their experience with the western school, the family decided to say nothing about Ruth's nationality. I accompanied her to the school myself. No placard of racial classifications was attached to either one of us and we let our faces speak for themselves. But a few months after Ruth had been attending school the following letter was received:

"My dear Madam: I regret very much the necessity that compels me to broach a matter that must prove a wrong done one of us and not pleasant to either. There is a conviction growing up among the members of our student body that Miss R bears other than Caucasian blood. If this be true, her presence here would be contrary to our precedent and would be received by our alumnae and corporation with disfavor. Miss R is a quiet, studious young woman, and while her schoolmates do not approve of race intermingling, they have suspended judgment in her case, and she is treated with due respect. Should what we fear prove true, the school would, of course, refund all money paid in after deducting for her room and tuition while here. If we are mistaken in this matter I shall be very sorry to have caused you this annoyance and will take steps to set the matter right before all concerned. Awaiting your early reply, I am very truly yours."

This letter was unexpected. I myself had taken Ruth to this school, feeling certain that the authorities would know that

I had "other than Caucasian blood," as soon as they saw me. The family had had a very disagreeable experience because Ruth's nationality had been disclosed to the principal of the western institution, so they asked me to accompany her to this school, feeling sure that if there were any objection to receiving a colored girl the authorities would notify me on the spot.

The opening sentence of the principal's letter, in which he declared that he regretted the necessity of broaching a matter that "must prove a wrong done one of us," threw a flood of light upon his attitude toward Ruth.

The family feared Ruth was being treated like an outcast by the pupils. In their mind's eye they saw the averted glances, the scornful smiles or the hard, cold stare of anger directed toward her. They asked me to go to Philadelphia as quickly as I could. The principal and I had a lengthy interview in which he told me he had no idea of my racial identity because I seemed to be highly educated and spoke correct English. He had never seen an educated colored woman before, he said.

"There are some southern girls here," he told me, "and the sight of a colored girl to southern pupils throws them into fits." According to the catalog, there were only five out of a total of 300. What a fine thing it would be if the North were as loyal to what it claims to be its principles as the South is to its views. If a petition should be circulated among northern pupils of a southern school praying for the admission of a colored girl, does anybody believe it would have the desired effect?

The mother of one of the southern girls visited the school, said the principal, and admired Ruth very much. Learning her name, however, and the town she came from, the southern woman grew very excited. She declared Ruth's family was well known and she was sure she was colored. "I denied it," said the principal, "but I promised to write for the facts, which explains my letter to you. Once before, we admitted a colored girl into the school by mistake—a fine young woman who sang divinely—but when we discovered she was not white we asked her to leave."

"But she was white, was she not?" I inquired. "Well, yes," was the quick reply, "white to the eye, but she had African blood in her veins, so we could not have her here."

That afternoon Ruth and I took the train for her home.

She had been very finely treated by a few of the girls, she said—by all of them, in fact, till the mother of the southern girl had circulated the report that she was colored and then her trials began. She had made it a rule not to seek the companionship of any of the girls. She let them make all the advances to her, she said. But she did not repel those who showed a disposition to be friendly.

In a burst of confidence the girl who liked Ruth best told her that some of the girls had tried to make fun of her. "I hope you won't feel bad, Ruth, if I tell you what they say. They say you are a nigger. I told them I didn't care if you were a Hottentot, you were far better bred and more congenial to me than they were."

Ruth's family were more determined than ever that the girl should enjoy the advantages she craved and for which they were able to pay. Suddenly I thought of a man who is a well-known author living in a Massachusetts college town where there is a fine fitting school for girls. We attended Oberlin College together. He and his wife once came to hear me speak, invited me to visit them and we spent several pleasant days together. Knowing how broad and just he was, I wrote him to ask the school officials to admit Ruth, feeling that a request from such a man would have its effect. He gave a cheerful assent.

Ruth was very happy when she learned that so distinguished a gentleman was interested in her and was willing to intercede for her. My author friend went personally to see the principal of the fitting school in Ruth's behalf. Then one day I received the following letter:

"I have been to see Miss Caswell of the Caswell-Brewster School" (this is not the real name of either the teacher or the school) "and I dare say I have nothing to add to your wisdom or experience in such matters. It is the same old story—modified in this case as in many others—by good wishes and regrets and a real desire to have things different. But they are not different and the world moves slowly. Miss Caswell says Miss R would have a very unhappy time at her school and nothing but harm, as things are at present, could come on both sides by her joining it. By the time girls get to college they are different. But the finishing schools, as you know, are very differently constituted, and have a very different spirit and purpose. Even the best of them are more or less implicated in the fashion business instead of education, and they furbish up their prejudices accordingly. If Miss R could prepare under tutors or abroad or in a high school—and skip over the main difficulty—there is little doubt that in the colleges themselves she would strike a higher stratum of culture and civilization and share all the benefits and pleasures in proportion."

I shall not try to describe how this letter affected Ruth.

Then a friend told me of another academy in Massachusetts which is one of the oldest in the country. "It is a very expensive school," she said, "but a few colored girls from well-to-do families have attended it nevertheless." We felt that the problem of finding a school for Ruth had been solved at last. Colored girls had actually attended the school. There was no doubt about that. I went to make arrangements with the principal and gave several personal references which I felt sure would enable her to classify me with ease, even if her eyesight were poor. She courteously showed me the really luxurious apartments occupied by the girls and was anxious to have Ruth's family send her at once.

The dormitory was arranged in suites of three rooms—two bedrooms opposite each other which were separated by a sitting room that was shared by the two girls. "Are you quite sure," asked Ruth, when I explained the arrangement to her, "that colored girls who have attended the academy have shared a sitting room with a white girl?" That set me to thinking. I had heard nothing about single rooms and I had seen none. I decided that whatever else happened there should be no misunderstanding. Ruth should not be humiliated again if I could prevent it. I wrote the principal that while Ruth was as fair as the average white girl and fairer than many, she was colored. I had not mentioned that when I talked to her, I wrote, because I took it for granted she could see I am a colored woman, and because I had heard on reliable authority that three or four colored girls had already attended the school.

The reply to this letter read as follows:

"I was greatly surprised at receiving your letter this morning. I had not the slightest suspicion that Miss R had any colored blood. Blessing Academy has always been friendly to the colored race and to all races. I have no reason to think that any one would object to Miss R's presence as a student. But we have just one vacancy in the building, and the student who takes this place will be put in the same suite of rooms with another student. You can easily see the embarrassment we might have been caused if Miss R had come here and had gone into a room with a white girl.

"Certainly it would have made a great deal of trouble, as soon as her roommate discovered that Miss R had colored blood and all the talk and the widespread criticism resulting would have reacted most unfavorably upon our school as well as upon Miss R and her race. Hence it is most fortunate that you wrote me as plainly as you did about the matter. We have three or four single rooms in the building, but they are all occupied. Hence it will be utterly impossible for us to admit Miss R at this time. I am very sorry and I want to repeat that it is not because she belongs to the colored race, but because we cannot give her a room.

"Sincerely yours."

Would there have been widespread criticism reacting unfavorably on Blessing Academy, on Ruth and her race if she had simply shared a sitting room with a white girl, while each one slept alone and they were separated from each other by a large room?

Ruth's disappointment was all the keener, because she felt sure she could attend a school to which other colored girls had been admitted. Then we heard about a fitting school in Massachusetts which Harriet Beecher Stowe helped to found. Surely an institution which that sainted woman helped to establish would not debar a member of the race whose emancipation was largely due to her energy, her heart and her brain. We wrote and received a most cordial invitation to send Ruth to Anson Academy. I requested a distinguished pastor to write to the principal stating to what race she belonged.

A few days afterward the following letter was received:

"It gives me pain to write that on hearing from Rev. Boston that Miss R had colored blood, I must refuse her entrance here. I regret that I had not known it from the first. There is no prejudice on the part of the trustees—far from it—but as our girls come from all parts of the country on behalf of Miss R's comfort and standing, as well as on behalf of the school, they feel it necessary to take this resolution. They have had to make this resolve before. I am sure she would suffer in many ways which I could not possibly prevent. I hope you had not made many preparations on the basis of my last letter and especially hope that she had not started to come here. Very sincerely yours."

There was not a single southern girl in Anson Academy at the time Ruth was refused admission on any terms. Feeling sure she would be admitted we had already bought our ticket when the fatal letter arrived. Ruth's state of mind was such that her family and I determined to send her to a fitting school such as she wished to attend if there were a single one in the United States that would admit her.

By the merest chance I met the mother of a young woman who was attending a girls' academy in Massachusetts of which I had never heard. She expatiated at length on the advantages to be derived from attending this particular school. The arrangements were made and Ruth went to this academy unaccompanied. She was admitted without any trouble and remained there a term. The girls were very fond of her and she maintained a high standard in her studies. But the thought that she was there under false pretenses was so disagreeable to Ruth, and the situation was so distasteful to us all that she did not return.

There were good high schools in the North and good institutions for colored youth at which Ruth might have prepared for college. But since she had been a small child, her family had told her they were going to send her to a northern academy to prepare for college. She and the rest of us had set our hearts on it. But I am sorry we were all so ignorant about conditions in the North. Our experience caused us many heartaches.

CHAPTER 30

TRAVELING UNDER DIFFICULTIES

THE FIRST TIME I FILLED lecture engagements for my own group in the South I would not try to get a berth in a sleeper. I argued that I was no better than other colored women, and if they had to travel without them, I would also. I had to sit up all night three nights in one week. At the end of that time I was so worn and weary I realized that I would have to do one of two things. Either I would have to decline engagements in the South which required me to travel long distances or I would be obliged to get a berth. An elderly woman with whom I lived when I first came to Washington had to take a long journey from there to a far southern State and was obliged to sit up several nights, because she was unable to get a berth on a Pullman. It made her quite ill; her life was despaired of for a long time and she never recovered completely from the hardships which she endured on the journey.

There are few experiences more embarrassing and painful than those through which a colored woman passes while traveling in the South. There are few ordeals more nerve-racking than the one which confronts a colored woman when she tries to secure a Pullman reservation in the South and even in some parts of the North. I have already related the first experience I had on the railroad when I was a small child.

An amusing one occurred when I was about twelve. My father was taking me from Memphis to Hot Springs, Arkansas, during a summer vacation. Instead of keeping close behind him, as he instructed me to do, I lagged behind him a few minutes to look at something which interested me. As I was hurrying to catch up with him, a very tall brakeman stopped me and told me to turn around and go the other way. "That's the car for you," he said, as he pointed in the opposite direction. "But I want to go with my father who is in front of me," I insisted, as I tried to get away from him. But he had a tight hold upon me and I could not loosen his grip. Seeing I could not pull away from him, I began to belabor him with my parasol with all my might, until it was broken. Several times I had called my father, who had gone ahead into the car for white people, thinking I was directly behind him. When he discovered I was not with him he came running back to find me. The brakeman saw him coming and beat a hasty retreat. He had intended to force me into the little cubby hole set aside for colored people. I had another taste of the Jim Crow arrangement when I was about sixteen years old and was coming from Oberlin College to spend my vacation in Memphis. I had to change cars in Bowling Green, Kentucky, and when I had detrained I asked a porter who was standing on the platform which car I should take for Memphis. As soon as I had entered the one to which he directed me, I observed that it was different from any coach I had ever seen. It was a regular day coach divided into two parts—the front being used as a smoker for white men and the rear half serving as a coach for colored women and men.

Instantly I knew this was the Jim Crow coach which I had never seen but about which I had heard. I realized that I had been trapped and I resolved that I would not remain in it. I tried to leave it and go into the car ahead of me, but the conductor barred the way. When he came through the Jim Crow car to collect the tickets, I told him I did not want to remain in the coach, and that I wished he would give me a seat in the coach ahead. The conductor sternly informed me that I was in the coach to which I belonged. "But I have a first class ticket," I protested, "and this is not a first class coach."

"This is first class enough for you," he replied sarcastically, "and you stay just where you are," with a look calculated to freeze the very marrow of my bones. I tried hard to compose myself and to decide to remain where I was. I kept telling myself that changing cars was not worth the fight for it I would undoubtedly have to make. I had entered the Jim Crow car in the afternoon, and it was well filled for several hours. But as evening wore on, the number of passengers dwindled until I was the only one left. I had to travel all night, and when I thought that during the whole night or even a part of it I might be in that car alone at the mercy of the conductor or any man who entered I was frightened and horrified. As young as I was, I had heard about awful tragedies which had overtaken colored girls who had been obliged to travel alone on these cars at night.

I decided to ask the conductor once more to allow me to go into the coach ahead. But he was obdurate. When I told him how frightened I would be with nobody in the car but myself during the night or a portion of it, he assured me with a significant look that he himself would keep me company and remain in there with me. "I should much rather be left to myself," I summoned courage enough to reply, "than to have you stay with me." By that time I was so agitated I felt that anything would be preferable to remaining alone in that car with the conductor during the night—even death itself. But what could I do? All at once I made up my mind to leave the train. I had heard the conductor announce that the next stop would be Erie, Tennessee, where passengers going to certain destinations would have to change cars. I decided I would get off there, wire my plight to my father and await instructions from him.

I was well aware that I was taking a desperate chance. I knew that any colored girl would run a great risk of having an unpleasant experience or of falling into danger of some kind by getting off at night at a strange town in the South, where she was acquainted with nobody and where she might have difficulty in finding a decent place to stay. But of the two evils, I decided that leaving the train was the less. When we reached Erie, therefore, I took my valise and started toward the door. But the conductor was there before me and refused to let me pass.

"What are you going to do?" he asked. "I am getting off here," I replied, "to wire my father that you are forcing me to ride all night in a Jim Crow car. He will sue the railroad for compelling his daughter who has a first class ticket to ride in a second class car."

"Do you know where you are going?" he inquired.

"Do you require all your passengers who leave the train to tell you their business?" I countered.

When the conductor saw how agitated I was and how determined I was not to remain on the train, his manner toward me changed completely. He tried to wrench my valise from my hand, but I held onto it with a vise-like grip. Seeing he was attracting the attention of some of the passengers, he let go of my valise and said, "You can go ahead into that car if you want to." By the time I had found a seat in the center of the first class coach I was on the verge of collapse, but I possessed sufficient self control not to burst into tears. When we reached Memphis the next morning, my father was walking up and down the platform waiting for the train. I saw the conductor speak to him, and Father told me afterwards that he inquired, "Are you waiting for your daughter, sir? She's right in there," pointing to the first class coach.

At that time the Jim Crow car had not been legalized in the State of Tennessee, and colored people who bought first class tickets could get first class accommodations if they insisted upon their rights, without violating the State law. At present, however, when colored people holding first class tickets are thrust into the dirty, stuffy coaches set aside for them which lack proper accommodations for the two sexes, they are obliged to stay in them, because they are told that these are first class for them and that it is against the law for them to ride in the same coach with white people. Those who maintain that conditions are growing better for colored people in the South might do well to consider how much more seriously they are handicapped today when they travel in that section than they were thirty or forty years ago.

A few years after the incident occurred to which I have just referred I had an experience which proved conclusively that the necessity of spending the night in a Jim Crow car is a real peril for a colored girl. As the passengers reached their destination and left, one by one, I realized to my horror and dismay that I was left alone. A white man from the smoker came into the car and began to talk to me. I told him I was sleepy and requested him to leave me alone. He refused to do so and made some ugly remarks. I was terror stricken and started to the door when the train slowed down to stop. He seized me and threw me into a seat and then left the car. No pen can describe and no tongue portray the indignities, insults and assaults to which colored women and girls have been subjected in Jim

Crow cars. If I should dare relate some of the things which have happened, many would not believe me, and very serious objections to publishing them in a book would probably be raised.

Few colored women, and especially few young women, travel at night when it is possible to arrange a journey in any other way. But sometimes a young woman attending college gets an emergency call home on account of illness in her family, or death, or for some other reason, and then it is that she is obliged to face the nerve-racking, dangerous situation.

The first time I realized the ordeal through which colored women pass who are stranded at night in a strange city was when I was traveling from Shreveport, Louisiana, to Paris, Texas. I had boarded the coach for white people at Shreveport when I started early in the morning because I knew I would have to ride all day. The agent who sold me the ticket assured me that the train I was taking would go straight through from Shreveport to Paris and that I would reach my destination that night.

When I learned that I would be on the road all day, I remembered what had happened to me on a previous occasion. I left Hot Springs, Arkansas, one morning about five o'clock to go to Fort Smith. When I boarded the train I had eaten nothing since I had had my dinner about six the night before. I had gone into the Jim Crow car at Hot Springs, and had been unable to get a morsel of food all day long. When I reached Fort Smith that night, therefore, I had not eaten for twenty-four hours. For that reason, I resolved that in the future if I knew I would be traveling all day in the South, I would board a first class coach when I started on my journey and run the risk of getting into trouble, perhaps, so that it would be possible for me to get the service and necessities which passengers require.

This trip to Paris, Texas, proved the wisdom of that course. A short while before the train reached Texarkana, Arkansas, the conductor, who had talked to me several times en route, came to tell me that the train would not go through to Paris, as the agent in Shreveport had stated, but that it would be cut off in the city which we would soon reach. I was terribly upset by this news.

"What shall I do?" I asked in bewilderment. "I am acquainted with no one here. Where can I stop tonight?"

The conductor treated my dismay and confusion as a joke and replied, "Why you can stop at a hotel, of course. As much as you have traveled, surely you must have stopped at a hotel." Up to that night it had never occurred to me to attempt to stop at a hotel for white people in the South. The very suggestion from the conductor shocked and appalled me. Before I stopped to think, therefore, I said impulsively, "Why, I can't stop at a hotel in Texarkana."

"Certainly you can," he said emphatically. "Why not? There's a fine hotel just across from the station."

By that time the train had stopped. He picked up my suit case and walked toward the door with it. I followed involuntarily, not knowing what else to do. I was in a dilemma such as I never could have imagined would overtake me. Seeing a porter approaching us, the conductor said, "Here Jim, take this lady to the Rawling's House." (That is not the name of the hotel.) I could not refuse to go to the hotel. I had no idea where I could find a boarding place among colored people. I did not know whether the porter could or would direct me to one or not. But before I had time to reason the situation to a conclusion, the porter had my suit case and was leading me to the hotel just a few steps ahead of us.

In a trice I stood at the desk to register my name and to be assigned a room. As he was giving the key to the bellhop the clerk said to me, "Dinner is almost over, so if you want anything you had better go to the dining room immediately. You haven't much time." That information was a blessing in disguise, perhaps. I had been sitting by an open window in a common coach that hot day passing through Louisiana, while the smoke and dust were covering me with several coats of smudge. Therefore, I must have been several shades darker than I usually am, so I was far from being as fair as a lily when I appeared at that hotel. However, the fates seem to have been guiding me or misguiding me in this dilemma. Without changing my dress I simply refreshed myself a bit and went into the dining room, soliloquizing, "just as I am without one plea." The colored head waiter placed me at a table where a man and his wife were sitting. By the time I had gone that far I had to exercise great self control to keep my composure.

"Just bring me a simple dinner," I said to the waiter. "I

am so late I shall not have time to give you an order—something you like yourself." The fact that the man and his wife did not arise immediately and leave the table was very reassuring, indeed. If they had entertained the slightest suspicion that a monster in the shape of a real, live, honest-to-goodness colored woman had been placed in such close proximity to them at a table, they would have died the death, before they would have tamely submitted to such an outrage.

My room was on the first floor above the main entrance with a window which reached from the floor to the ceiling and led to a little veranda. After I removed my hat and had begun to get settled, I remembered that I had written my full name quite legibly in that register, and a great fear suddenly took possession of me. I had been filling engagements in that part of the South for three or four weeks, and it was quite possible that some of the waiters in the hotel had read the colored newspapers which gave rather full accounts both of my career and of my speeches. What if they should see my name and recognize who I was? If they did and should tell the management of the hotel, what would happen? I trembled with apprehension and fear. What a fatal mistake I had made by not registering under an assumed name! I tried to allay my alarm as best I could and retired. Finally I fell asleep. I had been in bed about two hours, perhaps, when a loud noise at my door awoke me out of a sound slumber.

"Your time has come," was the first thought that popped into my head. I was sure that the clerk or the proprietor had learned that I was a colored woman and had come to wreak vengeance upon me for daring to violate the traditions and the customs of the Southland by stopping at a white hotel. I did not answer and tried to plan what I should do The second knock sounded louder than the first. Then I decided I would not allow myself to be taken out of the room alive, to be beaten and disfigured or otherwise mistreated by an infuriated mob. It came to my mind with startling vividness that somebody had told me that Texarkana was the first city in the South in which a colored man had been burned to death. This thought did not comfort me at all.

I hastily resolved that I would rush to the little balcony and jump to the ground. If that did not kill me, I argued, it might stun me enough to prevent me from being so sensitive to pain as I would otherwise be. By the time I had planned what I would do, a third knock came. Then I mustered up enough courage and strength to say, "Who is it? What do you want?"

"Lady," came a soft, ingratiating voice, "did you ring for a pitcher of water?"

"No," I fairly shouted. "I did not!"

I hope I shall never pass through an experience like that again. It is said that it is possible for a human being to have certain feelings only once in a life time. If the feelings are of a harrowing, painful variety such as overwhelmed me at that hotel in Texarkana, that dispensation of Providence is a great blessing, indeed.

I had another experience when I was filling a lecture engagement in Florida which proved again how unreliable railroad schedules are sometimes in certain parts of the South. I was told that the train for which I bought my ticket would carry me through to Miami and I would arrive that night. As evening approached, the conductor told me that the schedule had been changed and that I would have to remain overnight at a small place which was a winter resort for Northerners and take a train for Miami the next day at noon. I had been riding all day in the first class coach and had met some interesting people from Chicago who were en route to this resort. They had spent several winters there and were charmed with it on general principles. When one of the women, who had been especially attracted to me, learned that I had to remain all night at this resort, she insisted immediately that I should put up at her little hotel—a small, exclusive hostelry for discriminating guests. My newly made acquaintances stated with pride that nobody but people highly recommended could secure accommodations at this little inn.

I demurred at first, saying I preferred to go to a regular hotel, since I should be in the place only one night. But my new friend insisted so vigorously that I should stop at her hotel that I finally consented to do so. I had been in the room assigned me but a short while when some one knocked at the door. Without opening it far I made a little crack wide enough to inquire what was wanted. It was my new acquaintance, who said she had told some of her friends about me and they were in the reception room waiting to meet me. I excused myself on the ground that I was a bit fatigued and had to do some work before I retired.

About ten minutes later the lady came again to urge me to come down to meet her friends, saying that since she had told them about the delightful day we had spent together on the train, they would be very much disappointed if I refused. But I excused myself again, expressing regret that I could not comply with her request.

The next morning I was placed at the table for transients and not at the one reserved for regular guests. My new friend and her husband came in a little late and greeted me pleasantly, as they sat down. While I was eating my breakfast I felt that somebody was gazing at me very hard. I had had that feeling elsewhere on several occasions, and when I had tried to find the cause of this rather uncanny sensation, I usually discovered that somebody's eyes had actually been fixed upon me. Anyone who has tried to attract the attention of a friend sitting opposite to him in an auditorium by fastening his eyes upon him and has seen him look up at him will understand this psychic force which is hard to explain.

When I glanced around the room to see whether anyone was really looking at me, I caught the eye of a woman seated at the table for regular guests whom I recognized immediately. She bowed very graciously and seemed pleased to see me. As I was leaving the room, she came towards me, called my name and expressed surprise at seeing me so far South. I had to admit that while I was sure I had met her before, I could not remember her name. "Why, I am Mrs. R.," she replied. "We have spoken more than once from the same platform." Then I recalled she was the president of a large woman's organization and that we actually had addressed the same national and international meetings several times.

We left the dining room together and after a short conversation she went up the street, while I took a seat on a large veranda in front of the hotel. In a few minutes my new acquaintance with whom I had traveled the whole of the previous day, and who had been so infatuated with me that she wanted all the hotel guests to meet me, came out where I was sitting, stared at me coldly and cut me dead. I understood perfectly what had happened. My old friend had undoubtedly told her who I was without intending to injure me or betray any terrible secret which would cause anybody to snub me. Being without prejudice herself, she forgot that others might have some. But the fact that unawares she had admired a colored woman so much, had taken such pains to show it and had tried to present the off-color individual to her friends was a blow from which it was evidently impossible for my Nordic traveling companion of the day before to recover.

Whenever I have recalled this incident I have been very happy about two things. In the first place, I was glad I had been loyal to my race in several discussions which we had en route. As we passed some of the dilapidated unsightly huts in which colored people commonly live in many parts of the South, particularly in the rural districts, this lady from the West who had spent three or four winters in Florida surprised me by the harsh opinions she expressed. The worst thing she could say about colored people seemed too good. She agreed thoroughly with the Southerner's point of view.

Negroes are a bad lot on general principles, she declared. Few if any could be trusted. And so on and so forth. I reminded her that human beings are the result both of heredity and of environment and entreated her to judge colored people according to that rule. But I had little success. She was one of those Northerners who, colored people say, are more hard-boiled when they come South to visit or to live than the Southerners themselves.

"Deliver me from Yankees who live down here," southern colored people declare emphatically. It is easy to understand why northern people assume that attitude when they cast their lot with their brethren in the South. If northern people want to succeed in business or desire social recognition, they must agree with the Southerner's point of view on the race question. The white South will allow nobody to differ with it, contradict it or oppose it on that subject. It were better for an individual who attempts it that a mill stone were hanged about his neck and that he were drowned in the depths of the sea.

It was a great satisfaction for me to know that I had not been tempted to agree with the northern woman's unjust estimate of my group while we were traveling together in the South under circumstances which would have caused me trouble and embarrassment if she had suspected who I was. Several times I injected so much feeling into what I said, I wondered why she did not ask me to explain why I sympathized so deeply with colored people and advocated their cause so strongly. I shuddered as I looked at the Jim Crow car when I boarded the train for Miami. It was dirtier and more forbidding than they usually are, and it would have been an ordeal through which I should not have liked to pass, if I had been ejected from the first class coach, which was none too good on this particular road, and forced to take a long tedious journey in the Jim Crow car.

I was glad also that I had not registered under an assumed name. When I took the register in that little Florida resort, I recalled my first experience in stopping at a white hotel in the South and how I wondered whether it would not have been wiser to use a fictitious name to avoid getting into trouble. But, although I thought I might be running a risk to write my name correctly, I could not persuade myself to do otherwise. If I had pursued a different course, I would have been greatly embarrassed to have an old friend discover I was traveling under an assumed name. No matter how tactful she may be, a colored woman who is obliged to make journeys through the South has troubles and trials galore.

Both my husband, who was fairer than myself, and I would secure Pullman accommodations for our friends who were in Washington en route to their southern homes and feared they could not get them for themselves. I have never known one of our group to refuse such accommodations when they needed them on a long journey and could get them. But, curiously enough, some colored people have been known to object to having representatives of their group travel in a Pullman car. I did not know this until I had an experience which proved conclusively that this is true.

I knew that I had to take a long and tedious journey to fill a lecture engagement in the South which would require at least one night and two days and, perhaps, two nights, as uncertain as schedules in that section sometimes are. So I secured a berth from Washington for the entire distance. When I reached my destination I found a committee had come to meet me. They had gone to the Jim Crow car, as they were accustomed to do, and discovered I was not there. They had concluded I had missed connections in some way and would arrive later. In the meantime I had left the train and met the committee on the station platform.

While I was welcomed with politeness, there was a certain stiffness and frigidity in the atmosphere. With a woman's intuition I felt that something was wrong somewhere, but I did not know what it was and I could not guess. I delivered my address, had a large audience and the engagement was pronounced a success from every point of view. The organization which had invited me to speak, so as to raise money for some project, was perfectly satisfied with the amount realized.

But when I was going to take the train for a city not far away, the minister who had met me with the committee and who had been foremost in making the arrangements told me that he wanted to ask as a special favor that I leave the city in the Jim Crow car. He said I had been severely criticized by some for arriving in a Pullman. I assured him that I intended to leave the city in the Jim Crow car. I explained that I never tried to ride in the white coach in the South when I was going a short distance; but that when I had to take a long journey, such as I made when I came to his city, I felt it was my duty to my family, to myself and to the audience I had been invited to address to keep as fit as possible by taking the proper rest, so that I could give the people the very best I had to offer.

It was very irritating and nerve-racking to be obliged to stand at the ticket window and wait till all the people in the white waiting room had purchased their tickets, before the agent would sell me mine, no matter how early I would come to the station. It was hard to exercise self control and banish from my mind such thoughts as I would be ashamed to acknowledge as my own. When I first filled lecture engagements in the South, I traveled with a trunk, and several times I barely secured my ticket in time to have it checked. Once I had to leave it, although I had reached the station early. Many white people were going to some special meeting and the ticket agent paid no attention to me whatever, as I stood waiting what seemed to me an interminable time at the window of the colored people's room. For that reason I usually went into the white waiting room when I was not accompanied by friends, whenever I had to purchase a railroad ticket in the South. How self-respecting colored people can patiently endure such treatment year in and year out without getting desperate is difficult to understand.

CHAPTER 31

POLITICAL ACTIVITIES—CHARGED WITH
DISORDERLY CONDUCT

MY APPOINTMENT AS Director of
Work among Colored Women was almost dramatic. As President of the Women's Republican League of Washington I went to New York with the secretary shortly after the 19th amendment granting suffrage to women had passed. Our League wanted to become a national organization. Since the Household of Ruth with its large membership from all over the United States happened to be meeting in New York and the National Republican Committee had just gone into its headquarters fo: the Harding-Coolidge campaign, we thought it would be an excellent opportunity to speak to that big organization of women on the political situation and to ask the National Republican Committee to help finance us to become national at one and the same time.

After distributing literature among members of the convention and addressing them we went to the National Republican Headquarters on 44th Street near Fifth Avenue to see some of the leaders and prefer our request. Just as my friend and I met the Honorable Henry Lincoln Johnson, the able and eloquent national committeeman from Georgia, he said without any preamble or introduction to the subject, "Mrs. Welch, I want to present you to Mrs. Mary Church Terrell, the director of the colored women of the East."

I considered this as a mere pleasantry or a joke, for I did not know there was to be such a position. But Committeeman Johnson seemed to be serious and stated that Senator Coleman Dupont from Delaware had already appointed me. There was no doubt, he said, that I was to direct the political campaign for the colored women of the East. When they heard the news, the colored men at National Headquarters were quite enthusiastic about my appointment. On the 23rd of September, 1920, my birthday, I received a letter from General Dupont saying that I had been appointed to take charge of the colored women of the East during the campaign, that he wanted me to come to New York at once and that he wished to talk to me as soon as I arrived. I considered this recognition by the Republican party as a birthday present.

Since I had believed in and advocated woman suffrage all my life, I was happy in the prospect of being able to practice what I preached. I could not do this literally, however, for, in the District of Columbia where I had lived for thirty years, everybody was disfranchised, men and women, black and white, old and young, crazy and sane alike. At least there was no political discrimination against anybody in the National Capital on account of race, sex, class or condition.

When I arrived at the National Republican headquarters in New York, no place could be found for the office of the woman who had been appointed Director of the Eastern Division. Up and down I went through the big building, peering into every nook and corner, into every crack and crevice, only to be told that every room had been pre-empted—everything had been assigned to somebody else. At last, I found an open space for my headquarters on the third floor which had no privacy whatever. But there were at least a few square feet which I could call my own and in which I could function.

First, I had an interview with many women who had been engaged in the political activities of the city, some of them being captains in their respective districts. Each and every one of them promised to cooperate with me. This encouraged and gratified me greatly, for I had heard that efforts had been made to prejudice the Eastern women against me, both because I had no vote myself and because some folks said I hailed originally from the South, and they weren't going to be led by a southern woman! I was also informed that a few disgruntled souls had tried to create sentiment against me on the ground that it was a reflection upon them to send a woman from anywhere to the East to teach them to vote. But I had been in office only a short while before all the women who had been active in politics gave me their support.

Then I began to build up an organization by appointing women to take charge of the political work in their respective States. I sent out letters saying we should reach each and every one in the State, so that they would all register and vote for the Republican candidates. Even though we were sure the Republicans would win, I said, a great deal of work had to be done and there was little time to do it. I begged them not to sleep at the switch nor rest on their oars and declared that if we worked as though we feared we would lose, we should be sure to win.

"By a miracle the 19th amendment has been ratified," I wrote. "We women have now a weapon of defense which we have never possessed before. It will be a shame and reproach to us if we do not use it. However much the white women of the country need suffrage, for many reasons which will immediately occur to you, colored women need it more.

"If we do not use the franchise we shall give our enemies a stick with which to break our heads, and we shall not be able to live down the reproach of our indifference for one hundred years. I am sure you are eager to discharge the duties and obligations of citizenship. Hold meetings! Every time you meet a woman, talk to her about going to the polls to vote."

In New York, New Jersey and Rhode Island I delivered a large number of political speeches. During the morning I would work in my office, take as late a train as possible for the place in which I was to talk that night so as to reach there on time, address the audience, then leave at midnight for New York. Sometimes I went directly to my office from the railroad station or from the boat in the morning and repeated the same performance on the next day.

I left New York one afternoon at 1:03 o'clock and reached Newport, Rhode Island, at 7 that evening. I rushed to my stopping place, began to dress at 7:35, ate dinner, repacked my suit case before leaving the house, went to the church, delivered my speech, was on the boat again at 9:45, reached New York about 7 the next morning, went to the office, got my mail, left for Dover, Delaware, at 11 and arrived at 4:22 to fill an engagement there that night.

The work appealed to me strongly. It was literally "the

way I long had sought and sighed because I found it not." There was a new experience in each place. Although I had been on the lecture bureau, the situations and the thrills in a political campaign seemed entirely different. The audiences were very responsive and enjoyed expressing their satisfaction and approbation. But there is no rose without a thorn.

And right here I must relate the only unpleasant experience I have ever had during a political campaign. Less than five minutes after I reached Dover, Delaware, I was threatened with arrest by the ticket agent there. The gentleman who was to meet me at the station did not appear, so I went to the telephone booth to 'phone him. Unfortunately for me, I looked into the Wilmington Directory in the front part of the book, thinking it was for Dover, and did not turn to the back part where the Dover numbers were. There was no Bureau of Information in the little station, so I went to the window of the ticket office and saw a young man standing there reading a magazine. Dover is not a large city and the man I wished to reach was well known there, because he was a first class paperhanger and had been actively engaged in politics for years.

"I am a stranger here," I began, "and I am trying to reach Mr. Ross, whom I expected to meet me. I cannot find his name in the telephone directory. Have you any idea how I could reach him?"

A man sitting in the ticket office behind the young man to whom I had spoken growled roughly, "Go look in the telephone directory."

"I have already looked there before I came to you, and I cannot find his name," I said.

"Go away from that window," the man stormed, "and don't bother me any more."

Thinking the ticket agent was provoked because he thought I had come to him for information before I sought it at the proper source, I tried to placate him by saying, "I did not come to you till I had looked in the telephone directory."

"Go away from that window," the man roared again, "or I'll have you arrested. I'll call the police."

"For what?" I asked.

Then he rushed angrily to the telephone, took down the receiver, and began to talk. Naturally, I thought he was carrying out his threat. Feeling sure that the police would soon come to arrest me, I decided to ask Information for the number I could not find in the directory. While I was 'phoning in the booth I glanced up and saw the ticket agent standing at the door, listening to what I was saying. At first, I thought he had come to strike me, he was in such a towering rage, but when he did not approach me I decided he had left the ticket office and had come to the telephone booth to prevent me from leaving the station till the police arrived.

I then resolved that he should not have the pleasure of forcibly detaining me. I would remain in the station till the police came. After that, every time the station door opened, I expected to see an officer of the law coming to arrest me. After waiting about fifteen minutes I inquired how much longer I would have to remain there, before the police came to get me.

"Take your seat," the ticket agent roared, shaking his fist at me.

"I am a busy woman," I replied, "and it is not right to keep me waiting here so long to be arrested."

Then the agent jumped from his chair, rushed to the telephone again and jerked the handle so viciously I thought he had surely broken it. He 'phoned for the police a second time. I waited patiently for what seemed to me a long time, expecting every minute to have an officer open the station door to arrest me.

Finally I arose from my seat and went to the ticket window. "I will not wait here any longer to be arrested," I said. "I shall leave this station."

"Go away from that window," shouted the agent. "Take your seat. You are disorderly. You know you are."

"No, I am not disorderly. I am simply obeying instructions. You told me to wait for the police, and that is what I am doing, but I shall wait no longer."

Then I left the waiting room, although I feared that the agent would run out, grab me and detain me in the station. I saw a white cabman standing at the door and I asked him if he knew where a paperhanger by the name of Ross lived. He said he did. I did not try to engage the cabman to take me to the man's home, for I was not certain that he would do so. In many southern cities white companies will not let colored people ride in their cabs. My mind was greatly relieved, therefore, when he inquired in a kindly tone, "Do you want to go to Ross' home?" I told him I did. "I will take you there," he said, and he did.

After I had waited on his porch about an hour, Mr. Ross finally came. He told me he had heard about the trouble I had had at the station, and he seemed deeply concerned. I did not urge him to tell me what he had heard because I wanted to focus my thoughts on the speech I was to deliver in a few hours.

After the meeting that evening Mr. Ross told me that the ticket agent had sworn out a warrant for disorderly conduct against me and that I would have to appear in Court about ten o'clock the next morning. Two railroad detectives from Clayton, which was several stations above Dover, had been sent for by the ticket agent, he told me, and they had actually come to the theater while I was speaking to arrest me, but after they had heard me talk, they refused to do so. And thereby hangs a tale. There was a reason.

During my address I expressed sympathy for Ireland and referred to the martyr, McSwiney, who had gone on a hunger strike in jail as a protest against England's treatment of his country and had starved himself to death in prison. I also made several references to the cruelties and barbarities perpetrated upon the Russian Jews. One of the detectives who had come to the meeting to arrest me happened to be an Irishman and reached the theater just in time to hear my tribute to McSwiney and my expression of hope that Ireland might soon be delivered from the English yoke. He stood in the back of the theater until I finished speaking.

"I'll be damned if I arrest that woman," he is quoted as saying, as he took his departure, leaving his jail prospect free. For once in my life, therefore, I literally talked myself out of jail. The next morning the Dover Republicans who had arranged the meeting sent me an attorney, James Hall Anderson, and I related the whole story to him. I emphasized the fact that I would never have remained in the waiting room at the station an hour after arriving, if I had not feared the agent would forcibly detain me, if I tried to escape, or, if that did not happen, that I would be arrested on the public streets after leaving the station and be followed to the jail by a crowd of boys.

My attorney and I went to the office of the Justice of the Peace and I was put under $200 bond. Dr. Herman, a Hebrew, went on the bond. He declared that if my bond had been much higher than it was—'way up in the thousands—he would have been glad to serve me just the same. The courtroom was filled with men and boys, but there was not a colored citizen present except Mr. Ross, who had accompanied me. To me such a situation seemed very significant indeed. It would have been natural for my group to come to the trial when one of their own women had been arrested for disorderly conduct, unless they feared disagreeable consequences if they did. After being arraigned that morning I took the train for Wilmington, where I was to speak that night. And there another entirely new experience awaited me. Several hundred women led by a real, sure enough brass band paraded in my honor in front of the residence of Mrs. Alice Dunbar-Nelson, once the wife of Paul Laurence Dunbar, by whom I was entertained.

Several months later the charge against me was dismissed. I went before a Notary Public and signed an agreement not to bring suit against the railroad company or its agents growing out of the "dispute" "in consideration of the premises of one dollar lawful money of the United States of America to me in hand paid by the said company."

Once I decided definitely to sue the railroad company, but both white and colored lawyers persuaded me not to do it. Among the lawyers I consulted it was the consensus that a colored woman's chance of winning such a suit in the courts of Delaware was too remote to attempt legal action, no matter how just might be her cause. The only expense in the case was borne by the Dover, Delaware, Committee. Since the payment to me of one dollar by the railroad company was an acknowledgment that their agent did wrong, I felt that it might be the better part of wisdom to be satisfied with that outcome of the case and let the matter drop there. But 'way down deep in my heart, I confess I was not satisfied at all.

This experience was very valuable to me. It proved to me how easily a serious charge based upon a trivial incident may be trumped up against a colored woman or a man. If I had not been a campaign speaker for the Republican Party, if General Dupont had not been personally interested in me and had not thrown the weight of his powerful influence in my favor, perhaps today I might have a record in Dover, Delaware, of having been convicted on a charge of disorderly conduct in which I "used abusive language" and had been guilty of several other heinous offenses. The little newspaper published in Dover represented me as being an obstreperous woman indeed and the poor, ill-treated ticket agent as a victim of my terrible misdeed.

Personally, I should not have been worried much if I had actually been arrested. For several reasons I think it would have been a good thing. It would have shocked white and black alike if I had been sent to jail on a charge of disorderly conduct. Then, when they had learned afterwards that the disorderly conduct consisted of asking the ticket agent a question, and remaining in the station till the police came to arrest me, as he had instructed me to do, both races would have learned some facts about the reason why the proportion of arrests among colored people is so much higher than is that among other racial groups.

But the attitude of some in my own racial group was both interesting and amusing. The men especially appeared horror-stricken at the thought of my being placed under arrest. When I told them I would not have cared very much if I had been taken to jail on a charge of disorderly conduct under the circumstances, they shook their heads in fierce disapproval of my brash point of view and assured me that such a disgraceful experience would have ruined me for life. Some of my personal friends were so horrified when they heard the story, I wondered whether they would have associated with me afterwards if I had actually been sent to jail.

I could not help contrasting the attitude assumed by English women concerning the ordeal of being arrested in a good cause with that manifested by some in my own group. In the ballroom of the Willard Hotel in Washington I once heard the daughter of a distinguished prelate, the Bishop of Canterbury, relate the experiences through which British women passed in their effort to secure suffrage. She was petite and dainty and wore a light gray gown which was modish and becoming. She looked so ethereal and fragile, as she stood on the platform, she gave one the impression she would be terribly frightened if an ordinary mortal said "boo" to her.

But she began her speech by saying, "How many of you in

this room have ever been arrested for the sake of suffrage? Will those of you who have been, please raise your hands?" She beamed encouragingly upon her audience and looked as though she confidently expected to see several hands go up at least. But not a hand was raised. The little woman seemed very much surprised, not to say disgusted. After waiting in vain for a few seconds she remarked with keen disappointment, apparent in her face and in her voice, "Why, if I were to ask English women such a question in an audience like this, at least half a dozen hands would be raised."

But, since citizens of the United States do not look with such indulgence upon those who have been arrested, perhaps it is just as well that I have never been sent to jail. The Dover, Delaware, episode, however, was not the only time in my life I came near being apprehended by the law. In the National Capital, before the nineteenth amendment was passed, I narrowly escaped the same fate.

The National Woman's Party, led by Alice Paul, used to picket the White House in the afternoon when the departments were closing and the clerks were passing by on their way home. On a bitter cold day the phone would ring and a voice from Headquarters, which were then at Jackson Place, opposite Lafayette Square, would inquire, "Will you come to picket the White House this afternoon?" As a rule, I complied with the request and several times Phyllis would come with me to swell the number. Sometimes it was necessary to stand on hot bricks supplied by a colored man employed expressly for that purpose to keep our feet from freezing.

But once it was impossible for me to respond to this call, and, as the Fates would have it, on that very day several women were arrested for picketing and sent to Occoquan, the workhouse, when I was absent from my post. The following letter, dated January 20, 1921, notified me that a pin was to be presented to me, along with others, for the service I had rendered the cause of woman suffrage. It read:

"DEAR FELLOW PICKET:

"The National Woman's Party wishes to present to each woman who has ever picketed, whether she was imprisoned or not, a picket pin in memory of our picket days together. We will present these pins on the evening of February 18th during our national convention, which meets in Washington, February 15th, and lasts through February 18th. We hope to make the ceremony of giving the pins a dignified and impressive one and want, by this ceremony, to show appreciation of the militant workers in our campaign of whom we are all proud. We ask each picket to wear upon this evening a white dress, if possible, white shoes and stockings. A room will be provided adjoining the hall in which wraps may be left during the ceremony."

And so it happened that on February 18, 1921, my daughter, Phyllis, and myself were each presented a pin at the Washington Hotel by the National Woman's Party because we helped picket the White House as a protest against the disfranchisement of women. There is no doubt that this gesture on the part of determined women called attention to the injustice perpetrated upon them by denying them the suffrage and hastened the passage of the nineteenth amendment the year before.

CHAPTER 32

WORK IN WAR CAMP COMMUNITY SERVICE

So QUICKLY did I find myself signed up for work in the War Camp Community Service, it made my head swim. A telephone call summoned me urgently to the Dewey Hotel one morning. The number of the room was given and I was instructed to come up without any ceremony whatever. Mrs. Jane Ogle, the representative, wasted neither time nor words telling why she wanted to see me.

The War Camp Community Service had decided, she said, to do something for the colored women and girls living in the cities where little or nothing had been done for them. The armistice had been signed and colored soldiers were returning from Europe. Establishing recreational centers in those cities in which they would be demobilized was one of the methods suggested for doing practical work for a neglected group. Mrs. Ogle said she wanted me to help her select the women who would have charge of the centers which were to be established, and so impressed was she that I could render the assistance that she needed, she persuaded me to try.

I got busy and with infinite care, terribly burdened with the great responsibility, I selected the women living in and near Washington. A "School" for these women who had been invited to consider entering the service was held at the old Ebbitt House, which has since been torn down to make way for the National Press Building, opposite the New Willard Hotel. For several days lectures were delivered by experts on the best methods of carrying out the intentions of the promoters of the enterprise, and they were attended by colored and white together, which was quite an innovation for prejudice-ridden

Washington. So far as I can recall, this was the first time such a thing was done.

Immediately after this school closed Mrs. Ogle interviewed several women I recommended while she was in Washington, accepted them and assigned them to the cities in which they were to work. Shortly after she returned to Headquarters in the Metropolitan Building, Madison Square, New York, I received a special-delivery letter directing me to leave for the South immediately. Mrs. Ogle named the cities which she wished me to visit, directed me to find and interview the women I thought competent to do the work planned by the War Camp Community Service, wire her my estimate of their respective qualifications as soon as I had talked with them, and have them ready to attend school which was to be held in Hampton, Virginia, fifteen days from the morning I received her letter.

How in the world could I do what was expected of me in such a short time? I did not see how it was humanly possible for me to visit so many cities, discover the women fitted to do the work, interview them, send the result to Headquarters and return from the South myself to attend the school in fifteen days. It was a hectic, thrilling. but interesting experience, was that search for women prepared to do the important piece of work planned. My commission was fulfilled to the letter. Fifteen days after galloping through the principal cities of Illinois, Alabama, Tennessee and Georgia I had gathered together at Hampton, Virginia, as fine, capable and progressive a group of colored women as could be collected in the United States.

Then Headquarters directed me to visit certain cities, nearly all of them in the South, to see whether the leading citizens thereof would allow the War Camp Community Service to work in the interest of colored women and girls. I was also instructed to study and report the need of making efforts to promote their welfare. "We desire you to visit the following cities on the dates indicated," read the letter. The name of the Community Organizer for the whole city and of the Community Organizer for the girls' division was given in each case. "We have allowed two days for each city," continued the letter, "with one day to go to the next and to provide opportunity for writing your report."

If I should give an exact and detailed account of the views

expressed by some of the men on the committee formed by the War Camp Community Service in the work it was trying to do in the South, many would believe I was drawing largely on my imagination instead of confining myself strictly to facts. Some of the leading citizens of the places visited were opposed to making any effort whatsoever in behalf of colored girls. If these citizens had been expected or requested to contribute money to the work, their opposition would have been easy to understand. But they were not called upon to foot the bills at all. The W. C. C. S. was willing and eager to finance the work.

The reasons which some of the leading citizens assigned for opposing the work were very remarkable indeed. Some declared that colored girls were so bad on general principles that it was useless to try to improve them. I asked them if they had ever heard of an effort being made in the city to uplift them, and almost invariably these men confessed that they had not. This admission was usually followed by an explanation that nobody in their place had ever attempted it because they knew that it would be time, effort and money wasted. In meeting this particular opinion I tried to impress upon these men that so long as they made no effort to improve a group of evil women in their midst, they were not only perpetrating a great injustice upon their own sons and upon the other white youth of their respective cities, inasmuch as they were allowing them to be subjected to temptations which it was somebody's duty at least to try to remove, but they were making it hard for their own women to be happy, so long as they did nothing to improve the morals of the community as a whole. In replying to this argument its advocates always assured me that southern people understand the "nigger" better than anybody else in the world, that they alone know how to deal with him and can solve their problem best themselves. In fact, I was warned that southern people would brook no "interference" from the people of other sections, no matter how pure their motives might be.

I was instructed by the War Camp Community Service to send in a typewritten report of the opinions expressed by the leading men of the cities visited. Therefore, as soon as I left the men with whom I talked I made a verbatim report of what they said. It was not always an easy matter to find a typist to whom I could entrust a statement which was of such a confidential nature, and it was often difficult to lay hands on a typewriter which I could use myself. I was by no means an expert typist, and it took an interminable time for me to write a few sentences. But, by hook or crook, somehow I managed to obey instructions to send in a résumé of my interviews, a copy of which I have retained. For that reason I can reproduce them today almost word for word as I received them. Many of my reports read something like this: "The Community Organizer told me that nothing is being done for colored girls in this city by the Y. W. C. A. or by any other organization. There is no recreational center for colored people. There is no clubroom or meeting place of any kind for the colored soldiers or sailors who have returned from the World War."

There were two notable exceptions to this condition. One was the fine club for colored soldiers in Montgomery, Alabama, and the other was in Chattanooga, Tennessee. "There is no playground for colored children," is the information given in nearly all my reports. "There is no public park for them in this city and colored people are not allowed to enter the park provided for white citizens."

Following instructions from Headquarters, I always talked first with the Community Organizer who had charge of all the work done by the W. C. C. S. in the respective cities. Replying to my questions concerning the conditions under which the colored people of Montgomery, Alabama, then lived, the Community Organizer told me that there was no high school for colored pupils, that the city provided only 50 teachers for 5,000 colored children, while it supplied 100 for the same number of white children and paid the white teachers twice as much as colored teachers received—sometimes three times as much.

"There is just one eighth grade for five thousand colored children in this city," he said. In Montgomery I secured the services of a white typist for my report and when I read this statement to her, she was visibly displeased—so much so that I wondered whether she would continue to typewrite for me. "Even if higher grades were provided for colored children, they would not attend them," she said indignantly. When I repeated this to the Community Organizer, he replied that it might as well be argued that colored children would not wear diamonds if a generous Providence had kindly supplied them.

In several instances the organizers, who were northern men, appeared genuinely shocked at the conditions under which colored people were forced to live. Such men would urge me to do everything in my power to induce the W. C. C. S. to send a worker for colored girls on account of the pressing need.

In one instance, however, I found a northern man who had sold himself body and soul to the South. During a meeting of the committee called to decide whether the members were willing to let the W. C. C. S. bring a colored woman to Gulfport, Mississippi, to establish a center for colored girls, he referred to them continually as "niggers." "I know all about niggers," he began. He was immediately rebuked by Chaplain Taylor, a northern man, who said, "I don't consider them niggers by any means. All you need to do is to call colored people 'niggers,' and I know immediately that you are originally from the South. I call them Negroes or colored people." It was an unusual exhibition of courage on the part of a northern man in the presence of southern people among whom he lived.

In the South it was then and still is strictly against custom and tradition to call a colored woman "Mrs.," no matter who she is. Knowing this, the Community Organizer kept referring to me as "She." Instead of saying "Mrs. Terrell has come for the purpose" or "Mrs. Terrell has proposed" something or other, he would say "She has come" or "She says."

A northern woman who had lived in Gulfport for thirteen years and was a member of the committee refused to be intimidated by the others and defied custom by treating me with the same courtesy she would have shown a woman of her own race. When I first met the Community Organizer he told me he hailed from the West and he did not hesitate to address me as he would have any other woman under similar circumstances. That is, he did so when we were alone and no one was listening. But during the meeting he insisted several times he was a Southerner, although there was nothing in his speech to indicate it. He drew himself up proudly and stated "I want you to spread this propaganda that both my wife and I are Southerners." And he declared with great show of pride that his "father-in-law had owned thirty slaves, which he lost in the Civil War."

This was the most striking and pathetic illustration of a northern man's complete surrender to the customs and traditions of the South which I have ever seen. A little northern woman who had been sent to work among white women and girls was greatly shocked by the way colored people were treated in Biloxi, Mississippi, just a few miles from Gulfport. She was amazed at some of the conditions which prevailed among white people themselves. An incident which had happened just before she talked to me amused her immensely. A former Community Organizer of Biloxi had written to a friend in the State describing the immoral conditions of the place. This letter was printed in a newspaper, which so incensed the citizens that they threatened to whip the man who exposed them, and the War Camp Community Service felt obliged to transfer him to another place. "These people down here will kill you," the young white woman said, "if you do the least thing to displease them. I am scared to death. If I didn't need the money I'd leave tomorrow. And I'm going to ask to be transferred right away."

The treatment accorded colored people shocked the young organizer more than anything else. She illustrated this by describing the punishment which her landlady had meted out to the colored cook. She had heard quite a commotion in the kitchen one day and she asked her landlady what had caused it. She was then informed that Alphonse, the colored cook, had been in bad temper and that every time he misbehaved she gave him a bottle of castor oil and forced him to take it. Alphonse was then twenty-four years old, was married and had several children.

"Do your best to get two workers for colored girls down here," she said. "Nothing is being done for them in Biloxi at all. But whatever you do, insist upon having two workers sent here. It would be cruel to assign only one colored woman to this place, because it would be impossible for her to endure the conditions which would confront her in this town, if she came alone."

The young organizer persuaded me to call on a banker, who was a prominent member of the Biloxi Committee, to see if I could induce him to consent to having the W. C. C. S. send a colored worker for the girls. With fear and trembling mixed with hope, I went.

"If a worker who came here would teach colored girls to cook," he said, after I had explained my mission to him as best

I could, "there would not be any great objection to it. But the more attention you pay to niggers, the more harm you do them. As soon as you try to do something for them, they try to set themselves on a level with white people. Remember, that whenever you try to do something for niggers, you have to exercise great care to keep from harming them. They can't live and be useful, unless they stay in their place. When they get away from that, they make things terrible. The greatest trouble is the nigger preacher. Every nigger wants to live easy himself and make the rest of the niggers work for him. The more ignorant he is and the more he influences the niggers against white people, the better the niggers like him.

"The nigger preacher is a fraud and is unpeaceable as a rule. Southern people have fed and clothed and taken care of the niggers for years. Just as soon as they get something done for them they get sassy. If a nigger woman came down here she would probably have her nose in the air and give a great deal of trouble. The nigger woman who came here would want to come to this bank, sit down in that chair where you are and talk to me as you are doing."

Then an indescribable feeling of surprise, disgust and terror came over me. But I controlled my feelings sufficiently to ask the bank president if he would object to talking to a colored woman. "Not if she knows she is a nigger and keeps her place," he replied. "You people who come down here from the North have more trouble with darkies than the Southerners do. There is a Mr. S. here who says his views about niggers have entirely changed. He has had a great deal of experience with them down here and he ought to know."

When I went to see this banker I had no idea he would fail to recognize with what race I am identified. Naturally, I thought the Community Organizer had told the committee who and what I am. Moreover, he was not blind and had a pair of perfectly good eyes. He could see my face and I used my hands, on which I wore no gloves, quite often during the conversation, as is my custom. In all my life I have never had a more uncomfortable moment than I did when the banker said with a great deal of feeling, "the nigger woman who came here would want to come to this bank, sit down in that chair where you are and talk to me as you are doing."

As a rule, the more dangerous the situation in which I find myself, the more self-control I possess till the trouble is over. Then I wither and wilt. But in this instance when I imagined the indignation and wrath which would take hold of this man who was talking to me, if he discovered I was precisely the kind of Negro woman whom he had described with such righteous indignation and whom he so cordially disliked, I almost lost my self-control in my desire to flee from his presence.

No better illustration of the falsity of the claim which Southerners make, when they insist they can always detect colored people, no matter how fair they are, can be cited than this one. There is no doubt the banker would have laughed anyone to scorn who would have suggested that he would mistake a colored woman whose complexion is as swarthy as mine for a white woman. It is well for me that I was not near him when he discovered his error.

The Community Organizer of Hattiesburg, Mississippi, was very eager to have a colored worker sent there. It seemed to him, he said, that there was more bitterness displayed by white people toward colored people in that city than anywhere he had ever been. In referring to the colored girls who had been arrested by the Law Enforcement League, he said that the first cases had been undoubtedly framed up. White soldiers employed for the purpose had paid them with marked bills which had been used as evidence against them.

In Pensacola, Florida, the same opinion was expressed as was heard in Mississippi. "The white people here want colored people to do their washing and ironing, and they get mad as fire when they don't. They don't care a whoop about trying to 'elevate' them." "So far as the nigger is concerned," one man told me, "he is like a mule. He is a good animal, so long as you keep him broken." "But the colored soldiers rendered great service to the Allies during the World War," I interjected. "And so did the mule," quickly retorted the speaker. "There is no animal in the world that did better service than the mule during the war. The mule is just like the nigger. He will do the work if you will furnish the brain."

"I am not opposed to niggers," said one member of the committee. "I would not like to live in a country where there are no niggers. But I want a nigger to stay in his place. There is as much difference between a white man and a nigger as there is between day and night. Conditions down here can never be changed."

As the Captain made that statement which brooked neither opposition nor difference of opinion, it seemed to me that I could hear voices from the past. I seemed to hear the Captain's ancestors telling both my grandmothers that "conditions down here can never be changed"; that not only would they themselves always be slaves, but their daughters and their granddaughters would be bondwomen till the end of time. It is safe to assert that the Captain's ancestors made this prophecy with the same cocksureness that their descendant was expressing to me. As the granddaughter of a slave grandmother and the daughter of a slave mother, I was not at all disturbed by the Captain's predictions when he assured me that conditions in the South would never change, and I did not accept them as inspired at all. I let him prophesy to his heart's content and remained perfectly silent. I did not attempt to argue the point with him, for trying to convert a southern gentleman on the Race Problem was not the mission on which I was sent. Moreover, I was well aware that I could split the Rock of Gibraltar with an icepick as easily as I could knock a pet opinion on the Race Problem out of a southern gentleman's head with so little a thing as an idea.

True to type, this Captain informed me with a great deal of pride he had a "black mammy" in his home. She had "raised" his daughter (who was then sixteen years old) from the time she was a baby only one month old, and she was considered a member of the family, he said.

All the interviews with the committee members by no means resembled those to which I have referred. Several of them told me that they heartily approved of having a colored worker sent to minister to the needs of neglected colored girls. "I do not see why anyone should not help any group of human beings who need assistance," was the way one member expressed himself.

But the opinions expressed by an official in the North were no more complimentary to colored people than were those presented to me by a few people in the South. I was sent by the Supervisor of the Girls' Department to talk with the woman who had charge of all the work among the women in New York City. I requested her to start some work among colored women and girls because there was urgent need of it in a city where the colored population was even then between one hundred and one hundred twenty-five thousand.

"Oh, Mrs. Terrell," she exclaimed, aghast at the proposition, "I couldn't possibly do any work among Negro women. I know nothing whatever about the Negro mind and psychology, and I would never know when a Negro woman was telling me the truth." "Would you know when a woman of any other race was telling the truth?" I inquired. "Oh yes," she replied, "I would know when an Irishman was telling the truth, but I know nothing whatever about Negroes, positively."

During the conversation she told me that "no matter what colored people know or may achieve, it is an accepted fact that nobody is willing to receive colored girls in this country." "We have been fighting to 'make the world safe for Democracy,' " I reminded her, "and so long as girls whose race represents one-tenth of the population are undesirable, ignorant and immoral, the standard of the whole American people will be dragged down, unless something is done to prevent it." "Oh," replied the Director of Girls in New York City, very lightly and flippantly, "the world is not ready for Democracy yet."

She then referred to one of her artist friends who had once conducted dances for colored girls in Pittsburgh, and who in this way learned a great deal about them. The things which this friend had once seen and heard, she declared, were too terrible to be described. She simply shivered and shuddered as she referred to them. Then I suggested that, since colored women and girls were so bad as she depicted them, they were a constant menace to the men and boys of all races, and for that reason, if for no other, some effort should be made to uplift them. But she waved aside that suggestion impatiently, saying "I am a positive pessimist, so far as Negroes are concerned."

If that lady in New York City had been talking about Patagonians or Hottentots, she could not have displayed more ignorance about their psychology or their minds than she did about the colored people of the United States. Neither could she have shown less concern about their welfare.

Altogether, my experiences while I was director of work

among colored women and girls for the War Camp Community Service were an education to me. Before I engaged in this work, if anybody had related to me the opinions I heard expressed about colored people by well-educated, presumably fair-minded people both North and South, it would have been hard for me to believe him. Although I knew the attitude of many Southerners toward the race, it had never occurred to me that it would be possible to find so many "best citizens" who were unalterably opposed to giving their consent to permit competent workers to lift colored women and girls to a higher plane, even though they were not called upon to defray the expense themselves.

CHAPTER 33

DELEGATE TO THE INTERNATIONAL PEACE CONGRESS

THE FOLLOWING LETTER, which was received one morning in December, 1918, thrilled me with surprise and joy. "Dear Mrs. Terrell," it read, "it gives me real pleasure to inform you that at a meeting of the Executive Board of the Woman's Peace Party, which is the section for the U. S. A. of the International Committee of Women for Permanent Peace, held in New York City November 24, you were elected as one of thirty delegates and alternates to the International Congress of Women which it was arranged at the Hague in 1915 should meet at the time of the Peace Conference at the end of the War." The letter stated that it was likely the meeting would be held either at Paris or the Hague and the time might be either the first week in February or early in May.

"We realize," the letter concluded, "that this is not an easy journey we are inviting you to take under crowded conditions in winter to war-worn countries. But we sincerely hope that your love of human welfare will minimize the difficulties and that you will be able to go with us. Faithfully yours, Alice Thatcher Post, Secretary of Delegates from the U. S. A." Mrs. Post was the wife of Mr. Louis Post, who was then Assistant Secretary of Labor under President Wilson.

I was working for the War Camp Community Service at the time and was in the South trying to induce some of the committees of the large cities to sanction the establishment of centers for colored women and girls, as has already been mentioned. After completing the summary of the conditions which obtained in these cities I sent it to Headquarters and asked for a leave of absence to go as a delegate to the Peace Congress which would soon be held in Europe. This was granted in the following letter: "My dear Mrs. Terrell: Thank you for the summary; it is a fine piece of work and the classification workers are delighted with it. It will help us materially in understanding the problems of the cities you visited. We wish to express our appreciation of the devoted service you have given the W. C. C. S. through the past months, and willingly grant you the leave of absence to enable you to make the important trip abroad. Wishing you success in your undertaking, very sincerely yours, George E. Dickie, Director Field Department."

Miss Jane Addams, president of the Women's International League for Peace and Freedom, Mr. Moorfield Storey, president of the National Association for the Advancement of Colored People, and others were genuinely interested in having me go abroad and assisted in making the voyage possible. For three or four years I was a member of the Executive Committee of the United States Section of the W. I. L. and several times I attended meetings in the residence of Mrs. Lucy Biddle Lewis, who was then chairman, and who lived in a delightful, old-fashioned home in the midst of spacious grounds a few miles from Philadelphia.

Securing a passport to go abroad shortly after the armistice was signed was no easy matter. It was especially difficult to get one for France. The State Department refused to give passports to the 30 delegates and alternates to the Peace Congress, as originally planned, and reduced the number to 15. Under the circumstances it would have been easy to leave the colored delegate out. There were many women who had been deeply interested in the peace movement, who had contributed liberally to the cause and were financially able to go. For that reason I felt a signal honor had been conferred upon me by the Peace Party, when my name was retained as a delegate.

I had worked for the War Camp Community Service till the last minute and I had only a few days in which to prepare for the voyage after I reached home from New York. Having secured my passport in Washington, I had to have ample time for the visas in New York. Some of the visa work had to be done at least 72 hours before sailing. But the fates were very kind to me and I went through the mill in two days.

I was fortunate also in securing a fine, large stateroom in which there was only one passenger, a young woman born in

Holland whose parents had grown rich in Java, one of the Dutch possessions. With a party consisting of Miss Jane Addams, Miss Jeannette Rankin, the first woman to be elected to the Congress of the United States, Dr. Alice Hamilton, the first woman who was ever invited to lecture at the Harvard School of Medicine and others, we sailed from New York on the *Noordam*, Holland-America line, April 9, 1919, almost five months to a day after the armistice was signed. All of us sat at the Captain's table and received as much attention as is good for any human being. Every morning we worked hard in Miss Addams' room trying to decide on the resolutions which should be presented to the Congress and in what language they should be couched. The necessity of typewriting these resolutions became apparent. But where was a typewriter to be found? Nobody knew. And who could type them, if happily we could locate a machine? I guaranteed to get a typewriter and promised to type the resolutions, confessing that I had never taken a prize as an expert typist, and had little hope of ever reaching that stage of proficiency.

The purser cheerfully consented to lend me his machine a short time each morning, and I used it. Framing some of the resolutions, so that everybody in the delegation approved of them, was by no means easy and considerable gray matter was consumed in that operation.

We reached Paris Easter morning and secured suitable quarters with difficulty because all the hostelries were full. It was finally decided to go to the Hotel Continental. We remained in Paris several weeks and paid a pretty penny for the rooms we occupied. After much discussion it was decided to meet in Zürich, Switzerland, from May 12 to 17.

Attending this Congress was as interesting, as illuminating and as gratifying an experience as it falls to the lot of the average woman to enjoy. In the first place, we were a group of women meeting to advocate peace after a war in which the major portion of the civilized world had engaged. I was about to say that women from all over the world were present. But on sober, second thought it is more truthful to say that women from all over the white world were present. There was not a single delegate from Japan, China, India or from any other country whose inhabitants were not white. For the second time in my life it was my privilege to represent, not only the colored women of the United States, but the whole continent of Africa as well, since I was the only one present at that meeting who had a drop of African blood in her veins. In fact, since I was the only delegate who gave any color to the occasion at all, it finally dawned upon me that I was representing the women of all the non-white countries in the world.

I shall not attempt to give a detailed account of the subjects discussed or the measures proposed or the work actually done after that unspeakable World War by the International Congress of Women which met in Zürich. No group of human beings could have made more earnest or conscientious efforts to solve the problems of reconstruction and readjustments incident to the war than did the women who took part in that Congress. A striking, never to be forgotten feature was the good feeling existing between the French and German women who were present. Owing to France's hostile attitude toward the Peace Congress, some of the French women who wished to attend as delegates were unable to secure passports. But the letters and sentiments exchanged between the women of those two hostile countries showed their breadth of view, their sincerity of purpose and their determination to heal the breach between them beyond question or doubt.

On the third day of the Congress Miss Addams called me to her and told me that the American delegates had voted unanimously to have me represent them the next night, Thursday. Although the notice for such an important effort was short, I decided immediately to deliver my address in German, since Zürich is in German Switzerland and I wanted as many as possible to understand what I had to say. Everybody connected with the Congress was as busy as a bee. The resolutions and the important papers which came before the delegates were all translated into three languages, French, German and English, so I knew it would be difficult to get one of the official translators to help me.

However, I finally found a young woman who said she would assist me a little that afternoon at three o'clock. She had to leave to take a new position, she said, so that we would have to work quickly. I had been allotted only fifteen minutes and I knew it would require more time to express myself in

German than it would in English. It was difficult for me to decide, therefore, what to include in my talk and what to omit. By six o'clock, however, I had definitely made up my mind what to say, and with the assistance of the clever, obliging Swiss girl it had been translated into German.

Wednesday night I did nothing but read and reread that speech till dawn. I was obliged to attend the meeting Thursday morning, for I had been notified my resolution would be called for at that session. Nothing but serious illness or death could have kept me from that meeting, not even the desire to appear well the same evening, so eager was I to be present when my precious resolution was read to the delegates. I had written, rewritten and then done it all over again many times on the steamer, before it was acceptable to the whole delegation.

After the other delegates on the *Noordam* had presented all the resolutions which they cared to offer, I told them I wanted to submit one in which I was very much interested. I then offered one protesting against the discriminations, humiliations and injustices perpetrated, not only upon the colored people of the United States, but upon the dark races all over the world. Several members of the delegation objected to mine and thought they could improve upon it, but none of them expressed exactly the thought which I wished to convey. It was finally agreed to let me present the following resolution to the Congress: "We believe no human being should be deprived of an education, prevented from earning a living, debarred from any legitimate pursuit in which he wishes to engage or be subjected to humiliations of various kinds on account of race, color or creed."

Anent this resolution an amusing incident occurred. Just before it was to be read to the delegates Miss Emily Balch, formerly a teacher at Wellesley College and then an officer in the W. I. L., came to me to tell me my resolution had been changed a little. I expressed surprise and regret that this had been done without notifying me, but she told me it was too late then to discuss the matter, for the resolution which had been substituted for mine had already been translated into German and French and there was nothing left for me to do but go upstairs to the office of the translators, get it and read it when the time came. I did as I was directed, feeling very much depressed, not knowing what change had been made in the original. But when I glanced at the German and French copies which were given to me by the translators I could scarcely believe that I was seeing aright, for there before my very eyes was my own dear resolution in which no change had been made at all. The translator had misunderstood the instructions given her and instead of translating the substitute resolution she had translated mine.

It was a proud and gratifying moment in my life when I read that resolution in person in Zürich, Switzerland, to the Women's International Congress for Peace and Freedom. The only delegate who represented the dark races of the world had a chance to speak in their behalf.

I delivered my address that same night. It was the first large meeting of the Congress. The previous sessions at night had been held in the lecture rooms of the University of Zürich, where comparatively few could be accommodated. But this Thursday night meeting had been staged in a magnificent old cathedral in which women had never been allowed to speak before. We stood in a pulpit that was high over the heads of the audience and looked down upon the people as we spoke. That wonderful old St. Peter's Cathedral was packed and jammed, for the citizens of Zürich were immensely interested in that Peace Congress.

There were six speakers on the program. Addresses had been delivered in French, German, Italian and English, when I was finally introduced to the audience as the last speaker, just after Mrs. Philip Snowden, the brilliant English orator, now the widow of the late Chancellor of the British Exchequer, had spoken. When Miss Addams presented me she made a slight reference to the Race Problem in the United States. She declared that the American delegation was glad to have a representative of the colored group with them and concluded by saying, "Although Mrs. Terrell speaks English at home, she is going to speak German tonight." That German audience gave unmistakable evidence of the fact that this bit of information pleased it.

When I had finished, there went up such an outburst of approbation as I had not heard since I addressed the International Congress of Women which had met in Berlin fifteen years previously almost to a month. No matter where I went after that, women and men, too, would grasp my hand cordially and compliment me upon what they called my "faultless" German and upon my speech.

But there was certainly nothing remarkable about that speech. It pleased the people because I told them a few facts they did not know. It was presented by a human mélange such as they had rarely seen in that part of the moral vineyard. That was all.

In the first place, I thanked the broad-minded white women of the United States for inviting me to the Congress, making it possible for me to come and for giving me the opportunity to speak. In dealing with less favored groups, I said, if people everywhere had been imbued with the same breadth which they had displayed in this instance, race problems and a few others would long ago have disappeared from the world. It was my duty and my pleasure to state, I declared, that ever since slavery had been abolished in the United States, thousands of white people had helped with money and by personal efforts both to educate the emancipated slaves and their descendants and to lift them to a higher plane.

Then I reviewed the marvelous progress which the group had made along all lines of human endeavor in spite of the almost insurmountable obstacles in certain sections, referred to the fearful injustices of which we are often the victims and reminded my audience that the thousands of colored soldiers who had crossed the sea "to make the world safe for democracy" had fought in Europe for a freedom for others which in some sections of their own country they themselves did not enjoy.

I appealed for justice and fair play for all the dark races of the earth. "You may talk about permanent peace till doomsday," I predicted, "but the world will never have it till the dark races are given a square deal." I expressed regret also that at the Peace Conference in Paris "the two most highly civilized and the most Christian nations" in the world had denied racial equality to Japan which she had a right to demand. It was a great opportunity to enlighten the people of Europe on conditions confronting colored people in the United States and I tried to avail myself of it as best I could.

For once in my life I was satisfied with my effort. I have always been a harsh critic of myself and I have suffered many times after I had tried my level best to reach a certain standard because I felt that I did not attain it. As a result of that effort in Zürich I had many invitations to speak in various parts of Europe, but I did not accept them, because my plans already made would consume all the time I wanted to remain abroad.

While I was in Switzerland I wanted very much to revisit Lausanne, where, as a young woman, I had spent so many happy, profitable days in school. I hoped to find the family with whom I stopped so many years ago. I went to the post office, therefore, and asked one of the officials if either Mademoiselle Sarah or Célie Gowthorpe still lived in Lausanne. He told me they did, gave me their address in a jiffy and in a few minutes I was standing before the door of their apartment. Although we had not seen each other for thirty years Célie answered the bell, and recognized me immediately. "Mademoiselle Church," she exclaimed. Then came dear Sarah, of whom I was especially fond, and we had a soulful reunion for a whole afternoon and evening reviewing old times.

CHAPTER 34

MEETING OLD FRIENDS AND NEW—PLUS A DOSE OF
RACE PREJUDICE ADMINISTERED BY
MY COUNTRYMEN

IN PARIS, where I spent five weeks
on my way home from the International Peace Congress, I
renewed my acquaintance with Monsieur Jean Finot, whom I had
met fifteen years before when I was returning from the International Congress of Women which had been held in Berlin. He
had been making an exhaustive study of the mental capacity of
the white and dark races respectively for years and had not
changed his point of view at all. The only change that had
been made was in the name of his magazine. He was now editor
of *La Revue Mondiale,* instead of *La Revue de la Revue.*

Nothing was more exhilarating and encouraging than to
talk with this great French writer who believed head, heart and
soul in the fine mental and spiritual endowment of the dark
races. Nobody has taken more pains to explode the theory of
the natural superiority of one group and the inevitable inferiority of another than Monsieur Finot. His large book on Race
Prejudice (*Le Préjugé des Races*) contains enough facts and
arguments proving the fallacy of this position to convince any
human being who is open to conviction, who thinks and is sane.
Nobody could take a more advanced stand on absolute equality
between the white and black races than did that great French
writer.

When I expressed the fear that the French might learn
from the large number of Americans in their country how to
discriminate against colored people he assured me that my fears
were groundless and repeated what he had previously said:

"The French can no more learn how to be prejudiced against human beings on account of their color than Americans can unlearn it." After publishing his large volume on Race Prejudice Monsieur Finot wrote a shorter book entitled *L'Agonie et la Mort des Races*, which his friend, William T. Stead, then editor of the British *Review of Reviews*, translated into English under the title *The Death Agony of the Science of Race*.

In this masterful production Monsieur Finot shows that "the good in man is constantly leading him onward through the international hatred and war towards the brotherhood of nations and races. The old dogmas, the effect of which was to estrange human beings," he says, "are crumbling to pieces and new ones are arising whose whole burden is the equality of all mankind." Monsieur Finot presented me with both French editions and the translation by Mr. Stead and gave me permission to have the English book reprinted in the United States.

He told me he had talked with several rich Americans who had offered to back him with money if he would stop his "foolish prattle" about the equality of races. A well-known woman who was at the head of one of the large organizations till she died had taken the time and the pains to call on him to argue against his stand and to convert him to her point of view.

Trying to teach Frenchmen to discriminate against colored people amounted to an obsession with some Americans during the World War. The proprietor of a hotel in Nancy told me she had been advised against accommodating colored people, and when she allowed a colored officer to stop there, she was warned that if she adopted that as her policy, no self-respecting Americans would patronize her. She simply shrugged her shoulders and replied, "So much the worse for the Americans," and refused to discriminate against the colored officers. "But Madam," she said, "they came to my hotel just the same. If I lost any guests I did not know it and I certainly did not need them." The French people, old and young, men and women, sing the praises of the colored soldiers who went to France. There was no use trying to explain American prejudice against colored people to the French, for they simply could not understand it.

Through the courtesy of the Honorable Blaise Diagne, Commissioner in charge of Colonial Affairs, I had the pleasure of visiting the French Chamber of Deputies. Tall, very dark (almost black), straight as an arrow, self-possessed, dignified and full of reserve power, this French African was a living, breathing illustration of the possibilities of his people under favorable conditions when given the opportunity of cultivating their brains, coupled with the chance of reaching any height to which their ability enables them to attain.

There were five or six Africans in the Chamber of Deputies and it was an object lesson to me on what may occur when white and black mingle on terms of absolute equality and neither group is thinking about the color of the other's skin. The black and white deputies talked with each other, mingled indiscriminately, exchanged views, laughed and joked together and every now and then one would place his hand familiarly on the other's shoulder, just as though there were no difference in race or color at all.

Nobody who has a drop of African blood in his veins can fail to honor and love France on account of the way she treats her black subjects, when they live on her own soil and mingle with other citizens of the great Republic. I do not claim that France has always treated her black subjects in Africa as she should have done. In order to get first hand information I made up my mind that I would question every black Frenchman whom I happened to meet in the street about their status in France, so as to ascertain whether they were discriminated against in any way and how they were treated on general principles. Each and every one assured me they were treated just like "other Frenchmen wherever they went, or whatever they wanted to do."

But a conversation with one French African cured me of this habit of propounding questions. I had asked whether he could attend any school he chose, whether he could be served in any restaurant he entered or accommodated in any hotel at which he wished to stop. The more I questioned him, the more puzzled he became. Finally, in a tone denoting he was both surprised and grieved, he replied, "Mais, Madame, les Français nous aiment!" "But, Madam, the French people love us!" His attitude toward me and his tone of voice were precisely what one would expect from a child who had been asked whether his mother and father gave him enough to eat, a bed to sleep in and decent clothes to wear. His faith in the Frenchman's affection for his group and the testimony he so cheerfully bore to prove it convinced me that the French really treat their dark citizens from their African colonies like brothers and men while they are in France.

For several reasons my interview with Baron Makino, Japan's representative at the Peace Conference in Paris, was indelibly stamped upon my mind. Naturally, we discussed the attitude of the proud, white races toward the dark. I was very outspoken, as usual, but the Japanese baron was reserved and conservative in his remarks. He was a diplomat to his finger tips. It was a great relief to my pent-up feelings to tell him personally how shocked and sorry I was that racial equality, to which she was entitled, had been denied Japan. After that interview, which lasted an hour and a half, I felt that I had been in the presence of a real statesman.

A few years after that I had an interview with Baron Naibe Kanda at the Shoreham Hotel in Washington when he was attending the Arms Limitation Conference, and I discussed with him the attitude which the Japanese usually assume toward colored people in this country. As a rule, I told him, the Japanese avoid colored people and seem unfriendly toward them. I explained that, personally, I felt that I could understand the reason why Japanese in the United States hold themselves aloof from colored people. As soon as they reach this country, they learn that in many parts of the United States colored people are debarred from hotels and restaurants, are denied privileges accorded to other people and nearly everywhere they are socially ostracized.

Under the circumstances, I admitted, it is quite natural that the Japanese, who have troubles of their own when they reach the United States, should not want to be closely affiliated with a group which is generally regarded as inferior and considered undesirable in the social circle of the dominant race. Baron Kanda immediately assured me that in their own country the Japanese have absolutely no prejudice against colored people. They know very little about them, of course, he said, but when colored people come among them they are received with the same cordiality as that extended to other races. He himself had once entertained the Jubilee Singers, he said, when they filled some engagements in Japan. He had invited them to dine with him and had given them a reception afterwards. I prize highly a card which Baron Kanda gave me when we parted, on which he had written a statement in Japanese characters.

But, to return to Paris. One day while I was looking with admiration and adoration at the statue of Joan of Arc, a friend from New York greeted me and told me that William Monroe Trotter, the editor of the *Boston Guardian*, was in Paris and was trying to tell the French people the truth about conditions under which colored people live in the United States. I resolved to see him as soon as I could, and learned that a Frenchman who admired him and believed in him had given him a desk in his office. Sure enough, there he was working like a beaver!

"Have you heard what a hard time I had getting to Europe?" Mr. Trotter inquired. I had heard nothing about it, but when he related it I realized that he had not sailed to Paris on flowery beds of ease. For reasons best known to the officials who decided who should and who should not be granted passports right after the World War, Mr. Trotter had been unable to secure one. But he was bound, bent and determined to go. He could not swim across the ocean, so he put his wits to work. A bright thought struck him. He would cross the ocean as a cook on a steamer. But, alas, he did not know how to boil water, even. He could learn, couldn't he? And that is exactly what he did. He changed the appearance of his name by omitting the middle portion thereof, got a job on a steamer as a cook and reached France in due course right side up with care. The rest was easy.

The National Equal Rights League had elected him as a delegate to represent it and he was also made the secretary of the Race Petitioners to the Peace Conference. So, as soon as he landed in Paris and had been offered a desk in a sympathizer's office near the French Stock Exchange, he went to work in earnest.

Shortly after the armistice was signed, there was a riot in Washington, D. C., started, it is claimed, by marines who didn't like to see colored men wearing the uniforms of soldiers so cockily about the streets and who wanted to teach them to keep their place. The lives of my family and myself and all of the other colored people in the city were in danger on that occasion. The slightest pretext for shooting any one of us would have been considered sufficient excuse for a member of that Negro-hating,

Negro-baiting mob to commit murder. One shot was fired into the home of a friend, a widow, which came from the second story of the house across the street.

Mr. Arthur Spingarn, a member of the National Association for the Advancement of Colored People, came from New York to secure some facts concerning the riot and asked me to go with him on a tour of inspection. As we walked along U Street, near 13th, on which many colored people lived, one of my friends told me that the feeling against white people was running so high on account of the brutal manner in which they had beaten, shot and otherwise maltreated colored people, it was not safe for us to be seen together and advised me to return home. But Mr. Spingarn and I continued on our way together till we reached what was then the 8th precinct because we wished to ask the captain whether the report was true that colored men had been arrested by policemen and had been badly beaten after they were placed in the cells at the station house. Reluctantly, he admitted that such an outrage had occurred several times that night. In some of the cities of the South colored soldiers were lynched simply because white people objected to having them wear the uniform of a United States soldier.

In spite of the exhilaration and enjoyment derived just from being in Paris there was one feature of my sojourn which made my stay there decidedly unpleasant. It harrowed my soul to see how cruelly the horses were treated. As far back as I can remember, I have loved animals intensely and nothing stirs me to the depths more than to see them suffer unnecessarily. The drivers in Paris have no mercy on their horses. They ply their whips vigorously in season and out. It made my heart ache to see the heavy loads which the poor animals had to carry. Rarely did I spend an entire day in Paris without remonstrating on the street with some Frenchman about his cruelty to a horse. I had to be tactful, of course, so as not to cause any friction, and I rarely got into trouble. The only exception to that record was an effort I made to prevent an unusually cruel driver from beating his horse because it could not pull a heavy load up a steep hill. In Italy, it seemed to me, the horses were treated worse than they were in France.

The remarks made by men in my own group in the United States who were explaining to me why they had to beat their horses have often been very amusing. When I have begged them to desist they have always justified their cruelty by imputing to the horses the malice, the craftiness, the desire for revenge and the diabolical determination to do all the evil in their power of which nothing but a master human criminal would be capable.

My husband always feared I would get into serious trouble some day because I would insist upon talking to men who were mistreating their horses. But I never did. Once when I was out near the middle of the street talking with a driver who was unmercifully belaboring a pitiable specimen of a horse, whom should I see coming down Pennsylvania Avenue but Robert H. Terrell, who, I thought, was in Court. When I see a horse whose head is held too high, I let the check rein down. By long practice I have grown to be an expert at this. I can run out to the curb and snatch the rein off the little hook so quickly that I can hardly detect myself. During a lecture tour many a time an otherwise enjoyable trip has been spoiled because I saw a dog in the neighborhood chained, either panting in the hot sun without water or shivering with cold.

While I was in Paris a big, allopathic dose of race prejudice was administered to me by Government officials stationed there. I wanted very much to take a trip through the devastated sections of France which was offered citizens "in good standing" by the Government and arranged by the Visitors' Bureau. Nearly all the delegates to the Peace Congress with whom I had crossed the ocean had taken the trip. I had not been invited to go with the party, not because any member of it would have objected to my presence, but because they probably took it for granted that the discrimination against colored people in the United States under similar circumstances would quite likely be displayed by its citizens in France. In other words a taboo on anything which might be twisted to mean "social equality" for Colored Americans would undoubtedly "follow the flag."

I have often observed that very broad-minded white people who have no prejudice against colored people at all cause trouble unwittingly by raising the issue themselves, because they ask questions about the colored people whom they have invited to accompany them somewhere. If they want a colored person to take a meal with them at a restaurant or at a hotel, for instance, they feel in duty bound to go to the proprietor beforehand to inquire whether he will serve colored people or not. This very question raises the ugly issue which he has never had to face before, perhaps, and which promptly scares him out of a year's growth. In a sort of paroxysm of fear he quickly states that he cannot serve colored people in his place. In ninety-nine cases out of a hundred the probability is that if the white individual had asked no questions about the policy pursued by the proprietor with reference to colored people and had gone calmly into the dining room with his colored friend, his swarthy guest would have been served. There are exceptions to this, of course. It seldom happens, however, that a colored person accompanied by a white friend is excluded from a dining room in the North, East or West.

I do not know whether the other delegates to the Peace Conference asked the officials in the Visitors' Bureau in Paris whether there would be any objection to having a colored woman accompany them on the trip and were told there would be. I simply know that I was not invited to go with them when they went.

I wanted very much to avail myself of the opportunity of seeing the devastated sections of France, but I did not so express myself to the party. They had gone without me, so I carefully concealed my feelings from my companions. The evening they returned from their trip I had a nice little lunch waiting for them because I thought they would be too tired to order a meal for themselves, and I listened to a report of what they had seen without showing how disappointed I was that I had not been invited to go.

I made up my mind, however, that I would do my level best to get a chance to go. About the last of April I went to the Visitors' Bureau to prefer my request. A friend employed there told me he felt certain I could go at the Government's expense as the others had done. I presented my credentials to a red-headed young man who asked for them and who seemed very favorably impressed with me indeed. I gave him the original letter written to me by Mr. George Dickie, Field Director for the War Camp Community Service, in which he complimented my summary of conditions in some southern cities I had been sent to visit. The young man took it and made two copies of it, giving me one and retaining one himself. Captain Platt, one of the higher ups in the Visitors' Bureau, came in person to the Hotel Continental and, not finding me there, wrote me a note telling me to be ready to take the trip to the devastated sections the following Thursday, May 1.

But late Thursday afternoon, when I had packed and was ready to start, I received a telephone message saying the trip had been given up and that I would hear from the Visitors' Bureau later. But not a word from the Visitors' Bureau did I hear. This was a great disappointment to me. I had remained at the Hotel Continental a whole week—rather an expensive procedure at that time—so as to be in Paris long enough to go on that trip. Soon afterward I was obliged to leave Paris to go to Zürich to attend the Peace Congress.

When I returned to Paris after the Congress adjourned, I resolved to try once more to go to the devastated section, feeling reasonably sure I would be granted the privilege, since Captain Platt had intimated when he broke his first promise to me that I might make the trip later on. It is barely possible that the captain might have thought that after I left Paris I would not return, so there would be no "later on" pledge to come back to tease him. Presenting myself at the Visitors' Bureau again I saw the same red-headed young man who had received me so cordially when I made my first appearance before him. I would not refer to the color of the young man's hair if I knew his name, or was certain what position he held. I might add that I like red hair very much.

How this young man's attitude toward me had changed! O, what a fall, my countrymen! or words to that effect. The moment I began to talk with him I knew the awful secret had leaked out. Either he was using his own eyes more effectively than he had at first, or he had learned from others the damning fact of my African descent. When I first appeared at the Bureau and my racial identity was not suspected I was most cordially received by the young man with the lurid locks. He was eager to have me take the trip and was very courteous indeed. Now, after the great light had dawned upon him, he was positively rude. He told me very sternly that they did not intend to arrange for any more trips.

I replied that Captain Platt had definitely promised that I could do so and that I had remained a whole week at the Hotel

Continental, expecting every day to be notified I could go, but had been disappointed. "Well, we are not taking any more people, I tell you," he said angrily. "You are discriminating against me, because I am a colored woman," I replied. "We don't stand for any such accusation against this office," he snapped, glaring at me fiercely, trying to intimidate me. "And I don't stand for any such treatment," I said. "You are discriminating against me because I am a colored woman," I repeated. "I don't care what you think," he said, as he raised his voice and grew so red in the face that his complexion matched his hair exactly. Then he strode angrily out of the room and entered what was evidently a private office. I did not see him any more.

After I had waited a very long time another young man entered the office and asked innocently, "Are you attended to?" "I want to see Captain Platt," I replied. "Well, I don't know whether Captain Platt is here or not," he said doubtfully, "but I'll try to find him." Pretty soon Captain Silsby, who acted and talked like a gentleman, came into the room and asked me very courteously what I wanted. I related the conversation between the young man and myself. "Captain Platt will be here very soon," he said reassuringly.

In a short while Captain Platt really arrived. He was very dignified and stern when I told him he had definitely promised to let me take the trip which the Government had given others and that I had come to request him to do so. "We are not sending anybody else on these trips," he said icily. "Then you mean to say," I replied, "that although you promised to let me take the trip which has been given to so many other Americans, you now refuse to do so." "You cannot go," he said. "Well, so let it be," I replied scarcely above a whisper in a tone tense with indignation and feeling. Then I quickly left the room. I must confess I should not like to describe the emotions which surged within me when I left Captain Platt.

The following day I saw Captain Boutté, a colored officer stationed in the Visitors' Bureau, who spoke French fluently, and he told me I would hear definitely the next day whether I could take the trip or not. Since Captain Platt had stated definitely I could not go, I was very much surprised to learn that there was even a remote possibility that this decision would be reversed.

The stern Captain evidently relented, for the trip was arranged and Captain Boutté was designated as my guide. Thus it was that I saw the devastated sections of France, the terrible destruction of the villages and towns, the miles upon miles of the wicked barbed wire with which the fields had been interlaced and the beautiful, age-old structures which had been shot to pieces. It was pathetic, but heartening to see the wonderful industry and the fixed, grim determination of the French who had already started to repair the awful destruction which had been wrought.

Those who saw the Argonne Forest right after the World War must have been impressed with the fact that the Germans felt absolutely certain they would win it. They had converted it into a regular town with cemented houses, some of them prettily decorated. There was a grandstand in which the soldiers could listen to band concerts and a regular tiled bathroom for his Royal Highness. The little spades and pewter spoons left by the Germans were still to be seen lying here and there on the ground where their owners left them, and I took the trouble to bring several of them home with me.

In the Argonne Forest I plucked a piece of ivy which grew near the grave of an American soldier and, although I carried it about with me a long time for many miles from pillar to post, several pieces of it survived, so that in two places I have living things to remind me constantly of France—a French ivy vine which climbs up the front wall of my residence in Washington and one which clings to the front of my summer home near Annapolis on the Chesapeake Bay.

I was glad I had struggled against the exhibition of race prejudice shown by my countrymen in France and finally had an opportunity to see for myself what it would have been a tragedy for me to miss and to gain valuable information first hand which I could have received in no other way. Incidentally, it was an object lesson in the horrors of war which I can never forget.

CHAPTER 35

A WEEK-END VISIT WITH MR. AND MRS. H. G. WELLS—
I MEET OTHER DISTINGUISHED PEOPLE IN ENGLAND

ONE MORNING WHEN I was in the Hotel
Continental in Paris before I had started for the Peace Conference at Zürich, I received a letter from Mrs. H. G. Wells extending me a cordial invitation to be her guest after I returned from
Switzerland on my way to the United States. The newspapers
had given the delegates a great deal of publicity, so that it was
not difficult for anybody who wished to communicate with us to
get our address. If there had been the slightest suspicion in my
mind that the invitation to visit her was purely perfunctory, or
that it had been extended just for the sake of politeness, it would
have been dispelled when I reached Zürich, for there I found
another letter from Mrs. Wells. Fearing that the first one might
not reach me while I was in Paris, she had sent me the second
one in care of the American Express Company there, which she
knew would forward it to the correct address in Zürich.

She instructed me to notify her, as soon as I reached London
after the Congress adjourned, for she wanted very much to have
me come out to see her. Consequently, the first thing I did after
reaching London was to write Mrs. Wells requesting her to command me when she wanted me to come. By return mail I
received a letter stating that Mrs. Wells wished me to be at a
certain station between London and Dunmow on a certain Saturday afternoon in June.

To an American unaccustomed to traveling in England
conditions are bewildering in a huge station like the Liverpool,
when she tries to buy a ticket for a small place at which trains

stop only by request. After finding the right coach one has to keep a sharp lookout to avoid going several stations beyond the one she wishes to reach, for nobody calls out small stations in England. But the fates were with me and when I left the train I found Mrs. Wells waiting for me. Lithe and willowy of form, gracious, vivacious, smiling and charming in manner, Mrs. Wells looked younger than she did in a photo of herself and her two little sons which she had sent me fifteen years before. Mrs. Wells greeted me cordially and said, "We will wait a few minutes for I am expecting two other guests on this train." Just then a young man on crutches with a young woman by his side approached us. And I was introduced to Mrs. St. John Irvine and her husband, who was already a well-known, promising young English playwright and novelist whose plays have enjoyed merited success both in England and in the United States. He had lost his leg in the World War, but apparently that had not affected his spirit in the least.

After her guests had seated themselves in the automobile Mrs. Wells proved herself to be a first class chauffeur and she whisked us to her home in the twinkling of an eye. When Mrs. Wells opened the gate through which the auto passed I saw we were entering a typical English estate covering I don't know how many acres of land, which I learned later had been leased from the Countess of Warwick. I shall not attempt to give an extended or an accurate description of the house in which Mr. and Mrs. Wells were then living except to say that it contained everything which comfort and good taste could suggest. But I do want to refer to the library. I could gush like a school girl about that.

It was literally a dream—a thing of beauty and a joy forever. It was an unusually large room extending half way across the wide house, having at least three doors and I don't know how many windows through which the light streamed in floods. As soon as one stepped into the hall and entered Mr. Wells' home, one saw the most inviting, alluring room with tufted divans, big and little chairs artistically upholstered, plus books and magazines galore. But a great disappointment awaited a guest who expected to find any of Mr. Wells' books lying around handy. They were conspicuous by their absence. After casting about with the determination to find one, at least,

I finally discovered a small one in which my famous author-host described a trip to Mars.

Mr. Wells did not arrive from London until fifteen minutes before dinner. It was hard to believe I was actually looking at a man who had won such fame as a writer and about whom I had been hearing such a long time. Please don't ask me to tell you how the English people keep looking so young! But they seem to find the fountain of youth somehow and never grow old. There was H. G. Wells in the flesh, beaming upon his guests, extending them a most cordial welcome to his home, grasping their hands warmly, as ruddy, as lively, as approachable as a man could possibly be. Without doubt Mr. Wells is the most human and unassuming man in the world.

We had tea on the lawn when Mr. Wells arrived with Mrs. Lamont, wife of Thomas Lamont, who had just bought the *Evening Post* from Oswald Garrison Villard. Mr. Lamont was also the European representative of J. Pierpont Morgan's firm and was a valued member of President Woodrow Wilson's party in the Paris Conference of the League of Nations. After hearing Mr. Lamont relate some of the difficulties encountered by this international effort to establish universal peace, I felt that I had acquired a liberal education in its purposes and aims.

I shall never cease to regret that I had not learned stenography before I became a member of that house party, so that for my own sake (and not for publication) I might have recorded some of the clever remarks and bons mots of those interesting, well-informed, delightful people gathered for three days and nights under one roof, at one table, and then, after dinner, in a sort of family circle for the whole evening. I would not publish them broadcast to the world, of course, but it would be a comfort and joy to refresh my memory in the sere and yellow leaf and live those delightful hours over again.

Mr. Wells was as fine an example of perpetual motion as one could meet in a day's march. He will never grow old. He seemed never to tire and was never happier than when he was engaged in some kind of physical exercise. I saw him play the game of ball described in *Mr. Britling Sees It Through* an entire morning, then later play tennis on the Countess of Warwick's estate the whole afternoon without showing the slightest signs of fatigue. While he was playing the game of ball Mr.

Wells would take one guest as his partner, till that guest was tired out, and then he would go for another, until that one was exhausted too.

Strolling through his spacious grounds was another kind of recreation which Mr. Wells thoroughly enjoyed. He took pleasure in showing his guests the rose garden, which happened to be in bloom the beautiful Sunday morning in June that he showed it to me, and we afterwards went to the vegetable garden while we were walking through the grounds. It was during this stroll that I confided to Mr. Wells that some day before I passed out I wanted to write the story of my life and call it "The Confessions of a Colored Woman." "I like the title," he said immediately. "It will be widely read in England. But write it dispassionately." I have tried to follow the advice of this distinguished author as best I could. I am well aware, however, that what the victim of race prejudice would call a "dispassionate" account of her life might be called by another name by the dominant group.

While I was a guest of Mr. and Mrs. Wells, the Countess of Warwick, whom I had met in London fifteen years before when I was returning from the International Congress of Women in Berlin and whom I later met while she was lecturing in the United States, invited us all to tea Sunday afternoon. The baby who was only three months old when I first met the Countess had grown to be a beautiful young woman and one of the most pleasant experiences of my visit was playing a rather exciting game of ball with the little Lady Mercy Greville in Mr. H. G. Wells' gymnasium one morning.

The Countess asked me to sit beside her at the big, round table while the delicious refreshments were being served and, without doing anything which smacked of patronizing her swarthy guest, she showed she was genuinely interested in me. On the estate was a cage of monkeys of which the Countess was very fond. She sometimes went into their cage, she said, and they knew her quite well. The Countess still liked dogs very much and carried a favorite Pekinese wherever she went.

On several occasions I met Sir Harry Johnston, the noted explorer, author, painter and pioneer in British colonization in Africa. I heard him speak when he presided at a dinner given by the African Society, of which he was president. I prize very highly a pamphlet entitled *The Africa of the Immediate Future,* which Sir Harry wrote and presented to me with the following note on the cover: "Mrs. Mary Church Terrell from the Author. When you get back to the States you should read my novel *The Gay Dombeys,* published by McMillan and Co., New York."

For several years Mr. John Harris, the parliamentary secretary of the Anti-Slavery and Aborigines Protection Society, had been sending me valuable pamphlets on conditions in Africa which that organization had issued. As its name indicates, this society is organized to secure justice for the Africans. When I went to thank him for his kindness he informed me that the African Society would give a dinner the next night. He feared all the places had been taken, he said, but he would try to arrange to have me go. He did so. The dinner cost $5 a plate, but that seemed very cheap to me when I thought what a wonderful opportunity I would have to come into direct contact with all those fine Africans of whom I felt sure that African Society was composed. With such great expectations in my mind, imagine my surprise when I reached the banquet hall to see nothing but Lords and Ladies of high degree, the ladies arrayed in the latest creations and sparkling with gems.

About 250 sat down to that dinner and not more than five, including myself, had a drop of African blood in their veins. So far as I can recall, there was only one full-blooded African in the large room and I had the pleasure of sitting at the table with him. I met Sir Hugh Clifford, who was Governor of the Gold Coast, and Lady Clifford, both of whom were cordial to the African representative from the United States. After I returned home, Lady Clifford sent me a book she had written.

Mrs. Philip Snowden, whom I met at the Peace Congress in Zürich and whose husband later became Chancellor of the Exchequer for the Labor Party, invited me to lunch with her at her club, and I gained much valuable information from her, as I listened to her opinions concerning conditions in England. Interesting people attended the reception given by the Lady Courtney of Penwith whose names have long escaped me, but whose personalities I shall not forget. Since I happened to be in London at the same time with Miss Jane Addams and several other members of the Peace Congress, together with them I was invited to some social functions given by people of distinction at which I met men and women prominent in important activities in England.

After a separation of fifteen years it was a rare privilege and a genuine pleasure to spend an afternoon with Mrs. Coleridge-Taylor and her two interesting children at their home in Croyden. Each of the children has inherited the talent and taste for music from both of their parents. Here is an illustration of what unusual heredity does in some cases, at least. The father was a genius and the mother an accomplished musician also. Both before and after her marriage Mrs. Coleridge-Taylor, who had a voice of great sweetness and power, often sang in recitals accompanied on the piano or violin by her famous composer-husband.

On my previous visit Coleridge-Taylor contributed greatly to my pleasure and now that he was no longer with us in the flesh I could not help thinking about the unspeakable loss sustained by the whole world and by people of African descent in particular.

Before I left the Conference at Zürich I decided to go to St. Etienne, France, to visit my classmate, Mrs. Ida Gibbs Hunt, whose husband, the Honorable William H. Hunt, was United States Consul at St. Etienne for twenty years. Mrs. Hunt and I were classmates from the eighth grade in the public schools of Oberlin through the high school, the Oberlin Academy and Oberlin College, nine years all together. I bought my ticket to Paris from Switzerland with the understanding that at a certain point I could leave the train, buy a ticket to St. Etienne and return to that station and then resume my journey to Paris.

Quite a while before I reached this station the conductor came to get my ticket. When I explained my plans to him he became very excited and told me firmly, not to say roughly, that I would not be allowed to go to St. Etienne to visit anybody, that I must positively remain on that train and go straight through to Paris. I was bitterly disappointed to learn that after coming so many thousand miles I could not go to see my friend who was just around the corner, so to speak.

There were about twenty French soldiers on the train. One of them overheard what I said to the conductor and came to me to learn more about my trouble. When I explained to him what

I wanted to do and he saw how unhappy I was because the conductor had forbidden me to go to St. Etienne, he became very indignant indeed and used language which would not look well in print. He called several of his comrades together and told them my tale of woe with embellishments. They held a council of war, gesticulated and talked, all of them, at the same time. It was an outrage, they said, or words to that effect. The idea of that conductor daring to keep me from visiting the friend of my childhood! Even if I wanted to stay on the train and go straight through to Paris, they said, they would not let me do it. When we reached the station at which I would have to change cars for St. Etienne, they snatched up my two suit cases and put me off bag and baggage, as soon as the train stopped, explaining in detail, as they did so, what I would have to do and what time my train would leave.

When I reached St. Etienne, it was about two o'clock in the morning, and everything was as black as midnight—not a ray of light anywhere. Just one man was at the station and no conveyance of any kind. I was greatly frightened and hardly knew what to do. I asked where was the nearest hotel, and the man directed me as best he could. With the two suit cases, neither of which was as light as a feather, the distance seemed interminable. I have never understood how I found that hotel. When I finally reached it I had to knock a long time before the door was opened. When I asked for a room, I was told that every one was occupied. I had heard that before. But this was France! and not the United States. I knew that my race would not prevent me from getting accommodations in a hotel in France. But I insisted that, room or no room, I would remain at that hotel. At that hour of the night there was no other place for me to go. I explained to the man that I was a friend of the United States Consul there, but that I did not want to disturb him. After waiting quite a while I was finally taken to a room at the top of the house in which there was no window at all. In the ceiling, however, there was a skylight which was opened a bit to admit air. I presume I would have had to close it if it had rained. The next morning I surprised my classmate and her distinguished husband. The short visit with them was enjoyed all the more because of the difficulties experienced in making it possible.

CHAPTER 36

EMPLOYED BY RUTH HANNA McCORMICK TO HELP IN
HER CAMPAIGN FOR THE UNITED STATES
SENATE. ABROAD WITH MY DAUGHTER

W HEN MRS. RUTH HANNA Mc-
CORMICK asked me to assist in her campaign for election to the
United States Senate I jumped at the chance. I cannot say truthfully it was the realization of a long-cherished dream. In the
wildest flight of a lurid imagination I had never dared to presume to dream that the opportunity of assisting the very first
woman in the country who had courage enough to try to break
into the United States Senate on her own merit would come to me.

I was engaged by Mrs. McCormick in May, 1929, to begin
my work for her in the fall. During the summer my son-in-law,
Dr. L. A. Tancil of Chicago, motored with his wife, my daughter
Mary, and with Phyllis and myself through Canada. Dr. Tancil
said he wanted to get as far from civilization as possible and
he succeeded admirably. We went through some of the sparsely
settled sections and saw the great, open spaces of that vast
domain. The dilapidated houses falling into ruins in villages
long since deserted were depressing. One could picture the
enthusiasm and visualize the energy of those who built the
houses and founded the village and see their defeated ambitions
and their blasted hopes when they finally realized they were
fighting a losing battle.

It was not an unusual experience for us to see a deer, or a
pretty black and white skunk or some other little wild creature
scampering across the road when we traveled at night. Of all
the Canadian cities we visited, Quebec with the antiquity of some
of its sections and the Frenchiness of the whole fascinated me

most. Shortly after we returned to Chicago from our motor trip I started my new job in earnest. I asked Mrs. McCormick to give me the names of the women in our group who were her best friends, so that I might be sure to bring them strongly into the political picture. But my chief refused to do so, saying that she wanted me to dig out all the facts for myself. She did give me the name of one woman, however, and that helped to lay the foundation on which an effective organization was soon built.

For a while nobody but two or three women to whom I had confided the secret knew why I was in Chicago. Then when it finally leaked out, a few held a meeting at which they drew up resolutions protesting against Mrs. McCormick's bringing an "outsider" to Illinois to "head up" her campaign, as they expressed it. They warned her they would not vote for her if she persisted in this course. The first time Mrs. McCormick spoke to a group of colored people after these resolutions were forwarded to her she touched upon several things for which she was criticized and explained them away.

"And Mrs. Terrell is here," she said. "Mrs. Terrell is my friend. All her life she has worked for black women and she has worked for white women, too. She has lived at the seat of Government and has been interested in politics for years. She knows better than some of you why a woman is needed in the Senate. I am prouder of having brought Mrs. Terrell to Illinois than anything I have ever done in my life."

An Executive Committee was formed of which Mrs. McCormick made me chairman. It consisted of thirty-six women living in different parts of the State. At my request two were appointed in Chicago to assist in the office. Mrs. McCormick granted my request to have a breakfast for the members of the Executive Committee. Although the call was sent out only two days before, thirty women were present. Seven of those were out of town guests who paid their own expenses to and from Chicago.

Then I began to speak all over the State. Letters were written to women notifying them that I would arrive at their respective cities on a certain date and requesting them to arrange a meeting for me in a private residence. I explained to the women when I arrived that Mrs. McCormick was allowed to spend only a certain sum in her campaign, so that she dared not rent churches and halls in which to hold meetings. But in several cities the people themselves rented places in which I could speak when it was possible for me to remain long enough for them to do so. I was delighted at the rapidity with which a large and successful meeting could be arranged when the people were interested and wanted to hear a cause presented.

When the thermometer registered nineteen degrees below zero I traveled just the same. I was so interested in my work I did not mind the extreme cold. I talked to the people by day, going from house to house to tell the leaders about Mrs. McCormick's qualifications for the office she was seeking. But if I had ever entertained a notion about running for office, my experience in Mrs. McCormick's campaign would have cured me completely. It is hard to understand how falsehoods about a candidate get started in the first place, and still harder to comprehend why people who are supposed to have the least bit of gray matter can believe them. Nothing is easier than to start a barefaced falsehood about a candidate and nothing is harder than to stop it.

It was a thrilling experience to listen to the returns as they came in at Mrs. McCormick's headquarters on Michigan Avenue the night of Primary election day. She rolled up a plurality of 200,000 votes, and received a larger majority than had ever been given before to any candidate for the Senate in the State of Illinois. Then, a few months after that unprecedented plurality on Primary day, Mrs. McCormick was defeated in the November election. There were many reasons why Mrs. McCormick failed to be elected to the United States Senate. But it is certain that the votes given to her Democratic opponent were not cast against HER, but against the conditions which prevailed in her party at that time. It was very hard for me to become reconciled to her defeat. By nature, education, training and experience she was so well qualified to discharge the duties and obligations which as a member of the Senate she would have been obliged to perform.

Shortly before Mrs. McCormick's term as Congresswoman at Large expired she sent me the following letter:

"My dear Mrs. Terrell: Before completing my Congressional duties in Washington, I want to make grateful acknowledgment of the many services performed by you in my behalf. I shall always feel that I was fortunate in having your assistance in the Illinois Senatorial primary campaign of 1930. You performed a double duty in that campaign, having been organizer of colored groups in Chicago and throughout the State. In this connection you also organized meetings in various towns and cities, and the press reports that came to our office showed that you had been able to interest large audiences. So successful were you in the down-State localities that requests came in from county managers to have you return to make speeches.

"Your work required the greatest industry, judgment, tact and loyalty, and you generously fulfilled all those requirements.

"If I knew of anybody, Mrs. Terrell, who was in need of the services that I know you are so perfectly qualified to perform, I should regard it as a pleasure to commend you to them. Although our official relations are at an end we shall both be deeply interested in various matters relating to public service and I hope to thus continue the very pleasant association that we have had.

"With my kindest personal regards, believe me,
"Very sincerely yours,
"RUTH HANNA MCCORMICK."

The last of June, 1930, several months after my service with Mrs. McCormick had terminated, my daughter Phyllis and I sailed for Europe. Seeing my daughter catch her first glimpse of the far-famed cities on the Continent rejuvenated me. And then we were fortunate in being abroad the year the Passion Play was presented and we went to Oberammergau to see it. Again the Countess of Warwick entertained me and extended my daughter a cordial welcome. Mr. H. G. Wells invited us to spend Sunday with him and some friends. Mrs. Wells had passed away several years before. My daughter had the pleasure of meeting Mr. Wells' sons and their wives, with whom she had an interesting outing in the afternoon. Once again I saw some of the friends whom I met when I was studying abroad. I took my daughter to Lausanne so that she might meet Sarah Gowthorpe, in whose home I lived when I was a girl.

CHAPTER 37

A FEW CASES OF FRICTION

ALTHOUGH I have been more or less intimately associated with white people all my life, have entertained views on the Race Problem which have been considered quite radical by some and have always expressed my opinion honestly, I have had no open break with them as a group, and I have had friction with individuals very few times.

As a member of the Board of Education I might easily have fallen out with a man whose friendship I prized highly, because he insisted upon dismissing a Supervising Principal who was an excellent officer and one of the finest teachers in the corps, but who in the kindness of his heart had given her salary to a teacher in dire need and distress in a manner not prescribed by the rules. My good friend was a prosperous business man, who believed so thoroughly in business methods that he insisted that any school officer who failed to observe them should be dismissed, no matter how fine an instructor he might be.

I valued this man's friendship because he was one of nature's noblemen and was always willing to assist me in my efforts to put through measures which I believed would improve the school system. And I could rely absolutely upon any promise he made because he was courageous and outspoken almost to a fault, and because he had as little race prejudice as it is possible for a man born in this country to have. When it looked as though our friendship could not weather this storm, after I had tried hard to convert him to my point of view and had failed, I resigned myself to my fate, but held firmly and desperately to my efforts to prevent the supervising principal from being dismissed. I finally succeeded in saving the school official and also in retaining the friendship of Mr. O. as well because he was a broad-minded man, and when he finally yielded a point, he let the dead past bury its dead.

During the eleven years I was a member of the Board of Education I often differed materially with the others, but I never had bitter words or an open break with anybody. Perhaps I came as near having friction with a few members of the Executive Committee of the International League for Peace and Freedom as with any white people with whom I was ever associated. I was asked to sign a petition requesting the removal of the black troops from occupied German territory. I was told that all the other members of the Executive Committee were willing to sign it, and that it was especially desirable for me to affix my signature because the committee wished to make the request unanimous. Since I was the only colored member of the committee it was natural for them to want me to fall in line.

One of them who talked with me about it was Mrs. La Follette, wife of the late Senator from Wisconsin, and mother of the present Senator and of a former Governor of Wisconsin. What she said in favor of the petition impressed me deeply. She seemed to have no race prejudice whatever and always had the courage of her convictions when she felt it was necessary to show where she stood on the Colored American's right to a square deal. Both by word and by deed, Mrs. La Follette often placed herself on record as being in favor of any legislation or of any effort designed to give colored people all the rights and privileges which other people enjoy. I knew she wanted the petition signed because she believed it would pour oil on the troubled waters to have France remove her black troops from German soil. In such high esteem did I hold that broad-minded woman that nothing would have afforded me greater pleasure than to comply with her request.

On the afternoon when Mrs. La Follette invited me to her beautiful home to have tea with her, therefore, I listened to her arguments in favor of it with an open mind. But, try as hard as I might, I could not see my way clear to sign that petition. I disliked, however, to be the only member of the committee to refuse to sign it and thus make it impossible for the others to say their petition was unanimous. After mature deliberation I decided it was my duty to resign and I wrote the following letter to Miss Addams:

"WASHINGTON, D. C., March 18, 1921.

"MY DEAR MISS ADDAMS:

"It is plainly my duty to write you concerning a matter in which you are deeply interested, I know. I have been requested to sign a petition asking for the removal of the black troops from German territory. The most horrible crimes are said to have been committed by these black troops against German women. I belong to a race whose women have been the victims of assaults committed upon them by men of all races. As a rule, these men have ruined and wrecked the women of my race with impunity. For that reason I sympathize deeply with the German women if they are really the victims of the passions of black men.

"I pity them in their present peril, as I pitied the French women when the newspapers told of the brutal treatment they received at the hands of the German soldiers who were quartered in France. Because the women of my race have suffered so terribly and so long from assaults committed with impunity by men of all races, I am all the more pained at the brutal treatment to which German women are now said to be subjected by black troops.

"However, I am certain that the black troops are committing no more assaults upon the German women than the German men committed upon the French women or that any race of soldiers would probably commit upon women in occupied territory. Our own American soldiers treated the Haitian women brutally. On good authority it is asserted that young Haitian girls were not only cruelly misused, but were actually murdered by some of our soldiers. I can not vouch for the truth of that statement, but it is not at all difficult for me to believe that white Americans would treat colored women as brutally as our soldiers are said to have treated Haitian women.

"I can not sign the petition asking for the removal

of the black troops because I believe it is a direct appeal to race prejudice. In all the statements concerning the matter, great emphasis is laid upon the fact that these troops are worse than white soldiers. That is a reflection upon them which I am sure they do not deserve. Charges are usually preferred against soldiers of all races who are quartered in the land they have conquered. I can readily understand that if a German woman had to be outraged, she would prefer to suffer at the hands of a white man rather than at the hands of a black man. But even though that may be true, I can not sign a petition asking for the removal of these troops because they are black.

"On good authority I have been informed that the charges preferred against black troops are not founded in fact. Mrs. Carrie Chapman Catt investigated the charges against black troops when she was in Geneva and found, according to the testimony of reputable people living in the regions where the atrocities were alleged to have been committed, that these black troops had conducted themselves with more courtesy and consideration than white troops which had been stationed there.

"Two German delegates told Mrs. Catt that there was no movement in Germany to ask France to remove these colored troops and that, so far as they knew, there was no complaint in Germany on that score. Mrs. Catt says that the German women with whom she talked in Geneva promised to investigate the charges against the colored troops, which were being circulated in this country, and to let her know later.

" 'I saw all three of them in London early in December,' says Mrs. Catt, 'and again they reiterated the same statement in Geneva, which was to the effect that atrocities such as are being described in the United States could not have been committed by the Army of Occupation without the masses of the people of Germany knowing about it, and that they had heard nothing which warranted such charges being made.'

"Moreover, some of the leading business men in the

Rhineland have recently issued an indignant disclaimer of the propaganda campaign against the black troops. Director Reutten declared that investigation by the Rhineland Traffic Association had shown that the stories of molestation of the population by the troops of occupation were untrue.

"I can not sign the petition asking for the removal of the black troops with these facts staring me in the face. The propaganda against the black troops is simply another violent and plausible appeal to race prejudice. It is very painful to me not to do anything which you or the organization that I love would like to have me do. Knowing you as well as I do, however, I feel sure you do not want me to be untrue to myself or to the race with which I am identified simply to please my friends.

"I do not want to be a stumbling block or a nuisance as a member of the Executive Committee. I am willing to resign. You have always been such a true friend to me, and my esteem and affection for you are so great, I do not want to do anything which will embarrass you as the head of the International League for Peace and Freedom. I am not at all sure I can be present at the annual meeting next month. I shall try to be there. Please speak frankly to me. I am not narrow. I want to know the truth and do right.

"With gratitude to you for many kindnesses to me in the past, and with the highest esteem, I am,
"Sincerely yours,
"MARY CHURCH TERRELL."

In a few days I received the following letter from Miss Addams, written by her own dear hand March 29, 1921:

"MY DEAR MRS. TERRELL:

"I was chairman of a committee in the Chicago Branch on the colored troops on the Rhine and came to exactly the same conclusion which you have reached—that we should protest against the occupation of enemy territory—not against any special troops. I am quite sure you will find the annual meeting absolutely fair on the subject and I hope that you will be able to attend the meeting on Monday, April 11th, when the matter will probably come up. I have just come back from St. Louis and found your letter here. Please excuse this late reply.

"Faithfully yours,

"JANE ADDAMS."

This letter was a great relief to my mind. I was glad not to be forced to resign from the Executive Committee of the League. I enjoyed working for peace, and the contacts with the fine women who were members were an education to me. It also afforded me an excellent opportunity of getting out of the "Ghetto" in Washington and mingling occasionally with the dominant race, as I had been accustomed to do during my childhood and youth.

But two years later the question of removing the black troops again disturbed the public mind, and this time France succumbed to the clamor that was raised. I felt it was my duty to let some of the French officials know how a colored woman in the United States felt about the matter. So I sent the following letter to Premier Poincaré:

"PREMIER POINCARÉ:

"Paris, France.

"DEAR SIR: The colored people of the United States are shocked, discouraged and pained beyond expression at the cablegram sent by you to give the American State Department the assurance that only white troops are being used or will be used in the Ruhr and that black troops from Morocco and Algeria will be barred.

"Many colored people in this country love France devotedly because they have experienced real liberty for the first time in their lives while traveling on French soil, and have there enjoyed privileges accorded only to white citizens in the United States. We love France also because, as a rule, she has treated her dark citizens with justice and consideration. She has never discriminated against people on account of color and has never placed insurmountable barriers in their path to progress, but has allowed them to reach any height which their ability and their efforts would enable them to attain.

"We are proud of the brilliant record which the African soldiers fighting under the French flag made during the World War. For African blood flows through the veins of the colored people of the United States. We recall with pride that, at the first battle of the Marne, it was the black troops who helped to save France from utter destruction and preserved the civilization of the world. The Marne ran red with the blood of those brave, black soldiers who fought so desperately and so effectively to save their beloved France.

"And now, in spite of the valiant service rendered by these troops, the Premier of the French Republic, which owes its salvation largely to their blood and sacrifice, takes the time and the pains to cable the world that they will be barred from the Ruhr in deference to race prejudice which certain countries practice in their treatment of colored people. Thus, for the first time in her history France publicly places a stigma upon her black citizens. Having preserved an unblemished record in this particular for centuries, France has at last publicly prostrated herself before the monster—Race Prejudice, and trailed her proud banner in the dust.

"For a long time some of us Colored-Americans who have loved France so dearly have feared that she would eventually be inoculated with the deadly germ of race prejudice through intimate association with other nations in which men, women and children are lynched with impunity, in many instances solely because their complexions are dark. But Frenchmen, both white and black, have always ridiculed the idea that this could ever happen in their land of liberty, equality and fraternity, and have assured me that I need give myself no concern on this account.

"When I was in Paris immediately after the World

War and expressed this fear to Monsieur Jean Finot, one of the most distinguished and well-known authors in France at that time, he replied, 'France can no more learn race prejudice than the average white person in the United States can unlearn it.'

"The colored people of the United States have no right to question the wisdom of France's decision to bar black troops from the Ruhr. We do not and cannot understand all the reasons why she has decided to pursue this course. Nor it is necessary for us to understand them. But, we submit, that if for good and sufficient reasons it was deemed wise to draw the line between white and black soldiers, the interest of her brave, black soldiers would have been better conserved if that fact had not been cabled broadcast throughout the world. Since France has always stood for absolute equality between her white and black citizens, her attitude in deliberately barring black troops from the Ruhr will not only be interpreted by the world as a reflection upon them, but it will give aid and comfort to those already steeped in prejudice against their race.

"The cablegram sent by your Excellency assuring the American State Department that only white troops are being or will be used in the Ruhr, and that the Colonial troops from Morocco and Algeria will be barred, certainly panders to the race prejudice which rages so violently and ruthlessly in the United States. It is a great blow to many colored women in this country, whose husbands and sons lost their lives in the World War to save France. We hope that France's decision to bar her black troops from the Ruhr does not portend any radical change in her attitude toward the dark races and we beseech the leaders of the great French Republic to do nothing more which will encourage the spread of race prejudice throughout the world.

"May the day never dawn when France will exchange her slogan of Liberty, Equality and Fraternity which colored people have always enjoyed on her beloved soil for one of discrimination, proscription and prejudice which handicap them so seriously and from which they suffer so terribly in the United States.

"Very sincerely yours,

"MARY CHURCH TERRELL."

I received no reply to this letter. But I had the satisfaction of knowing that some of the higher ups were acquainted with a colored woman's point of view concerning the treatment of the black troops.

The only time I have been openly attacked on the platform by a representative of the dominant race for something I have said in an address was in Baltimore, Maryland. I had been invited to deliver the Commencement address at the Baltimore High School for colored youth shortly after the United States entered the World War. There was a general understanding that the Government wished Commencement speakers to refer to the war, so as to interest the public in this country's efforts to aid the allies.

In complying with this request, I decided to take as my subject, "The Race Problem and the War." In order to encourage the young men in the graduating class, as well as the other men in the audience, to do everything in their power to win the war, I referred to the high stand this country had taken in the conflict. Since the United States was fighting to make the world safe for Democracy, I declared, if the Allies were victorious the status of the colored people in this country would be greatly improved. I held out the hope that the opportunities hitherto denied the race would be enjoyed. "For the first time in history," I said, "the major portion of the civilized world is fighting for freedom. If actions speak louder than words, 'Give us liberty or give us death' is the cry that rings from one end of the civilized world to the other." I referred to the gains which had recently been made by freedom. An old and strongly entrenched despotism like Russia had been overthrown, and a Republic had been set up in its place. England was about to listen to Ireland's prayers and entreaties to be allowed to govern herself. Great Britain had even promised the people of India the recognition which they felt had been deserved for years, but which had hitherto been denied.

I emphasized the attitude assumed by southern newspapers,

which were full of editorials asserting that the "War of Democracy against Autocracy had brought about the formation of a common brotherhood that knows neither race, religion nor people." I praised the white people of the South for the efforts they were making to set their house in order. In short, I assured my large audience that the condition of the group I was addressing would be improved because the people of the country were thinking about freedom and democracy as they had never thought before, that their consciences had been aroused on the subject and their hearts had been touched.

The Comptroller of Baltimore had been requested to represent the Mayor at the Commencement exercise, and when he arose to make some remarks he was so enraged that he could scarcely control himself. He complimented those who had spoken, those who had sung—in fact he had fair words for everybody but myself. He launched at once into a tirade against "the speaker of the evening." He almost jumped upon her with both feet. White with rage, he paced up and down the stage criticizing my speech.

"The speaker of the evening has predicted that the condition of the colored people of this country will be greatly improved," he declared with fierce indignation. He was too deeply stirred to proceed, so he paused a second. He shouted aloud and shook his fist at the audience, as he warned—"But I tell you people you will have no more rights after the war than you enjoy now." He shook his fist at the audience again, as he uttered this threat.

Then something occurred which I had never heard before in an audience of colored people and which I have never heard since. They hissed the Comptroller of Baltimore with all their might. But he shook his fist at them again and told them sarcastically that he knew all about colored people, that he understood them perfectly and that he didn't care a fig (or words to that effect) how much they hissed. The newspaper account of this disgraceful occurrence which appeared in the *Baltimore-American* was naturally very biased and gave the Comptroller's point of view, so I sent a letter to explain and correct it.

Under the headline "Meant To Be Optimistic" on June 28, 1917, the *Baltimore-American* published my letter as follows:

"The report of the Commencement exercises of the Colored High School which appeared in the *Baltimore-American* misinterprets the spirit and purpose of the address to the graduates and misrepresents the speaker. I am charged with having aimed scathing and bitter remarks at the white race and with having referred to certain lynchings and hangings.

"My address consumed fifty minutes of which about one minute and a half, perhaps, certainly not more, was consumed in referring to the recent riot in St. Louis. The Comptroller of Baltimore is reported to have said that it was my 'unwise reference to lynchings and hangings,' which caused him to rebuke me, and the *Baltimore-American* states that 'he denounced' me 'in no uncertain terms.' If less than two out of fifty minutes were devoted to one burning and one race riot, it is clear that one who reads the report of my address would get a decidedly inaccurate account of it.

"The part of the report which states 'the Comptroller of Baltimore denounced' me, the guest of the occasion, 'in no uncertain terms,' is literally true. I doubt that any colored man in the country would treat a woman of any race under such circumstances with such discourtesy. The *American* states that 'the white people who attended the exercises declared that my address should have been one of optimism, but it was just the opposite, and calculated to arouse anything but a feeling of good will.' It is difficult to believe that any fair-minded person who listened to my address made any such comment.

"By insisting that after the war there would be a better understanding between the two races, that efforts are already making in the South to ameliorate the condition of colored people, by reviewing the marvelous progress along all lines achieved by the race since the Civil War, by emphasizing the irreproachable record made by the colored soldiers from the Revolutionary War to the martyrdom into which brave, colored troops rushed last summer at Carrizal, I did everything in my power to create optimism and to inspire the members of the graduating class with hope.

"I have spoken in every State of the South, and rarely have I addressed an audience in that section in which no white people were present. I have always pleaded for my heavily-handicapped race and expressed the hope that they would enjoy greater freedom some day and be given an equal chance. But, up to date, the Comptroller of Baltimore is the first man, white or any other color, who has publicly 'denounced' me for anything I have said.

"It is possible to take a sentence or two from any address and distort it into meaning anything a hostile, illiberal, angry man wants it to mean. Moreover, some people cannot bear the truth, no matter how tactfully it is told. No doubt the haughty, the tyrannical, the unmerciful, the impure and the fomentors of discord take a fierce exception to the Sermon on the Mount.
"MARY CHURCH TERRELL."

With one exception the most serious friction which has ever occurred between white and colored club women was caused by the segregation of the race in the Washington Auditorium when the Quinquinnial of the International Council of Women met here in May, 1925. Mrs. Mary McLeod Bethune, who was then president of the National Association of Colored Women, had requested me to confer with the Chairman on Music appointed by the American Council of Women because she happened to be stopping at the Mayflower Hotel, while she was making out the program. A former president of the National Association of Colored Women had arranged to have 200 colored singers from the Richmond (Virginia) Treble Clef Club, the Hampton Institute Choir, the Howard Choral Society of Washington, D. C., and musicians of note like Nathaniel Dett, the well-known composer, and Professor Roy Tibbs of Howard University to take part in the program.

But the night on which the colored musicians were to appear, colored people who went to the auditorium discovered that they were not only segregated, but that nearly all of them were seated in the most undesirable section of the building.

When the singers learned this, they refused to appear. There was a large audience, and many of them who had gone expressly to hear the colored singers were greatly disappointed. This was especially true of the foreign women who had looked forward to this concert with great anticipation of pleasure. When they learned the cause of the trouble they were thoroughly disgusted. Among both white and colored people who were genuinely interested in the welfare of the race, opinions concerning the wisdom of the step taken by the singers differed widely.

Some felt that they had missed a glorious opportunity on a notable occasion of showing what they had accomplished in music and what they could do. But practically all the officers of the National Association as well as thoughtful people in the group felt that the drastic action had been forced upon them by those who subjected the race to the humiliation of segregation in the National Capital, adding insult to injury by doing so when a large number of foreign women were present to witness it.

The members of the choirs and the choruses who were to appear on the program at the Auditorium said that when they heard how representatives of their own race who had come to hear them were being treated, they were too depressed to sing.

CHAPTER 38

CROSSING THE COLOR LINE

As MY TWO DAUGHTERS grew up, the question of their education was often discussed. Several of my white friends urged me to send them to Europe. It was a revelation to me to see how clearly some of them saw the difficulties and disadvantages under which colored women labor in the United States. I was surprised also to see how keenly some of them felt about it.

Once I was invited to the Waldorf Astoria by Mrs. Warner, wife of the man who gave the money with which to build the Conservatory of Music at Oberlin College. During the conversation she asked me why Judge Terrell and myself did not go to Europe to live. She said she could not understand how colored people like ourselves could stand being discriminated against as we are. "You cannot get accommodations in hotels. You cannot be served in restaurants as a general rule. In many places you cannot go to the theatre or to the opera. In fact, you have no more privileges than are enjoyed by the most ignorant and the most unfortunate of your racial group." Then Mrs. Warner related a very amusing incident which happened when she and Dr. Warner went abroad one summer and took the colored valet.

"As soon as we reached our destination and stood on the railroad station, the porters would rush to the colored man and take all of his baggage, while we white people were scarcely noticed. We had to shift for ourselves the best way we could. I presume the porters thought he was some oriental potentate. Colored people certainly enjoy more privileges in Europe than they do in the United States," she said.

But I did not take the advice given me by some of my friends for several reasons. In the first place, I could not afford it. My husband's salary was not large enough to defray the expenses which going abroad with two daughters, living there and sending them to school entailed. I was well aware that if they were educated abroad and lived there they would know nothing about the disagreeable experiences which would sooner or later overtake them here, from which neither I nor anybody else could shield them. And that appealed to me greatly, of course. Then, too, I gave the matter more serious consideration than I might otherwise have done, because I was acquainted with several colored women who have married abroad and whose unions with foreigners seem to be a success from every point of view. But in spite of these successful marriages of colored women to white foreigners the idea did not appeal to me for my own daughters. I am also well acquainted with several colored women who have "crossed the line" and married white men in the United States. Some seem as happy as they would have been if they had mated men of their own race, and some do not.

When a colored person decides to "pass for white" in the United States it means that he must pursue a course which is both hazardous and hard. He must make up his mind to renounce his family if he has one, and give up his friends. Crossing the color line separates mother from daughter, father from son, sister from brother, and relatives from their nearest kin.

A fine woman who has worked with me in the National Association of Colored Women married a colored man in a large western city. Her sister married a white man in the same city. The sister who married a colored man does not dare call upon her sister who married a white man. The only time they can see each other, therefore, is when the sister who married the white man comes to see the one whose husband is colored.

One of my friends who was born, reared and educated in New England decided to go to a college in the East which had never admitted colored girls. Although she herself is fair enough to pass for white, the other members of her family are too dark to do so. This young woman entered college, made a fine record and graduated without either the students or the teachers suspecting her racial identity. I have been informed that the president of the college knew, but kept it a secret.

After graduating she obtained a good position in a large eastern city and married a colored physician who is fair enough to pass for white. They moved to a southern city where colored people are not allowed to use the public library. The conditions were so intolerable to the New England woman that she and her husband decided to return to the East, pass for white and rear their children as white. They have carried out their plan and their daughter graduated not long ago from the same institution in which her mother completed her course and under precisely the same conditions.

This woman who has so successfully crossed the color line has a sister with whom I am well acquainted, and this sister is too dark to conceal her racial identity. The only time these two sisters see each other is when the fair one calls on the one unmistakably colored. Every now and then a dear, old colored woman comes to her white daughter's house in New York City, but her grandchildren have no idea she is their grandmother. She simply poses as a helper in her fair daughter's family, and is perfectly willing to play this role to save her child and grandchildren from bearing the burdens which colored people have to carry and to permit them to avail themselves of innumerable opportunities which colored people are not allowed to enjoy.

But even if I had ever thought seriously of taking my daughters abroad with the intention of having one or both of them marry a foreigner, I would have been deterred by a tragedy which occurred in a family with which I am well acquainted. Two sisters studied abroad. One girl was fair enough to cross the color line and married white, while the other was too dark to do so. The darker girl, who was both comely and talented, returned to her home in New England and committed suicide shortly afterward.

Very often when I go downtown I see a woman whom I knew as a girl. She was colored then, but she is white now. She used to visit her sister who attended Oberlin when I did. She is fair enough to pass for white, although she is more oriental than Caucasian. She had a wonderful suit of hair which hung below her waist when long hair was fashionable and was still considered a woman's crown of glory. This woman married a colored man who looked like a Latin-American. The couple moved from a middle western city to Washington, where the husband secured a position as a Government clerk. They had three children and seemed to be getting along nicely. Suddenly it was rumored that the husband had fallen in love with a white woman and had deserted his wife and children. Several years afterward her friends observed that she, too, had crossed the color line and had taken her children with her. Quite a while after that I watched an inaugural parade pass up Pennsylvania Avenue one day, and I saw this colored woman's son leading the cadets of the white high school as the captain of his company.

"Don't look while I am talking to you," my husband said to me one day after we had boarded a street car. "Pretty soon I want you to notice a man who sits near the entrance of the car on the opposite side to us. He and I used to be very close friends when he was known as a colored man. We went to New York together when President Grant was buried and we roomed together in a New York hotel. He has crossed the color line completely and is white now. When we meet on the street I do not speak to him because I do not want to embarrass him in any way. But, occasionally we come together in some out-of-the-way place and then we have the time of our lives talking about his metamorphosis and the many advantages it has brought. As a colored man he could not find a position he cared to fill. He was turned away everywhere he applied. Then he decided he would allow himself to be handicapped no longer, moved from his colored boarding house, took a room run by and for white people and found a good job in a very short while."

An old Washingtonian with whom I am well acquainted related an experience she had which was both amusing and a bit pathetic. She went to a large middle western city to visit her son who had married a white woman and to see her grandchildren. Even in her old age the grandmother was very fair indeed. One day one of her grandsons who was being prepared for college rushed to her in great distress of mind.

"See here, Grandma," said he, "what do you think? Jack won't consent to go to Harvard. I wouldn't give a rap to go anywhere else." "Where does Jack want to go?" asked the grandmother. "Jack wants to go to the University of Virginia. He says he wants to go somewhere—any old place—where niggers can't come." The feelings of the grandmother, who kept a boarding house for colored people in Washington at that time, can better be imagined than described.

A real estate man who lives in Washington told me a very amusing experience he had when he went to visit his sister who lives in Charleston, South Carolina. An exposition was being held there at the time. His sister gave him a list of things which he must see without fail. But she was very enthusiastic about an East Indian with an unpronounceable name who had astounded the natives with his wonderful feats of legerdemain. The most exclusive lady in that most exclusive social circle, she said, had invited him to her home, where he transported her guests with wonder and joy by his adroitness and extraordinary skill.

"Herbert," said the man's sister, "I want you to meet this clever East Indian very much. Come with me and let me introduce you to him. He is at leisure just about this time." Then they wended their way to the celebrity's office.

"Mr. So and So," said his sister, "let me present my brother to you." The eyes of the two men met in instant recognition. "Hello, Bert," said the great East Indian reaching out his hand. "We haven't seen each other since we used to play marbles together when we were boys." This case was all the more remarkable, because the "East Indian" had been born and brought up as a colored boy in that very southern city and some of his relatives were still living there. He visited them almost every night after dark when he removed his costume. But he grew so bold about it that a friend in his own racial group warned him to exercise more caution.

When I was a child I was well acquainted with a young woman in Memphis whose marriage was the cause of one of the most remarkable cases in the history of American jurisprudence. A well-to-do young white man of French extraction fell deeply in love with her. In spite of threats made by both white and colored people and in spite of the entreaties of his family and friends he decided to make this colored woman his wife. Without benefit of clergy they had several children. They could not marry legally in Memphis.

In order to legitimize his children he went to Arkansas,

where there was no penalty attached to the intermarriage of the races at that time, and had the marriage ceremony performed. When the two young people returned to Memphis, a penitentiary sentence of seven years stared them both in the face.

Without going into the full details of the case, it was proved in court that the young colored woman was white. She had a soft creamy complexion with red cheeks, but she was far from fair. She had been reared all her life by a mulatto aunt with very curly hair. She had attended the schools for colored children in Memphis and Fisk University in Nashville, Tennessee, which was established for the education of colored youth. But certain witnesses who claimed to know her parents testified that her mother was Spanish and her father, who was quite swarthy, was a Mexican. So the court decided she was white, and white she was, as long as she remained in the city where she was reared as a colored girl and where she could hardly walk down the street without meeting some of her colored friends with whom she had associated all her life. Although she herself had attended the colored schools, her children were sent to the white schools.

The father of the woman with whom I lived when I first came to Washington was white, but her mother was colored. Against his will he had been forced into the Confederate Army. Although all of his children were colored, they showed no trace of belonging to their mother's race. When he entered the Army this white father took his eldest son with him. The father was killed.

After the war the colored son continued to play the role of white man which he had assumed when he entered the Confederate Army with his father. He married into one of the aristocratic families of a southern State. In spite of forty years of exile from his mother's family, the desire to see his only living brother and his sister's children became so great that he journeyed to the National Capital to gratify it.

"The door-bell rang one day," said my friend, whose husband was a skillful physician, "and the maid told me that an old gentleman who refused to give his name wanted to see me on important business. The moment I laid eyes on him," said she, "I noticed a striking resemblance to Uncle Milton, with whom you are acquainted and who has lived here for years. 'Is this Sarah's child?' said the stranger, rising and holding out his hand.

'Yes,' I said. 'Well, I am your Uncle John. Surely your mother has told you about me.' After I told him my mother was dead and we had reviewed the history of the various members of the family, he wanted to see my children. 'Whatever you do, don't tell them who I am,' said he. He refused flatly to see my husband for fear he might betray him in some way. 'My husband is a gentleman,' I said, 'and he would not harm you if he could.' When he saw one of my boys (who, as you know, is quite fair) pass through the room, he lamented deeply that such a fine-looking lad should be brought up as colored under the existing condition of things in this country. 'All of my children do not look like that boy,' I said. 'Three of them are a little darker than he is. Surely you would not advise me to rear one-half of my children as colored and the other half white.'

"As I looked at that old man," said my friend, "I could not help noticing the difference between my handsome, courageous, manly Uncle Milton, who is just as fair as Uncle John, but who has never deserted his family and his group, and this newly-found uncle who has lived a falsehood all his life. His manner was nervous. He seemed uncertain of himself. About his eyes there was a haunted, fearsome look which is said to be characteristic of men who have served a term in a penitentiary. As I noticed these points of difference, if I had ever been tempted to rear any of my children as white, I should have changed my mind immediately."

Not only do fair colored people cross the color line when they wish to do so, but even those whose complexions are quite dark sometimes manage by hook or crook to escape the fate which confronts their race in the United States. A man who has recently passed away was almost black. But he decided to call himself a Hindu and had quite a following of white people who believed in him thoroughly and admired him greatly. Of all the people in my group he stands out in my mind as the one who was more impatient with the restrictions imposed upon him, more peeved and irked than anybody I can recall. Then he learned the cult which he advocated, so that he knew it backward and forward, was well versed in oriental lore, dressed in white from his head to his heels and went places as a Hindu which he could not penetrate as a Negro. A Fact-Finding Commission studying this subject would be forced to conclude that people of African descent are not discriminated against in the United States because their complexions are dark.

Even though there is absolute certainty that the chances of success are much greater for a colored person who forswears his race than for the individual who remains loyal to it, many do not yield to the temptation to pass for white. A young woman who is one of my friends is a musician of distinction and has written a book. She could easily pass for white if she wished to do so. Her complexion is modeled after the Spanish or French. Her hair and eyes are as black as midnight.

She married a young physician who can also pass for white. They went to a western city, where the doctor had a large and growing practice. He suddenly decided that he would shake off the body of the dusky death, so to speak, and cast his lot with the dominant race. When he revealed his plan to his wife, she told him she would rather live on a small income, if necessary, than have a large one if she were obliged to forsake her family and friends. The husband could not be shaken from his purpose and the wife could not be persuaded to turn her back on her family and friends. So they separated. She came here to Washington, remained here a while and then went to a large eastern city where race prejudice is less acute than it is here. When I used to see this accomplished young woman, as I often did, and her little daughter, who was both fair and pretty, I could not help wondering how the husband and father could have summoned the strength and courage to tear himself away from them and bid them good-bye.

In this particular phase of the Race Problem a very unusual thing occurred in a western city not many years ago. A couple had been happily married a long time. The husband was a physician with a lucrative practice and the wife, a college graduate, had been a teacher in a high school. Suddenly the wife noticed that her husband seemed very much worried about something. He had a far away look, was distraught and evidently very unhappy. She feared that he no longer loved her. She questioned him repeatedly and begged him to tell her what was the matter.

Replying to her questions he told her he was not in financial straits. Money matters were not troubling him and there certainly was no other woman in the case. He admitted that he was greatly worried about something. But he begged her not to insist upon knowing what was the cause of his mental distress on the ground that if he told her she would be much more unhappy than she was. But the wife assured her husband that no matter what was the cause of the trouble, she would rather know what it was than remain in ignorance and suspense.

"Very well," said he, "since you insist and will not let me alone I'll tell you. I am a colored man." The wife ran to him quickly, threw her arms around his neck and exclaimed, "Thank God! Thank God! I am a colored woman and I feared that in some way you had discovered the truth and were unhappy because I had deceived you."

At first blush it would seem that a camel with a hump could literally pass through a cambric needle's eye easier than an individual with even a drop of the fatal African tincture could palm himself off as a white man in the United States. And yet colored people are doing this in droves every year. Here is one of them who has tried to find employment in an occupation for which he has been trained. He has knocked first at one door and then at another which he finds can be opened only by a white man's hand. He becomes discouraged.

"What a curse it is to be a Negro in this country," he mutters. Suddenly he looks into the mirror. He has done so before, perhaps. He has always been identified with the struggling race, but he has a fair skin and straight hair. Something asserts itself. There are those who say it is his white blood. "What's the use of trying to row against the tide?" he asks. "Nobody but a giant can accomplish the impossible, and I am not a giant." He quickly reaches a decision. He has thought of it before, but he has always put it behind him as a last resort, too contemptible and cowardly to be considered seriously. He is out of work now. Inability to get a good position has become chronic. The long, lingering look occurred, let us say, Tuesday evening at eight o'clock. On Wednesday morning at precisely that hour he is a white man, made so by virtue of last night's decision and nature's gifts. Where does he go?

If the man happens to have no family in the city and the city is large, in many instances he stays right there. How does he do it? Among other things, he ceases to frequent the old resorts. He changes his lodging house and betakes him to a section of the city diametrically opposite to the one in which he formerly lived. His old friends see him no more. That is, they don't if he can help it. They think he has left the city. When he sees them approaching he makes it convenient to cross to the other side of the street. He isolates himself completely. He scrapes up acquaintances with white people among whom he is living and they do not suspect he has the fatal drop. Finally, he gets a good job which it would be impossible for him either to have or to hold, if his employer knew the truth.

The more one investigates the matter, the more certain does one become that many whom the world accepts as white are in reality colored, according to established standards in this country. "If I were white," said one of my friends, "and felt toward colored people as many Caucasians do, I should be perfectly miserable. I should be constantly tormented by the fear that some day I might discover a trace of Negro blood in my veins. Only last week a young woman who thought she was white committed suicide in a southern hotel because, in settling her estate, the lawyer made the startling discovery that her grandmother was a slave."

A short while ago I saw Fannie Hurst's *Imitation of Life*, which was named among the twelve nominations for the most outstanding motion picture in 1934. It is the story of a colored girl fair enough to pass for white who disowns her dark-skinned mother. This picture drew large crowds everywhere, called attention to a phase of the Race Problem not generally known, and created much comment.

Long before slaves were emancipated, it was no uncommon thing for colored boys and girls to be sent to Europe by their masters, who were also their fathers, but who loved their children born of a slave mother too fondly to allow them to remain in the United States where they would have to bear the hard and humiliating lot of a slave. These children were educated abroad, where most of them married. Their descendents are living in Europe today, not dreaming they have a drop of African blood in their veins.

It is often stated that if a white woman marries a black man, or vice versa, one of the children of such a union is quite likely to be black. If the curse does not settle directly upon the offspring of this intermarriage, it will certainly fall upon the second generation, according to this theory. One of the grandchildren of this black and white pair will certainly "take after" its African progenitor, it is claimed. This is a kind of propaganda spread broadcast, it is said, for the purpose of frightening white women from marrying colored men.

All my life I have associated with people who were the children of white fathers and colored mothers and never in the same family have I seen one of the children black, while their brothers and sisters were yellow or white. Nor have I ever heard that there is a single black person in England or Europe who is a descendant of an ancestor in the United States whose father was white and whose mother was black. There are different types and shades in colored families as there are in families of other racial groups.

In white families some of the children have black hair, while others are blonds. Some have blue eyes, while the eyes of others are black. Some are very fair in complexion, while others are much darker. In the same way there are slight differences of complexion in the families of colored people. There is also a difference in the texture of the hair and in the color of the eyes. But there is no such reversion to type as some people claim, so that the child of two fair colored people or the offspring of a white person and one of African descent is "apt to be black."

CHAPTER 39

THE COLORED MAN'S PARADISE

ONCE UPON A TIME Washington was called "The Colored Man's Paradise." But I certainly hope the angels in Heaven will be a little more kindly disposed towards me than some of the good people in my home town are, although from their point of view, I am sure they feel they have dealt with me very generously, indeed.

Washington might have been given the beautiful name in bitter irony by some member of the handicapped race, as he reviewed his limitations and rebuffs. Or, it might have been given immediately after the Civil War by an ex-slaveholder who for the first time in his life saw colored people walking about like freemen, minus overseer and whip. But it would be difficult to find a worse misnomer for Washington than the "Colored Man's Paradise" if one knew the facts and had any regard for the truth.

I have lived in Washington for fifty years, and while it was far from being "a paradise" for colored people when I first touched these shores, it has done a great deal since then to make conditions for them intolerable. As a colored woman, I might enter Washington any night, a stranger in a strange land, and walk miles without finding a place to lay my head. Unless I happened to know colored people who live here or ran across a colored man or woman who could recommend a colored boarding house or hotel to me, I should be obliged to spend the night wandering around. Indians, Japanese, Chinese, Filipinos and representatives of other dark races can find hotel accommodations, as a rule, if they can pay for them. The colored man or woman is the only one thrust out of the hotels of the National Capital like a leper.

As a colored woman I may walk from the Capitol to the White House ravenously hungry and supplied with money to purchase a meal without finding a single restaurant in which I would be permitted to take a morsel of food if it was patronized by white people, unless I were willing to sit behind a screen. And in some places I would not be allowed to do even that. I am almost ashamed to admit that more than once when I have been downtown attending a meeting or transacting business, and have been both hungry and weary, I have stood in front of a restaurant or a cafeteria in the National Capital looking with longing eyes at a special menu offered for that day at a price I could afford to pay, and have been unable to summon the courage to go in and get what I needed. Being physically weak, I presume, I did not have the grit to run the risk of being recognized by someone and refused. I was not always in the frame of mind that I felt I could stand a slap in the face. Sometimes when I am provoked with colored people who are too timid to insist upon their rights as citizens, I remember those lapses of my own when I have lost my nerve. But I have never stopped trying to get what I knew was just and right for me to have.

During a meeting of the Women's International League for Peace and Freedom, Miss B., a delegate from Chicago, invited Mr. L., a colored man who is a Rhodes scholar, and myself to dine with her and several friends at a hotel near the Union Station. It was a good hotel, but was not listed as first class. A first-class hotel will often serve a colored person when the others will not. Miss B. was a guest at this hotel as were several others attending the meeting.

Miss B., the other three white women, the colored man and myself had been seated at the table but a short while when I noticed that the proprietor was standing at the dining room door looking at us very hard and wearing an expression which showed he was far from being pleased. I understood what was the matter, of course. My hostess sat with her back to the door, so that she did not see the proprietor there.

We were allowed to finish our meal. As soon as we did so, I wanted to leave the hotel, but my hostess insisted that we should go into the reception room with her and the other guests and I was obliged to yield. We had been sitting there but a few minutes when the colored elevator boy came to tell Miss B. the proprietor wanted to see her immediately. She left the room and remained a long time. When Miss B. returned we all arose and left the room without saying a word. When we reached the street our hostess told us that the proprietor had rebuked her for inviting colored people to dine at the hotel and stated that it was strictly against the rule to serve them. He was especially provoked with Mr. L. and declared that he should have known better than to come, no matter how cordially he had been invited.

I did not shed any briny tears at the discomfiture of a man who was violating an amendment to the Constitution every day in the Capital of the United States. I was glad Miss B. had not made the mistake of asking him to allow her to bring two colored guests. He would have refused her, of course. As it was, they enjoyed their dinner, as they had a right to do. And their presence in the dining room established a principle.

As a colored woman I cannot visit George Washington's home and last resting place without being forced to sit in a Jim Crow section on a bus which starts from the very heart of the city, midway between the Capitol and the White House. If I refuse thus to be humiliated, I am cast into jail in Virginia and forced to pay a fine for violating the laws of that State. Every hour in the day Jim Crow cars enter and leave the National Capital. Intelligent and well-to-do colored people are forced to ride in them.

With a party of friends I boarded a Mount Vernon car one day and we refused to sit in the rear seat to which colored people are relegated, as soon as they reach Virginia. After we had been riding about seven minutes we came to Highway Bridge in that State. Then the conductor ordered us to move to the rear from the seats we had taken when we entered the car. Nobody in our party was willing to submit to that humiliation and we returned home. I have always regretted that the Capital of the United States was moved from New York or Philadelphia. If it had been located in the North, East or West the status of colored people would be far better than it is.

As a colored woman, I may enter more than one white church in Washington without receiving the welcome which any human being has a right to expect in the sanctuary of God. Sometimes the usher is stricken with a peculiar kind of color blindness which prevents a dark face from making any impression on his retina, so that it is impossible for him to see colored people at all. Or, if his eyesight happens to be normal, he will keep these dusky Christians waiting a long time when they have had the temerity to thrust themselves into a temple where only fair faces are expected to worship. Then he will ungraciously show them a seat in the rear—the Jim Crow section of the house of God.

There is no way for me to earn an honest living in the National Capital, unless I am willing to be a domestic servant, if I am not a trained nurse or a dressmaker, or unless I can secure a position in the public schools. This is exceedingly difficult to do, for, as a rule, the supply of colored teachers in every city is greater than the demand. It matters not what my intellectual attainments may be or how great may be the need of the services of a competent person, if I try to enter any one of the numerous vocations in which my white sisters are allowed to engage, the door is shut in my face.

I can not go to see the plays which I should like to witness and I can not hear the operas and artists I long to hear, unless I am willing to be Jim Crowed in the theatres, or run the risk of being ejected with the humiliating publicity it would cause if, in some round-about way, I can get a ticket. From the white theatres and movies colored people are excluded altogether. One of my friends was so eager to see a play that she decided to go as a nurse for a little white girl she knew. She asked me to telephone to the ticket seller just before the matinee to inquire whether a good-looking, neat-appearing colored nurse would be allowed to sit in the parquet with her little white charge. I did so and the answer rushed quickly and positively through the receiver, "NO."

When I remonstrated with him and told him that in some of the theatres of the South colored nurses were allowed to sit with the white children for whom they cared, the ticket seller told me it was very poor policy to employ colored nurses in Washington. "They are excluded from every place to which white nurses are allowed to take children for pleasure."

There is a fine conservatory of music at Howard University

from which some of the most successful colored pianists, singers and composers have graduated. For a long time both the teachers and the students of this institution were deprived of the advantage and the privilege of hearing the great artists who come to Washington. Later some of these restrictions were removed so that conditions are much better today than they once were. For several years, however, Howard University has offered a series of recitals in which the finest artists in the country may be heard by the colored citizens of Washington without being subjected to the humiliation of being Jim Crowed in any auditorium. Marian Anderson, one of the greatest artists this country has produced, was not allowed to sing in Constitution Hall because she is a colored woman. With two exceptions, there is not a single white college or university in the National Capital which will admit colored students. It matters not how great the ability, how lofty the ambition, how unexceptionable the character, or how keen the thirst for knowledge may be, the door of educational opportunity is slammed by the white institutions in a colored person's face.

Before the Art Department of Howard University was opened one of my friends wanted very much to study drawing and painting. But she was unable to do so because the art schools of Washington refused to admit her. She possessed great talent and submitted some drawings to the Corcoran School of Art. They were accepted by the Committee of Awards, who sent her a ticket entitling her to a course in the school. But when the committee discovered that my friend was colored they declined to admit her. Without mincing matters at all, they told her that if they had suspected her drawings had been made by a colored woman they would not have examined them. The efforts of Frederick Douglass and a lawyer of repute were unavailing.

In order to cultivate her talent this woman was forced to leave her home and incur the expense of going to New York. She entered the Woman's Art School of Cooper Union, graduated with honor and then went to Paris to continue her studies. There she achieved signal success and was complimented by some of the greatest artists of France.

A young woman who had already attracted attention in the literary world by her volume of short stories answered an advertisement which appeared in a Washington newspaper. It called for the services of a skillful stenographer and expert typist. The applicants were requested to send specimens of their work and answer certain questions concerning their experience and speed before they called in person. The young colored woman, who was fair and attractive, received a letter from the firm stating that her experience and references were the most satisfactory that had been submitted and requesting her to call.

When she presented herself there was some doubt in the mind of the man interviewing her concerning her racial pedigree, so he asked her point blank whether she was colored or white. When she confessed the truth the merchant expressed deep sorrow and regret that he could not avail himself of the services of so competent a person. He frankly admitted that employing a colored person in his establishment in any except a menial position was simply out of the question.

One of my daughters had a similar experience. She answered an advertisement and was appointed a clerk in the credit department of a large department store where we had traded for years. Her father had often assisted the head of the firm by advising him gratuitously concerning matters which the latter did not care to take into the courts. Without the knowledge of either one of us, she secured this position on her merit. But she had been employed less than a week before she was called to the office of the manager and questioned concerning her race. An employee of the store, who was well acquainted with our family, had reported that a colored girl was working in the credit department and had told who she was. Then my young daughter promptly lost her job. Naturally, it shook me to the very foundation of my being to see her the victim of such cruel race prejudice, but I was helpless to shield her from the embarrassment and humiliation to which she had been subjected.

In order to get a good job one of my young friends left Washington and went to New York. There she worked her way up in one of the largest dry-goods stores till she was placed as saleswoman in the cloak department. Tired of being separated from her family, she decided to return to Washington, feeling sure that with her experience and fine recommendations from the New York firm she could easily secure employment at home. Nor was she overconfident, for the proprietor of a large dry-goods store in her native city was glad to secure the services of a young woman who had brought such glowing credentials as she had from New York.

She had not been in this store very long, however, before she called upon me one day and asked me to intercede with her proprietor in her behalf. She had just been discharged that afternoon because it had been discovered that she was colored. When I called upon my young friend's employer, he made no effort to avoid the issue, as I feared he would. He did not say that he had discharged the young woman because she had not given satisfaction, as he might easily have done. On the contrary, he admitted without the slightest hesitation that the young woman he had just discharged was one of the best clerks he had ever had. In the cloak department, where she had been assigned, she had been a brilliant success, he said.

"But I can not keep Miss Smith in my employ," he concluded. "Are you not master of your own store?" I ventured to inquire. The proprietor of this store was a Jew, and I felt that it was particularly cruel, unnatural and cold-blooded for the representative of one oppressed race to deal so harshly with another. I had intended to make this point very strong when I decided to intercede for my young friend. But when I thought how a reference to the persecution of his own race would wound his feelings, the words froze on my lips.

"When I first heard your friend was colored," he explained, "I did not believe it and said so to the clerks who made the statement. Finally, the girls who had been most pronounced in their opposition to working in a store with a colored girl came to me in a body and threatened to strike. 'Strike away,' I said. 'Your places can be easily filled.' Then they started on another tack. Delegation after delegation began to file down to my office. Some of the women were my best customers, and they protested vehemently against my employing a colored girl. Moreover, they threatened to boycott my store if I did not discharge her at once. Then it became a question of bread and butter with me and I yielded to the inevitable. Now," said he concluding, "if I lived in a great cosmopolitan city like New York, I should do as I pleased, and refuse to discharge a girl simply because she was colored."

That recalled to my mind a similar incident that happened

in New York. I remembered that a woman, who was a leading member of the National Association of Colored Women, had been a saleswoman in a large department store in New York City. She was very efficient, attractive and fair, but she was summarily discharged, after she had held this position for years, when the proprietor accidentally discovered that a fatal drop of African blood was percolating somewhere through her veins.

When my kneecap was fractured in an automobile accident I was taken to a certain hospital. While I was being wheeled along a corridor on a stretcher, a nurse told me I could not have a private room. I was a bit dazed and did not understand that she meant to tell me I could not have a private room because I am a colored woman. Some years before my accident I had secured a private room for my mother and I had not heard that the hospital had changed its policy in that particular.

"Good morning, Mary," said the head nurse to me next morning. I could scarcely believe my ears. It was the first time I had been called "Mary" by anybody except my family and friends since I had grown to womanhood. I objected to being called Mary and asked the nurse to treat me with the same courtesy she would accord women of other racial groups. Several nurses came to my bed and addressed me as "Mary" also. When I objected to being addressed in this way they sent for the superintendent. He came quickly and angrily. In the presence of the sixteen other women in the ward he said loudly, "I hear you are making trouble and creating a disturbance." I told him I had not done this, but I had politely requested the nurses not to call me "Mary." "The nurses have been instructed to call you 'Mary'," he fairly shouted. "But the nurses do not address women of other racial groups by their Christian names," I said. "No," he said, "they don't. But there is a vast difference between white women and colored women," he said. He also suggested that I had better go to some other hospital. But my leg was in a cast and I dared not move. I asked the nurses not to call me anything. I told them to obey their instructions, for I did not want them to do anything which would get them into trouble. But several of them addressed me as "Mrs. Terrell" in a low tone of voice in spite of my request not to do so.

So far as I have been able to ascertain, in no hospital in Washington are colored women addressed as "Mrs." or "Miss."

They are called by their first names by everybody who attends them. Colored men are treated in the same way, no matter how distinguished they may be or how high a position they may hold.

During the World War colored girls ran the elevators in some of the department stores. But after the war, when the Minimum Wage Committee decided that working girls should receive a certain amount for their services, colored girls were dismissed in most of the stores because there was a strong sentiment against giving them $16 per week. The jobs were given to white girls. In one large store, however, colored girls still run the elevators.

Colored women customers are not infrequently treated with discourtesy by the clerks and sometimes by the proprietor himself. There is a restaurant in one of the large department stores. It was established by a man who hailed from Boston, once the home of William Lloyd Garrison, Wendell Phillips and Charles Sumner. A colored teacher, good-looking, well-dressed and fair, took a seat at one of the tables of the restaurant of this Boston store. She sat unnoticed for a long time. Finally, she asked a waiter who passed by her if she would not take her order. She was quickly informed that colored people could not be served in that restaurant and was obliged to leave in confusion and shame, much to the amusement of the waiters and guests who had observed the incident.

In one of the Washington theatres colored people have been viciously assaulted several times. The proprietor knows well that they have no redress for such discriminations against them in the District Courts. A colored clerk in one of the Government Departments bought a ticket for the parquet of this theatre in which colored people are nowhere welcome. Incidentally, this clerk looks more like his paternal ancestors who fought for the "Lost Cause" than his grandmothers who were the victims of the "peculiar institution." He also bought a ticket for his mother, whose complexion was noticeably swarthy.

The usher refused to allow the young man to take the seats for which his tickets called and tried to snatch the coupons from him. A scuffle ensued. Both mother and son were ejected by force. A suit was brought against the proprietor, who lost the case. The damages awarded the injured man and his mother amounted to the munificent sum of one cent. One of the teachers of the colored high school who went to see a play which would help him in his class work was similarly treated in the same theatre, but he did not sue the proprietor, so that he might get damages for one cent.

When my daughters were children, one of their little friends figured in one of the most pathetic incidents of which I have ever heard. A member of my family who is very fond of children promised to take six little girls in his neighborhood to a matinee. It happened that he himself and five of his little friends were fair enough to pass muster, as they stood in judgment before the ticket seller and the ticket taker. Three of the little girls were sisters, two of whom were very fair and the other a bit darker. Just as this little girl, who happened to be last in the procession, went by the ticket taker, that argus-eyed, sophisticated gentleman detected something which caused a deep, dark frown to mantle his brow and he did not let her pass. "I guess you have made a mistake," he called to the host of the theatre party. "Those little girls," pointing to the fair ones, "may be admitted, but this one," pointing to the swarthy one, "can't."

But the colored man was quite equal to the emergency. "What do you mean? What are you trying to insinuate about that little girl? Do you mean to say that Filipinos are excluded from the theatres of Washington?" This little ruse succeeded brilliantly, as he knew it would. "Beg your pardon," said the ticket taker, "don't know what I was thinking about."

"What was the matter with me this afternoon, Mother?" asked the little off-color girl innocently, when she mentioned the affair at home. "Why did the man at the theatre let my two sisters and the other girls in and try to keep me out?" The child's mother related this incident to me and told me her little daughter's question completely unnerved her for a time. It showed such blissful ignorance of the depressing, cruel conditions which confronted her and which she would have to face continually, she said.

White and colored teachers are under the same Board of Education and the system for the children of both races is said to be uniform. Nevertheless, race prejudice bobs up to tease the colored teachers every now and then. From 1870 to 1900 there was a colored superintendent at the head of the colored schools. During all that time the directors of the cooking, sewing, physical culture, manual training, music and art departments were colored people. A change was made. The colored superintendent was legislated out of office, and the directorships, without a single exception, were taken from the colored teachers and given to the whites.

There was no complaint about the work of the colored directors—no more than is heard about every officer in every school—as a general rule. The directors of several departments were particularly fine. Now, no matter how competent or superior the colored teachers in our public schools may be, they know they can never rise to the height of a directorship. They can never hope to be more than an assistant and receive the salary therefor, unless the present regime is radically changed. And it is not likely that will occur.

A distinguished kindergartner came to deliver a course of lectures in Washington a few years ago. The colored teachers were eager to attend, but they could not buy the coveted privilege for love or money. They appealed to the director of kindergartens and were told that the expert kindergartner had come to Washington under the auspices of private individuals so that she could not possibly have them admitted. But one of the white teachers realized what a loss her colored colleagues had sustained in being deprived of the information and inspiration which these lectures afforded, so she volunteered to repeat them as best she could for the benefit of the colored teachers for half the price she herself had paid, and the proposition was eagerly accepted by some.

For years strenuous efforts have been made to run Jim Crow street cars in Washington. "Resolved that a Jim Crow Law should be adopted and enforced in the District of Columbia," was once the subject engaged in by the Columbian Debating Society of the George Washington University in our National Capital, and the decision was rendered in favor of the affirmative.

When Senator Heflin of Alabama, who was defeated several years ago for reelection to the United States Senate, was a representative in Congress, he introduced a bill providing for Jim Crow street cars in the District of Columbia. He received a letter from the East Brookland Citizens Association, "indorsing the movement for separate street cars and sincerely hoping that you will be successful in getting this enacted into law as soon as possible." Brookland is a suburb of Washington. But Heflin of Alabama is not the only man in Congress that has introduced a bill to force colored people in the National Capital to ride in certain cars especially provided for them. It is a sort of indoor sport often indulged in by the men who represent in the national Congress that section of the country in which Jim Crow laws and other similar products are indigenous to the soil.

Once, Senator Heflin was so incensed at seeing a colored man in a Washington street car that he shot at him but struck a white man, who came near dying from the wound which he inflicted.

In Washington the colored laborer's path to a decent livelihood is by no means smooth. Into some of the trades unions here he is admitted, while from others he is excluded altogether. By the white union men this is sometimes denied. But I am personally acquainted with skilled workmen who tell me they are not admitted into the unions because they are colored. Even when they are allowed to join the unions they often derive little benefit, owing to certain tricks of the trade. When the word is passed around that help is needed and colored laborers apply, they are often told by the union officials that they have secured all the men they needed. The jobs are reserved for white men and colored men must remain idle, unless the supply of white men is too small.

In the middle of the front page of the May 15, 1940, issue of the *Washington Evening Star,* the following notice appeared with the headline, "WANTED: MEN FOR JOBS NOW AVAILABLE. Wanted: Not jobs, but men to fill them."

"The District Employment Center, which usually finds things the other way around, announced today it had more jobs than men in certain fields. If you're a white, experienced bricklayer, carpenter, paperhanger or automobile mechanic, you can walk into the Employment Center and walk out with a job.

"The Employment Center also is in need of experienced white men and women for all types of hotel and restaurant work.

"Edwin W. Jones, acting director of the center, said it looked like more jobs were opening up, that the need for more men was more than a seasonal shortage.

"The number of calls, he said, had shown a consistent increase over last year. May, 1939, was the biggest placement month in the history of the service, he said, and this month seems to be even bigger."

The District Employment Center in the Capital of the United States thus serves notice on colored men that no matter how skillful they may be in the trades mentioned or how much they may need jobs so as to support their families and themselves, they dare not apply to it for them, even though it admits it has more jobs than men. How disastrously such flagrant, cruel discrimination against their group affects the youth of the race can not be estimated or expressed in words. It crushes their aspirations, paralyzes their energy and blasts their hopes.

And yet, colored people are constantly being criticized and blamed in the National Capital because so many of them are on relief. But if colored men are not given jobs, even when there are not enough white men to fill them, and colored women know that the Employment Center wants only white women "for all types of hotel and restaurant work," it is difficult, if not impossible, for many of them to earn their living. They must either go on relief or let their families and themselves starve.

I am personally acquainted with one of the most skillful laborers in the hardware business in Washington. For 30 years he worked for the same firm. He told me he could not join the union, and that his employer had been almost forced to discharge him, because the union men threatened to boycott his store if he did not. If a white man could have been found to take his place, he would have lost his job, he said. When no other human being could bring a refractory chimney or a balking stove to its senses, this colored man was called upon as a court of last appeal. If he failed to subdue it, it was pronounced a hopeless case at once. And yet, this expert workman received much less for his services than did white men who could not compare with him in skill.

And so I might go on citing instance after instance to show the various ways in which our group is sacrificed on the altar of race prejudice in the capital of the United States and how huge are the obstacles which block the colored man's path to success. Early in life many a colored youth is so appalled by the helplessness and the hopelessness of the situation in this country that in a sort of stoical despair he resigns himself to his fate.

When I taught in the high school of Washington the thoughtful boys would sometimes come to me and say: "What is the good of our trying to get an education? We can't all be preachers, teachers, doctors and lawyers. Besides those professions, there is almost nothing for colored men to do but engage in menial occupations, and we do not need an education for that." Such remarks uttered by young men and women in our public schools who possess brilliant intellects have often wrung my heart.

CHAPTER 40

SOCIAL ACTIVITIES

THROUGHOUT OUR MARRIED LIFE until shortly before he was stricken, my husband and I belonged to some social club which generally gave three or four dances during the season. Judge Terrell danced divinely and enjoyed it. As I have already said, I cannot remember a time when I would not rather dance than eat. If I had an opportunity to indulge in that delightful recreation now, I am sure I would get as much pleasure out of it as I ever did.

Until the Wilson administration, there were always many social functions given for the strangers by our group during the inauguration of a president. There were breakfasts in the morning, luncheons, musicales, teas, card parties in the afternoons, dances, card parties and banquets at night. My husband and I missed very few of these functions. We made it a point to attend as many as we could during these inaugural festivities. We felt it our duty to do so, and we certainly derived great pleasure from meeting the strangers. Judge Terrell's social nature was highly developed, and so was mine. Our tastes were similar in practically every respect—in music, literature and the drama. I can recall only one instance in which our tastes differed with respect to music.

There are more well-educated colored people to the square inch in Washington than in any other city in the United States. There was a time when some of the leaders were considered quite well to do. Among our friends and acquaintances were doctors, whose practice was lucrative and large, lawyers, dentists, plus real estate men, not to mention the Government clerks, who had secured their positions through competitive examinations rather than political influence, as a rule, and not forgetting the officers and teachers in the public schools, some of whom wear Phi Beta Kappa keys given them by the best universities and colleges in the United States.

Often when I looked at a group of these people at a social function I used to recall what a physician said one day, when my father told him I wanted to go to college to get a degree. "Bob," said he, "you ought to be proud of a girl who has ambition enough to go to college. But, if you send her, you will only be laying up a lot of unhappiness for her because you will be educating her away from her people. There will be nobody for her to associate with, when she completes her college course. There will be no colored man well enough educated for her to marry."

Over and over again I have wished this physician might have looked in on some of the colored functions in Washington and have seen the distinguished men and women gathered there. He could have been convinced that the guests observed the same standards of conduct and culture as do those in the best social circles in the United States. At one time or another he might have seen the Register of the Treasury, whose name appeared on the paper money of this country, the recorder of deeds, a judge of the municipal court and a literary light or two. Then, too, he might have seen a handsome man who had once been governor of Louisiana for a day. The equally handsome grandson of this man is now a well-known writer who has crossed on the other side of the racial line, where he has married and feels he belongs.

The colored people of Washington probably took the lead in employing physicians of their own race. Some years ago in the average city what is called the "best class" of colored people could not have been persuaded to employ one of their own physicians because they had no confidence in their skill. "I shall never forget with what fear and trembling I called a colored physician for the first time," said one of my friends. "If I had ordered a dynamite bomb, and it had come suddenly rolling in upon me to destroy me, I could not have been much more agitated than I was when my first colored physician entered my room, felt my pulse and told me to stick out my tongue."

Although I myself did not feel so dubious about it as that, nevertheless, I wondered whether I was dealing justly by myself when I called in a physician of my own racial group for the first time because I thought it was my duty to do so and because I realized that I would be very inconsistent and false to my standards if I did not. To such a lamentable extent are colored people themselves, from the wisest of us to the silliest goose that masquerades as a sentient human being, the victims of a narrow, prejudice-producing, mind-murdering, soul-crushing environment.

In all our large cities today, however, colored physicians are well patronized by members of their race, some of whom are even beginning to think that they can be healed a little quicker and a little better by their own doctors than by anybody else.

When my husband began to practice law, after he had lost his position as Chief of Division in the Treasury Department, when the Democratic party won with Grover Cleveland, he used to tell me that every now and then some colored man who had employed him would come back and ask him to return the papers in the case that had been given him. His client had changed his mind because he had not sufficient confidence in a colored lawyer's ability and skill to trust him with the case, and had placed it in the hands of a white lawyer. Sometimes the white lawyer would charge a great deal more for his services than my husband did, but the colored client was usually willing to pay the difference in price. On several occasions, however, the colored Doubting Thomas, on sober, second thought, changed his mind once more and tried to re-employ my husband. But he made it a rule not to accept the case under such circumstances.

Colored people in Washington, and everywhere else for that matter, are gradually gaining more confidence in all their professional men, are employing their own tradesmen more and are dealing more and more at the colored stores.

For a long time I belonged to a Booklovers' Club which had a membership of 12 women. As its name implies, our club was organized for the purpose of reading, reviewing and discussing books. There are a goodly number of literary and art clubs among the older and younger members of our group with some civic and political organizations thrown in for good measure.

Judge Terrell belonged to the Mu-So-Lit Club, which includes among its members some of the cleverest and most intelligent men of the race. This club annually celebrates the birthday of Frederick Douglass. Speeches laudatory of the life and services of this Moses of his people are made. And then, at the expense of the guests and members, quips, jokes and witticisms are indulged in which are as clever as are those made by recognized leaders in this line.

There are musical organizations galore among all classes and kinds and conditions of the colored people of Washington. Notable among these is the Coleridge-Taylor Society, the purpose of which is to cultivate a taste for the best music and to learn to sing it well. I have already referred to the occasion when Coleridge-Taylor himself, the great Anglo-African composer, came from London to conduct the chorus of this society which was named in his honor, when it rendered "Hiawatha" and the Marine Band accompanied the singers under his baton.

For years I attended regularly the weekly meetings of the Bethel Literary and Historical Society, which is the oldest organization established by colored people in this country. In fact, I was the first woman to be elected president. Some of the most distinguished men, without regard to race or color, have appeared in this forum. After the speaker has finished his address, the audience is allowed to discuss the subject from the floor.

I belong to the oldest woman's card club formed by our group in Washington. When I was first invited to join it I was so serious-minded I thought it would be wrong to accept the invitation. Playing cards seemed to me to be a wicked waste of time. I was then a member of the Board of Education, which consumed a great deal of my time. I thought that all the extra minutes I could scrape together should be devoted to my children, to my home and to reading, so as to keep abreast of the times. I thought the inaugural festivities once in four years plus the dances usually given during the season were quite sufficient to satisfy all my social needs.

But Mother insisted that I needed the kind of recreation which a card game with friends one afternoon every other week would afford. I took her advice and joined the club and I have never regretted it. I owe cards a debt of gratitude which it would be hard to pay. When my husband was ill four and a half years I could never banish the impending tragedy from my mind except when I tried to fix it on a game of cards. Even when I did not succeed entirely in doing so, spending an afternoon or an evening with congenial friends at a card game occasionally cheered me greatly and helped me to view more philosophically the visitation of sorrow through which I was passing.

As one grows older, there is nothing which can give her greater pleasure than a card game with friends. A quilting bee would undoubtedly answer the same purpose, but that form of recreation is not so popular as it once was. The need of quilts is not so great now-a-days. To be sure, I am not an expert at cards. I have discovered that there is such a thing as "card sense" which some people naturally possess and some do not. And I am in the latter class. But I enjoy trying to match wits with the gifted ones just the same. I find myself feeling sorry for a woman who does not know the joy of playing cards when she is no longer able to indulge in the more active, strenuous forms of recreation which she enjoyed in her youth.

I feel that my intellectual and social needs have been well ministered to ever since I made Washington my home. I have enjoyed my friends immensely and, generally speaking, I have had a good time. I have worked hard to do my bit, and my efforts have been appreciated as well as I had any right to expect.

Occasionally when I have indulged in a panegyric of Washington society, somebody either in the city or out of it has fixed me with a cold eye and has opined that it is a great pity some of the socialites are not more civic-minded than they are. An unbelievably large number of the leading citizens, says the critic, manifest no interest whatsoever in any effort to promote the welfare of their group. They do not attend meetings called to devise ways and means of removing unjust restrictions imposed upon them and to improve their condition. They do not contribute as largely as they should to charitable organizations. Those who have enjoyed unusual educational facilities, continues our critic, do not attend meetings to which they would be welcome and which would increase their knowledge of science, art, literature, government affairs and other important matters.

I regret that I dare not say each and every one of these charges is false. But I can say that such criticism of leading citizens, both white and black, may be heard in practically every city in the United States.

CHAPTER 41

I ADDRESS THE INTERNATIONAL ASSEMBLY OF THE WORLD FELLOWSHIP OF FAITHS IN LONDON AND MEET HAILE SELASSIE

IN JULY, 1937, I delivered an address before the International Assembly of the World Fellowship of Faiths in London. I had definitely decided I could not accept the invitation for several reasons. My brother had died suddenly in January in New York City and shortly afterwards I had to settle his affairs. In addition to that I had had a severe and stubborn case of bronchitis and had had my tonsils removed in May. The Court appointed me Guardian of my brother's nine-year-old son, Thomas Junior, who seems to have inherited his father's talent for drawing. At twelve years of age he is cartoonist for his school paper, of which he is a member of the editorial staff, has drawn a series of cartoons for it and has written a story.

Late the last Friday night in June, 1937, I showed my daughter Phyllis a letter from Mr. Charles F. Weller, one of the general secretaries of the Fellowship, urging me to come, and saying he was depending upon me to represent my racial group. "Mother," she exclaimed, "do you mean to tell me after receiving such a letter as that you are not going to London? You must go." I felt condemned. But I declared that even if I wanted to go, it was too late to book passage on a steamer that would put me in London by July 7, when Mr. Weller wanted me to extend greetings at the opening meeting. "You must try to get a steamer," insisted my daughter. "Telephone to all the steamship companies the first thing tomorrow morning, and see if you can't get one."

I obeyed my daughter and not a single line had anything to offer which would put me in London July 7. Then I decided it was not intended that I should go. Finally, about noon the telephone rang and a man said "Are you the lady trying to get to London?" "I am," I replied. "Well," said he, "I can guarantee you a berth on the *Aquitania*, which sails next Wednesday at noon." "Where will my cabin be?" I inquired. "Cabin," he said laughing. "You will have no cabin. All I can do is to guarantee you a berth somewhere and that you will reach Southampton July 6. Then you can surely be in London on the 7th.

"I know Saturday is a half holiday," I said, "but please don't close your office till I come for my ticket." I didn't know when I bought the ticket whether I would be put in the kitchen or hang in a hammock till I reached Southampton. But the fates were kind to me and I had a two-berth cabin all to myself.

Even if I had the space to describe such a meeting I could not do it justice. The theme of the whole conference was Peace and Progress Through World Fellowship and no subject which could bear even remotely upon that slogan was omitted. People of all races and religions were there. There were 54 speakers all together: eighteen from America, nineteen from the British Isles, one from Canada, one from Ceylon, two from Germany, one from Hungary, two from Holland, nine from India and one from Mexico. I was greatly interested in the East Indians because the attitude of the English toward that dark race is exactly like that of the dominant race in this country toward colored people. If you had closed your eyes and listened to the speeches of protest made by the East Indians, you might easily have thought you were listening to a colored man describing the conditions in the United States. Several times I was invited to preside over the meetings. And I especially enjoyed having the privilege of introducing Mr. Laurence Housman, author and dramatist, whose play, *Victoria Regina*, has enjoyed such deserved success both in the United States and Great Britain.

I delivered my address the last night of the Assembly.

Viscountess Snowden, widow of the late Chancellor of the Exchequer, invited me to luncheon at the Lancaster Club. And then I received a note from Lady Astor inviting me to tea on the terrace of the House of Commons. Among the eight guests were two southern gentlemen from Virginia, where Lady Astor was born and reared. When I was shown to her Ladyship's table I found her daughter, Lady Willoughby, there receiving the guests for her mother, who was attending a session in the House of Commons. When our hostess came to greet her guests she sat beside me so that I would be on her right. Nothing could be formal or dull in a group where Lady Astor appears. She is full of information and her witticisms drive home clearly and strongly any point she wishes to make. She is too broad to be fettered by race prejudice and she enjoys poking fun at the South every now and then. Owing to the presence of the two southern gentlemen, at first I was afraid to laugh. But when I saw them enjoying Lady Astor's sallies I joined them most heartily. The repast which our hostess had spread before us was delicious.

When she arose to leave she asked me whether I would like to attend the session of Parliament. I assured her I would. Eager as she was to return, she rushed off somewhere to get me a ticket for the "Stranger's Gallery." When I entered I saw a young man speaking. "Do you know who that is?" said a woman who sat next to me. "That is Lady Astor's son." So his distinguished mother reached Parliament just in time to hear her young son address the House of Commons. I appreciated the courtesy shown me by Lady Astor all the more, because she not only left an important session of Parliament to extend it, but ran the risk of being absent when her son spoke. It is hard to imagine a woman more natural, informal, progressive and charming than Lady Astor.

I was glad to accept an invitation to tea extended me by Mr. H. G. Wells, with whom I have been acquainted for more than 25 years and whose hospitality I have enjoyed every time I have been in London. It was a pleasure to meet Miss Philippa Strachey, who is the Secretary of the London and National Society for Women's Service, a very useful and powerful organization. I accepted her invitation to luncheon, but was unable to accept an invitation extended me by the Junior Council of that Society to join the science group on an expedition to the port of London, to which they were going by steamer to cruise the busiest parts of London River and the Royal Albert and King George Docks, because I left London for Southampton the day before they were going, to take the steamer for New York.

But the high point of my latest sojourn in England was my visit with Haile Selassie I, Elect of God, King of Kings, The

Conquering Lion from the Tribe of Judah, Emperor of Ethiopia. He was living in Bath, about an hour and a half's ride by train from London, on a beautiful estate located on an elevation in the suburb of the city. The attendants were expecting me and ushered me immediately into the room where His Majesty receives his visitors. Promptly at 4 o'clock Haile Selassie appeared and greeted me cordially. As soon as this preliminary was over I sat down. Not being accustomed to be ushered into the presence of emperors and kings, I am not at all sure this was the proper caper. Everybody else who came into the room remained standing.

Haile Selassie looks like an aristocrat from his head to his heels. He really looks like a king and is much younger and handsomer than his pictures represent him to be. He conversed with me in French. I do not know whether he speaks English or not. But French is the language used in most of the foreign courts, and I presume he prefers to use it whenever he can. I did not tear passion to tatters, but I told Haile Selassie that rightminded, justice-loving people all over the world considered Italy a highway robber, sympathized deeply with Ethiopia and hoped that some day, somehow, justice would triumph in the end.

Haile Selassie is a philosopher. Without going into details he left me under the impression that he hopes to return to his country and regain his throne. Of course I do not know whether, deep down in his heart, he really believes the fates will smile upon him to that extent or not. But he certainly assumes the attitude of hopefulness rather than that of despair. Fearing I was consuming too much of his time I arose to leave. But he urged me to be seated, said something to his attendant, and soon a man servant brought in tea and dainty little cakes.

The empress and both his daughters were away. One of his daughters was studying to be a nurse in an English institution. The other, whose husband was shot to death by Italians, has two children. Wishing to say something pleasant I referred to the beautiful surroundings in which he was living. In an undertone he made a remark to his attendant in his native language, I presume. Then the attendant said, "Although this is a pretty place, it does not compare with the emperor's palace in Addis Ababa." The ex-Emperor of Ethiopia is a pathetic figure indeed, in spite of the dignity and philosophy with which he accepts his cruel fate.

If an organization of powerful dark races had treated one of its Caucasian members as the League of Nations has treated Haile Selassie, the Hitler Aryans would have cited that as proof positive of the inherent, inevitable cowardice and dishonor of all non-Aryans.

CHAPTER 42

CARRYING ON

I AM STILL CARRYING ON in the same old way, just as busy as a bee all the time, working at one thing and then another, continually wishing I could do some of the things I have longed to do for so many years, and hoping that "after a while" I shall have self-control and grit enough to put aside everything except what I have planned to do "some day."

Instead of slowing down, as a woman who is older than she used to be is supposed to do, I seem to be taking on new responsibilities every day in every way. I do not feel old. I intend never to grow old. My friends are constantly telling me that I must put the soft pedal on some of my activities and I try to take their advice. But I cannot. I am just not built that way. I can walk faster and farther than either one of my daughters without feeling it. And I have greater power of endurance than either one of them has.

I can dance as long and as well as I ever did, although I get very few chances to do so. There seems to be sort of a tradition that after a woman reaches a certain age she should not want to trip the light fantastic, and that even if she is anachronistic enough to wish to do such an unseemly thing, she should not be allowed to indulge in this healthful and fascinating exercise. I believe if a woman could dance or swim a half hour every day, her span of life would be greatly lengthened, her health materially improved and the joy of living decidedly increased.

When I attended the World's Fair in Chicago—the second one for me—I visited my daughter, Mary, who lives there. While the fair was undoubtedly very fine, the exhibits did not interest me as much as did those I saw 40 years before at the first World's Fair. That is easily explained, perhaps. I was a few years older and seeing sights was less a novelty to me in 1933 than it was in 1893. I went to the fair grounds only once with one of my daughters. I preferred to go alone because when I set out to see a huge exhibit covering a wide space I like to look at as many things as possible. I enjoy walking and do not tire easily. My dear daughters do not "take after" their mother in that respect. I feared that if anybody accompanied me on these rounds of sightseeing I might want to walk farther and longer than my companion felt she could or should do. I get more tired "resting" very often than I do continuing my tour till I really feel the necessity of taking a seat.

I was especially interested in the plans for the second World's Fair because some of the officials once thought of making a display of the progress of the Negro in America. While I was in Chicago serving Mrs. Ruth Hanna McCormick (now Mrs. Simms) as director of work among the colored women of Illinois during her senatorial primary campaign, I was requested by Dr. Allen D. Albert to give him the names of ten or twelve outstanding colored men who would be invited to serve on the committee designated to make plans for the display. I complied with this request and was introduced to Mr. Rufus C. Dawes, the President of the Chicago World's Fair Centennial Celebration, 1933, by Dr. Albert, his assistant. Mr. Julius Rosenwald was also interested in this matter. But, for some reason, the plan did not materialize and there was no display showing the progress made by the colored people of this country.

My public work is still going on. Several times in recent years I have appeared before committees in Congress to urge the necessity of passing the anti-lynching bill. "What effect do you think lynching will have upon the white women of the South?" somebody asked me. "We all believe in heredity," I replied. "There is no escape from that. More than once white women in the South have applied the torch to burn colored men to death. Those women are being brutalized by the crimes in which they themselves participate. Their children will undoubtedly inherit the brutal instinct from their mothers and it will be more difficult to stop lynching on that account."

At a hearing before a committee on public building and grounds I recently urged Congress to appropriate a sum of money with which to buy a site and erect a building in which colored people may have a place where they can give tangible evidence of their contributions to the growth and prosperity of this country as well as furnish proof of the marvellous progress which they have made themselves. The colored soldiers have fought with a patriotism and died with a courage surpassed by none. Although the first blood spilled for the independence of this country was shed by Crispus Attucks, a colored man, who was the first to lead the American patriots against the British troops and fought desperately for the independence of the Colonies till the enemy shot him down, there is not a public building in the capital of the nation for which Crispus Attucks fought and died in which his statue or that of any other hero of African descent may be placed. In not a single building of the Federal Government may colored people hang a picture or place a statue or bust of the representatives of their group who have distinguished themselves in science, literature, art, industry or in any other field of human endeavor.

I did not cultivate the habit of interviewing Congressmen, but when it seemed necessary and wise I did not hesitate to do so. Sometimes I went alone and sometimes I went with a delegation. I learned once that there was an Anti-Intermarriage Bill in Congress which would make it illegal for white and colored people to intermarry in any State of the Union. Although I have never advocated intermarriage of the races, I have always stoutly maintained that marriage is a question which should be settled by the individual and not by the State. Five colored women, including myself, decided to talk to Senator Capper of Kansas, who introduced the bill and who, we knew, was and is friendly and just to our group. We told him that the bill was objectionable because it would deprive a colored woman of protection, no matter what a man of any other racial group might do to injure her. Senator Capper was greatly surprised to learn from our small delegation that he had introduced an Anti-Intermarriage Bill. He had been requested by a large organization, he said, to introduce a bill which would make the laws bearing on divorce the same in all the States—a National Divorce Bill— and he thought he had done so. He did not know that hidden away in that bill was a provision preventing intermarriage of the races. This bill died at the end of that session of Congress and it was not introduced again by Senator Capper.

It is pleasant to recall that the first time I went to the White

House to see a President of the United States I went with Frederick Douglass to urge President Harrison to speak out boldly against lynching in his annual message. Since then I have been to see every President who has sat in the White House except Woodrow Wilson. I have not yet seen President Franklin Roosevelt, but Mrs. Roosevelt has granted me a personal interview in the White House which was greatly appreciated.

During the Sesquicentennial Exposition held in Philadelphia I took part in a pageant which was given in an auditorium that seated 16,000 people. Every seat was occupied and scarcely standing room was left. "Loyalty's Gift" was undoubtedly one of the finest evidences of progress made by the colored people of this country which has ever been witnessed. With appropriate music and costumes, the history of the African was presented from the beginning—his enslavement in this country—and his progress since he was emancipated from bondage. Especially interesting was the achievement scene, in which persons who had won special distinction, or who had been pioneers in race movements, were mentioned and appeared in person when the roll was called.

My heart beat faster and my pulse was considerably quickened when I received a letter dated January 14, 1928, from my alma mater. "For this year's *Hi-O-Hi*, which is published in May," it read, "we are using as a motif the contribution of Oberlin's alumni to the world. Your name is on the list of 100 famous alumni, some of whose pictures we are planning to work into one section of the book. Would it be possible for you to send us a photograph of yourself? As it is rather late and near the closing time of our engraving copy we would appreciate it greatly if you could give attention to this soon. Thanking you in advance for your courtesy, I remain, yours very truly, Margaret L. Heimbach, alumni editor."

When the National Association of Colored Women celebrated its thirty-second anniversary, the opening meeting was held in the church in which it was organized in 1896 and in which I was elected its first president. I was invited to preside over part of the session. I thanked God that my life had been spared so long and that I had lived to see the organization reach such wonderful proportions. Its development and growth, for which, together with other women, I had worked so hard, seemed like a miracle of modern times, as I listened to the reports of some of the things which had been done.

Commissioner Hazen, who is president of the Board of Commissioners of the District of Columbia, made me a member of the Advisory Council on Playgrounds and Recreation several years ago. It was the duty of this council to advise with the commissioners on affairs relating to the administration of playgrounds and to study proposals offered for the unification of recreation for the District of Columbia. I was also appointed a member of the District of Columbia Advisory Committee on Women's Participation in the New York World's Fair, 1939-40.

For a long time I was president of the Southwest Community House, a character building institution, in a section of the National Capital where little is being done for colored people living there, compared with efforts exerted in behalf of their group in other parts of the city. If I should start to talk about the clubs and the work done there for the children for whom this house is conducted, I should not know where to stop.

Until recently I was secretary of the Race Relations Committee of the Washington Federation of Churches, of which Canon Phelps Stokes was chairman for a long time. This committee is trying to establish a better understanding between the two races in the National Capital and to make it possible for colored people to enjoy some of the privileges of which they are deprived. With Canon Stokes as chairman, a committee composed exclusively of white people called upon the managers of several theatres in an effort to remove restrictions imposed upon colored people. While the committee did not succeed in this undertaking, their effort was commendable just the same.

Under the auspices of this Race Relations Committee a study of the housing conditions of colored people was made and the facts thus obtained were published in book form. Partly as a result of this effort made by our committee, the slums are being cleared and the people living in the alleys, 90 percent of whom are colored, are being moved to more sanitary and decent quarters.

During the celebration of the George Washington Bi-Centennial I wrote a pageant based on the life of Phyllis Wheatley, a slave, to whom the Father of His Country was courteous and kind. I wanted to show colored children that George Washington had done something commendable for a representative of their group, so that they would feel they had at least one reason to revere his memory as the children of other groups did. As a rule, colored people have no great love for George Washington because from their youth up they are taught that he was a slaveholder.

When I was a member of the Board of Education and was invited to speak to the colored children of the public schools on Washington's birthday, I always impressed upon them that George Washington was a victim of his environment and that he was a slaveholder because it was the custom of his section of the country and of his time and that he freed his slaves in his will.

Phyllis Wheatley greatly admired George Washington, wrote a poem in his honor and sent it to him. When he replied to her letter he addressed the young slave as "Miss Phyllis," complimented her on her talent as a poetess and closed his letter by saying: "If you ever come to Cambridge or near headquarters, I shall be happy to see a person so favored by the muses and to whom nature has been so liberal and beneficent in her dispensations. I am with great respect, your obedient, humble servant, George Washington."

This was clearly and strongly brought out in my pageant, so that colored children might see that although the Father of His Country was a slaveholder, in accordance with the deplorable custom of his time, nevertheless, he was broad-minded, generous-hearted and just enough to give credit where credit was due, to make written acknowledgement of the talent of an African girl and to pay homage to her while she was still being held as a slave.

This pageant was produced by the pupils of the public schools of Washington for colored children, assisted by a few citizens. Mrs. Marie Moore Forrest, who is recognized as an expert in this field, directed it. The District of Columbia George Washington Bi-Centennial Commission donated $1,000 to defray the expenses incident to staging it. The pageant also was produced by the Booker T. Washington Junior High School of Baltimore.

Mr. Cloyd H. Marvin, who is president of the George Washington University in Washington, D. C., and was also president of the District of Columbia George Washington Bi-Centennial Commission, sent me the following letter, dated January 31, 1933:

"My dear Mrs. Terrell: On behalf of the District of Columbia George Washington Bi-Centennial Commission it is my pleasure to transmit to you under separate cover, a copy of the report of the commission in which I know you will be interested.

"Further, on behalf of our commission, it is my privilege to acknowledge your splendid cooperation and to call to your attention what the commission believes to be your outstanding service to the community. There is not one member of the commission but what feels that a great deal has been added to our citizenship by your splendid effort by bringing closer to this generation the principles for which the father of this nation stood.

"To this letter may I add my own personal expression of appreciation.

"Sincerely yours,

"CLOYD H. MARVIN."

During the Hoover campaign in 1932 for the second time the Republican National Committee appointed me director of work among the colored women of the East. My office was in the beautiful Waldorf Astoria Hotel in New York City and the work which I did was similar to that which was performed in 1920, right after the woman suffrage amendment was passed, when Mr. Harding, the Republican candidate, was elected by a large majority.

I am still interested in Howard University, Miner Teachers' College and the other public schools in Washington. I am still being invited to address these institutions, and I always cheerfully accept the invitations. In 1939 I was very busy when the seventy-fifth anniversary of establishing public schools for colored children in the District of Columbia was celebrated.

For many years there was nothing I enjoyed more than beautifying and looking after my home. But housekeeping finally began to pall on my taste and to get on my nerves more and more. I found myself regretting that even though I had employed some help, so much of my own time and strength had been consumed in cooking, dishwashing, sweeping, dusting, painting woodwork and sewing instead of being devoted to activities for which I had trained myself and which appealed more strongly to my taste. I have heard other women say that, as the years crept upon them, they were affected in a similar way. It is comforting, therefore, to feel that I am no exception to a general rule in this respect, even though, because I dislike housework, some may think I am an awful example of what a nice, old lady should not be.

For six months I worked for the Emergency Relief Division in Washington, doing first one kind of clerical work and then another. Then the head of the department told me he had been ordered to reduce the force and for that reason my services would be dispensed with the first of August, 1934. I was the only colored woman working on the files at that time and I was the only woman dismissed. And then, in trying to get employment elsewhere I had to swallow the same bitter dose of race prejudice in my old days that I did in my youth.

Several days before my appointment expired the man who had charge of the division where I worked told me he would help me get another job which would pay me more. I knew he had asked to have me work in his department and would have kept me if it had been possible. "I have strongly recommended you," he said, "and the man to whom I am sending you needs clerks. He will be glad to take you." I did not have the courage to inquire whether my chief, who was a northern man, had mentioned the little matter of my race, while he was setting forth my qualifications to my prospective employer, but I took it for granted that he had. I would not allow myself to go with fear and trembling to the man I was told would employ me, although I was beset by doubts. I called upon all the Christian Science and Unity that I knew and "held on to the thought" with a kind of desperate tenacity.

It was not easy to see the man for whom I was searching. At first I was told that he was not in. But when I reported that Mr. W. had made a definite engagement for me at 9 o'clock that morning I was directed to the place where he could be found. I had to walk down a very long room full of clerks, all of whom were white and most of them women. To me that was painfully significant. When I reached the man to whom I had been sent for a personal interview I told him what I had been instructed by my chief to say. The gentleman was courteous and attentive, but he informed me immediately he had all the clerks he needed.

When I reported this ultimatum to my chief he said he

would speak to the head of that department again. He kept his promise and after he had seen him he told me that I had made "a very fine impression upon him" and repeated something complimentary he had said about my "personality," "my bearing," my "evident fitness for the job," but he could not employ me. "What reason did he assign for not employing me in his department, since he says he needs clerks?" I inquired. "He gave no reason at all. He simply said he couldn't take you."

When my chief requested the director of the department to employ me he evidently had not thought that the fact that I am a colored woman would prevent me from getting the job, and he was greatly embarrassed—too much so to admit frankly why I was rejected. But we both understood what was the trouble perfectly.

I do not mean to say that there are no colored women employed in the various activities in which the Government is engaged to cure the depression and restore conditions to normalcy. But I do say there are very, very few, and that it is exceedingly difficult for a colored woman to secure employment, no matter what her fitness may be, what service she may have rendered her community or her country and no matter how great her need.

I am well aware that the inability to secure employment for its citizens without regard to race, religion or sex is a vexatious problem which not only the United States, but nearly all the countries in the world are trying to solve today. But the average broad-minded citizen in this country does not know or does not realize that for every difficulty experienced by a white woman or a white man seeking a way to earn his or her daily bread, at least 50 times that many confront his brothers and sisters of a darker hue. Colored people are the last to be hired and the first to be fired. Nobody conversant with existing conditions can doubt or dispute it. This is one of the things which make me apprehensive of the future. If the discrimination against colored people in the various pursuits and occupations continues much longer I fear that the youth of our group may become so discouraged that they will no longer try to secure as thorough an education as possible, or to fit themselves properly for any particular pursuit. I could relate many conversations I have had with our young people which show that this state of mind is getting to be alarmingly common among them.

Another fear haunts me constantly. I fear the youth of the

race may lose their faith in religion, unless the church takes a more active part in trying to bring about a better understanding between the racial groups and is itself more careful to avoid discriminating against colored people. Faith in religion has been a great factor in helping to make the race patient throughout its sufferings during slavery and its grueling struggles, since it was emancipated.

But I am constantly meeting young men and women, particularly those in high schools and colleges, who express themselves as being very skeptical about the church's attitude toward them. "I don't see how you, as an intelligent woman, can have any faith in religion or the church," said a young man to me after the officers of the Sunday School Convention which met in Washington a few years ago had refused to allow colored children to march in the parade and to seat colored delegates. I told the young man that "God is no respecter of persons," and that the officials who had excluded colored children from the Sunday School Convention parade and who had refused to seat the colored delegates were not acting according to the principles either of the Christian church or of the Christian religion. I hope that the church will do everything in its power to increase the faith of the youth of our group in its desire to help the race rather than generate doubts and distrust in their minds by discriminations of any kind. "Do you know?" a young girl challenged me not long ago, "that the Christian church is the only one in the world which discriminates against its members on account of the color of their skin?" "That is not the fault of the church," I replied, "but it is the fault of those who administer the affairs of the church."

In writing the story of my life I might have related many more incidents than I have, showing my discouragement and despair at the obstacles interposed and the limitations placed upon me because I am a colored woman. Several times I have been desperate and wondered which way I should turn. I have purposely refrained from entering too deeply into particulars and emphasizing this phase of my life. I have given the bitter with the sweet, the sweet predominating, I think. While I have presented the barriers raised against my entering certain pursuits and the difficulties encountered in an effort to buy a home which we needed and which appealed to my taste, I have also given a faithful account of the opportunities afforded me to develop what talent I may have possessed. Some people will feel, perhaps, that I have reveled too much in the fact that I have been able to accomplish as much as I have in spite of the prejudice encountered because of both my race and my sex. Colored women are the only group in this country who have two heavy handicaps to overcome, that of race as well as that of sex. Colored men have only one handicap to hurdle—that of race.

But if I had failed to relate the success I have been able to achieve, largely because broad-minded representatives of the dominant race gave me a chance to make good, I should have been accused of ingratitude. And justly so. Now that I have done so, some people will declare I have been trying to tell the world how "smart" I am, and will call me a conceited prig. It is impossible to strike the golden mean. No matter what I say I shall be accused either of "whining" too much or of boasting too much.

I have not referred to the attacks made upon me several times by white men who were angry with me and who were determined to punish me for some fancied offense. I shall relate just two of these experiences. I boarded a street car in Washington one day with my arm full of bundles. I was on my way to Opequon, a little summer resort near Winchester, Va., to join my small daughters. There was ample space for me to sit between two white men, but neither one of them would move an inch. I requested them politely to do so, but they refused to budge. Then I seated myself in the space anyway, for I could no longer stand up holding the bundles.

Both of the men became very angry because I sat down, and one of them talked loudly about "a nigger woman daring to sit by me," and he said he had a good mind to slap me. He was about to do so, when a colored woman with whom I was not acquainted and have never seen since remonstrated with him and warned the men they "would get into a lot of trouble" if they struck me. Then they desisted. But there was not a man in that car who came to my defense. I am sure that if an Indian woman, or a Japanese woman or a woman of any other dark race had been bullied in that way by two men, some gentleman in the car would have come to her defense.

On another occasion, I was in a street car alone and rang the bell to stop it. It passed the corner, however, without stopping and I rang again. Just before I reached the door to leave the car, the conductor caught hold of me roughly, pushed me toward the door and tore my dress badly, as I tried to loosen his hold. In some parts of the country I would have been arrested for "disturbing the peace," or for "disorderly conduct," fined, perhaps, or sent to jail. The word of a colored woman, no matter what her standing in the community may be, counts for nothing against the word of a white man or woman, no matter what or who they may be, in many parts of the United States. This is one of the reasons why statistics showing the number of colored people arrested and convicted is so much larger in proportion to their number than are those for other groups.

My daughter and I, accompanied by a fine musician, who was an instructor in Howard University, went to hear a concert in the Scottish Rite Temple, which is considered one of the sights of the Capital. An unusually fine pipe organ was to be used for the first time, and we were all eager to hear it. After the concert the audience was invited to inspect certain parts of the Temple which were thrown open to the public. As we were about to enter one of the rooms, an attendant rudely ordered us away. I told him we had come because the newspapers had stated that the public was invited to inspect the Temple. He caught hold of me and would have pushed me down a long flight of stone steps in front of the building if I had not wrenched myself from his grasp with a strength born of fright and desperation, just before he had dragged me to the edge.

In November, 1930, President Hoover called a Child Welfare Conference, which was held in Washington, and I attended it. Two of my friends came from the South as delegates. At noon one day they told me they were hungry and asked me where they could get a bite to eat. They had had nothing since the previous afternoon, they said. I was greatly embarrassed, for the sessions of the conference were held in Constitution Hall, which is in a section of the Capital where there are no restaurants kept by those who will serve colored people.

I explained the situation to my friends, one of whom was a teacher in Tuskegee and the other the wife of a distinguished physician in Atlanta, Ga. I did not mind being refused myself, I told my friends, but it would pain me to see them humiliated. Then they said they had already asked a colored porter in the building where they could get something to eat and he had directed them to the cafeteria across the street from Constitution Hall. I felt certain that my friends would not be served there and I told them so. But they insisted that the colored porter must have known what he was talking about and were eager to go. I had eaten a late breakfast and I did not intend to get lunch. But it seemed very ungracious on my part, as a resident of the National Capital, not to be willing to take strangers across the street to satisfy their hunger.

I went ahead, entered the cafeteria, took the tray, put some silver on it and asked the colored woman who was serving to give me a sandwich and a cup of coffee. They did not serve sandwiches and coffee at that counter, she said, but I could get them at the lunch counter in the hall. Then I told my friends to take what they wanted. I waited till they had put the food on the trays and had started to take a seat at a nearby table. Feeling sure that everything was all right I went out of the room to get my sandwich and coffee at the lunch counter in the hall, so that I could return to my friends and have lunch with them. I told the colored woman who had served me that I would take my tray into the cafeteria, so that I might be with my friends who were having their meal there.

"You can go into the cafeteria, all right," said the woman, "but you won't find your friends in there. They are over there in the hall." "You are mistaken," I replied. "I was with them in the cafeteria when they were served and saw them go to a table." "Yes, ma'am," said the woman, "maybe you did see them go to a table, but they show didn't sit down, for they are right out there this minute in that hall." I looked where she was pointing, and sure enough there they were!

"Why did you leave the cafeteria?" I inquired. "Well," said one of my friends, "a woman who seemed to have charge of the cafeteria told us that colored people could not sit at the table there and that we must eat upstairs. I told her we were delegates to the Child Welfare Conference which had been called by President Hoover and thought we could eat in a building owned by the United States Government. 'That makes no difference,' she replied, 'you cannot eat in here!' So we put our trays down and left. We did not want to have any trouble."

As we were talking in the hall, one of my friends looked up and exclaimed, "There is the woman who told us we could not take seats at a table in the cafeteria." I went up to her and asked her if she had refused to let my friends eat their lunch in the cafeteria. "Yes, I did," she replied with a great deal of emphasis. "Colored people must go up stairs." "Well, that cafeteria is in a building owned by the United States Government," I said, "and my friends and I are going to be served in it right away." I invited the two women to come with me and I went into the cafeteria, put the food I had selected on the tray and took my seat at an unoccupied table. The women refused to follow me, but returned hungry to Constitution Hall, which, ironically enough, is named for that very instrument that has an amendment granting them the privilege of eating in that cafeteria, but which is violated in the National Capital every day in the week and every minute in the day.

Just as I was finishing my meal and was about to arise from the table I saw a policeman standing in the door, looking at me. I knew immediately the woman had sent for him to intimidate me. I waited till he came to the table. He stood there beside me without saying a word. Several craned their necks to see what was about to happen. There are many people in Washington coming from other cities who do not know that colored people cannot eat in cafeterias and restaurants where white people are served. "Why did you come in here, Mr. Officer?" I inquired. "Oh, I just came in to see what was going on," he replied. "No, I beg your pardon," I said, "you came in here to intimidate me, and here I am right here for you." "You haven't broken any law, have you?" "No," I agreed, "I haven't broken any law, but you came in here for me just the same." Then I arose and started toward the door. I left the room with the officer walking beside me. When we reached the hall I saw the woman who had undoubtedly sent for the policeman and we exchanged a few sharp words with each other, while the policeman listened to us in silence. It had been rumored that I was being arrested and the colored waitresses gathered in one of the hall doors to witness the spectacle. Seeing me walking along with the policeman they took it for granted that what they had heard was true. The policeman walked with me down what seemed to me an interminable corridor. I asked him the name of the woman who had charge of the cafeteria. He gave it to me very obligingly and we bade each other good-bye.

I went to the Secretary of President Hoover and to the Secretary of the Interior, Dr. Ray Lyman Wilbur, and related the story to them. But I have heard nothing from either one of them up to date. I was advised against instituting a law suit for damages in this case, as I was in another. A colored woman who sues a white individual or a white firm has only a slight chance to win her case. For that reason when the firm whose truck wrecked my automobile and broke my kneecap offered to settle out of court, after the first trial resulted in a hung jury, I accepted the sum paid me, although it was ridiculously small. It did not even cover my surgeon's bill. My husband was in the hospital, paralyzed at the time, and I could not force myself to carry the litigation any further. My lawyer was a Jew. And I am colored. With a fatal combination like that one or two members of the Ku Klux Klan sitting on a jury would have made it impossible for me to win. Colored people seldom mention incidents showing they are denied service in restaurants, refused accommodations in hotels, or are insulted or assaulted by the dominant race. They have a sort of pride which makes them feel it is a reflection upon themselves to let anybody know they have been humiliated or discriminated against and they prefer to keep these painful facts to themselves.

And now I am about to confess something which I hesitate to admit, because I may be misunderstood. I should like to belong to several organizations in Washington from which I am excluded on account of my race. I should like to join them, not because the members are all white, but because they were formed to consider things in which I am deeply interested and to plan work which I should like to do. One of them is a literary organization. I would have derived great benefit from the discussions in which these women have engaged and from the methods of doing their work which they have used. I would have received many valuable points which I need and which would have helped me.

I can more than fulfill all the requirements for admission to this literary league. In fact, I have more of these requirements than some who are members. I lack only one. I am not white. If I could have joined it I would have been benefited by the atmosphere which is always created when people of similar tastes meet together and exchange points of view. American artists go abroad, not because there are no teachers in this country capable of instructing them, but because they feel the need of living in an atmosphere conducive to developing and encouraging their talent. It is hard to create an atmosphere all by one's self, as a spider spins his web from the silk glands within him. And atmosphere means so much to the success of an individual who is trying to do creative work. Over and over again I have wished I lived some place in which people would be received on their merit in organizations they wished to join and not be excluded on account of their race.

I thought I was actually living in such a city when I opened my mail one bright October morning a little more than a year ago and received a pressing invitation to join the largest woman's club in the city. I could scarcely believe my eyes, for I knew colored women were not admitted to this club. But I also knew that the day of miracles had not entirely passed. I could not see how the membership committee could fail to know that I am a colored woman. There was my name in full with the proper address. I have been working actively in Washington for years and I am well acquainted with many of the women who belong to this club. However, I called up headquarters several times, said I had received the invitation, was glad to get it and agreed that it would be a decided advantage to me to join the club, as the invitation stated.

But I waited a while before sending my check. Even though in my case I did not see how the membership committee could have made a mistake, nevertheless, with a woman's intuition I was uncomfortable. The officer who acknowledged the check wrote me the following letter with her own hand: "Dear Mrs. Terrell: So glad to welcome you as a member of the Women's ————— Club. I hope you will use the club this coming winter and enjoy our many interesting activities. Drop into tea this Sunday, November 8, 4:30. A very lovely program I'm sure you would enjoy. I am answering your letter in Mrs. W's absence. I would appreciate if you would send me for our club records your phone number, business address, if any; Miss or Mrs. I am enclosing a bulletin for November. I hope to meet you very soon. Sincerely yours, (Mrs.) M—————, Secretary-Manager."

Inclosed in this cordial letter was a card of admission. I accepted the invitation to the tea Sunday evening and enjoyed the musical program very much. I talked with several women whom I have known for years. One of them was the president of the club, the widow of a man whose name a few years ago was a household word among those interested in pure food and pure drugs. Three days after the Sunday evening tea I received the following typewritten letter: "My dear Mrs. Terrell: According to the By-Laws of the Women's ———— Club, the names of proposed members must be accepted unanimously by the Board of Directors. I am sorry to say your application has not received the necessary approval of the board. I am therefore returning your check in the amount of $12.50. Very truly yours, Membership Committee."

In the first place, I did not make an application. I simply accepted an invitation to become a member. It never occurred to me that a fine organization like the one which turned me down would invite a woman to become a member without knowing her pedigree from start to finish—especially her race affiliation, since that, of course, was of paramount importance. A short while after my check was returned I met the president of the club and told her how sorry I was that I had accepted the invitation of the membership committee and emphasized the fact that I did not apply for membership myself. I felt it would be narrow and ungracious for me to decline the invitation, I said, if the club had decided to be broad and just enough to include in its membership colored women whom they deemed worthy and capable enough to join. The president expressed genuine regret that the mistake was made.

Under no circumstances would I force myself into a club whose members would object to my presence because I am a colored woman. I have too much self respect for that. But every now and then I find myself wishing that my lines had been cast in some pleasant place where I might have joined a few organizations which would have been an education to me and an inspiration at the same time. Knowing that I am barred from them on account of my race, I bow to the inevitable as philosophically as I can.

There are many cases of assault and battery committed upon the feelings and self respect of colored people and I am no exception to a general rule. Assault and battery committed upon a human being's soul often leave wounds which are deeper and more painful than are those inflicted upon the body, while they are harder to heal and do greater harm.

On one occasion I was invited to become a member of a Committee which decided to do something to see that the law was better enforced in the National Capital than it had been. A dinner at the Mayflower Hotel was planned to launch the movement and I was invited to attend. Several times I had been invited to dinners on similar occasions and since I was eager to hear the speakers who were to outline the plans for the new organization established in behalf of law enforcement and justice, I sent my check for three dollars, as I was requested to do. The day on which the dinner was to be given, my door bell rang about noon. The man who had come to see me told me he had been sent to ask me not to attend the dinner that night and he handed me my check. "I have already received the ticket for the dinner," I said. "Why are you returning my check?" "It is feared," he explained, "that a number of people might leave the room immediately, if they knew colored people were seated at a table."

I asked the man if other colored people had been invited to attend the dinner. He told me he had made the same request of two colored men, both prominent; one of them was an ex-judge of the Municipal Court and the other was holding an important position in a well-known university and was an assistant to the Secretary of War during the World War. I was shocked and humiliated, of course. After the man left I called up one of my white friends and related the incident to her. She evidently got busy right away and phoned the wife of the wealthy Jew who was at the head of this organization, telling her how unjust it was to humiliate the two colored men and me by practically forbidding us to attend the dinner to which we had been invited by people organized to enforce the law and promote justice in the Courts, after our checks had been accepted and the tickets to the dinner had been sent to us.

Something evidently happened as the result of this protest. The dinner was to be given at eight o'clock. And just about two minutes before eight one of the colored men phoned me that the wife of the chief promoter of the organization had called him to ask him to escort me to the dinner and to sit at her table. But I could not generate enough spirit and courage to go. Even if I had, by the time I had dressed and reached the hotel it would have been too late to enter the dining room without attracting the attention of the guests to my escort and myself, and I was not willing to pass through such an ordeal under the circumstances.

[424]

In striking contrast to the exhibitions of prejudice to which I have just referred was the action taken by the Washington Branch of the Oberlin Alumnae Association. On Tuesday, January 23, 1934, it "Voted Unanimously to Request the President of Oberlin College, Oberlin, Ohio, to Confer an Honorary Degree upon Mary Church Terrell for the Services She Has Rendered Her Race and for the Efforts She Has Made to Create a Better Understanding and Feeling between the Two Races in the United States."

Since Oberlin had named me as "one of its one hundred most famous alumni" shortly before it celebrated its one hundredth anniversary, the Association believed it would confer the degree which was requested. I was not a member of the Association and was, of course, not at the meeting when the motion was passed.

Some of the Trustees of Oberlin College wrote a friend who was very much interested in the matter that they voted for the degree and regretted that it was not conferred. I am very grateful to them, to the Washington Branch of the Oberlin Alumnae Association and to my dear friend for the efforts they made in my behalf, even though they failed.

In the midst of a brilliant career my husband was suddenly stricken and remained an invalid for four years. After a union of thirty years we were finally separated by death. Since then I have been carrying on alone. Throughout his illness he was a philosopher. No man ever bore a similar affliction more cheerfully than he did. I did not realize until he had passed away how dependent upon him I was for information of every kind. About matters pertaining to the Government, to politics and to every phase of the Race Problem he was a veritable encyclopedia. Now that he is gone it is very gratifying to see the estimate placed upon him by those among whom he lived and labored. Two schools have been named for him—the Terrell Junior High School and the Robert H. Terrell Law School.

A few years ago the members of the Delta Sigma Theta Sorority of Howard University, which made me an honorary member, requested me to write a creed for them. I complied and embodied in it the following rules of conduct by which, I think, every colored woman in the United States should try to guide her life. With varying success mixed with failure I have attempted to abide by the following precepts myself.

I will strive to reach the highest educational, moral and spiritual efficiency which I can possibly attain.

I will never lower my aims for any temporary benefit which might be gained.

I will endeavor to preserve my health, for, however great one's mental and moral strength may be, physical weakness prevents the accomplishment of much that might otherwise be done.

I will close my ears and seal my lips to slanderous gossip.

I will labor to ennoble the ideals and purify the atmosphere of the home.

I will always protest against the double standard of morals.

I will take an active interest in the welfare of my country, using my influence toward the enactment of laws for the protection of the unfortunate and weak and for the repeal of those depriving human beings of their privileges and rights.

I will never belittle my race, but encourage all to hold it in honor and esteem.

I will not shrink from undertaking what seems wise and good, because I labor under the double handicap of race and sex; but, striving to preserve a calm mind with a courageous, cheerful spirit, barring bitterness from my heart, I will struggle all the more earnestly to reach the goal.

Considering that I have lived in a country in which my race is regarded as inferior, whose representatives are terribly circumscribed and limited in various ways and are socially ostracized in the bargain, I have had a fairly fortunate existence and my lot might have been much harder, I must confess. Early in life I realized that a wonderful opportunity was presented to me of rendering valuable service to my own group which needed it. This has helped me face many unpleasant situations and cruel rebuffs with a kind of rebellious resignation and a more or less genuine smile.

I have sometimes taken advantage of my ability to get certain necessities and comforts and I have occasionally availed myself of opportunities to which I was entitled by outwitting those who are obsessed with race prejudice and would have withheld them from me, if they had been perfectly sure of my racial status. But never once in my life have I even been tempted to "cross the color line" and deny my racial identity. I could not have maintained my self respect if I had continuously masqueraded as being something I am not.

So far as possible, I have tried to forget the limitations imposed upon me on account of my race and have gone ahead striving to accomplish what I wanted to do. But always before me, written in letters of flaming, inextinguishable light, was that mandate like unto the laws of the Medes and Persians which warned me: "Thus far shalt thou go and no farther."

Finally, I want to insist again with all the emphasis that I can command that I have never allowed myself to become bitter. Naturally, I have been pained and grieved that a powerful group of human beings has limited my activities and has prevented me from entering fields in which I should have liked to work. But the blow has been greatly softened by the efforts which broad-minded, justice-loving representatives of that group have made to give me a fair chance and a square deal. If it had not been my good fortune to come into contact with such people, my life would scarcely have been worth living, and I would have been a miserable woman indeed.

While I am grateful for the blessings which have been bestowed upon me and for the opportunities which have been offered, I cannot help wondering sometimes what I might have become and might have done if I had lived in a country which had not circumscribed and handicapped me on account of my race, but had allowed me to reach any height I was able to attain.

INDEX

A

Addams, Jane, 153, 154, 330, 331, 334, 352, 361-364.
Addis, Ababa, 405.
Adler, Dr. Felix, 181.
Aelioian, Society, Oberlin College, 44, 221.
Ætna Building, Washington, D. C., 250.
African Society, England, 351-352.
African Prince, Paris, 83.
Afro-American, 222.
L'Agonie et la Mort des Races, Finot, 338.
Agricultural College, England, 218.
Albert, Dr. Allen D., 408.
Allies, First World War, 325.
Colored Soldiers, 325.
A. M. E. Church Review, 222.
Amendments, Fourteenth and Fifteenth, 99, 167.
Amendment, Nineteenth, Woman Suffrage, 310, 413.
Amenia Conference, 195.
American Express Company, 348.
American Missionary Society, 171, 184.
American Magazine, 233.
Anderson, James Hall; Dover, Delaware, 313.
Anderson, Marian, 387.
Anson, Academy, 293, 294.
Anti-Lynching Bureau, Director, 182.
Anthony, Mary, 145, 169.
Anthony, Susan B., 143, 144, 145, 146, 169, 182, 200, 245. Memorial Meeting, 182.
Anti-Intermarriage Bill, 409.
Anti-Slavery and Aborigines Society, England, 352.
Appropriation Committee of Congress, 140.
Aquitania, 402.
Argonne Forest, 347.
Arnold, Matthew, 41.
Arms Limitation Conference, 340.
Associated Press Report, 183.
Astor, Lady, 403, 404.
Atlanta Constitution, 227.
Atlanta University, 191.
Attucks, Crispus, 161, 409.
"Aunt Liza," Grandmother, Eliza Ayres, 10.
Austrian Reporter, 202.

B

Baker, Ray Stannard, 233.
Balch, Emily, 333.
Ball Rent Act, 266-267.
Baltimore, High School, 367-370.
Commencement Address, 369.
"Race Problem and the War," 367, 368.

Comptroller of Baltimore, 370.
Baltimore-American, 368-370.
Bank of England, 165.
Baptist Woman's Home Missionary Society, 226.
Bar Association, District of Columbia, 261.
Barber, Max, 222-223.
Voice of the Negro, 222.
John Brown, 222.
"Being a Colored Woman in the United States," 229.
Bénédit, Monsieur, Paris, France, 210.
Berea College, 41.
Berlin, Germany, 73-80, 84-90, 197-199, 201-209.
Bethel Literary and Historical Society, 400.
Bethune, Mary McLeod, 370.
Biloxi, Miss., 323-325.
Bishop of Canterbury, 315.
Bismarck, 205.
Blackwell, Alice Stone, 145.
Blackwell, Henry, 145.
Blatch, Harriet Stanton, 145, 169.
Blessing, Academy, 293.
Boas, Professor, Columbia University, 181.
Board of Education, District of Columbia, 127-146, 158, 233, 266, 271, 359-360, 400, 412.
Boissevain, Inez Milholland, 212.
Bone, Scott, 193.
Booklovers', Club, 399.
Booth, Maud Ballington, 159, 162.
Boston Globe, 223.
Boston Guardian, 341.
Boston Herald, 228.
Boston Transcript, 146, 229.
Boutté, Captain, 346, 347.
Boyden, Philip, 233.
Brewer, Justice, United States Supreme Court, 171.
Briggs, Dean, Harvard University, 178.
Bright Side of a Dark Subject, the, 160, 163.
Brooklyn Institute of Arts and Sciences, 180, 181.
Brown, John, 239.
Brown, Private, 272.
Brownsville, Texas, 268-276.
Bruce, Senator, B. K., 49, 50.
Bruce, Mrs. B. K., 49, 50.
Bryan, William Jennings, 159.
Bryn Mawr, College, 177.
Buffalo Convention, National Association of Colored Women, 153.
Bulletin, the, 261.

[429]

Bunting, Mr., Editor, Contemporary Review, 213.
Burt, Brigadier General A. B., 273, 274, 279.
Burton, Senator Theodore, 264-265.

C

Cafeteria in Washington, D. C., 419.
Calhoun Club, Boston, 183.
Campaign, primary, senatorial, Illinois, 355-358.
Canada, 355.
Capitol, Washington, D. C., 384.
Capper, Senator Arthur, 409.
Carpenter, Secretary to Secretary of War, Taft, 269.
Caswell-Brewster School, 291.
Catt, Carrie Chapman, 145, 362.
Census Bureau, Washington, D. C., 256-258. Resign, 258.
Centenary, Harriet Beecher Stowe, 279-281.
Centennial Exposition, Philadelphia, 22.
Chancellor of the British Exchequer, 334, 352.
Charleston, South Carolina, 376.
Chattanooga, Tenn., Club for Colored Soldiers, 321.
Chautauquas, 160.
Chesapeake Bay, 239, 347.
Chicago Biennial, National Association of Colored Women, 125-156.
Chicago Daily News, 152.
Chicago Defender, 222.
Chicago, Illinois, 356-358.
Chicago Times-Herald, 152.
Chicago, Tribune, 154, 228, 274.
Chicago World's Fair (first) 109.
Chief of Division, Treasury Department, Washington, D. C., 399.
Child Welfare Conference, Washington, D. C., 418-420.
Choral Society, Howard University, 370.
Christmas in the White House, 223. Voice of the Negro, 223.
Church, Annette, 97.
Church, Anna Wright, 58-59.
Church, Captain, C. B., 1, 2.
Church, Louisa Ayres, 1, 8, 9, 10, 12 ,13, 16, 17, 18, 27, 36, 48, 50, 56, 58, 67, 79, 80-83, 100, 104, 115, 125, 126, 197, 242, 400.
Church, Mary Eliza, 1-427.
Church, "Miss Mollie," (namesake), 13.
Church, Robert Reed, 1, 2, 5, 6, 7, 10, 11, 12, 14, 15, 16, 25, 32, 36, 37, 38, 56, 57, 58, 59, 62, 63, 64, 66, 67, 68, 69, 74, 84, 91, 97, 104, 109, 122, 154, 197, 283, 298.
Church, Robert, Jr., 97.
Church, Thomas Ayres, 10, 42, 232, 233, 277, 402.
Church, Thomas, Jr., 402.

Church, First Congregational, Oberlin, Ohio, 31.
Church, First Congregational, Washington, D. C., 157.
Churches, in United States, 106.
Civil War, 2, 7, 13.
Clerk, Colored in Washington, D. C., theatre, 391.
Clifford, Sir Hugh, 352.
Clifford, Lady, 352.
Cole, Bob, 247.
Coleman, George, 164.
Coleman, Mrs. George, 164, 168.
Coleridge-Taylor, Society, 400.
College Alumnae Club, 281.
College, Antioch, 18, 19.
Colored American, Washington, D. C., 222.
Colored People of Washington, D. C., 183.
Colored Soldiers, Clubs for, Chattanooga, Tenn., Montgomery, Ala., 321.
Columbian Debating Society, George Washington University, Washington, D. C., 393.
Columbia Hospital, Washington, D. C., 237.
Columbia Law School, Washington, D. C., 232.
Commissioners, District of Columbia, 127, 137, 411.
Hazen, Commissioner, 411.
Community Organizer, War Camp Community Service, 319, 321, 325.
Comptroller of Baltimore, 369, 370.
"Confessions of a Colored Woman," 351.
Congregational Association of Maryland and the District of Columbia, 157.
Confederate Army, 11, 377.
Congress, 127, 137, 140, 167, 408, 409.
Congressional Library, 227.
Conservatory of Music, Oberlin, Ohio, 31, 244, 372.
Constitution Hall, Washington, D. C., 367, 418.
Constitution League, 212, 269, 271, 272, 273.
"Conspiracy of Silence," 269.
Contemporary Review, 213.
Continental Hotel, Paris, France, 67, 331, 345, 346, 348.
Contract Labor System, 217.
Conventions of National Association of Colored Women, 152.
Nashville, Chicago, Buffalo, 152.
Convict Lease Camp, 176.
Convict Lease System, 153, 162, 168, 217, 227.
Peonage in the United States, (Nineteenth Century and After), August, 1907, 227
Cook, George F. T., 101, 138.
Cook, Joseph, 285.
Cook, Will Marion, 78.
Cook Tour through Europe, 66.
Coolidge, President and Mrs. Calvin, 157.
Coolidge, T. Jefferson, 105.

Cooper, Edward (Editor, Colored American) Washington, D. C., 222.
Cooper Union, 172, 182, 212, 387.
Woman's Art School, 387.
Cornell University, 178.
Court of Inquiry, 275.
Crane, Mrs. Murray, 281.
Crisis, the, 177.
Crosby, Mr., 181.
Crozier, General, 250-252.
Cruger, Mrs. Van Renssalaer, 230, 245 (Mrs. Chance).
Cuba, 273, 274.
Czolgosz, 172.

D

Von D—, Berlin, Germany, 88, 91, 92.
Darrow, Clarence, 181.
Dawes, Rufus C., 408.
Day, Alice Hooker, 169.
Death Agony of the Science of Race, the, W. T. Stead, 338.
Declaration of Independence, 183.
Delta Sigma Theta, Sorority Creed, 425.
Detective Refuses to Arrest Me, 313.
Dett, Nathaniel, 370.
Diagne, Honorable Blaise, Paris, France, Commissioner in Charge of Colonial Affairs, 338.
Dickie, George E., War Camp Community Service, letter from, 329, 330, 344.
Director of Political Activities of Colored Women of Eastern Division, Harding-Coolidge Campaign, 308-315.
Disfranchisement, 166, 167.
District of Columbia Court of Appeals, 267.
Divorce Bill, National, 409.
Dixon, Tom, 160.
Douglas, Major Charles, 239.
Douglas, Frederick, 51, 92, 93, 110, 116, 125, 133, 134, 169, 170, 171, 239, 279, 387, 399, 410.
Douglass, Lewis, 125.
Douglass Day, 134.
Washington Public Schools for Colored Children, 134.
Dover, Delaware, ticket agent calls police, 311-315.
DuBois, W. E. B., 191, 192, 212.
Dunbar, Paul, 110-112, 239, 314.
Dunmow, England, 348.
Dupont, Senator Coleman, 308, 309, 314.
Dyer, Anti-Lynching Bill, 108, 408.

E

Easter Holiday, Washington, D. C., public schools, 133.
Ebbitt House, Washington, D. C., 318.
"Effect of the Disfranchisement of Colored Men Upon Colored Women in the South," (address), 181.

Emancipation Proclamation, 166, 187-195.
Emergency Relief Division, Washington, D. C., 414.
Emmeline, R. R. Church's mother, 2-4, 283, 284.
Employment Center, District of Columbia, advertises for white men only, 394, 395.
Erie, Tenn., 297.
Essay, "Resolved There Should Be a Sixteenth Amendment to the Constitution Granting Suffrage to Women," 144. (Written in freshman year, Oberlin College).
Etienne, St., France, 353, 354.
Eula, 124.
Evans, Admiral, 189.
Evening Star, Washington, D. C., 223, 232, 271, 272, 279, 394.
Executive Board, Woman's Peace Party, U. S. A., 329.
International Committee of Women for Permanent Peace, 329.

F

Fairbrother, Isaac, Supervising Principal, Eighth Division, Washington, D. C., Public Schools, 135.
Federation of Afro-American Women, 149.
von Finck, Fräulein, 84-87.
Finot, Jean, Editor, 209.
La Revue de la Revue, 209.
La Revue Mondiale, 337.
Le Préjugé des Races, 337.
First Congregational Church, Washington, D. C., 31, 114, 157.
Fisk University, 179, 377.
Fleetwood, Major, 114.
Florence, Italy, 94, 96, 97.
Florida, 303-305.
Foraker, Senator Joseph B., 276.
Ford Hall, 164, 165.
Boston, Massachusetts.
Forrest, Marie Moore, 412.
Fort Reno, 270.
Fort Smith, Ark., 299.
Fortune, T. Thomas, Editor, 222.
France, 209.
Francis, Dr. John R. 64, 65, 66.
Frederick, Empress, Berlin, Germany, 76.
Freedmen's Hospital, 139.
French Chamber of Deputies, 338, 339.
Frost, Professor, 41, 64.

G

Garfield's Inauguration, Washington, D. C., 49, 50.
Garlington, Lieutenant Colonel, 275.
Garrison, Francis, 177, 178.
Garrison, William Lloyd, 169, 196, 391.
Genoa, Italy, 95.

George Washington Bi-Centennial Commission, District of Columbia, 412.
Letter from, 413.
Germany, Dresden, Munich, 71, 72.
Gibbs, Ida, 52 (Mrs. William H. Hunt), 353, 354.
Ginsberg, Herr and Frau Dr., Berlin, Germany, 201, 207.
Goethe, 209.
Goldman, Emma, 172.
Gowthorpe, Célie, 336.
Gowthorpe, Sarah, 336, 358.
Grandfather Clause, 195.
Grandmother, Eliza Ayres, 10, 11, 17, 36, 37.
Grant, General, 27.
Greeley, Horace, 27.
Greenwich, Connecticut, 187.
Greville, Lady Mercy, 351.
Groton Academy, 288.
Guiteau, 172.
Gulfport, Miss., 322.

H

Hague, the, 329.
Haile Selassie, First, 405, 406.
Hampton Institute Choir, 189.
Harding-Coolidge Campaign, 308.
Harding, President Warren, 260, 413.
Harper, Ida Husted, 145, 200.
Biography of Susan B. Anthony, 145.
Harper Publications, 225.
Harper's Weekly, 231.
Harpers Ferry, 239-242.
Harris, John, Parliamentary Secretary, Anti-Slavery and Aborigines Protection Society, 352.
Harrison, President Benjamin, 275, 410.
Hart, Professor Albert Bushnell, 181.
Harvard University, 161, 165, 166, 181, 286, 375.
Harvey, Colonel, 231.
Harper's Weekly.
Hattiesburg, Mississippi, 325.
Hay, Mrs. John, 281.
Hayes, Roland, 248.
Hazen, Commissioner, District of Columbia, 411.
Headquarters, National Republican, 308, 309.
Heflin, Senator, Alabama, 393, 394.
Herman, Dr., Dover, Delaware, 313.
Highland Beach, Maryland, 239, 240.
Highway Bridge, Va., 385.
Hi-O-Hi, Alumni Magazine, Oberlin College, 410.
Margaret Heimbach, editor, 410.
History of Woman Suffrage, 145, 245.
Hitler, 92.
Hooker, Dr. Edward, 280.
Hooker, Isabella Beecher, 67, 68, 169, 282.
Hooper, Franklin, W., Brooklyn Institute of Arts and Sciences, 180, 181.

Hoover, President Herbert, 119, 413, 418. 420.
Hospital in Washington, D. C., 390, 391.
Fractured kneecap.
Hospital, Rochester, Minn., 244.
Hot Springs, Ark., 299.
Houghton-Mifflin's Publishing House, 179.
House of Commons, 403, 404.
Housman, Laurence, 403.
Victoria, Regina, 403.
"How, Why, When and Where Black Becomes White," Boston Herald, Chicago Tribune, 228.
Howard Magazine, 222.
Thomas A. Church, Editor.
Howard, General O. O., 113.
Howard University, 179, 212, 244, 413, 418.
Choral Society, 370.
Conservatory of Music, 244.
Art Department, 387.
Howells, William Dean, 225, 231.
Hunster, Mr. and Mrs., 18, 24.
Hunt, Ida Gibbs, 353, 354.
Hunt, Honorable William H., 353, 354.
United States Consul to St. Etienne.
Hurst, Fannie, Imitation of Life, 381.

I

Idylls of the Gass, 234.
Independent (magazine), 277.
"Taft and the Negro Soldiers," 277.
Indianapolis, Freeman, 222.
Ingersoll, Robert G., 116, 232, 233.
Ingersoll, Mrs. Robert G., 232, 233.
Instructive Visiting Nurse Society, Washington, D. C., 236.
Intermarriage, 165, 166, 409.
International Committee of Women for Permanent Peace, 329.
International Congress of Women, Berlin, Germany, 197-208, 213, 220, 334, 351.
"The Progress of Colored Women" (address), 203, 204.
International League for Peace and Freedom (Women's), 329, 336.
Member of Executive Committee, 360-363.
Irish Riot in Memphis, 7.
Irvine, Mr. and Mrs. St. John, 349.
Ithaca, N. Y., Unitarian Church, address in, 178.

J

Java, 331.
Jay, John, 190.
Jefferson, President Thomas, 105.
Jenks, Professor, Cornell University, 178.
Jews, 74, 89, 90, 207, 234, 255, 313, 389, 421, 424.
Jim Crow, 15, 16, 296-299, 305, 306, 383-396.
Joachim, Germany, 78.

Job Hunting, 46, 47, 414, 415.
Johnson, Charles A., teacher, 8th Division, Washington, D. C., Public Schools, 135.
Johnson, Henry Lincoln, 308.
Johnson, Rosamond, 247.
Johnston, Mrs. A. A. F., Oberlin, 52, 64, 67, 103, 174.
Johnston, Sir Harry, 351, 352.
"The Africa of the Immediate Future," 352.
Joint Committee of Colored Women's League and Federation of Afro-American Women, 151, 152.
Jones, Edwin, Jr., Acting Director, Employment Center, Washington, D. C., 394.
Jubilee Singers in Japan, 340.
Judiciary Committee, 261.
Congress.
Judges, District Supreme Court, 137, 142.
Justice of the Peace, Dover, Del.
Justice, The, of Woman Suffrage (address), 146, 147.

K

Kanda, Baron Naibe, 340, 341.
Kinnaird, Lord, 165, 166.
Kneecap Suit in Court, Washington, D. C., 421.
Ku Klux Klan, 421.

L

La Follette, Senator Robert, Sr., 360.
La Follette, Senator Robert, Jr., 360.
La Follette, Mrs. Robert, Sr., 360.
Lamont, Thomas, 350.
Lamont, Mrs. Thomas, 350.
Lancaster, Ohio, Chautauqua, 242, 243.
Law Enforcement League, Hattiesburg, Miss., 325.
Law Enforcement Organization, Washington, D. C., invites me to dinner at Mayflower Hotel, then recalls the invitation, 424.
League, Colored Women's, Washington, D. C., 148-150.
League, Women's International for Peace and Freedom, 329, 336.
Member of Executive Committee, 360.
Leave of absence from War Camp Community Service requested and granted, 329.
LeDroit Park, Washington, D. C., 113, 114.
Letter from master of Grandmother Emmeline, 2-5.
Lewis, Lucy Biddle, 330.
Liberal Club, Harvard University, 178.
Lincoln Congregational Temple, 114, 279.
Lincoln Memorial Congregational Church, 114.
Lincoln, President Abraham, 106, 154, 179, 280, 281.
Liverpool, England, 348.
London, 211-220, 348, 353, 402-406.

London and National Society for Women's Service, 404.
Lorain, Ohio, 54.
Louvre, Paris, 67, 211.
"Loyalty's Gift," 410.
Sesquicentennial.
Luxembourg Gallery, 210.
Lynching, 172.
"Lynching from a Negro's Point of View," 225, 230, 231, 234.
North American Review, June, 1904.

M

McCormack, John, 159.
McCormick, Ruth, Hanna (Simms), 355-358, 408.
McReynolds, Attorney General, 261.
Judge, United States Supreme Court.
McSwiney, 313.
M Street High School, Washington, D. C., 251.
Magistrate's Court, New York City, 222.
Makino, Baron, 340.
Malay Princess, 3.
Mann, Horace, 18.
Mannheimer, Max, 79.
Marietta, Ohio, 100.
Martin, Prof. Charles Martin, 174.
Marvin, Pres. Cloyd H., 413.
President, George Washington University, Washington, D. C.
Mayo, Dr. Will, Rochester, Minnesota, 244.
Medium, a, 283-285.
Memphis Commercial Appeal, 104.
Memphis, An interesting race case, 376, 377.
Metropolitan Building, New York City, 319.
Miami, Florida, 305.
Milwaukee Normal School, 173.
Milholland, John, 177, 211, 212, 269.
Milholland, Mrs. John, 211, 212.
Milholland, Inez, 212.
Miller, Elizabeth Smith, 171.
Miner Teachers College, 413.
Minimum Wage Committee, 391.
Mississippi, 167, 176.
Montgomery, Ala., Club for Colored Soldiers, 321.
Morgan, J. Pierpont, 350.
Moss, Tom, 105, 108.
Memphis, Tennessee.
Most, Johann, 172.
Mott Lucretia, 144.
Mount Holyoke College, 177.
Mount Vernon, Home of George Washington, 385.
Municipal Court, District of Columbia, 256, 260.
Munro, Editor, North American Review, 225-227.
Musical Union, Oberlin College, 31.
Mu-So-Lit Club, Washington, D. C., 399.

N

Nancy, France, 338.
Nashville Convention, National Association of Colored Women, 152.
National Afro-American Council, 182.
National American Woman Suffrage Association, 143, 145, 153, 158.
National Association of Colored Women, 146, 151-156, 160, 179, 281, 370, 371, 390, 410.
Conventions, Nashville, Chicago, Buffalo.
National Association for the Advancement of Colored People, 177, 193-195.
Washington Branch, 212, 342.
National Council of Women, 111, 145, 370.
National Equal Rights League, 341.
National Federation of Afro-American Women, 150.
National Negro Conference, 181.
National Press Building, 318.
National Purity Congress, La Crosse, Wisconsin, 172.
National Woman's Party, 316, 317.
Alice Paul, 316.
Negerin, die, Berlin, Germany, 198, 199, 207.
Negro Woman and the Church, the, (address), 191.
Atlanta University.
Nelson, Mrs. Alice Dunbar, 314.
New Era Magazine, 222.
News and Courier, Charleston, South Carolina, 184.
New York Age, 133.
New York Journal and American, 232.
New York Sun, 261.
New York World's Fair, 1939-40, 411.
Nineteenth Century and After, 226, 227.
A Plea for the White South by a Colored Woman, July, 1906, 226.
Peonage in the United States (Convict Lease System), August, 1907, 227.
Noordam, Holland-America Line, 331.
Nord Deutscher Lloyd, 198, 201.
Norfolk, Va., Journal and Guide, 222.
North American Review, June, 1904, 213, 216, 224-227, 231, 234.
"Lynching from a Negro's Point of View."
Nourse, Robert, Falls Church, Virginia, 157-159.

O

Oak Bluffs, Massachusetts, 239.
Oberammergau, 358.
Passion Play.
Oberlin Alumnae Association, 425.
Washington branch requests president to confer degree, 425.
Oberlin Alumni Magazine, 145.
Mrs. Catt's article—"Mary Church Terrell, An Appreciation."

Oberlin College, 39-48.
Senior preparatory and college departments.
Activities and honors, 39-48, 51-54, 60, 65, 92, 145, 146, 161, 174, 182, 243, 245, 251, 277, 291, 296.
Oberlin Academy, 40, 244, 353.
Conservatory of Music, 31, 244, 372.
Oberlin Review, 221.
Oberlin News, 182.
Oberprediger, Frau H., Berlin, Germany, 88-90.
Officers, Colored, Training Camp for, 196.
Ogle, Jane, 318, 319.
Ohio State Federation of Colored Women's Clubs, 112.
Oliver, Assistant Secretary of War, 270.
Opequon, Virginia, 239.
Osborne, Eliza Wright, 169.

P

Page, Thomas Nelson, 225.
Pageant, Phyllis Wheatley, 411-413.
Booker T. Washington High School, Baltimore, Maryland, 412.
Washington, D. C. public schools for colored children, 412.
Paine, Robert Treat, 183.
Panama-Pacific Exposition, San Francisco, 184.
Paris, France, 67-69, 82, 83, 209-211, 331, 335, 337-347, 348, 353, 354.
Exposition, 83.
Paris, Texas, 299.
Parkhurst, Dr. C. H., 182.
Parliament, London, 404.
Patterson, Raymond, 228, 274.
Paul, Alice, 316.
Peace Conference, Paris, France, 335, 340, 341, 344.
Peace Congress, Zürich, 329-336, 343, 345, 348, 352.
Pensacola, Florida, 325.
Peonage in the United States (Convict Lease System), 227.
Nineteenth Century and After, August, 1907.
Philharmonie, Berlin, Germany, 204, 205.
Address, The Progress and Problems of Colored Women, 203-204.
International Congress of Women, 197-208.
Philippines, 273, 274.
Phillips, Wendell, 391.
Picketing the White House, 316.
Pitts, Helen, 92; (Mrs. Frederick Douglass).
Platt, Captain, Paris, France, 344-347.
Plea, a, for the White South by a Colored Woman, 226, 231.
Nineteenth Century and After, July, 1906.
Poincaré, Premier, 364-367.

Policeman, a, in Washington, D. C., cafeteria, 420.
Political Equality Club, 169.
Porter, Bruce, San Francisco, 234.
von Posodonsky, Minister of the Interior, Germany, 205.
Post, Louis, Assistant Secretary of Labor under President Woodrow Wilson, 329.
Post, Alice Thatcher, Secretary of Delegates from the U. S. A., 329.
Post, Washington, 193, 205, 223, 224, 266, 271, 279.
Le Préjugé des Races, Finot, 207.
Primary Election Day, Illinois, 357.
Prince Henry of Prussia, 189, 190.
"Progress of Colored Women, the," 153, 157, 158, 160, 168.
Purity Congress, International, Battle Creek, Michigan, 183.
Purvis, Dr. C. B., 127.

Q

Quebec, Canada, 355.
Queen Victoria, 190.
Quinn Chapel, Chicago, Illinois, 154.
Quinquennial, International Congress of Women, Berlin, Germany, 197-208.

R

Race Prejudice, by Jean Finot, 337, 338.
Race Problem, 162, 165, 172-175, 181, 184, 209, 213, 216, 224, 228, 234, 379.
Race Relations Committee, Washington, D. C., 411.
Washington Federation of Churches, 411.
Radcliffe College, 178.
Railroad detective refuses to arrest me, 313.
Dover, Delaware, 313.
"Raising of Lazarus," Paris, France, 209-211.
Henry O. Tanner, 209.
Randolph-Macon Institute, 176.
Rankin, Honorable Jeannette, 331.
"Rawling's House," Texarkana, Arkansas, 300.
Reed, Senator James A., 260, 266.
Registrar, Oberlin College, 103, 174.
Republican Committee, National, 308, 309, 413.
Republican League, Women's, Washington, D. C., 308.
Review of Reviews, England, W. T. Stead, editor, 245.
Rhineland Traffic Association, Germany, 363.
Rice, Prof. Fenelon B., Oberlin Conservatory of Music, 31.
Riley, Elizabeth, teacher, Eighth Division, Washington, D. C., public schools.
Rinehart, Mary Roberts, 231.
Ringwood's Afro-American Journal of Fashion, 149.
Riot in Washington, D. C., 341-342.

Rockefeller, John D., Sr., 164.
Rogers, Will, 150.
Rohan, Princess Maria, 220.
Rosenwald, Julius, 408.
Ross, Commissioner, District of Columbia, 127, 128.
Ross, Mr., Dover, Delaware, 312, 314.
Roosevelt, President Theodore, 193, 223, 260, 268, 278.
Assistant Secretary of the Navy, 277.
Editor, Kansas City Star, 277.
Roosevelt, Mrs. Eleanor, 410.
Ruffin, Mrs. Josephine St. Pierre, 148, 150, 222.
Rush Medical College, Chicago, 244.
Dr. L. A. Tancil.
Ruth, 287-294.

S

Sage College, 178.
St. Johnsbury Academy, Vermont, 185, 244.
St. Nicholas (magazine), 221.
St. Peter's Cathedral, Zürich, 334.
(International Congress of Women).
St. Louis Globe Democrat, 272.
Saunders, Mingo, 272, 273.
Scottish Rite Temple, Washington, D. C., 418.
Seneca Falls Woman's Rights Convention, 169-171.
Seneca Falls Historical Society.
Schools, childhood and youth.
Yellow Springs, Ohio, model school and public school, 18-28.
Oberlin, Ohio, public schools, 29-36.
Oberlin Academy, 40, 244, 353.
Oberlin College, 39-48.
School, Western High, Washington, D. C., 137.
Sesquicentennial, "Loyalty's Gift," 410.
Sewall, May Wright, 145.
Shaw, Rev. Anna Howard, 145.
Sherman, Mrs., Vice President, 281.
Shreveport, Louisiana, 299.
Slayton Lyceum Bureau, 159.
Smith College, 177.
Smith, Gerritt, 171.
"Smith, Miss," colored clerk, department store, Washington, D. C., 388, 389.
Smith, Senator Hoke, 260.
Socialism, 217, 218.
Southern Workman (magazine), 222.
Southwest Community House, Washington, D. C., 411.
Spanish-American War, 274.
Spelman, Seminary, 164.
Spencer, J. W., Fort Worth, Texas, 175.
President, Farmers and Mechanics Bank, 175.
Spingarn, Arthur, National Association for the Advancement of Colored People, 342.
Spingarn, Joel, National Association for the

Advancement of Colored People, 195, 196.
State Teachers Associations, Colored, Kentucky and Tennessee, 183.
Stenographer, skillful, Washington, D. C., rejected on account of race, 388.
Stokes, Canon Phelps, 411.
Storer College, 239.
Storey, Moorfield, 177, 178, 195, 330.
Stowe, Rev. Charles, 280.
Stowe, Harriet Beecher, 158, 162, 169.
  Centenary, 279-282.
  "Appreciation of Harriet Beecher Stowe," 280.
Stowe, Lyman Beecher, 279.
Strachey, Philippa, Sec'y, London and National Society for Women's Service, 404.
Stranger's Gallery, London, 404.
Sumner, Charles, 276, 391.
Sunday School Convention Parade, Washington, D. C., 416.
Supervising Principal, Colored Schools, Washington, D. C., 359.
Supervisor, Girls Department, War Camp Community Service, New York City, 327.
Supreme Court, Louisiana, 249.
Supreme Court, United States, 195, 267.
Sutherland, Duchess of, 218.
Swift, Rev. Clarence, 183.
Swift, Mrs. Clarence, 183.

T

Taft, President William Howard, 260.
  Secretary of War, 268-272, 274.
Taft and the Negro Soldiers, 277.
  Article in Independent Magazine, July 23, 1908.
Tancil, Dr. L. A., 355.
Tanner, H. O., 209-211.
  "Raising of Lazarus," Paris, France.
Taylor, Chaplain, Gulf Port, Mississippi, 322.
Taylor, Samuel Coleridge, 123, 218-220, 353.
Taylor, Mrs. Samuel Coleridge, 218, 219, 353.
  Gwendolyn and Hiawatha.
Teachers, Washington, D. C., public schools, colored and white, 135-141.
Tennessee Conference, A. M. E. Church, 184.
Terrell Junior High School, 425.
Terrell, Mary Louise, 116, 117, 241, 234, 246, 355, 372, 374, 407, 408.
Terrell, Phyllis Church, 145, 185, 198, 238, 244, 247, 316, 317, 355, 358, 372, 388, 402, 403, 408, 418.
Terrell, Robert Heberton, 65, 66, 101, 102, 103, 106, 107, 115, 116, 121, 122, 127, 128, 137, 151, 154, 157, 158, 159, 177, 187, 193, 194, 197, 242, 245, 256, 260-267, 277, 288, 305, 342, 343, 372, 373, 388, 397, 399, 421, 425.
Terrell, Robert Heberton Law School, 425.

Testimonial given by citizens of Washington, D. C., 414.
Texarkana, Ark., 299-302.
Tillman, Senator Ben., 260.
Treble Clef Club, Richmond, Virginia, 370.
Tremain, General, 172.
Tribune Chicago, 154, 228, 274.
Troops, Black, in Germany, 359.
Trotter, William Monroe, Editor, Boston Guardian, Secretary of the Race Petitioners to Paris Peace Conference, 341.
Tuskegee, 190-193.
Twenty-fifth Infantry, Companies B, C and D dismissed without honor by President Theodore Roosevelt, 268-278.
Twentieth Century Club, Boston, 183.
Twentieth Century Club, Pittsburgh, 183.

U

"Uncle Sam and the Sons of Ham" (address), 160-162.
Uncle Tom's Cabin, 233, 246, 279, 280, 281.
Union Army, 203.
University Park Temple, 114.
  Washington, D. C.
University of Chicago, 289.
University of Virginia, 375.

V

Vanderbilt, Mrs. Cornelius, 190.
Van Horn, Annie, 135.
  Teacher, Eighth Division, public schools, Washington, D. C.
Vardaman, Senator James K., 260, 262, 263, 266.
  Vardaman's Weekly.
Vassar College, 177.
Venus and the Night Doctors (story), Washington Post, 224.
Villard, Mrs. Henry, 169, 177.
Villard, Oswald Garrison, 196, 350.
Visitor's Bureau, Paris, France, 343-346.
Voice of the Negro, 222, 223.
  Christmas in the White House, 223.
  Max Barber, Editor, 222-223.

W

Wagner, Charles, 159.
Waldorf Astoria Hotel, 372, 413.
Walla Walla Case, 257.
Wainer, Colonel, War Risk Insurance Bureau, 255, 256.
War Camp Community Service, 277, 318-350.
War Department, 268-278.
Ward, William Hayes, Editor of the Independent magazine, 276.
Warner, Mrs. Charles Dudley, 280.
Warner, Dr. Lucien C., 372.
Warner, Mrs. Lucien C., 372.

War of the Rebellion, 172, 203.
War Risk Insurance Bureau, 252-256.
Experience as clerk, in, 252-256.
Warwick Castle, 218.
Warwick, Countess of, 214-219, 349, 357, 358.
Warwick, Earl of, 218.
Washington, Booker T., 189-194, 229, 277.
Washington, Mrs. Booker T., 149.
Washington, D. C., "Colored Man's Paradise," 383-396.
Washington, D. C., Federation of Churches, 411.
Race Relations Committee, 411.
Washington Evening Star, 223, 232, 271, 272, 279, 394.
Washington, President George, 385, 411, 412.
Washington, George, Bi-Centennial, 411.
Washington, Hotel, 317.
Washington Post, 193, 205, 223, 224, 266, 271, 279.
Washington Tribune, 222.
Welch, Mrs. Daisy, 308.
Wellesley College, 176, 177, 333.
Weller, Charles F., 402.
Wells, H. G., 349-351, 358, 404.
Wells, Mrs. H. G., 348, 349, 358.
Von Wenckstern, Frau General, 85, 86, 87, 88.
Westcott, Miss, Principal Western High School, Washington, D. C., 136, 137.
Wheatley, Phyllis, 411, 412.
Pageant, 412.
White, Mrs. Andrew D., 178.
White House, 114, 193, 233, 277, 316, 384.
White, "Prin," Oberlin Academy, 29.
Whittier Historical and Literary Association, Memphis, Tenn., 158.
Wilberforce University, 60-63.
Wilbur, Ray Lyman, Secretary of the Interior, 420.
Wilcox, Ella Wheeler, 231.
Wilhelm, Emperor of Germany, 189, 190.
Willard, Frances, 245.

Willard Hotel, 232, 315, 318.
Williams, John Sharp, 173.
Willoughby, Lady, 404.
Winchester, Virginia, 239.
Wilson, James, 11.
Wilson, President Woodrow, 119, 261, 263, 350.
Woman's Art School, Cooper Union, 387.
Woman's Club, Washington, D. C., invites me to join.
Board of Directors rejects me, 423.
Woman's Club, Fall River, Mass., 183.
Woman's Congress of Missions, San Francisco, 184, 185.
Woman's Rights Convention, first, 169.
Woman Suffrage, 143-147, 169, 170, 245, 309, 316.
Women, Haitien, 361.
Women's International League for Peace and Freedom, 329-334, 384.
Member of Executive Committee, 330.
Women's Republican League, Washington, D. C., 308.
Women's Henry George League, New York City, 179.
World Fellowship of Faiths, International Assembly, London, England, 402, 403.
World's Fair, New York, 1939-40, member of District of Columbia Advisory Committee on Women's Participation in, 411.
World War, first, 256, 259, 332, 338, 341, 349, 391.

Y

Yale, 161.
Y.M.C.A., West Side Branch, New York City, 187.
Yellow Fever in Memphis, 36, 37.
Yellow Springs, Ohio, 18-28.
Model school and public school, 18-28.

Z

Zürich, Switzerland, 331-336, 348, 353.

ABOUT THE EDITORS

Henry Louis Gates, Jr., is the W. E. B. Du Bois Professor of the Humanities, Chair of the Afro-American Studies Department, and Director of the W. E. B. Du Bois Institute for Afro-American Research at Harvard University. One of the leading scholars of African-American literature and culture, he is the author of *Figures in Black: Words, Signs, and the Racial Self* (1987), *The Signifying Monkey: A Theory of Afro-American Literary Criticism* (1988), *Loose Canons: Notes on the Culture Wars* (1992), and the memoir *Colored People* (1994).

Jennifer Burton is in the Ph.D. program in English Language and Literature at Harvard University. She is the volume editor of *The Prize Plays and Other One-Acts* in this series. She is a contributor to *The Oxford Companion to African American Literature* and to *Great Lives from History: American Women*. With her mother and sister she coauthored two one-act plays, *Rita's Haircut* and *Litany of the Clothes*. Her creative non-fiction has appeared in *There and Back* and *Buffalo*, the Sunday magazine of the *Buffalo News*.

Nellie Y. McKay is Professor of American and Afro-American Literature at the University of Wisconsin-Madison. She serves as associate editor for *African American Review* and is the author of *Jean Toomer—the Artist: A Study of His Literary Life and Work* (1984), the editor of *Critical Essays on Toni Morrison* (1988), and has published numerous articles and essays on African-American writers of the nineteenth and twentieth centuries.